Social Skills and
Adaptive Behavior in Learners
with Autism Spectrum Disorders

D1564245

ORGANIZATION FOR
AUTISM RESEARCH

Social Skills and
Adaptive Behavior in Learners
with Autism Spectrum Disorders

edited by

Peter F. Gerhardt, Ed.D.
McCarton School
New York

and

Daniel Crimmins, Ph.D.
Georgia State University
Atlanta

·P·A·U·L·H·
BROOKES
PUBLISHING Co ®

Baltimore • London • Sydney

Paul H. Brookes Publishing Co.
Post Office Box 10624
Baltimore, Maryland 21285-0624

www.brookespublishing.com

Typeset by Network Publishing Partners, Inc., Glenview, Illinois.
Manufactured in the United States of America by
Sheridan Books, Inc., Chelsea, Michigan.

Photograph on the cover copyright © Corbis Photography/Veer.

The individuals described in this book are real people whose situations are based on the
authors' experiences. Names and identifying details are used by permission.

Quotation on page 225 from Butler, C. (1997). You're standing on my neck. *Sidewalk
Bubblegum*. Retrieved from http://sidewalkbubblegum.com/wp-content/uploads/2010/03/
sidewalk_bubblegum_150.gif; reprinted by permission.

Library of Congress Cataloging-in-Publication Data

Social skills and adaptive behavior in learners with autism spectrum disorders /[edited] by
Peter F. Gerhardt and Daniel Crimmins.
    p.   cm.
  Includes bibliographical references and index.
  ISBN 978-1-59857-060-1 (perfect binding)—ISBN 1-59857-060-9 (perfect binding)
  1. Autistic children—Behavior modification.   2. Autistic youth—Behavior modification.
  3. Youth with autism spectrum disorders—Behavior modification.   4. Social skills—Study
  and teaching.   I. Gerhardt, Peter F. II. Crimmins, Daniel B. (Daniel Bernard), 1952–
RJ506.A9S633 2013
618.92'85882—dc23   2012022033

British Library Cataloguing in Publication data are available from the British Library.

2016   2015   2014   2013   2012

10   9   8   7   6   5   4   3   2   1

Contents

About the Editors

Peter F. Gerhardt, Ed.D., is the director of education at the Upper School of the McCarton School and the founding chair of the Scientific Council for the Organization for Autism Research (OAR). He has more than 30 years of experience using the principles of applied behavior analysis in supporting adolescents and adults with autism spectrum disorders (ASDs) in educational, employment, residential, and community-based settings. Dr. Gerhardt is the author or the coauthor of articles and book chapters on the needs of adolescents and adults with ASDs and has presented nationally and internationally on this topic. He serves on the editorial board of *Behavior Analysis in Practice* and on numerous professional advisory boards. Dr. Gerhardt received his doctorate from Rutgers, The State University of New Jersey, Graduate School of Education.

Daniel Crimmins, Ph.D., is Director of the Center for Leadership in Disability, a University Center for Excellence in Developmental Disabilities program; Director of the Georgia Leadership Education in Neurodevelopmental Disabilities program; and Clinical Professor of Public Health at Georgia State University. He has a career-long interest in working with organizations to adopt evidence-based behavioral and educational interventions for children and adults with autism and related neurodevelopmental disabilities. Dr. Crimmins has taught extensively at the graduate level in special education and public health and has a long involvement with interdisciplinary postgraduate training. He has a particular interest in issues that reflect the intersection of research, practice, and policy. Dr. Crimmins received his B.A., M.A., and Ph.D. degrees in psychology from Binghamton University; completed an internship in clinical psychology at the University of Mississippi Medical Center; and is a licensed psychologist in New York. In 2002 and 2003, he was a Robert Wood Johnson Health Policy Fellow in Washington, D.C., where he worked in the office of Senator Jim Jeffords on health and education policy.

About the Contributors

Shahla Ala'i-Rosales, Ph.D., is an associate professor of behavior analysis in the College of Public Affairs and Community Service at the University of North Texas in Denton. She teaches classes on applied behavior analysis, parent training, early intervention, and ethics. During the past 25 years, she has overseen applied research and interventions that have successfully improved the lives of children with autism and their families.

Stephen R. Anderson, Ph.D., BCBA, is the chief executive officer of Summit Educational Resources in Getzville, New York. He serves as an adjunct assistant professor at several universities and has published journal articles, book chapters, and one book on the education and treatment of children with developmental disabilities. As a licensed psychologist, he has worked in the autism field for more than 35 years.

Rosa I. Arriaga, Ph.D., is a senior research scientist and the director of pediatric research at the School of Interactive Computing of the Health Systems Institute at the Georgia Institute of Technology in Atlanta. She investigates fundamental topics of human–computer interaction with an emphasis on using psychological theory and methods.

Pei-Yu Chen, Ph.D., BCBA, is an assistant professor at the National Taipei University of Education of the Da-an District in Taipei City, Taiwan. Her research focuses on helping children with disabilities build positive behaviors and social relationships in school settings.

Joanne Gerenser, Ph.D., CCC-SLP, is the executive director of the Eden II Programs in Staten Island, New York. She has published numerous articles and book chapters on autism, language disorders, and related subjects.

Walt Guthrie, of Decatur, Georgia, is an autism advocate.

Eric H. Ishijima, Ph.D., is a post-doctoral student in the Kasari Research Lab of the Semel Institute for Neuroscience and Human Behavior of the University of California–Los Angeles. His research focuses on joint attention, joint engagement, imitation, and social skills of children with autism.

Connie Kasari, Ph.D., is a professor at University of California–Los Angeles' Semel Institute for Neuroscience and Human Behavior who examines the effects of targeted interventions for improving core developmental areas associated with autism spectrum disorders. She studies how to move effective interventions into the community with traditionally underserved and underrepresented populations of children with autism.

Kathleen Koenig, M.S.N., is a clinical nurse specialist in psychiatry and an advanced practice registered nurse at the Yale Child Study Center in New Haven, Connecticut. She is involved in research and clinical work with children and adults with autism spectrum disorders, examining interventions related to improving social and communication skills.

Mark Kretzmann, Ph.D., conducts postdoctoral research at University of California–Los Angeles' Semel Institute for Neuroscience and Human Behavior. His research centers on testing novel interventions to improve social functioning for children with autism, particularly in the school setting.

Patricia Lanaspa is a Hispanic Services Supervisor with the Parent to Parent of Georgia organization in Atlanta. She is the mother of a teenager with autism and serves as a resource to Hispanic families in Georgia whose children receive this diagnosis.

Suzanne Letso, M.A., is the chief executive officer and cofounder of the Connecticut Center for Child Development in Milford, Connecticut. She is a registered lobbyist for the Connecticut General Assembly and has worked as an advocate on legislative issues within Connecticut. She is also a parent of a son with autism.

Jill Locke, Ph.D., is a postdoctoral fellow at the Center for Mental Health Policy and Service Research at the University of Pennsylvania in Philadelphia. Her research focuses on developing and implementing interventions designed to address social ability in children with autism spectrum disorders in community settings as well as exploring the ways in which treatment gains in intervention programs are generalized and sustained over time.

John R. Lutzker, Ph.D., is the director and a professor at the Center for Healthy Development of the School of Public Health at Georgia State University in Atlanta. He serves on professional editorial boards and is a fellow in five divisions of the American Psychological Association.

Erik A. Mayville, Ph.D., BCBA-D, is the clinical director of the Institute for Educational Planning and Connecticut Center for Child Development in Milford, Connecticut. His research focuses on curriculum content in applied behavior analysis, problem behavior, social skills, psychiatric disorders, and psychotropic medication for people with autism and developmental disabilities.

Robert L. "Bob" Morris, B.S., had a long first career as an engineer in Atlanta, Georgia. Bob also had autism, and beginning in the 1980s, as he recognized the unique problem-solving talents in his "autistic cousins," he began a second career in mentoring others toward independence and respect.

Daniel Openden, Ph.D., BCBA-D, is the vice president and clinical services director of the Southwest Autism Research and Resource Center and an adjunct faculty member at Arizona State University in Phoenix. He leads a programmatic line of research on implementing Pivotal Response Treatment in real-world settings.

Stacey Ramirez, B.S., is the director of individual and family supports at the Center for Leadership in Disability at Georgia State University in Atlanta. She has a career interest in community inclusion, person-centered planning, culturally competent family supports, and furthering the human rights of people with intellectual disabilities. She is the proud mother of three teenage boys, one of whom has autism.

Roy Q. Sanders, M.D., is the medical director of the Marcus Autism Center in Atlanta, Georgia. He works in the field of developmental disabilities and is committed to the full inclusion of people with differences and disabilities in all aspects of public and private life. He is the father of a son diagnosed with an autism spectrum disorder and cognitive disabilities.

Gloria M. Satriale is the executive director of the Preparing Adolescents and Adults for Life Program, a community-based life skills program in Downington, Pennsylvania, and is the president and founder of Mission for Educating Children with Autism. She is a parent of a child diagnosed with autism.

Ilene S. Schwartz, Ph.D., is the chair of special education at the University of Washington–Seattle and the director of the Norris and Dorothy Haring Center for Applied Research and Training in Education. She started the Developmentally Appropriate Treatment for Autism Project in 1997 to provide an effective school-based intervention model for young children with autism.

Linda Styles is an Atlanta-based autism advocate, as well as a graphic artist, a writer, and a photographer.

Ginny L. Van Rie, Ph.D., is an assistant professor of special education at the Georgia College & State University in Milledgeville, Georgia. She teaches behavior management courses to preservice undergraduate- and graduate-level teacher candidates to help them intervene positively and proactively to minimize challenging behaviors in the classroom and support student achievement.

Mary Jane Weiss, Ph.D., is a professor of education at Endicott College in Beverly, Massachusetts, where she directs the graduate programs in applied behavior analysis and autism. Her clinical and research focus is on identifying best practices in educating learners with autism, on using evidence-based practices to remediate all deficits associated with autism spectrum disorders, and on aiding family adaptation.

Thomas Zane, Ph.D., is a professor of education and director of the Applied Behavior Analysis Online Program at the Institute for Behavioral Studies, Van Loan Graduate School, Endicott College in Beverly, Massachusetts. His research interests include teacher training, staff development, and evidence-based practice in autism. As part of his duties at Endicott College, he offers a BCBA certificate program through distance learning.

Jessica M. Zawacki, M.Ed., BCBA, is a senior behavior analyst of the Preparing Adolescents and Adults for Life Program in Downington, Pennsylvania. She works with preschool children with and without autism spectrum disorders.

Preface

Social skills and adaptive behavior are critical areas of focus in individuals with autism spectrum disorders (ASDs) and areas in which there is exceptional focus in research and intervention. This book features prominent researchers who discuss the state of the science in autism research with individuals with ASDs, family members, professionals, educators, and others. The ultimate purpose is that this comprehensive review of research on the ranges of topics related to social skills and adaptive behavior should lead to improvements in understanding, increased access to effective services and supports, and the identification of future research priorities. The Organization for Autism Research (OAR) hosted the contributors to this volume as part of a research convocation, *Social Skills and Adaptive Behavior in Individuals with an Autism Spectrum Disorder (ASD)*. The event was cosponsored by the University Center for Excellence in Developmental Disabilities, then at the Marcus Institute and now the Center for Leadership in Disability at Georgia State University. As is evidenced by the chapters that follow, important research is highlighted, as are the experiences and opinions of those affected most by ASDs. By all accounts, this convocation was an extraordinary success.

CONTEXT AND DEFINITIONS

For the purposes of this convocation, the following definitions were used as a starting point of reference:

- *Social skills* are defined as interpersonal responses with specific operational definitions that allow an individual to adapt to the environment through verbal and nonverbal communication (Matson, Matson, & Rivet, 2007).
- *Adaptive behavior* is defined as those skills or abilities that enable an individual to meet standards of personal independence and responsibility that would be expected of his or her age and social group. It also refers to the typical performance of individuals without disabilities in meeting environmental expectations. Adaptive behavior changes according to a person's age, cultural expectations, and environmental demands (Heward, 2005).

THE PRESENTERS

Each presenter was asked to follow a structured format in which he or she briefly reviewed the status of research on a specific aspect of the topic, discussed the relevant implications of the research, and offered recommendations for future research and practice. The presenters (who were joined by colleagues to prepare chapters based on these subjects) and focal topics were as follows:

- Erik Mayville: the assessment of social skills
- Suzanne Letso: social and adaptive behaviors in the context of family life
- Mary Jane Weiss: behavior analytic interventions in the development of social skills
- Kathy Koenig: the complexity of social skills training and the range of possible changes
- Joanne Gerenser: the junction of joint attention and communicative or social competence
- Ilene Schwartz: building social skills and social relationships in school settings
- Daniel Openden: Pivotal Response Treatment and the development of social competence
- Stephen Anderson: adaptive behavior in young learners with ASDs
- Peter Gerhardt: adaptive behavior in adolescents and adults—life in the community
- Connie Kasari: peer relationships, friendships, and loneliness at school for children with ASDs
- Roy Sanders: impact of psychopharmacology on adaptive and social responding in learners with ASDs
- Thomas Zane: pseudoscience in social skills research and intervention

The convocation offered short periods of discussion after every two presentations. The final presentations offered a perspective on taking evidence-based practices to scale (Daniel Crimmins and John Lutzker) and a summary of the common themes from the convocation and the discussions from both days, along with challenges for the future (Shahla Ala'i-Rosales).

PANELISTS

In addition to the scientific presenters, the convocation included several panelists representing the perspectives of individuals with autism, family members, and service providers. These individuals were asked to commit to attending for the full 2 days, listen carefully, actively participate in the discussions, and review the final results and recommendations from the convocation. We wish to thank our panelists for their attention, diligence, and efforts on behalf of the convocation agenda: Rosa Arriaga, Nate Call, Clair Dees, Evelyn Falconer, Walt Guthrie, Patricia Lanaspa, Will McKeen, Michael Morrier, Bob Morris, Georgina Peacock, Stacey Ramirez, Cheryl Rhodes, Sherry Richardson, Tom Robertson, Opal Simmons, Linda Styles, and Toni Thomas. Six of these individuals provided commentaries that are included in Section II of this book.

CONTROVERSIES AND QUESTIONS

It would seem a simple thing to bring a group of applied scientists together to discuss their work and identify new areas for exploration. But applied scientists do not speak with one voice, nor did the panelists, and with the whole mix, there were many strained moments and bruised feelings. Although they will be discussed in some detail in the Afterword section, several questions emerged early in the convocation that resonated in later discussions.

Who participates in the research process? Because the lack of social relatedness is among the earliest signs of an ASD, social skills interventions often target relatively young children. Much of the research presented at the convocation focused on preschool and early-school-age children. This represents a commitment to providing these children with skills to access the broadest range of social environments within their families, at school, and in their communities. However, it begged the following question: Where are youth, young adults, and even older adults in the research process? One panelist—an older individual with autism—raised the concern that 70% of life is spent in adulthood, yet little research addresses the needs and supports for adults with ASDs. So, although research on social skills may naturally focus on younger children, the broader research community must consider the needs of all ages.

How do we view individuals with autism in the research process? At the risk of overgeneralizing, our research scientist presenters look at children with ASDs who interact poorly or not at all, who have difficulties communicating using language, and have a range of behaviors that interfere with their participation in social venues. The self-advocates viewed themselves as having strengths and the potential to contribute—just as they are—in a society that is often intolerant of differences. Practitioners work with people with learning and communication difficulties that have to be addressed directly for these individuals to succeed. Family members advocate for interventions that respect the individual, promote inclusion and self-confidence, and want what is best, understanding that means very different things to and for all involved. These different viewpoints contributed to lively discussions.

What is the ultimate goal of our research? Any single research study tends to be narrowly focused, often asking a single question, with one or two measures, and the results go only so far. Scientists know this and realize that one accumulates information across dozens of studies to form the big picture. Unfortunately, when science is taken out of the big-picture context and the results of a single research study or a series of studies are presented, a lay audience responds, "You have to do research to prove that?" Our panelists expressed frustration at times with the narrow focus of research, which was—to a large degree—agreed on by *all.* It underscored the importance of future research increasingly needing to take place in the natural ecology of social relationships and take into account context, meaningful outcomes, and clinical significance. In particular, the field must move from targeting individual social skills to targeting contextual social competence.

Who sets the research agenda? The convocation provided a forum for research scientists to present a synthesis of their work—reflecting the evolution of their thinking and the increasing sophistication of methods. The convocation provided an opportunity to hear others' perspectives and incorporate their contributions and findings into an even better understanding, which provides a powerful platform for a deepened understanding of the topics under study. We found that the convocation also offered the prospect of identifying new areas and directions for research. Our discussions highlighted the need, for example, to go beyond current measures of generalization and the maintenance of social skills to include assessments of "broader" change, including social competence, independence, and quality of life. It was clear that this area could be enriched by greater input from individuals on the spectrum and their families.

REFERENCES

Heward, W.H. (2005). *Exceptional children: An introduction to special education* (8th ed.). Upper Saddle River, NJ: Prentice Hall.

Matson, J.L., Matson, M.L., & Rivet, T.T. (2007). Social skills treatments with children with autism spectrum disorders. *Behavior Modification, 31*, 682–707.

Acknowledgments

The book you are now holding is the collective effort of many people beyond the noted chapter authors. First and foremost are James Sack, the chairman of the Organization for Autism Research (OAR), and Michael Maloney, OAR's executive director. Without their support and vision, OAR, let alone this volume, would not have been possible. The many runners who have slogged through marathons, half marathons, triathlons, and various other acts of self-abuse to raise money for autism intervention research must be duly recognized. All the parents, professionals, and, most important, individuals on the autism spectrum who have supported the work of OAR since its founding must be repeatedly thanked for all they have done—and continue to do—to promote research to improve quality of life of individuals with autism.

We would like to thank the chapter authors and all those who wrote commentaries on the convocation; they collectively offered testimony to how much we have to learn from each other. In the time since the convocation, Daniel Crimmins's professional world went through a dramatic transition to Georgia State University. He thanks those in the university who made this go smoothly, recognizes the support of colleagues in the Center for Healthy Development and the National SafeCare Training and Research Center who shared the transition, and particularly appreciates his colleagues in the Center for Leadership in Disability and the Morehouse School of Medicine who have supported and expanded the mission.

We would like to specifically thank Stacey Ramirez, who works tirelessly to ensure that the voices of people with autism and other disabilities are heard and that their families are supported. Stacey served as a liaison to the individuals, family members, and community professionals who participated in the convocation. We also want to acknowledge the late Bob Morris. His commitment to improving the lives of adults with autism took him into the difficult realm of having to deal with people like us—he is missed. Finally, we want to thank Rebecca Lazo of Paul H. Brookes Publishing Co. for her infinite patience and perseverance at bringing this book to completion.

To my parents, Fred and Janet Gerhardt—
thanks for all the love, support, and encouragement

—PFG

In memory of Bob Morris (1937–2010)—
autistic cousin, eccentric expert, guide, and colleague

—DC

Current Research and Recommendations on Social Skills and Adaptive Behavior

Social and Adaptive Behavior in the Context of Family Life

Suzanne Letso

Roger and I were just starting our family. I had some complications early in my first pregnancy, so my doctor sent me for every test imaginable. I was relieved when my test results indicated that my baby did not have Down syndrome or any other recognizable genetic defect.

My son Tyler was born 2 months premature. When I held him in my arms for the first time, I noticed that he looked devoid of emotion, almost like a wise old man, not what I imagined a newborn to be like at all. I chalked it up to his being as startled as I was by his early arrival. I had no worries about him at all. My first twinge of concern came when Tyler was 4 months old. I was feeding him and trying to put my finger on the little kernel of worry I was having but could not name. I finally realized that I just could not imagine him ever having a friend, yet I had no definitive reason for this concern. I made the mistake of talking to Tyler's pediatrician about my worries. He immediately labeled me as one of "those parents" who, as he later put it, "had a penchant for the perfect child."

At every well-baby checkup thereafter, I would identify little things that seemed unique to my child. But because my doctor pegged me as the "yuppie mom whose kid did not talk because she worked with a nanny who spoke English as a second language," my concerns fell on deaf ears. The doctor assured me that Tyler was fine. As a "preemie," he could be expected to be slow to achieve various developmental milestones, and I should not give it a moment's thought because "Einstein didn't talk until he was 5 years old."

When Tyler was 3 years old, he was finally diagnosed with autism. The bullet I thought I had dodged had hit its mark after all. Our lives have been forever changed. We are now that family at the mall that mothers notice and protectively hug their babies. Roger and I sometimes refer to ourselves as the "traveling Letso comedy hour." Yet somehow we manage to muddle through and even sometimes have moments of magnificence.

I have learned that being the parent of a child with autism is a very challenging, never-ending task that will be my responsibility until the day I die. In fact, I intend to affect Tyler's life from the grave if I can. I believe the best way for me to ensure that my beloved son leads a full and satisfying existence now, as well as after I die, is by working each day to help him become as functional and independent as possible. My goal for Tyler is not necessarily education in the least restrictive environment but *life* in the least restrictive environment now and in adulthood.

To accomplish this goal, I turned to research and the practical interpretations of how this seemingly fractured body of information is translated into better educational practices to improve the quality of life for each member of my family.

There is nothing exceptional about my story. On the contrary, the same scenario is playing out in households across the United States. As both a parent of a child with autism and a service provider, I see the beneficial effects of the existing body of research and its translation into practical application in classrooms, homes, and community settings. But there are still many more problems than solutions and more holes than fabric in the patchwork of the existing tapestry of autism research.

Although a scholarly enterprise, the Organization for Autism Research is really about what happens to a child with autism and the family when both the parents and the child with autism are home alone without assistance or support. We attempt to answer the following questions:

- Does having a child with autism affect families differently than do other disabilities?
- As researchers and practitioners, what do we already know about social and adaptive deficits and skill development that can help families manage better today?
- Where are the holes in the existing body of research, policy, and practice in the areas of social skill development and adaptive behavior?
- What can researchers do over the next 5–10 years to close some of the gaps in this body of knowledge relative to social skills and adaptive skills?
- How can we better translate what has already been learned through research to enhance autism education?
- How can we more efficiently translate ongoing practices to generate new research questions that will ultimately enhance outcomes for children, families, and the broader community?

The remainder of this chapter focuses on these important questions by discussing social and adaptive skills within the context of family life. For me, the ultimate question, which is the focus of this chapter, is as follows: "How does what we know, what we do, and how we do it make a difference in a home where a parent is alone with his or her child with autism?"

EVEN HARDER THAN THE "HARDEST TO DO"

Research is generally identified as either basic research, which is conducted in a laboratory or another very controlled setting, or applied research, which is conducted in real-life situations. However, applied research might be better conceptualized as occurring across a continuum of environments that can range from highly controllable situations to highly variable and uncontrollable situations. This variability has significant implications in choosing the research questions to be pursued, the financial and human resources required to produce compelling scientific evidence, and the generalization of research results to other individuals and environments (Guralnick, 1999). Although special education research has been dubbed the "hardest of the hard-to-do science" (Berliner, 2002), school environments are conceptualized as the more controllable end of the applied continuum of environments in applied research. Research conducted in homes and community settings is even more difficult to control than research in school settings and is considered to be in the middle of that continuum of environmental complexity. The most difficult research to conduct, measure, and replicate is related to adaptive skills that are performed when someone is alone, applicable across multiple settings, occurring without applying an extrinsic motivation system, or occurring in conjunction with other behavioral repertoires. The initial instruction of a child—and the associated research concerning social and adaptive skill development—might first take place in a school setting when the ultimate measure of program relevance and effectiveness is best measured by the effect of that instruction in the child's home. Further complicating matters, research related to social and adaptive behavior includes other areas of consideration beyond the utility of those behaviors. Two areas of great research importance that overlap with assessing children with autism and their adaptive and social skills within the context of family life are parental stress and parent training.

EFFECTIVE TEACHING STRATEGIES

In spite of the challenges facing applied researchers, many research articles have been published in peer-reviewed journals that assess the teaching of social and adaptive strategies applicable to family life. In particular, the effects of instructional strategies based on the principles of applied behavior analysis, which, by definition, seek to generate socially important outcomes for people and society at large, have been particularly well documented in the literature. For example, multiple studies assess the development of specific social and adaptive skills, such as leisure and recreation (Hurren, 1994; Jerome, Frantino, & Strumey, 2007; Wall & Gast, 1997), the fear of doctors and participation in medical care (Shabani & Fisher, 2006), nail and skin care (Ellis, Ala'i-Rosales, & Glenn, 2006), improving sleep patterns (Durand,

2002; Durand & Christodulu, 2004; Weiskop, Richdale, & Matthews, 2005), shopping (Alcantara, 1994), self-determination (Field & Hoffman, 1999; Fullerton & Coyne, 1999; Held, Thoma, & Thomas, 2004; Sakamoto, Muto, & Mochizuki, 2003), requesting assistance (Reichle, McComas, & Dahl, 2005), helping others (Reeve, Reeve, Buffington-Townsend, & Pouson, 2007), food selectivity and other eating problems (Ahearn, 2003; Anglesea, Hoch, & Taylor, 2008; Luiselli, Ricciardi, & Gilligan, 2005; Paul, Williams, & Riegel, 2007; Schreck & Williams, 2006), increasing personal independence (Bouxsein, Tiger, & Fisher, 2008), toileting and restroom use (Bainbridge & Myles, 1999; Keen, Brannigan, & Cuskelly, 2007; Taylor, Cipani, & Clardy, 1994), using social language (Akmanoglu-Uludag & Batu, 2005; Jones, Feeley, & Takacs, 2007; Maione & Mirenda, 2006; Newman, Reinecke, & Meinberg, 2000), and play skills (Boelter et al., 2007; Bruzek & Thompson, 2007; Legoff & Sherman, 2006).

However, when practitioners are reviewing the literature, it is often impossible to identify the effect of teaching protocols relative only to social and adaptive skills versus other skill sets. As Matson, Matson, and Rivet noted, "The definition of social skills is the difficulty in sorting out what are social skills versus communication skills versus behavior problems and abnormalities. The literature describes procedures that overlap all three of these major domains" (2007, p. 684). Research produced related to teaching social skills and the generalization of academic- or school-related repertoires can also overlap with development of basic "learning to learn" skills, such as attending to a verbal instruction, following multistep instructions, and joint attention. The effective remediation of a maladaptive behavior necessitates replacing that behavior with at least one (or more than one) more functional and socially appropriate behavior (e.g., adaptive replacement behavior; Snell & Brown, 2006). There are several comprehensive studies in the literature that include but are not limited to teaching social and adaptive skills (Eikeseth, Smith, Jahr, & Eldevick, 2002; Green, Brennan, & Fein, 2002; Howard, Sparkman, Cohen, Green, & Stanislaw, 2005; Perry, Cohen, & De Carlo, 1995; Sallows & Graupner, 2005; Smith, 1999; Smith, Groen, & Wynne, 2000) and a vast amount of both basic and applied research applicable to the human race in general, including individuals with autism (Cooper, Heron, & Heward, 2007). Indeed, changes in social and adaptive behavior are frequently measured to determine the efficacy of special education placements and behavioral intervention protocols (Remington et al., 2007).

Osnes and Lieblein conducted a literature review and determined that the empirical assessment of the generalization of behavioral interventions "continues to be an elusive entity" (2003, p. 371). Generalizing and maintaining social and adaptive skills and assessing long-term outcomes within the context of family life are necessary for evaluating specific instructional strategies and measuring programmatic effectiveness in general. Critical measures of emerging social and adaptive skills that enhance the personal independence of individuals with autism are the effect of these repertoires on the level of moment-to-moment supervision required to maintain them safely at home and the measurement of the effects on parental stress and anxiety associated with raising a child with an autism spectrum disorder.

PARENTAL ANXIETY AND STRESS

Education professionals generally have direct student contact with children with autism spectrum disorders no more than 5–6 hours per day (equivalent to 25–30 hours per week); they are often tired and eager for their charges to go home by the end of the school day. However, the existing social system and established educational processes require parents to shoulder the burden of teaching adaptive and social skills for much greater periods of time and be primarily responsible for generalizing those skills across a variety of home circumstances and community settings. If these children are in school 30 hours per week and sleep 8 hours per night, then their parents may have primary care and educational responsibility for them 74 hours per week when school is in session and 104 hours per week when school is not in session, in addition to competing priorities (e.g., work, other children, aging parents). Many children with autism also have atypical sleep patterns and may sleep less than children who are typically developing or those with other developmental disabilities (Goodlin-Jones, Tang, Liu, & Anders, 2008). As a result, many parents do not get adequate sleep each night as they ensure the safety and well-being of their children throughout the night.

The demands of raising a child with autism can be overwhelming—even to the most highly educated and dedicated parent. There is a sizable body of research that evaluates parental anxiety and stress relative to raising one or more children with autism spectrum disorders (Cassidy, McConkey, Truesdale-Kennedy, & Slevin, 2008; Fitzgerald, Birkbeck, & Matthews, 2002; Gray, 2006; Liwag, 1989). Increased parental stress has been correlated with the presence or the absence of adaptive skills in their children with autism (Gray, 1997; Robbins, Dunlap, & Plienis, 1991).

Parents are responsible not only for the everyday parenting of their children but also for performing many other duties—such as filling the role of program administrator, education advocate, and teacher—that may contribute to increased levels of parental stress. In addition to teaching new repertoires of skill sets without the benefit of formal training, parents face myriad difficult decisions across their life span that can affect their levels of stress, such as having to choose among taking out a second mortgage on their home to pay for therapeutic services, addressing sibling

issues (Senel & Akkok, 1995), advocating and hiring legal counsel to protect their child's due process rights, or obtaining placement for their child
in a nonfamily residential setting (Benderix, Nordstrom, & Sivberg, 2006;
Holroyd, Brown, Wikler, & Simmons, 1975).

Certainly parents of children who are typically developing experience
anxiety and stress related to their children from time to time, and parents
of children with serious medical conditions or disabilities will experience
elevated levels of anxiety and stress. However, families of children with
autism experience higher levels of anxiety and stress than parents of children with other medical issues or severe disabilities (Bouma & Schweitzer,
1990; Brown, MacAdam-Crisp, Wang, & Iaroci, 2006; Holroyd et al., 1975;
Sanders & Morgan, 1997) and for longer periods of time (Gray, 2006). The
factors that result in the greatest increases of anxiety and stress have not been
fully evaluated. The effect of potential stressors—such as the socioeconomic
status of the family; a family's race, culture, or ethnicity; the availability or
the quality of educational services; the availability of home-based supports
and services; the configuration of family units; preexisting parental psychopathology; or the availability of an extended family presence—has not been
adequately evaluated to date.

Research assessing the efficacy of strategies to alleviate or remediate parental stress is needed, although there is some evidence that parental resilience might be a critical factor (Bayat, 2007; Gray, 2006; Twoy,
Connolly, & Novak, 2007). Other research questions of interest include
the following:

- Is there a correlation between the parents' and the child's adaptive
  repertoires?
- Do families whose child has a dual diagnosis or those with more than
  one child with a disability have increased anxiety and parental stress?
- Is the divorce rate for parents of children with autism spectrum disorders
  higher than, lower than, or the same as that of the general population
  or of parents whose children are medically fragile or have other serious
  impairments?
- Is parental anxiety and stress different for those with children with
  high-functioning autism or Asperger syndrome versus those more significantly affected by autism?
- What services or supports positively influence the quality of life for
  children and their families?
- Can parent training reduce anxiety and stress? If so, what specific skill
  sets generate the most positive outcomes and enhance familial quality
  of life?

- Is there a correlation between parental stress and a child's level of stress? If so, how does this correspond to the level of a child's cognitive impairment?
- Do emerging medical issues related to the aging process of either the parents or the child increase anxiety and stress?
- What is the effect of the death of a parent on surviving family members, including the siblings of the child with autism?

Unlike people with some other disabilities, people with autism do not typically experience specific constellations of other medical complications that will significantly shorten people's life expectancy (Shavelle & Strauss, 1998). It is highly probable that people with autism will outlive their parents, consistent with the life expectancies of the population at large. Expanding the concept of family life in both research and practice to include issues related to groups associated by affinity or coresidence rather than solely by genetic association is also needed. Research questions specific to alternative residential settings include the following:

- Does placement in a nonfamily residential setting reduce aging parent or sibling anxiety and stress?
- Does the level of staffing, staff training, or the length of employment correlate to increased or decreased anxiety and stress for caregivers of people with autism or cohabitants?
- Does the number of cohabitants per residence or the similarity in the adaptive skill levels of the cohabitants affect the anxiety and the stress of either the caregivers or the cohabitants?
- Do the caregivers of adolescents and adults with autism spectrum disorders in residential homes experience increases in anxiety and stress as do family members or guardians?
- If the caregivers of adolescents and adults with autism spectrum disorders experience increased anxiety and stress, is it due to the same variables? Will the same remedies generate the most positive outcomes and enhance the residential quality of life for caregivers and clients as those used to assist the parents of people with autism?

There are many unanswered questions regarding what can be done to reduce stress and anxiety among families of children with autism and in individuals with autism themselves. There is some evidence that teaching individuals with autism new social and adaptive skills can reduce familial stress, and one promising method of accelerating the development of these skills is by enlisting the parents as partners in the educational process.

PARENT TRAINING

Given the reliance on parents as the primary agents of behavior change, it is not surprising that parent training has received considerable attention from both practitioners and researchers (Koegel, Bimbela, & Schreibman, 1996; Lerman, Swiezy, & Perkins-Parks, 2000; Phaneuf & McIntyre, 2007; Schertz & Odom, 2007). Many autism professionals consider parent training to be one of the hallmarks of a comprehensive educational program. Fitzgerald et al. (2002) found that parent training designed to increase self-care and independence can help remediate parental stress.

The assessment of parent training strategies, however, suffers from several fatal flaws and has yet to be translated into the generation of comprehensive, effective protocols that can be widely implemented. For example, a parent training curriculum is often conceptualized as a modification of information tidbits and strategies based on existing staff training programs, even though these two populations are wildly different across many critical features. Autism professionals select their instructional staff based on their education, experience, interests, and skills. Parents are not preselected based on any criteria—other than having a child with autism—and may represent a much broader range of skills, cognitive abilities, motivations, and competing priorities. As noted previously, the total amount of time that parents spend with their children is far greater than the amount of time that these children are in school. This difference alone may contribute to parental inability to consistently implement educational strategies across a longer period of time and a greater number of environmental conditions. For example, a complex data collection system designed to monitor the acquisition of an emerging social behavior, such as physically orienting toward a speaker, that can be accurately implemented across a 6-hour school day by multiple instructors may be impossible for a single parent to consistently implement in home and community settings.

There is evidence in the literature that instructional staff require ongoing supervision and training to prevent instructional "drift" (Cooper et al., 2007, p. 235). Effective employee training protocols include evaluating levels of performance and providing additional training as needed to maintain or improve teaching skills. Yet parent training is often conceived of as a "one-shot deal." One area for future research is assessing the durability of the effects of parent training. Another important question for future researchers to address is whether parent training that targets adaptive skills results in enhanced quality of family life and increased parental motivation to sustain their training efforts over time.

FROM RESEARCH TO
PRACTICE; FROM PRACTICE TO RESEARCH

Although far from complete, a substantive body of research already exists in the areas of social and adaptive skill development for children with autism spectrum disorders and their families. A wide array of recommended practices is also implemented in schools and homes. These practices are both derived from that body of research and employed in spite of that research and a host of strategies and methodologies that are, as yet, untested by scientific inquiry. The circle of research leading to better practice and practice generating novel research questions is fractured and incomplete.

Much of the existing body of research has not been translated into the "lingua franca" of public school educators, parents, administrators, health and human service professionals, special education attorneys, mass media, the community at large, or even other researchers working in related fields. Cross-communication between researchers and practitioners or among professional disciplines occurs sporadically and accidentally, not through a concerted effort to translate what is known into usable information for a variety of constituencies. For example, a behavior analyst might define an early learning to learn social skill as orienting toward an adult, whereas a parent might define social behavior as being able to sustain play with a sibling or have a friend. Because of differing perspectives, a parent might erroneously conclude that a behavior analyst is not teaching social skills to his or her child with autism.

Enhanced communication among various groups of stakeholders may facilitate the better use of the evidence-based practices that autism service providers already have in their arsenal and generate novel research questions that are socially relevant to the lives of families and school communities. Medical practitioners and research have historically confronted the same dilemma and have learned to modify their terminology to be more understandable to both patients and lay audiences. In addition to translating the results of and the implications of research, both applied and basic researchers can aid this communication process by disseminating their results beyond scholarly venues and into the publications of other related fields of interest.

Autism service providers usually think of the social effects of autism in relation to the child rather than the child's family. Scientists, educators, administrators, and policy makers have not yet focused sufficient attention and resources on the broader family impact of this devastating disorder. Perhaps someday, in addition to a diagnosis and a copy of their due process rights, the parents of children with autism will be provided with a bill of rights as follows.

The Parents' Bill of Rights

Parents of a child with autism are guaranteed to have the following:

- Timely, accurate, and complete evaluations for their child and specific recommendations that are tied to known research
- Timely and effective intervention, medical treatments, and family supports based on recommended practices and evidence
- Administrative and accountability systems aligned with best practices, research, and legal mandates
- Community acceptance
- Life for their child and family in the least restrictive environment
- A fulfilling and joyful life without undue guilt and regret
- Hope for the future
- The gift of going to their graves at peace knowing that their child will lead his or her life with dignity, purpose, and grace

REFERENCES

Ahearn, W. (2003). Using simultaneous presentation to increase vegetable consumption in a mildly selective child with autism. *Journal of Applied Behavior Analysis, 36*(3), 361–365.

Akmanoglu-Uludag, N., & Batu, S. (2005). Teaching naming relatives to individuals with autism using simultaneous prompting. *Education and Training in Developmental Disabilities, 40*(4), 401–410.

Alcantara, P. (1994). Effects of videotape instructional package on purchasing skills of children with autism. *Exceptional Children, 61*(1), 40–55.

Anglesea, M., Hoch, H., & Taylor, B. (2008). Reducing rapid eating in teenagers with autism: Use of a pager prompt. *Journal of Applied Behavior Analysis, 41*, 107–111.

Bainbridge, N., & Myles, B. (1999). The use of priming to introduce toilet training to a child with autism. *Focus on Autism and Other Developmental Disabilities, 14*(2), 106–109.

Bayat, M. (2007). Evidence of resilience in families of children with autism. *Journal of Intellectual Disability Research, 51*(9), 702–714.

Benderix, Y., Nordstrom, B., & Sivberg, B. (2006). Parents' experience of having a child with autism and learning disabilities living in a group home. *Autism, 10*(6), 629–641.

Berliner, D. (2002). Educational research: The hardest science of all. *Educational Researchers, 31*(8), 18–20.

Boelter, E., Wacker, D., Call, J., Ringdahl, J., Kopelman, T., & Gardner, A. (2007). Effects of antecedent variables on disruptive behavior and accurate responding in young children in outpatient settings. *Journal of Applied Behavior Analysis, 40*, 321–326.

Bouma, R., & Schweitzer, R. (1990). The impact of chronic childhood illness on family stress: A comparison between autism and cystic fibrosis. *Journal of Clinical Psychology, 46*(6), 722–730.

Bouxsein, K., Tiger, J., & Fisher, W. (2008). A comparison of general and specific instructions to promote task engagement and completion by a young man with Asperger syndrome. *Journal of Applied Behavior Analysis, 41*, 133–146.

Brown, R., MacAdam-Crisp, J., Wang, M., & Iaroci, G. (2006). Family quality of life when there is a child with a developmental disability. *Journal of Policy and Practice in Intellectual Disabilities, 3*(4), 238–245.

Bruzek, J., & Thompson, R. (2007). Antecedent effects of observing peer play. *Journal of Applied Behavior Analysis, 40*, 327–331.

Cassidy, A., McConkey, R., Truesdale-Kennedy, M., & Slevin, E. (2008). Pre-schoolers with autism spectrum disorders: The impact on families and the supports available to them. *Early Child Development and Care, 178*(2), 115–128.

Cooper, J., Heron, T., & Heward, W. (2007). *Applied behavior analysis.* Upper Saddle River, NJ: Prentice Hall.

Durand, M. (2002). Treating sleep terrors in children with autism. *Journal of Positive Behavior Interventions, 4*(2), 66–72.

Durand, M., & Christodulu, K. (2004). Description of a sleep-restriction program to reduce bedtime disturbances and night waking. *Journal of Positive Behavior Interventions, 6*(2), 83–91.

Eikeseth, S., Smith, T., Jahr, E., & Eldevik, S. (2002). Intensive behavioral treatment at school for 4–7-year-old children with autism: A 1-year comparison control study. *Behavior Modification, 31*, 49–68.

Ellis, E., Ala'i-Rosales, S., & Glenn, S. (2006). The effects of graduated exposure, modeling, and contingent social attention on tolerance to skin care products with two children with autism. *Research in Developmental Disabilities, 27*(6), 585–598.

Field, S., & Hoffman, A. (1999). The importance of family involvement for promoting self-determination in adolescents with autism and other developmental disabilities. *Focus on Autism and Other Developmental Disabilities, 14*(1), 36–41.

Fitzgerald, M., Birkbeck, G., & Matthews, P. (2002). Maternal burden in families with children with autistic spectrum disorder. *Irish Journal of Psychology, 23*(1–2), 2–17.

Fullerton, A., & Coyne, P. (1999). Developing skills and concepts for self-determination in young adults with autism. *Focus on Autism and Other Developmental Disabilities, 14*(1), 42–52.

Goodlin-Jones, B., Tang, K., Liu, J., & Anders, T. (2008). Sleep patterns in pre-school age children with autism, developmental delay, and typical development. *Journal of the American Academy of Child & Adolescent Psychiatry, 47*(8), 932–940.

Gray, D. (1997). High functioning autistic children and the construction of "normal family life." *Social Science & Medicine, 44*(8), 1097–1106.

Gray, D. (2006). Coping over time: The parents of children with autism. *Journal of Mental Disability Research, 50*(12), 970–976.

Green, G., Brennan, L.C., & Fein, D. (2002). Intensive behavioral treatment for a toddler at high risk for autism. *Behavior Modification, 26*, 69–102.

Guralnick, M.J. (1999). Family and child influences on the peer-related social competence of young children with developmental delays. *Mental Retardation and Developmental Disabilities Research Reviews, 5,* 21–29.

Held, M., Thoma, C., & Thomas, K. (2004). "The John Jones Show": How one teacher facilitated self-determined transition planning for a young man with autism. *Focus on Autism and Other Developmental Disabilities, 19*(3), 177–188.

Holroyd, J., Brown, N., Wikler, L., & Simmons, J. (1975). Stress in families of institutionalized and noninstitutionalized autistic children. *Journal of Community Psychology, 3*(1), 26–31.

Howard, J.S., Sparkman, C.R., Cohen, H.G., Green, G., & Stanislaw, H. (2005). A comparison of intensive behavior analytic and eclectic treatments for young children with autism. *Research in Developmental Disabilities, 26,* 359–383.

Hurren, J. (1994). The therapeutic use of play, recreation and leisure for children with autism and developmental disorders. *Journal on Developmental Disabilities, 3*(1), 51–62.

Jerome, J., Frantino, E., & Strumey, P. (2007). The effects of errorless learning and backward chaining on the acquisition of internet skills in adults with developmental disabilities. *Journal of Applied Behavior Analysis, 40*(1), 185–189.

Jones, E., Feeley, K., & Takacs, J. (2007). Teaching spontaneous responses to young children with autism. *Journal of Applied Behavior Analysis, 40,* 565–570.

Keen, D., Brannigan, K., & Cuskelly, M. (2007). Toilet training for children with autism: The effects of video modeling category. *Journal of Developmental and Physical Disabilities, 19*(4), 291–303.

Koegel, R., Bimbela, A., & Schreibman, L. (1996). Collateral effects of parent training on family interactions. *Journal of Autism and Developmental Disorders, 26*(3), 347–359.

Legoff, D., & Sherman, M. (2006). Long-term outcome of social skills intervention based on interactive LEGO play. *Autism, 10*(4), 317–329.

Lerman, D., Swiezy, N., & Perkins-Parks, S. (2000). Skill acquisition in parents of children with developmental disabilities: Interaction between skill type and instructional format. *Research in Developmental Disabilities, 21*(3), 183–196.

Liwag, M. (1989). Mothers and fathers of autistic children: An exploratory study of family stress and coping. *Philippine Journal of Psychology, 22,* 3–16.

Luiselli, J., Ricciardi, J., & Gilligan, K. (2005). Liquid fading to establish mild consumption by a child with autism. *Behavioral Interventions, 20*(2), 155–163.

Maione, L., & Mirenda, P. (2006). Effects of video modeling and video feedback on peer-directed social language skills of a child with autism. *Journal of Positive Behavior Interventions, 8*(2), 106–118.

Matson, J., Matson, M., & Rivet, T. (2007). Social-skills treatments for children with autism spectrum disorders. *Behavior Modification, 31*(5), 682–707.

Newman, B., Reinecke, D., & Meinberg, D. (2000). Self-management of varied responding in three students with autism. *Behavioral Interventions, 15*(2), 145–151.

Osnes, P., & Lieblein, T. (2003). An explicit technology of generalization. *The Behavior Analyst Today, 3*(4), 364–374.

Paul, C., Williams, K., & Riegel, K. (2007). Combining repeated taste exposure and escape prevention: An intervention for the treatment of extreme food selectivity. *Appetite, 49*(3), 708–711.

Perry, R., Cohen, I., & De Carlo, R. (1995). Case study: Deterioration, autism, and recovery in two siblings. *Journal of the American Academy of Child and Adolescent Psychiatry, 34*, 232–237.

Phaneuf, L., & McIntyre, L. (2007). Effects of individualized video feedback combined with group parent training on inappropriate maternal behavior. *Journal of Applied Behavior Analysis, 40*, 737–741.

Reeve, S., Reeve, K., Buffington-Townsend, D., & Poulson, C. (2007). Establishing a generalized repertoire of helping behavior in children with autism. *Journal of Applied Behavior Analysis, 40*, 123–136.

Reichle, J., McComas, J., & Dahl, N. (2005). Teaching an individual with severe intellectual delay to request assistance conditionally. *Educational Psychology, 25*(2–3), 275–286.

Remington, B., Hastings, R., Kovshoff, H., Espinosa, F., Jahr, E., Brown, T.,…Ward, N. (2007). Early intensive behavioral intervention: Outcomes for children with autism and their parents after two years. *Journal on Mental Retardation, 112*(6), 418–438.

Robbins, F., Dunlap, G., & Plienis, A. (1991). Family characteristics, family training, and the progress of young children with autism. *Journal of Early Intervention, 15*(2), 173–184.

Sakamoto, M., Muto, T., & Mochizuki, A. (2003). Enhancing the self-determination of students with autism: Evaluation of a training package for teachers. *Japanese Journal of Behavior Analysis, 18*(1), 25–37.

Sallows, G., & Graupner, T. (2005). Intensive behavioral treatment for children with autism: Four-year outcome and predictors. *American Journal on Mental Retardation, 110*(6), 417–438.

Sanders, J., & Morgan, S. (1997). Family stress and adjustment as perceived by parents of children with autism and Down syndrome: Implications for intervention. *Child & Family Behavior Therapy, 19*(4), 15–32.

Schertz, H., & Odom, S. (2007). Promoting joint attention in toddlers with autism: A parent-mediated developmental model. *Journal of Autism and Developmental Disorders, 37*(8), 1562–1575.

Schreck, K., & Williams, K. (2006). Food preferences and factors influencing food selectivity for children with autism spectrum disorders. *Research in Developmental Disabilities, 27*(4), 353–363.

Senel, H., & Akkok, F. (1995). Stress levels and attitudes of normal siblings of children with disabilities. *International Journal for the Advancement of Counseling, 18*(2), 61–68.

Shabani, D., & Fisher, W. (2006). Stimulus fading and differential reinforcement for the treatment of needle phobia in a youth with autism. *Journal of Applied Behavior Analysis, 39*, 449–452.

Shavelle, R., & Strauss, D. (1998). Comparative mortality of persons with autism in California, 1980–1996. *Journal of Insurance Medicine, 30*, 220–225.

Smith, T. (1999). Outcome of early intervention for children with autism. *Clinical Psychology: Science and Practice, 6*, 33–49.

Smith, T., Groen, A., & Wynne, J. (2000). Randomized trial of intensive early intervention for children with pervasive developmental disorder. *American Journal on Mental Retardation, 105*(4), 269–285.

Snell, M., & Brown, F. (2006). *Instruction of students with severe disabilities* (6th ed.). Upper Saddle River, NJ: Prentice Hall.

Taylor, S., Cipani, E., & Clardy, A. (1994). A stimulus control technique for improving the efficacy of an established toilet training program. *Journal of Behavior Therapy and Experimental Psychiatry, 25*(2), 155–160.

Twoy, R., Connolly, P., & Novak, J. (2007). Coping strategies used by parents of children with autism. *Journal of the American Academy of Nurse Practitioners, 19*(5), 251–260.

Wall, M., & Gast, D. (1997). Caregivers' use of constant time delay to teach leisure skills to adolescents or young adults with moderate or severe intellectual disabilities. *Education & Training in Mental Retardation & Developmental Disabilities, 32*(4), 340–356.

Weiskop, S., Richdale, A., & Matthews, J. (2005). Behavioral treatment to reduce sleep problems in children with autism or fragile X syndrome. *Developmental Medicine & Child Neurology, 47*(2), 94–104.

The Assessment of Social Skills

Erik A. Mayville

There are few behaviors that as broadly affect human functioning as those that serve as the basis for social interaction. Such behaviors are numerous, spanning nonverbal and verbal topographical domains and a multitude of environment–behavior relationships. The process of assessing social behaviors that facilitate successful social interaction (i.e., social skills) is therefore complex, particularly when the difficulties in social interaction characteristic of autism spectrum disorders (ASDs) are considered. In this chapter, I describe the particular challenges of assessing social skills in individuals with ASDs and examine the existing measures that are suitable for this task. I conclude with suggestions for needed research on assessment practices in both research and clinical contexts.

SOCIAL SKILLS AND SOCIAL COMPETENCE DEFINED

Social skills are commonly characterized as verbal and nonverbal behaviors that enable a person to interact positively with others (Elliott & Gresham, 1987; Matson, Matson, & Rivet, 2007) and avoid negative consequences (Gesten, Weisberg, Amish, & Smith, 1987). A survey of several commonly used measures of social skills reveals several constituent constructs, such as cooperation, assertiveness, self-control, and responsibility (Gresham & Elliott, 1990); interpersonal relationships (Sparrow, Ciccetti, & Balla, 2005); and inappropriate assertiveness/impulsiveness (Matson, 1994). Elliott and Gresham (1987) described categories of social skills definitions based on outcomes of social behavior (i.e., ratings of peer acceptance), observed behaviors and their context, and skills that are perceived by a child to influence a certain positive outcome. The term *social competency* is sometimes used interchangeably with *social skills*, although social competency can be distinguished from social skills in judging the degree to which a person skillfully exhibits social behaviors and achieves important outcomes, including establishing and maintaining

17

satisfactory interpersonal relationships, gaining peer acceptance, and terminating harmful personal relationships (Gesten et al., 1987; Gresham, 1983). Determining the degree to which a person is socially competent is often a goal in assessing social skills, which is achieved by assessing both the presence and the absence of positive skills (e.g., attempts household tasks before asking for help, accepts others' ideas for help; Gresham & Elliott, 1990) and negative skills (e.g., becomes angry easily, always wants to be first; Matson, 1994).

Social Skills and Autism Spectrum Disorders

In the *Diagnostic and Statistical Manual of Mental Disorders, Fourth Edition, Text Revision* (*DSM-IV-TR*; American Psychiatric Association [APA], 2000), impairment in social functioning is commonly described as a secondary result of a disorder, not a core feature of a disorder. Exceptions to this are the criteria for autism and other pervasive developmental disorders (henceforth collectively described as ASDs) in which impairment in social interaction is a primary aspect. Such impairment translates to impairments in social skills. For example, when comparing scores among children with ASDs and children who are typically developing on a social skills measure designed for populations that are typically developing, Matson, Stabinsky Compton, and Sevin (1991) found a greater degree of negative social behavior and a lesser degree of positive social skills in the group with ASDs compared with the group that is typically developing. However, social skill impairment in ASDs often includes impairments that extend beyond those often relevant in populations that are typically developing. In particular, the four criteria in the impairment in social interaction domain described in *DSM-IV-TR* represent a fundamental disturbance in relating to others, including impairment in using multiple nonverbal gestures, in spontaneous sharing of interests and occurrences, and in exhibiting social or emotional reciprocity (APA, 2000).

A repertoire consisting of all these behaviors is joint attention, which is defined as the capacity of an individual to coordinate attention with a partner for the purposes of sharing an event or an object (Mundy & Burnette, 2005). For example, when seeing an airplane fly overhead, a child might point to the plane, look back to her mother while smiling and exclaiming "Plane!" and then look back to the plane as her mother directs her own gaze toward it. Research suggests that competency in this domain predicts competency in others, such as language, imitation, and play skills (Jones, Carr, & Feeley, 2006; Whalen, Schreibman, & Ingersoll, 2006), and children with ASDs are more likely than children who are typically developing to exhibit impairments in joint attention (Mundy & Crowson, 1997; Sigman & Kasari, 1995).

Joint attention has been considered as a component of a larger category of behavior known as social cognition, which is defined as an ability to recognize, manipulate, and behave with respect to socially relevant information (Adolphs, Sears, & Piven, 2001). Social cognition and the domain of communication known as pragmatic language—which involves comprehending and expressing language in conversational contexts—represent relatively rudimentary concepts that individuals who are typically developing usually acquire and use daily. However, such behavior is often very difficult for people with ASDs to understand and exhibit and constitutes a "hidden curriculum" of frequently changing rules and expectations. For example, researchers have found that people with ASDs have impairments in describing others' reasons for behaving in accordance with emotional and informational states (i.e., perspective taking; Dawson & Fernald, 1987; Klin, Volkmar, & Sparrow, 1992); in recognizing and discriminating among faces and facial expressions (Dawson, Webb, & McPartland, 2005; Kasari & Sigman, 1996); in understanding intention and related concepts, such as deception (Baron-Cohen, 1992); and in "binding" details as a whole as opposed to focusing on only a few in problem solving (cf. Baron-Cohen & Belmonte, 2005; Rincover, Feldman, & Eason, 1986), among others. Such impairments can be viewed as some of the key repertoires described in *DSM-IV-TR* as significant impairment in social interaction.

There are also several areas of impairments within the other two *DSM-IV-TR* diagnostic criteria categories—communication and repetitive and restricted interests—as well as associated features of ASDs that can affect social competence. People with ASDs have been found to have difficulties in multiple aspects of pragmatic language, including understanding inference (Dennis, Lazenby, & Lockyear, 2001); comprehending the influence of the tone of voice on language meaning (Happe, 1993); maintaining cohesion in topics within conversation (Fine, Bartolucci, Szatmari, & Ginsberg, 1994); and using mental state verbs, such as believing, knowing, imagining, and remembering (Tager-Flusberg, 1992). Individuals with ASDs may also display impairments in aspects of language production, such as intonation, volume, rate, stress, and rhythm (Shriberg et al., 2001), that may compromise attempts to verbally socialize. In addition, preoccupation with restricted interests may manifest in atypical play behavior and one-sided conversation on topics of little or no interest to others (APA, 2000). Finally, impairments in personal daily-living skills, including toileting, grooming, and bathing, are not uncommon among people with ASDs (Bölte & Poustka, 2002) and can compromise social competency (cf. Stokes, Cameron, Dorsey, & Fleming, 2004).

One of the most important aspects of a social skill repertoire is the ability to implement skills with relative precision, that is, under select conditions informed by conditional stimuli, such as a communicative partner's nonverbal or verbal behavior and a multitude of environmental setting variables. Relevant aspects of behavior include latency (i.e., the amount of time passing between stimuli indicating a particular social behavior and the execution of that behavior), discrimination, generalization, and motivation; these aspects are at least as important when assessing behavioral topography in considering one's degree of social competence. (For an example of a multidimensional conceptual model of social competence in ASD, see Romanczyk, White, & Gillis, 2005.) Generalization, the degree to which responding reinforced in the presence of particular stimulus conditions extends to similar stimuli beyond the initial acquisition context, has proven an elusive outcome thus far in group-based social skill interventions (Bellini, Peters, Benner, & Hopf, 2007; Rao, Beidel, & Murray, 2008). Conversely, overgeneralization (i.e., a lack of discrimination) is another crucial issue (e.g., starting small talk with others in inappropriate places, such as at adjacent urinals in a men's restroom). The issue of motivation is a crucial but often overlooked assessment dimension; that is, does the individual appear interested in social contact and, most important, under what conditions? In a discussion of interventions to increase joint attention in children with ASDs, Jones and Carr noted that the natural consequence for joint attention—social interaction about the object of joint attention—"is typically not reinforcing to children with autism" (2004, p. 22). This underscores the importance of assessing reinforcement contingencies underlying social interactions and what social stimuli might be reinforcing to the individual with an ASD.

In summary, the types of social difficulties common to people with ASDs may necessitate assessments of different topographies and features of behavior than are typical for people without ASDs. In the next section, I discuss the tools that have been created for this process.

SOCIAL SKILLS ASSESSMENT METHODS

The most common social skills assessment modalities are direct observation of social behavior in natural or analog environments and rating scales completed in interview format or independently by people who know the participant. The assessment tools described in this section either have been evaluated for use with people with ASDs or have been employed in research with this population (with the exception of curriculum-based assessment tools) and were selected from among several social skills assessments for this reason. (For a more detailed review, see Gerhardt & Mayville, 2010.) Because of space limitations, the assessment tools of constructs related to social skills in people with ASDs (e.g., problem solving, nonverbal behavior comprehension, paralinguistic behavior, language) are not described here. Judgments regarding reliability and validity properties (i.e., excellent, good, fair) are adapted from Cicchetti (1994).

Rating Scales for Autism Spectrum Disorder Populations

Rating scales constitute a "first-line" assessment modality in assessing social skills in children who are typically developing, primarily because of their suitability for assessment of low-rate behavior and the high reliability of many scales (Merrell, 2001), as well as a variety of behaviors that can be covered quickly from multiple sources (Elliott, Malecki, & Demaray, 2001). Using rating scales for individuals with ASDs as a component of the assessment process makes sense for the same reasons. However, almost no rating scales are designed to measure social skills for people with ASDs, and no scales have been established as sensitive to social skill effects, an ironic state of affairs given the centrality of social functioning to ASDs. Two measures that are composed of relevant social behavior, the Social Responsiveness Scale (SRS; Constantino, 2002) and the Children's Social Behavior Questionnaire (CSBQ; Hartman, Luteijn, Serra, & Minderaa, 2006; Luteijn, Jackson, Volkmar, & Minderaa, 1998) were designed as diagnostic measures but can function as measures of social skills. Only one measure—the Autism Social Skills Profile (ASSP; Bellini & Hopf, 2007)—was designed as a measure of social skills for intervention planning and monitoring purposes.

The SRS is a brief screening assessment for ASDs that emphasizes social reciprocity behaviors in individuals between 4 and 18 years old. Subscales include Social Awareness, Social Cognition, Social Communication, Social Motivation, and Autistic Mannerisms. Normative data for the SRS are based on a sample of more than 1,600 children; T-scores are produced for all subscales and the total score. Interrater and test–retest reliability is excellent (i.e., >.80; Constantino, Przybeck, Friesen, & Todd, 2000). Research on convergent validity has illustrated that the SRS correlates well with established measures of autistic symptomatology (Constantino et al., 2003).

The CSBQ was designed to assist in identifying individuals with pervasive developmental disorder-not otherwise specified (PDD-NOS), which is a diagnostic category typically characterized by relatively subtle reciprocal social impairment compared with other ASDs (Luteijn et al., 1998). The original 135-item questionnaire was reduced to 49 items, a process guided by factor analysis and clinical judgment (Hartman et al., 2006). Normative data for the CSBQ are not readily available. The overall internal consistency of the CSBQ is excellent (Cronbach's alpha = .94), with subscale internal consistency ranging from fair (e.g., alpha = .76 for stereotyped behavior) to excellent (e.g., alpha = .90 for not optimally tuned to the social situation; Luteijn, Luteijn, Jackson, Volkmar, & Minderaa, 2000). Interrater and test–retest reliabilities for overall and subscale scores were also excellent (e.g., overall correlations of .86 and .90, respectively; Luteijn et al., 2000). Regarding validity, the CSBQ has been assessed as having a stable, six-factor solution and has been found to discriminate among individuals with PDD-NOS and other difficulties (e.g., attention-deficit/hyperactivity disorder, intellectual disability; Hartman et al., 2006).

The ASSP was designed primarily as a tool for quick and precise identification of social skill impairments in children with ASDs and for monitoring intervention effects in the areas of social behavior and communication
(Bellini & Hopf, 2007). In a preliminary evaluation of psychometric properties, the ASSP was found to have excellent test–retest reliability and internal
consistency for subscale and total scores. It consists of three subscales derived
from factor analysis: Social Reciprocity (e.g., recognizes the facial expressions of others, joins a conversation without interrupting, maintains personal
hygiene), Social Participation/Avoidance (e.g., exhibits fear or anxiety about
social interactions, engages in solitary actions near peers), and Detrimental
Social Behaviors (e.g., misinterprets the intentions of others, recognizes the
body language of others). Additional research on the ASSP is needed to investigate its interrater reliability, validity, and sensitivity to change given its
purpose of assessing intervention effects.

Rating Scales for
Populations Without Autism Spectrum Disorders

Rating scales designed for populations without ASDs (e.g., children who
are typically developing, adults without disabilities) may be useful in identifying a wider ranger of behaviors representative of social competence.
They can also be particularly helpful in measuring the degree to which
social skills interventions lead to outcomes that are socially valid, that is,
outcomes that are of great social importance and have a great impact on an
individual's everyday life (Gresham, 1983; Wolf, 1978). The Social Skills
Rating System (SSRS; Gresham & Elliott, 1990) is commonly used in social skills research with children who are typically developing, and with
people with ASD as a measure of improvement in global social functioning
(cf. Barry, Zeber, Blow, & Valenstein, 2003; Bauminger, 2002). Estimates
of reliability and validity of the SSRS vary somewhat across response formats. Internal consistency estimates are low to excellent (.63 to .90) for the
parent and the student forms and good to excellent for the teacher forms.
Test–retest reliability is excellent for the teacher form (.75 to .93), fair to
excellent for the parent form (.48 to .87), and fair to good for the student
form (.52 to .68). The SSRS has been assessed as valid regarding content,
construct, and criterion validity (Gresham & Elliott, 1990, pp. 112–141).
Norms exist for ages 3–10; 4,170 children's ratings, 1,027 parent ratings,
and 259 teacher ratings were included.

The Vineland Adaptive Behavior Scales (Sparrow, Balla, & Cicchetti,
1984; Sparrow et al., 2005) are commonly used to rate adaptive behavior in
clinical settings for people with ASDs (Luiselli et al., 2001) and are widely
used in evaluations of early intensive behavioral intervention (cf. Eikeseth,
Smith, Jahr, & Eldevik, 2002, 2007; Howard, Sparkman, Cohen, Green, &

Stanislaw, 2005). Supplementary normative data for individuals with autism are available for the first edition of the Vineland Adaptive Behavior Scales (Carter et al., 1998) and on a smaller scale for the second edition of the Vineland Adaptive Behavior Scales. The socialization domain is well suited for assessing broadly defined social skills and includes items representing behavior relevant to people with ASDs, including nonverbal communication to regulate social interaction and the ability to keep and maintain personal relationships (Sparrow et al., 2005, p. 4). Psychometric data on both editions of the Vineland Adaptive Behavior Scales are extensive and largely reflective of very sound psychometric properties.

Direct Observation

Direct observation of behavior is another first-line assessment method of social skills (Merrell, 2001) and is a hallmark of interventions based on applied behavior analysis (ABA), which is an intervention approach yielding voluminous efficacy evidence for individuals with ASDs (cf. Eikeseth, 2009; Matson, Benavidez, Compton, Paclawskyj, & Baglio, 1996; Strain & Schwartz, 2001). Although direct observation may be an inefficient means of assessing low-frequency behaviors, it is perhaps the only means of conducting a detailed assessment of the contribution of multiple aspects of social behavior to social competence in particular contexts, as well as interpreting the influence of contextual variables on social behavior skills (i.e., functional assessment). This method can also be useful in confirming others' interpretations of an individual's skill repertoire produced from an informant-completed rating scale and has long been the method of choice in single-subject research on social skill outcomes (cf. Strain & Schwartz, 2001; Taylor, 2001).

Direct observation can occur under "naturalistic" conditions (e.g., playground, classroom, workplace) or in analog settings (e.g., under contrived conditions designed to simulate a particular context). For naturalistic observations, three conditions are desirable: observing and recording behaviors at the time of occurrence; using trained, objective observers; and a behavioral description system involving a minimal level of inference by the observers (Jones, Reid, & Patterson, 1979). Investigators have developed systems of coding behavior of children with ASDs in naturalistic settings for use in research (e.g., Anderson, Moore, Godfrey, & Fletcher-Flynn, 2004; Hauck, Fein, Waterhouse, & Feinstein, 1995) and typically report acceptable estimates of reliability for such procedures. However, target behaviors within these systems tend to account for potentially diverse behaviors under summary categories, such as initiations and responses, because accounting for the multiple levels of social behavior (e.g., nonverbal, verbal), the type of behavior (e.g., comments, questions), and the quality of social behavior (e.g., comments on- and off-topic, questions within and outside areas of repetitive interest, linguistic structure of vocalizations) can be an overwhelming task. Technological advances have yielded computer-based tools for direct observation that can potentially address these challenges (cf. Kaiser et al., 2000), although the observation of social behavior of children and adolescents with ASDs is not common in research or clinical settings.

The Autism Diagnostic Observation Scale (ADOS; Lord, Rutter, DiLavore, & Risi, 1999) is perhaps the most widely used tool for assessing social behavior in analog settings. The ADOS was designed to assist in diagnosing ASDs and consists of four different modules that vary in analog assessment methods according to an individual's language ability. The domains language and communication and reciprocal social interaction allow the assessment of several ASD-related social communicative behaviors, including eye contact, shared enjoyment in interaction, initiation of and response to joint attention, the quality of social overtures, language production and linked nonverbal communication, and insight. The ADOS is a reliable and valid diagnostic instrument (Gotham et al., 2008; Lord et al., 1999).

The Autism Screening Instrument for Educational Planning, Third Edition (ASIEP-III; Krug, Arick, & Almond, 2008) is another analog setting observation tool that has been formally evaluated for individuals with ASDs. The Interaction Assessment subtest is designed to "elicit an individual's social responses in a controlled setting with stimuli presented in a systematic fashion" (Krug et al., 2008, p. 2) and uses a variety of observation methodologies, including time sampling, anecdotal recording, and frequency recording. A child's behavior is assessed across three phases (Active Modeling, Passive No Initiation, and Direct Cues) and is recorded with respect to four variables in each phase: Interaction, Constructive Independent Play, No Response, and Aggressive Negative. Initial estimates of reliability (i.e., percent agreement) suggest that trained raters can (in most cases) reliably assign ratings to social behavior (i.e., percent agreement scores range from 73% to 100% for 77 of 87 trainees in the reliability sample), and rating items appear homogeneous and valid (i.e., Kuder-Richardson estimate = .86). The Interaction Assessment also appears capable of discriminating among children with ASDs and children with a severe disability without ASDs (Krug et al., 2008).

Curriculum-Based Assessment

When the purpose of assessment is to identify a sequence of behaviors for instruction, it is advisable to review the target individual's behavioral repertoire with respect to a curriculum. Although the term *curriculum* is most often associated with academic instruction, curriculum-based assessment (CBA) is described here because of the potential importance of curricula in designing and evaluating social skill interventions, as well as the likely frequent use of curricula in designing and implementing interventions in multiple functioning domains for children with ASDs (Love, Carr, Almason, & Petursdottir, 2009).

The term *curriculum* has multiple definitions, many of which incorporate instructional content, assessment procedures, and the means of selecting objectives, among others (Olley, 2005). The family of procedures known as CBA was developed as a means of using data on student performance to make decisions about instruction. (For a review, see Dunlap, Kern, & Worcester, 2001.) Specific procedures include using a series of brief tests in measuring student fluency in reading, math, spelling, and writing (i.e., curriculum-based measurement); designing and administering criterion-referenced tests corresponding to a series of sequentially arranged short objectives from a student's curriculum (i.e., criterion-referenced CBA); and employing direct observation and task-and-error analyses in task-analyzing skills and identifying student strengths and weaknesses in a curriculum (i.e., curriculum-based evaluation), among others (Dunlap et al., 2001).

Data-based CBA methods for selecting social skill objectives and assessing social skills intervention outcomes have not been described. In the only paper to use the term *CBA* for social skills assessment, Rubin and Laurent (2004) described a social-communication curriculum designed for individuals with ASDs that includes suggestions for assessment procedures. However, as of 2003 (Prizant, Wetherby, Rubin, & Laurent, 2003), data on the utility of a CBA approach with their curriculum—Social Communication, Emotional Regulation, and Transactional Support (SCERTS®)—had not been published. Practitioners using an ABA instructional approach are likely to approximate CBA procedures for social skills instruction given the emphasis on data-based decision making and the widespread use of curricula in such programs (Love et al., 2009). However, many of the curricula commonly used in these programs (Leaf & McEachin, 1999; Lovaas, 2003; Sundberg & Partington, 1998) do not offer detailed descriptions of the wide variety of social behavior likely to be relevant to the diverse needs of people with ASDs.

CHALLENGES TO TRANSLATING RESEARCH FINDINGS INTO EFFECTIVE PRACTICE

Perhaps the biggest challenge in translating research on social skills assessment into practice is the relative paucity of research on assessment methods. Only one ASD-specific social skills rating scale exists, and it has yet to be evaluated for one of the primary purposes for which it was created (i.e., measuring outcomes). Several diagnostic assessments may be effective for planning and in measuring outcomes (e.g., SRS, CSBQ, ADOS), but as of today, they are untested for these purposes. In the area of direct observation, no attention has been devoted to which observational procedures might yield the most reliable and valid results for which behaviors, an important variable given the expansiveness and the complexity of the social behavior domain. Although the number of commercially available ASD-specific social skills curricula is increasing, no data-based CBA procedures have been described. Thus, identifying challenges to putting research-based practices into action in clinical practice is a somewhat preliminary task.

Despite these needs, the voluminous body of single-subject research could serve as a valuable resource for practitioners wishing to design direct observation assessment procedures. However, these studies are spread throughout several journals, which pose access difficulty for clinicians. A paper or a book chapter compiling detailed descriptions of the direct observation procedures employed in these studies would be a helpful tool for research-based social skills assessment and intervention efforts.

RESEARCH-BASED RECOMMENDED PRACTICES

Although additional research in various aspects of social skills assessment is needed, some initial best-practice recommendations can be offered. In the field of social skills assessment and interventions with youthful, non-ASD populations, recommended practice suggestions have included employing a combination of rating scales and behavioral observation (Merrell, 2001). This recommendation has been echoed for people with ASDs (Gerhardt & Mayville, 2010) and is reiterated here. Administering only one assessment method, particularly rating scales, runs the risk of missing important information. For example, on the Vineland Adaptive Behavior Scales, Second Edition (Sparrow et al., 2005), a commonly used measure of adaptive behavior, an item on the interpersonal relationships subdomain requires an informant to indicate the degree to which an individual answers small-talk questions appropriately. "Appropriately" in this case would likely constitute multiple behaviors, including responding within an appropriate period of time following the question, emitting an acceptable length of response given the context (e.g., "Hi" might be an appropriate response when passing a coworker in the hallway but curt at a party when lengthier discussion might be expected), coordinating the response with multiple nonverbal behaviors (e.g., eye contact, head nodding, hand waving, smiling), and answering the question without significant errors in syntax and pragmatic language. Thus, the details about which aspects of behavior are relevant in this scenario would not be thoroughly informed by a response of "sometimes or partially true" on the small-talk item but would require one to observe how the target individual actually responds in context(s).

Furthermore, when using rating scales, it is important to administer measures surveying social behavior of particular relevance to populations with ASDs, rather than using measures only designed for general populations. For example, a school-age child with an ASD may be assessed on the SSRS (Gresham & Elliott, 1990)—an assessment for children who are typically developing—as not congratulating family members on accomplishments, not joining group activities without being asked, and not accepting others' ideas for playing. However, that same child could be assessed on the SRS (Constantino, 2002)—a measure designed for populations with ASDs—as not seeming to mind being "out of step" with others, avoiding starting social interactions, and not understanding others' tone of voice and facial expressions. The impairments on the latter scale may inform those reported on the former and might suggest a different course of intervention (e.g., conditioning basic social contact to be reinforcing; learning to initiate very limited contact with others and having it be reinforced before learning to join group activities).

RECOMMENDATIONS FOR FUTURE RESEARCH

A theme emerging from this review is the need for additional research on social skills assessment for people with ASDs. For clinical settings, additional research is needed on assessment practices. It is likely that people with ASDs are receiving assistance in social interaction to a greater degree than ever before, yet almost no studies inform what assessment or intervention practices are implemented in different resource venues (e.g., schools, clinics). From the available data, it appears that curricula are commonly used in behavioral intervention with children (Love et al., 2009). Research on CBA procedures for social skills for people with ASDs is very much needed given the importance of tools to guide the clinician in assessing which of the hundreds of social behaviors might be important to teach, in what order, and under what conditions and procedures for assessing progress and the need to modify instructional curricula. The majority of standardized social skills assessment tools are not likely to inform a clear course of intervention in this complicated area. Social skills assessments designed to monitor the effects of intervention for people with ASDs are also needed. This could be achieved by validating the existing intervention and diagnostic measures and constructing new measures for which intervention item selection rules are implemented (Meier, 1997, 2004). It is recommended that these measures contain items representing repertoires central to the impairments common to ASDs (e.g., joint attention). Research on the viability of different behavioral observation methods for different social behaviors is also needed, particularly those employing computer-based technology (cf. Thompson, Felce, & Symons, 2000).

Finally, a striking feature of the social skills literature is that the majority of studies are focused on assessing the social skills of children and some adolescents. Adults are chronically underrepresented in the social skills assessment literature, yet they constitute a sizable proportion of the population with ASDs in need of assistance in this area. Thus, subsequent efforts should include adult populations, particularly in developing methods that facilitate the assessment of socially valid behaviors in higher education and vocational settings, as well as those likely to result in the acquisition of other important behaviors (i.e., behavioral cusps) in such settings. (For an example with adults with developmental disabilities, see Hughes, Rodi, & Lorden, 2000.)

REFERENCES

Adolphs, R., Sears, L., & Piven, J. (2001). Abnormal processing of social information from faces in autism. *Journal of Cognitive Neuroscience, 13*, 232–240.

American Psychiatric Association. (2000). *Diagnostic and statistical manual of mental disorders* (4th ed., text rev.). Washington, DC: Author.

Anderson, A., Moore, D.W., Godfrey, R., & Fletcher-Flynn, C.M. (2004). Social skill assessment of some children with autism in free-play situations. *Autism, 8*, 333–349.

Baron-Cohen, S. (1992). Out of sight or out of mind? Another look at deception in autism. *Journal of Child Psychology and Psychiatry, 33*, 1141–1155.

Baron-Cohen, S., & Belmonte, M.K. (2005). Autism: A window onto the development of the social and the analytic brain. *Annual Review of Neuroscience, 28*, 109–126.

Barry, K.L., Zeber, J.E., Blow, F.C., & Valenstein, M. (2003). Effect of strengths model versus assertive community treatment model on participant outcomes and utilization: Two-year followup. *Psychiatric Rehabilitation Journal, 26*(3), 268–277.

Bauminger, N. (2002). The facilitation of social-emotional understanding and social interaction in high-functioning children with autism: Intervention outcomes. *Journal of Autism and Developmental Disorders, 32*(4), 283-298.

Bellini, S., & Hopf, A. (2007). The development of the autism social skills profile: A preliminary analysis of psychometric properties. *Focus on Autism and Other Developmental Disabilities, 22*, 80–87.

Bellini, S., Peters, J.K., Benner, L., & Hopf, A. (2007). A meta-analysis of school-based social skills interventions for children with autism spectrum disorders. *Remedial and Special Education, 28*, 153–162.

Bölte, S., & Poustka, F. (2002). The relation between general cognitive level and adaptive behavior domains in individuals with autism with and without co-morbid mental retardation. *Child Psychiatry and Human Development, 33*, 165–172.

Carter, A.S., Volkmar, F.R., Sparrow, S.S., Wang, J., Lord, C., Dawson, G.,… Schopler, E.(1998). The Vineland Adaptive Behavior Scales: Supplementary norms for individuals with autism. *Journal of Autism and Developmental Disorders, 28*, 287–302.

Cicchetti, D.V. (1994). Guidelines, criteria, and rules of thumb for evaluating normed and standardized assessment instruments in psychology. *Psychological Assessment, 6*, 284–290.

Constantino, J.N. (2002). *The Social Responsiveness Scale*. Los Angeles, CA: Western Psychological Services.

Constantino, J.N., Davis, S.A., Todd, R.D., Schindler, M.K., Gross, M.M., Brophy, S.L.,...Reich, W. (2003). Validation of a brief quantitative measure of autistic traits: Comparison of the Social Responsiveness Scale with the Autism Diagnostic Interview—Revised. *Journal of Autism and Developmental Disorders, 33*, 427–433.

Constantino, J.N., Przybeck, T., Friesen, D., & Todd, R.D. (2000). Reciprocal social behavior in children with and without pervasive developmental disorders. *Journal of Developmental and Behavioral Pediatrics, 21*, 2–11.

Dawson, G., & Fernald, M. (1987). Perspective-taking ability and its relationship to the social behavior of autistic children. *Journal of Autism Developmental Disorders, 17*, 487–498.

Dawson, G., Webb, S.J., & McPartland, J. (2005). Understanding the nature of face processing impairment in autism: Insights from behavioral and electrophysiological studies. *Developmental Neuropsychology, 27*, 403–424.

Dennis, M., Lazenby, A.L., & Lockyear, L. (2001). Inferential language in high-function children with autism. *Journal of Autism and Developmental Disorders, 31*, 47–54.

Dunlap, G., Kern, L., & Worcester, J. (2001). ABA and academic instruction. *Focus on Autism and Other Developmental Disabilities, 16*, 129–136.

Eikeseth, S. (2009). Outcome of comprehensive psycho-educational interventions for young children with autism. *Research in Developmental Disabilities, 30*, 158–178.

Eikeseth, S., Smith, T., Jahr, E., & Eldevik, S. (2002). Intensive behavioral treatment at school for 4- to 7-year-old children with autism: A 1-year comparison controlled study. *Behavior Modification, 26*, 49–68.

Eikeseth, S., Smith, T., Jahr, E., & Eldevik, S. (2007). Outcome for children with autism who began intensive behavioral treatment between ages 4 and 7: A comparison controlled study. *Behavior Modification, 31*, 264–278.

Elliott, S.N., & Gresham, F.M. (1987). Children's social skills: Assessment and classification practices. *Journal of Counseling and Development, 66*, 96–99.

Elliott, S.N., Malecki, C.K., & Demaray, M.K. (2001). New directions in social skills assessment and intervention for elementary and middle school students. *Exceptionality, 9*, 19–32.

Fine, J., Bartolucci, G., Szatmari, P., & Ginsberg, G. (1994). Cohesive discourse in pervasive developmental disorders. *Journal of Autism and Developmental Disorders, 24*, 315–329.

Gerhardt, P.F., & Mayville, E.A. (2010). Autism spectrum disorders and social skills. In D.W. Nangle, D.J. Hansen, C.A. Erdley, & P.J. Norton (Eds.), *Practitioner's guide to empirically based measures of social skills* (pp. 193–206). New York, NY: Springer.

Gesten, E.L., Weisberg, R.P., Amish, P.L., & Smith, J.K. (1987). Social problem solving training: A skills based approach to prevention and treatment. In C.A. Maher & J.E. Zins (Eds.), *Psychoeducational evaluations in schools: Methods and procedures for enhancing student competence* (pp. 197–210). New York, NY: Pergamon.

Gotham, K., Risi, S., Dawson, G., Tager-Flusberg, H., Joseph, R., Carter, A.,... Lord, C. (2008). A replication of the Autism Diagnostic Observation Schedule (ADOS) algorithms. *Journal of the American Academy of Child and Adolescent Psychiatry, 47*, 642–651.

Gresham, F.M. (1983). Social validity in the assessment of children's social skills: Establishing standards for social competency. *Journal of Psychoeducational Assessment, 1*, 297–307.

Gresham, F.M., & Elliott, S.N. (1990). *The Social Skills Rating System*. Circle Pines, MN: American Guidance Service.

Happe, F.G.E. (1993). Communicative competence and theory of mind: A test of relevance theory. *Cognition, 48*, 101–119.

Hartman, C.A., Luteijn, E., Serra, M., & Minderaa, R. (2006). Refinement of the Children's Social Behavior Questionnaire (CSBQ): An instrument that describes the diverse problems seen in milder forms of PDD. *Journal of Autism and Developmental Disorders, 36*, 325–342.

Hauck, M., Fein, D., Waterhouse, L., & Feinstein, C. (1995). Social initiations by autistic children to adults and other children. *Journal of Autism and Developmental Disorders, 25*, 579–595.

Howard, J.S., Sparkman, C.R., Cohen, H.G., Green, G., & Stanislaw, H. (2005). A comparison of intensive behavior analytic and eclectic treatments for young children with autism. *Research in Developmental Disabilities, 26*, 359–383.

Hughes, C., Rodi, M.S., & Lorden, S.W. (2000). Social interaction in high school and supported employment settings: Observational research application and issues. In T. Thompson, D. Felce, & F.J. Symons (Eds.), *Behavioral observation: Technology and applications in developmental disabilities* (pp. 253–269). Baltimore, MD: Paul H. Brookes Publishing Co.

Jones, E.A., & Carr, E.G. (2004). Joint attention in children with autism: Theory and intervention. *Focus on Autism and Other Developmental Disabilities, 19*, 13–26.

Jones, E.A., Carr, E.G., & Feeley, K.M. (2006). Multiple effects of joint attention intervention for children with autism. *Behavior Modification, 30*, 782–834.

Jones, R.R., Reid, J.B., & Patterson, G.R. (1979). Naturalistic observation in clinical assessment. In P. McReynolds (Ed.), *Advances in psychological assessment* (Vol. 3, pp. 42–95). San Francisco, CA: Jossey-Bass.

Kaiser, A.P., Tapp, J., Solomon, N.A., Delaney, E.M., Ezell, S.S., Hester, P.P.,... Hancock, T.B. (2000). Observing complex adult-child interactions: Computer-supported coding, analysis, and graphing. In T. Thompson, D. Felce, & F.J. Symons (Eds.), *Behavioral observation: Technology and applications in developmental disabilities* (pp. 177–192). Baltimore, MD: Paul H. Brookes Publishing Co.

Kasari, C., & Sigman, M. (1996). Expression and understanding of emotion in atypical development: Autism and Down syndrome. In M. Lewis & M. Wolan Sullivan (Eds.), *Emotional development in atypical children* (pp. 109–130). Mahwah, NJ: Lawrence Erlbaum Associates.

Klin, A., Volkmar, F.R., & Sparrow, S. (1992). Autistic social dysfunction: Some limitations of the theory of mind hypothesis. *Journal of Child Psychology and Psychiatry, 33*, 861–876.

Krug, D.A., Arick, J., & Almond, P. (2008). *Autism Screening Instrument for Educational Planning, Third Edition*. Austin, TX: PRO-ED.

Leaf, R., & McEachin, J. (1999). *A work in progress: Behavior management strategies and a curriculum for intensive behavioral treatment of autism*. New York, NY: DRL Books.

Lord, C., Rutter, M., DiLavore, P., & Risi, S. (1999). *The Autism Diagnostic Observation Schedule.* Los Angeles, CA: Western Psychological Services.

Lovaas, O.I. (2003). *Teaching individuals with developmental delays: Basic intervention techniques.* Austin, TX: PRO-ED.

Love, J.R., Carr, J.E., Almason, S.M., & Petursdottir, A.I. (2009). Early and intensive behavioral intervention for autism: A survey of clinical practices. *Research in Autism Spectrum Disorders, 3,* 421–428.

Luiselli, J.K., Campbell, S., Cannon, B., DiPietro, E., Ellis, J.T., Taras, M., & Lifter, K. (2001). Assessment instruments used in the education and treatment of persons with autism: Brief report of a survey of national service centers. *Research in Developmental Disabilities, 22,* 389–398.

Luteijn, E.F., Jackson, A.E., Volkmar, F.R., & Minderaa, R.B. (1998). The development of the Children's Social Behavior Questionnaire: Preliminary data. *Journal of Autism and Developmental Disorders, 28,* 559–565.

Luteijn, E., Luteijn, F., Jackson, S., Volkmar, F., & Minderaa, R. (2000). The Children's Social Behavior Questionnaire for milder variants of PDD problems: Evaluation of the psychometric characteristics. *Journal of Autism and Developmental Disorders, 30,* 317–330.

Matson, J.L. (1994). *The Matson evaluation of social skills for youngsters* (2nd ed.). Orland Park, IL: International Diagnostic Systems.

Matson, J.L., Benavidez, D.A., Compton, L.S., Paclawskyj, T., & Baglio, C.S. (1996). Behavioral treatment of autistic persons: A review of research from 1980 to the present. *Research in Developmental Disabilities, 17,* 433–465.

Matson, J.L., Matson, M.L., & Rivet, T.T. (2007). Social skills treatments for children with autism spectrum disorders: An overview. *Behavior Modification, 31,* 682–707.

Matson, J.L., Stabinsky Compton, L., & Sevin, J.A. (1991). Comparison and item analysis of the MESSY for autistic and normal children. *Research in Developmental Disabilities, 12,* 361–369.

Meier, S. (1997). Nomothetic item selection rules for tests of psychological interventions. *Psychotherapy Research, 7,* 419–427.

Meier, S.T. (2004). Improving design sensitivity through intervention-sensitive measures. *American Journal of Evaluation, 25,* 321–334.

Merrell, K.W. (2001). Assessment of children's social skills: Recent developments, best practices, and new directions. *Exceptionality, 9,* 3–18.

Mundy, P., & Burnette, C. (2005). Joint attention and neurodevelopmental models of autism. In F.R. Volkmar, R. Paul, A. Klin, & D. Cohen (Eds.), *Handbook of autism and pervasive developmental disorders* (3rd ed., pp. 650–681). New York, NY: Wiley.

Mundy, P., & Crowson, M. (1997). Joint attention and early social communication: Implications for research on intervention with autism. *Journal of Autism and Developmental Disabilities, 27,* 653–676.

Olley, J.G. (2005). Curriculum and classroom structure. In F.R. Volkmar, R. Paul, A. Klin, & D. Cohen (Eds.), *Handbook of autism and pervasive developmental disorders, Vol. 2: Assessment, interventions, and policy* (3rd ed., pp. 863–881). Hoboken, NJ: Wiley.

Prizant, B.M., Wetherby, A.M., Rubin, E., & Laurent, A.C. (2003). The SCERTS model: A family centered, transactional approach to enhancing communication and socioemotional abilities of young children with ASD. *Infants and Young Children, 16*, 296–316.

Rao, P.A., Beidel, D.C., & Murray, M.J. (2008). Social skills interventions for children with Asperger's syndrome or high-functioning autism: A review and recommendations. *Journal of Autism and Developmental Disorders, 38*, 353–361.

Rincover, A., Feldman, M., & Eason, L. (1986). "Tunnel vision": A possible keystone stimulus control deficit in autistic children. *Analysis and Intervention in Developmental Disabilities, 6*, 283–304.

Romanczyk, R.G., White, S., & Gillis, J.M. (2005). Social skills versus skilled social behavior: A problematic distinction in autism spectrum disorders. *Journal of Early Intensive Behavioral Intervention, 2*, 177–193.

Rubin, E., & Laurent, A.C. (2004). Implementing a curriculum-based assessment to prioritize learning objectives in Asperger syndrome and high functioning autism. *Topics in Language Disorders, 24*, 298–315.

Shriberg, L., Paul, R., McSweeny, J., Klin, A., Cohen, D., & Volkmar, F. (2001). Speech and prosody characteristics of adolescents and adults with high-functioning autism and Asperger's syndrome. *Journal of Speech, Language, and Hearing Research, 44*, 1097–1115.

Sigman, M., & Kasari, C. (1995). Joint attention across contexts in normal and autistic children. In C. Moore & P.J. Dunham (Eds.), *Joint attention: Its origins and role in development* (pp. 189–203). Hillsdale, NJ: Lawrence Erlbaum Associates.

Sparrow, S.S., Balla, D.A., & Cicchetti, D.V. (1984). *Vineland Adaptive Behavior Scales: Interview edition survey form.* Circle Pines, MN: American Guidance Service.

Sparrow, S.S., Ciccetti, D.V., & Balla, D.A. (2005). *Vineland Adaptive Behavior Scales, Second Edition: Survey forms manual.* Circle Pines, MN: American Guidance Service.

Stokes, J., Cameron, M., Dorsey, M., & Fleming, E. (2004). Task analysis, correspondence training, and general case instruction for teaching personal hygiene skills. *Behavioral Interventions, 19*, 121–135.

Strain, P.S., & Schwartz, I. (2001). ABA and the development of meaningful social relations for children with autism. *Focus on Autism and Other Developmental Disabilities, 16*, 120–128.

Sundberg, M.L., & Partington, J.W. (1998). *Teaching language to children with autism or other developmental disabilities.* Danville, CA: Behavior Analysts.

Tager-Flusberg, H. (1992). Autistic children's talk about psychological states: Deficits in the early acquisition of a theory of mind. *Child Development, 63*, 161–172.

Taylor, B.A. (2001). Teaching peer social skills to children with autism. In C. Maurice, G. Green, & R.M. Foxx (Eds.), *Making a difference: Behavioral intervention for autism* (pp. 83–96). Austin, TX: PRO-ED.

Thompson, T., Felce, D., & Symons, F.J. (Eds.) (2000). *Behavioral observation: Technology and applications in developmental disabilities.* Baltimore, MD: Paul H. Brookes Publishing Co.

Whalen, C., Schreibman, L., & Ingersoll, B. (2006). The collateral effects of joint attention training on social initiations, positive affect, imitation, and spontaneous speech for young children with autism. *Journal of Autism and Developmental Disorders, 36*, 655–664.

Wolf, M.M. (1978). The case for subjective measurement, or how behavior analysis is finding its heart. *Journal of Applied Behavior Analysis, 11*, 203–214.

Behavior Analytic Interventions for Developing Social Skills in Individuals with Autism

Mary Jane Weiss

THE CHALLENGES OF
LEARNING AND TEACHING SOCIAL SKILLS

Social skills intervention for children with autism is an area in which gains have been modest and the development of innovative clinical approaches has been limited (Rao, Beidel, & Murray, 2008). Social skills are among the most elusive targets to teach. One impediment to teaching social skills is that there may be limited intrinsic interest on the part of individuals with autism spectrum disorders (ASDs) to learn these skills. Many individuals with ASDs lack social interest and fail to comprehend social nuances. In addition, they often exhibit little social initiation, as well as reduced social responsiveness.

It is often difficult to identify the best methods for teaching social skills. Most social skills are multielement skills that require an individual to engage in multiple behaviors and distinct tasks. Also, most social skills involve an element of judgment in determining whether and when to use each skill (e.g., Is it appropriate to engage in this behavior at this time?). Such complexities make it difficult to teach such skills effectively and thoroughly. How can practitioners operationally define social judgment? How can practitioners best prepare learners for the endless possibilities that exist in the natural social environment?

This chapter examines the components of social skills necessary for effective social functioning. In addition, commonly used approaches for teaching social skills are reviewed. The importance of identifying the critical elements of intervention is discussed.

BASIC COMPONENTS OF SOCIAL SKILLS

Social initiations include skills such as greeting others, asking questions of others, commenting to others, and asking to join ongoing activities. Social responses include responding to the social overtures of others, which may include greetings, questions, and offers to join activities. In individuals with ASDs, social initiations are generally weaker than social responses. Applied behavior analysis (ABA) has been shown to be extremely effective in building social initiations and social responses.

Social skill impairments include impairments in making social initiations, responding to social overtures, and demonstrating social comprehension (i.e., behaving appropriately in circumstances that require complex or multicomponent initiations and responses). Impairments in these central skills limit the success of social integration and can negatively affect how an individual interacts with others in his or her environment.

One of the common questions posed regarding social skills training is when such training should actually commence. Often, clinicians conceptualize social skills as being complex or later-stage curricular targets. However, many of the initial emphases and core foundation skills are essentially social in nature. Consider three main early foci of educational programs: play skills, imitation, and manding/requesting training. Each skill is social in nature and focuses on attention to and interaction with another person.

Play skills have long been a focus of early intervention and instruction. Aberrant play skills distinguish children with autism from peers who are typically developing and make it difficult to promote parallel and cooperative play skills. Furthermore, training children with autism in the functional and intended uses of objects facilitates a wide variety of functional and play skills. Children with well-established play repertoires are also more likely to engage in productive activities (and less likely to engage in purposeless or stereotypic behaviors) when less supervision is available. For children, socialization is play and play is socialization. Play is emphasized in curricular programming because it serves as a very effective bridge to social contact with peers.

Imitation has also been a strong historical emphasis in programming for children with autism (Leaf & McEachin, 1999; Lovaas, 1981; Sundberg & Partington, 1998; Taylor & McDonough, 1996). A deficit in imitation is an early and clear sign of autism. Although children who are typically developing are constantly watching and doing, such behavior is exceedingly rare in children with autism (Ingersoll & Schreibman, 2006). Teaching imitation is important for building a wide variety of skills in all areas, and teaching attention to a model facilitates the development of more complex imitation skills and the use of peers as a source of information in social and school settings. Several curricula have emphasized the importance of assessing imitation skills and systematic instruction in imitation as a foundation skill (Leaf & McEachin, 1999; Sundberg & Partington, 1998; Taylor & McDonough, 1996).

In general, clinicians have approached imitation training through discrete trial instruction. However, there is evidence that naturalistic approaches to teaching imitation skills enhance generalization and increase other social-communicative behaviors (Ingersoll & Schreibman, 2006). Perhaps a combination of formal and informal instruction is best. Formal instruction provides multiple learning opportunities that are simply not available in naturalistic instruction. In addition, formal instruction can systematically build aspects of imitation that are central to developing a strong imitative response class. Examples of such elements of imitation include delayed imitation, sequenced imitation, and complex imitation. Naturalistic instruction ensures that imitation training is integrated into natural interactions, and all naturally occurring learning opportunities are captured. The social and generalization benefits should increase the extent to which naturalistic imitative training is integrated into interventions.

Manding/requesting has become an increasingly prominent focus of instruction because the field has recognized the importance of methods to build initiation skills. Historically, discrete trial instruction built social responsivity, not social initiation. Sundberg and Partington (1998, 1999) integrated Skinner's classification of verbal behavior into teaching language to children with autism. In this context, they highlighted the importance of mand training to increase initiation.

These emphases and developments have strengthened the quality and the scope of social skills programming at young ages and have created a good foundation for working on social responsivity and social initiation in other ways (Leaf & McEachin, 1999; Maurice, Green, & Luce, 1996; Sundberg & Partington, 1998).

QUALITATIVE ASPECTS OF SOCIAL BEHAVIORS

Qualitative aspects of social initiations and responses affect the functional utility of social skills learned, regardless of how they are taught. Social initiations and responses emitted may lack clarity (e.g., a child who waits near the water table as a mand to join) or be blatantly inappropriate (e.g., a child who initiates a game of chase by pulling another child's hair). Such children may lack independence and require facilitation from an adult. Such assistance may be subtle (e.g., encouragement) or intrusive (e.g., scripting).

When skills lack clarity or are inappropriate, they typically do not result in social interaction. In fact, ineffective social initiations and inappropriate social behaviors often reduce the extent to which an individual is approached, leading to increased isolation (Mesibov, Adams, & Klinger, 1997).

Another qualitative aspect of social skills is the latency to respond. For a social response to be functional, it must occur within an acceptable time frame. If there is a delay of 5 or 10 seconds after a child is greeted and before he or she responds, many social opportunities are lost. Peers will often leave the social interaction when they do not receive a timely response. They may also infer that their friend is not interested in or able to respond to them, reducing the likelihood of future initiations with them. These attributions or explanations of a child's failure to respond further reduce the likelihood of future attempts to interact. Ensuring a quick latency to respond is a very important aspect of skill mastery that is often overlooked.

Another time-based aspect of social responding is the duration of interactions. Although many individuals with autism successfully master simple conversation or play exchanges, they falter when the interaction continues. An exchange of one or two back-and-forth communications may be successful, but individuals with autism may be unable to continue the interaction beyond these simple and preliminary exchanges. It is important to target the duration of conversational and play skills to increase the success of learners with autism in social exchanges.

SOCIAL COMPREHENSION

Social comprehension describes the complicated social responses and initiations that are part of navigating the social world. Individuals are required to understand social rules, engage in behaviors that are expected in given contexts, and interpret social nuances. Social comprehension skills are essential in making meaningful progress in effectively navigating the social world. (In essence, what is often referred to as social comprehension is simply more complex forms of social responding. From an ABA perspective, such comprehension is conceptualized as sequenced or complex social responses.)

Some commercially available curricula target the development of such skills and have clearly defined lessons for teaching a variety of behaviors (Baker, 2003a, 2003b; McGinnis & Goldstein, 1990; Richardson, 1996; Taylor & Jasper, 2001). Many of these curricula are written from a behavior analytic point of view, outline precise and well-defined teaching strategies, and require the collection of data to guide decisions.

Whether or not such commercially available curricula are used, social comprehension interventions are generally layered approaches involving a variety of instructional strategies. Often, several approaches are used together, in a combination or packaged approach, to address such issues. Such packages may include both empirically validated and nonempirically validated techniques. Strategies commonly used in such packages include video modeling, Social Stories, rule cards, and role playing.

Video Modeling

Video modeling is an effective means of teaching a wide variety of skills, including the imitation of peers (Haring, Kennedy, Adams, & Pitts-Conway, 1987), learning sign language (Watkins, Sprafkin, & Krolikowski, 1993), developing play skills (Charlop-Christy, Le, & Freeman, 2000), and building conversation skills (Charlop & Milstein, 1989; Sherer et al., 2001). The research base in this area has led to clinical extensions of video modeling to teach academic skills, community-relevant skills, conversational exchanges, and play skills (Snell & Brown, 2000; Taylor, 2001; Weiss & Harris, 2001).

Many students with ASDs are strong visual learners, enjoy watching videos, and attend well to a model presented in a video clip. Clinically, video modeling is often done with an adult demonstrating the skill first. From a practical perspective, an adult model controls the instructional variables and ensures that the salient aspects of the target behavior are highlighted. Alternately, older peer tutors or mature peers can be used as models. These choices have obvious advantages because of the similarities of peers to the target students.

In video modeling, learners observe a video clip of the desired actions and are prompted to engage in the behaviors depicted on the video. Initially, there may be simultaneous imitation of what is being watched (doing the actions along with the model on the video), followed by delayed imitation of what was observed (watching the clip and then engaging in the behaviors). Rote response can be a significant concern because many learners will precisely imitate the sequence from memory, so it is essential to program variability into the video modeling protocol. Such variability in programming ensures that the response class of imitation is strengthened.

Another extension of video instruction is to use videos to provide feedback to learners on their performance during play activities. Reinforcement and corrective feedback can be provided. In addition, areas of weakness can be targeted for additional training (Taylor, 2001).

Guidelines for using videos with learners exist (Krantz, MacDuff, Wadstrom, & McClannahan, 1991). Suggestions include ensuring the presence of prerequisite skills, removing extraneous stimuli from the enactment, and considering cognitive level as a possible factor influencing the appropriateness of the intervention.

Social Stories

Social Stories can be used to both increase and decrease behavior. For example, Social Stories can be used to explain the actions required to buy food at a grocery store, order meals in a restaurant, or explain the contingencies required to access a desired reinforcer (e.g., time on the computer is earned through worksheet completion). Social Stories are often used to convey behavioral expectations for multielement situations (which change frequently), for fear situations, and to reduce challenging behaviors.

Learners with autism often have difficulty understanding expectations in social situations. Social Stories have become increasingly popular as an instructional strategy for learners with ASDs (Barry & Burlew, 2004; Delano & Snell, 2006; Sansosti, Powell-Smith, & Kincaid, 2004). Social Stories are brief descriptions of expectations that are explained in the context of a story created for an individual to describe a specific scenario the learner will encounter (Gray, 1993, 1994, 2008). Typically, the story is written from the perspective of the learner, in a meaningful format for people with ASDs (Gray, 2000). Social Stories are often supplemented with pictorial cues or photos in addition to textual information (Reynhout & Carter, 2006).

Gray (2000) outlined suggestions for developing effective Social Stories and included guidelines about the types of sentences to be used. There are seven recognized sentence types for creating Social Stories (Barry & Burlew, 2004; Crozier & Tincani, 2007; Reynhout & Carter, 2006):

1. *Descriptive* sentences provide factual information.
2. *Perspective* sentences provide insight regarding the thoughts, the feelings, and the behaviors of others.
3. *Affirmative* sentences are used to reassure learners.
4. *Directive* sentences tell learners what specific behaviors are expected.
5. *Control* sentences use analogies to explain situations.
6. *Cooperative* sentences give learners information about who can help them in different situations.
7. *Consequence* sentences give learners information about what will happen as a result of actions.

Although using Social Stories is common in clinical practice, the number of carefully controlled investigations is relatively small. Most clinical guidelines for using Social Stories have not been empirically validated and require more comprehensive investigation.

Barry and Burlew (2004) used a multiple-baseline design across two participants to evaluate the effects of Social Stories on independent choice making and appropriate play. The authors reported that the level of prompting required for choice making decreased for both participants, and the duration of appropriate play increased. However, the study did not control for other ongoing interventions in the classroom at the time of the intervention, thus significantly limiting the power of the findings.

Thiemann and Goldstein (2001) used Social Stories with text cards, visual cues, and video feedback to increase the social behaviors of five learners with autism. The targeted social behaviors included contingent responses, securing attention, commenting, and requesting. The effects of Social Stories were evaluated using a multiple-baseline-across-skills design. Small group instruction was done with two typically developing peers and the children with autism. The results indicated that Social Stories effectively increased the targeted social behavior of the learners with autism. In addition, two learners demonstrated generalization to other social skills. This was encouraging, even though these effects may have been caused by the similarity of the targeted skills. Although the data on acquisition were encouraging, there was a general lack of maintenance across skills and learners.

Social Stories are often used in combination with other interventions as part of a packaged social skills intervention (Reynhout & Carter, 2006). When Social Stories have been examined as part of packaged interventions, some gains have been noted (Sansosti & Powell-Smith, 2008; Swaggart et al., 1995). However, the existence of multiple, simultaneous interventions in these studies limits the extent to which the effects of intervention can be attributed to any one variable, including Social Stories.

When studies employ more than one intervention method (Barry & Burlew, 2004; Burke, Kuhn, & Peterson, 2004; Thiemann & Goldstein, 2001), the degree to which Social Stories are responsible for an effect is unclear. Delano and Snell (2006) extended the research of Thiemann and Goldstein (2001) by using the same social skills but isolating Social Stories as the only intervention. During intervention, social skills increased for all three learners. However, as the Social Stories were faded out, the effects disappeared. Two learners showed generalization of social skills to their general education classroom. The effects were higher than baseline but were not maintained at levels achieved during intervention.

The tendency for Social Stories to be implemented concurrently with other interventions is a serious challenge to understanding their potential efficacy. Another major challenge in the use of Social Stories is the lack of available data on the essential elements of their use. Clinical implementation and the development of the Social Stories are highly variable, presentation to a student is highly idiosyncratic, and staff training procedures are largely ignored. There have been no controlled studies examining the length of each intervention phase.

The literature describes a variety of formats designed for implementing Social Stories. They include having a teacher or a parent read to a child (Crozier & Tincani, 2007), having a child read the story (Thiemann & Goldstein, 2001), listening or watching a story on a computer or a television (More, 2008; Sansosti & Powell-Smith, 2008), and listening to a story embedded in a song (Brownell, 2002). Crozier and Tincani (2007) outlined specific strategies for ensuring appropriate instruction, including getting the learner's attention.

The widespread use of Social Stories is not in line with the limited data available regarding their efficacy. Despite the paucity of data, they remain a very popular tool for intervention. Parents and teachers generally report liking Social Stories (Burke, Kuhn, & Peterson, 2004; Dodd, Hupp, Jewell, & Krohn, 2008) and do implement them. Are there potential benefits to this likelihood of implementation? Perhaps Social Stories enhance parent and teacher attention to targeted behaviors, which may result in more prompting and reinforcement of the targeted skills. Social Stories may also result in the use of more direct behavior change procedures by teachers and caregivers.

There also appears to be a discrepancy between the perceived effects of intervention and the future use of Social Stories. Dodd, Hupp, Jewell, and Krohn (2008) reported that the parents in their study were not certain whether the Social Stories had improved the target behaviors, but they planned to continue using them and extending their use.

Crozier and Tincani (2007) reported that teachers liked using Social Stories and found their outcomes to be favorable, although the teachers did not always continue to use them. When the results are promising, it is difficult to identify the critical components of such effectiveness. Developing more effective methods for evaluating Social Stories will lead to improvements in creating and implementing them. It is possible that their effectiveness may be a result of other elements of the packaged interventions, and this should be systematically studied.

Rule Cards

Another strategy for increasing social skills is a rule card or a similar approach known as the Power Card strategy (Gagnon, 2001). The Power Card is a small card that a learner carries that summarizes a strategy to use when a particular problematic circumstance occurs. The card is generally individualized for a learner with a picture of a preference or a strong interest. The behavior or skill is encouraged through its connection to the special interest (Keeling, Smith Myles, Gagnon, & Simpson, 2003).

Keeling et al. (2003) used the Power Card strategy to decrease the whines and the screams of a 10-year-old student with autism in game playing. A multiple-baseline design was implemented across three game activities. On the first day of the intervention, a full Power Card script was read, in which the student's favorite cartoon character modeled appropriate responses for both winning and losing games. Prior to all other intervention sessions, a shorter version of the Power Card was read, which listed three strategies for winning and three strategies for losing (all of which came from the longer script). The Power Card was effective in decreasing the whines and the screams, and the intervention generalized to the third activity, which had never been targeted with the Power Card. The student used the strategies described on the card in new settings with peers and even modeled the responses for a classmate. A limitation of the study was that data were presented only for problem behavior.

A closely related intervention is the script-fading procedure, in which textual prompts can be embedded into a picture activity schedule or a conversational exchange (Krantz & McClannahan, 1993, 1998). Scripts can increase the number of social initiations made by learners with autism, the length of the social interactions, and the number of unscripted interactions. Behaviors developed with scripts have been shown to be maintained and generalize to new activities. Stevenson, Krantz, and McClannahan (2000) used an audiotaped script to increase the social interactions of four students, ages 10–15. Every participant was able to produce high levels of unscripted responses, and the results were maintained after the scripts were faded.

Summary of Strategies to Build Social Comprehension

Social skills are difficult to define and challenging to teach. Furthermore, it is often difficult to evaluate the impact of the instructional methods used. Social skills are often targeted in a wide variety of ways, and they may be addressed through a package of instructional strategies. Some of the commonly used approaches include Social Stories, rule cards, and video modeling. Although probably the most widely used approach, Social Stories have little data supporting their effectiveness. Even though there have been some reports of success, it is not clear whether using Social Stories is the critical element responsible for the effects. In fact, it is likely that other procedures used in combination with Social Stories were responsible for those effects. Conducting component analyses would help to isolate the unique contribution of Social Stories. In addition, research is needed on the critical elements of Social Stories as an intervention approach. Video modeling and social scripting have good empirical support. It is essential that variability be included in scripts and models to ensure generalized and functional results. The use of rule cards is an interesting clinical direction, particularly when used in combination with role playing or other behavioral rehearsal techniques.

Often, these strategies are used as part of a package of interventions designed to address a specific deficit or issue. For example, Social Stories or rule cards may be used in combination with other procedures in a package of behavioral teaching interventions. Such package interventions may assist the clinician in teaching these multielement skills. In addition, they may provide more practice and learning opportunities and increase the degree to which training prepares learners for the range of possible experiences in the social world. As is the case with all interventions, direct behavior change procedures should always be used to effect behavior. In addition, data on the effectiveness of all strategies used with individual learners should be collected and used to determine which elements of an intervention should be used with a learner in the future.

OTHER TARGETS

Other approaches to social skills training may have utility for learners with ASDs. Some of these approaches have been demonstrated as effective with other populations of learners, whereas others are theoretically compelling. In particular, a great deal of attention has been paid to interventions designed to increase perspective taking, problem solving, and joint attention.

Perspective Taking

Perspective taking refers to the capacity to understand the thoughts and the feelings (or perspectives) of others (Baron-Cohen, 1989; Baron-Cohen, Leslie, & Frith, 1985). In typical development, perspective taking emerges during the preschool years, but children with autism often have significant impairments in their ability to understand the perspectives of others. This skill is of particular importance because of its relationship to other critical social skills, such as turn-taking, empathy, sharing, conversational exchange, and social initiations (LeBlanc et al., 2003).

   Theory of mind is a theoretical construct encompassing many skills and mental capacities. A person is said to have a theory of mind when he or she can infer and understand others' desires, beliefs, and feelings (Ozonoff & Miller, 1995). Research on theory of mind often uses measures of appearance reality, false belief, and representational change to operationally define perspective taking and theory of mind (Charlop-Christy & Daneshvar, 2003; Taylor & Carlson, 1997). Such tests measure an individual's ability to distinguish between what something may appear to be and what it truly is. Similarly, tests may assess a person's ability to accurately label what people believe about a situation, particularly when they have different or incomplete information.

   Literature on the teaching of perspective taking is limited. Two studies have used video modeling to teach perspective taking (Charlop-Christy & Daneshvar, 2003; LeBlanc et al., 2003). In these studies, children with autism ranging in age from 6 to 13 years old were taught to answer questions by watching videos of others answering the questions correctly. Charlop-Christy and Daneshvar (2003) used three false-belief tasks, referred to in the literature as the Sally-Ann task, the M&M's task, and the hide-and-seek task. As an example, in the Sally-Ann task, Ann moves a ball belonging to Sally from a basket to a box. The child is asked where Sally will look for the ball when she reenters the room. Children with autism will usually not demonstrate awareness that Sally's knowledge base is different from Ann's and will not factor in the difference in their observation of the object's movement. In other words, people with autism assume that Sally will answer based on the reality of the object's location, not on the basis of her experience.

In the Charlop-Christy and Daneshvar study, training was provided on each task until the children were able to demonstrate generalization of the skill on a similar example. All three participants were able to learn the tasks and correctly answer questions on similar tasks. Only two participants were able to pass the posttest (an untrained Sally-Ann task) at the conclusion of the training. LeBlanc et al. (2003) used a similar method with the addition of reinforcers delivered for correct answers. The results were similar to those of Charlop-Christy and Daneshvar. Two out of three of their participants passed the untrained Sally-Ann task at the end. These studies lend support to using video modeling and suggest that multiple exemplar training may be a useful component of social skills training packages.

Two interesting clinical question arise: Who might best be helped by tasks involving perspective taking? Which learner characteristics predict acquisition and generalization? Anecdotally, Charlop-Christy and Daneshvar (2003) reported that the participant who did not pass the posttest also had the most difficulty answering questions about what he or she had seen in the video and was the least social and verbal of the three participants. The nonpassing participant in the LeBlanc et al. (2003) study was the oldest participant at 13 years old (the other participants were both 7 years old), perhaps pointing to limits imposed by age (or a combination of age and ability). There is, in fact, some evidence of a correlation between performance on perspective taking and age-equivalent scores on the Daily Living scale of the Vineland Adaptive Behavior Scales (Rehfeldt, Dillen, Ziomek, & Kowalchuk, 2007).

Perspective taking is theoretically compelling because the interventions are designed to address what is perhaps the central social deficit of autism. There is great potential clinical utility in this area. However, more research is needed to understand how to best teach such skills and, most important, how to teach them in ways that transfer to natural social situations.

Problem Solving

The navigation of conflict situations is often very difficult for individuals with ASDs. Difficulties in managing such situations can lead to serious negative social consequences. The term *problem solving* refers to the ability to use available information to develop strategies to solve problems (Agran, Blanhard, Wehmeyer, & Hughes, 2002). Learners with autism often exhibit a lack of problem-solving abilities, including difficulty in selecting the appropriate strategy for a situation, generating alternative solutions, and knowing when to change strategies (Gagnon, 2001). When solutions are generated, they may not be socially appropriate (Channon, Charman, Heap, Crawford, & Rios, 2001).

Practitioners agree that problem-solving skills are essential to success in school and community settings. However, there is a paucity of information about what to teach and how to teach it. Teachers are often simply not providing the necessary learning opportunities or experiences that would help students to improve in this area (Agran et al., 2002).

Goddard, Howlin, Dritschel, and Patel (2007) found that individuals with Asperger syndrome were less likely than their neurotypical counterparts to develop detailed and effective solutions to social problems. These researchers suggested that one component of successful problem solving may be autobiographical memory. They found that those with Asperger syndrome demonstrated significantly longer latencies to recall memories and had a fewer number of memories recalled overall compared with neurotypical peers. It is possible that such characteristics are somewhat related to deficient problem solving because individuals may be less able to draw from memories of past experiences.

Problem solving is indeed important in school and is central to navigating the social world. Many students with other types of difficulties (e.g., attention-deficit/hyperactivity disorder) have benefited substantially from problem-solving approaches. Problem-solving training usually involves helping learners identify problems and select appropriate solutions. Children with ASDs often have difficulties with deciphering the ambiguity of social problems and evaluating options for a course of action. They may fail to see the range of options or respond impulsively. Problem-solving training (Shure, 2001a, 2001b, 2004) can help students identify problems, generate alternative solutions, evaluate the effectiveness of different potential courses of action, and choose the best option. This can be done as a whole-class intervention or as an individual intervention.

The social autopsy is a variation of problem solving commonly used with students with high-functioning autism or Asperger syndrome (Bieber, 1994). This approach helps to identify cause-and-effect relationships between one's behavior and the reactions of others. This clinical approach involves reviewing the situation in detail after the event and creating a plan to prevent further instances (Dunn, 2006). The specificity of the application to real-world difficulties encountered by the individual may increase the effectiveness of this approach.

Joint Attention

Children are often initially referred for an autism evaluation when they exhibit language delays. However, social delays are also often observed at an early age. One such deficit is a lack of joint attention. Joint attention typically develops before a child speaks his or her first words. The topic of joint attention has received much attention in the literature because it may have important implications for early diagnosis and intervention (Bruinsma, Koegel, & Koegel, 2004; Dawson et al., 2004). The concept of joint attention consists of a variety of behaviors (e.g., gaze following, social referencing, protoimperative gestures, protodeclarative gestures, monitoring). Joint attention is frequently described as a coordinated shift in attention between an object or an event and another person that occurs in a social context. The term is used to refer to both recruiting (or initiating) attention and responding to the bids of others. For instance, a child recruiting attention may point to a toy while saying "Look." Other examples related to joint attention include a child responding to bids for attention from others, turning to look when the child hears his or her name called, or looking both at a toy being offered and at the person holding it. In addition to the many operational definitions used in the literature, joint attention is also often used colloquially to mean sharing attention or understanding what another person is interested in. Children with autism typically exhibit significant impairments in joint attention.

Whalen and Shreibman (2003) distinguished between two main types of recruiting attention: protoimperative and protodeclarative. Although both types of attention recruitment may be similar in topography, the function of each is different. Whalen and Shreibman described protoimperative gestures and vocalizations as those used to request access to an object, whereas protodeclarative gestures and vocalizations are used to recruit attention for sharing or mutual attending to an object. Mundy et al. (2007) described the concepts of protoimperative and protodeclarative gestures and vocalizations as initiating behavior regulation/requests and initiating joint attention, respectively. In addition, they described the response to joint attention and the response to behavior requests to characterize the responding to others' bids for joint attention.

Joint attention is considered an important skill partly because of its possible relationship to several domains of development. Joint attention has been linked to language development, socioemotional development (Sheinkopf, Mundy, Claussen & Willoughby, 2004), and frontal lobe function (Mundy & Crawson, 1997). Joint attention has been suggested as important in understanding language outcomes later in childhood. Morales et al. (2000) found that response to joint attention was directly related to vocabulary development in learners between 6 and 24 months. Bruinsma, Koegel, and Koegel (2004) reported that the time spent engaging in joint attention behaviors was positively related to the size of a child's vocabulary in the future.

There is some evidence to suggest that joint attention can be taught. Kasari, Freeman, and Paparella (2006) assigned children to one of three experimental groups: a joint attention intervention group, a symbolic play intervention group, and a control group. The groups differed in their primary intervention goals, focusing on teaching either joint attention or symbolic play. Sessions were conducted daily for 30 minutes for 5–6 weeks. Improvements in joint attention and joint engagement were found for both treatment groups as compared with the control group, and they were generalized from the instructor to the child's caregiver. The authors recommended that early intervention programs should incorporate play and joint attention into their targets of intervention.

In a similar study by Kasari, Paparella, Freeman, and Jahromi (2008), the authors compared the effects of different interventions (joint attention intervention and symbolic play intervention) on expressive language development in 3- and 4-year-old learners with autism. They found that children in both the joint attention and the symbolic play intervention groups made gains in expressive language relative to the control group. In addition to the initial improvements, the effects grew stronger across time (12-month follow-up compared with the control group). This suggests that there may be significant benefits to including training on joint attention and symbolic play when designing interventions for young children with autism.

Joint attention interventions are compelling for reasons similar to those reviewed for teaching perspective taking. Yet much work remains to be done to identify how to teach such skills and how to generalize such skills to natural interactions and contexts. However, if researchers can target these core impairments with focused interventions, they may be able to significantly increase the magnitude of socially significant changes achieved.

SUMMARY

Compared with strides in addressing other impairments in individuals with ASDs, the results demonstrated in remediating social skill impairments are modest. Individuals with ASDs have very significant social impairments, including problems in responding to others and making social overtures. In addition, there are often problems in the quality of social initiations and responses made by individuals with autism. Initiations and responses may be unclear, inappropriate, prompted, or delayed. Poor-quality responses result in less social success.

In addition, many social skills are complex, multielement skills, requiring a variety of component skills. The demonstration of social skills also requires social judgment regarding when and how to use the skills.

It has been more difficult to operationally define social skills because of the subskills involved and the necessary skills in social judgment that are intrinsic to successful mastery.

Many techniques are commonly used for teaching social skills to individuals with ASDs. ABA approaches have been demonstrated to be highly effective in teaching discrete social responses and initiations. Numerous behavioral and nonbehavioral techniques are commonly used to build more complex social responses involving the understanding of social rules and the interpretation of nuances. Some of those techniques are not empirically validated or have been used primarily with other populations. Many of these techniques are used in packaged or combination approaches. It is important to identify the unique contributions that each strategy is making to skill acquisition to ensure efficient and effective instruction.

Newer directions for social skill intervention include addressing impairments in problem solving, perspective taking, and joint attention. More research is needed to identify the critical elements of these targeted interventions and strategies for enhancing the generalization of learned skills to real-life social exchanges in the natural environment.

REFERENCES

Agran, M., Blanhard, C., Wehmeyer, M.L., & Hughes, C. (2002). Increasing the problem-solving skills of students with developmental disabilities participating in special education. *Remedial and Special Education, 23,* 279–288.

Baker, J.E. (2003a). *Social skills picture book: Teaching play, emotion, and communication to children with autism.* Arlington, TX: Future Horizons.

Baker, J.E. (2003b). *Social skills training.* Overland Park, KS: Autism Asperger Publishing.

Baron-Cohen, S. (1989). Joint-attention deficits in autism: Towards a cognitive analysis. *Development and Psychopathology, 1,* 185–189.

Baron-Cohen, S., Leslie, A.M., & Frith, U. (1985). Does the autistic child have a "theory of mind"? *Cognition, 21(1),* 37–46.

Barry, L.M., & Burlew, S.B. (2004). Using Social Stories to teach choice and play skills to children with autism. *Focus on Autism and Other Developmental Disabilities, 19,* 45–51.

Bieber, J. (1994). *Learning disabilities and social skills with Richard Lavoie: Last one picked...first one picked on.* Washington, DC: Public Broadcasting Service.

Brownell, M.D. (2002). Musically adapted Social Stories to modify behaviors in students with autism: Four case studies. *Journal of Music Therapy, 39,* 117–144.

Bruinsma, Y., Koegel, R.L., & Koegel, L.K. (2004). Joint attention and children with autism: A review of the literature. *Mental Retardation and Developmental Disorders, 10,* 169–175.

Burke, R.V., Kuhn, B.R., & Peterson, J.L. (2004). Brief report: A storybook ending to children's bedtime problems—the use of a rewarding Social Story to reduce bedtime resistance and frequent night waking. *Journal of Pediatric Psychology, 29,* 389–396.

Channon, S., Charman, T., Heap, J., Crawford, S., & Rios, P. (2001). Real-life-type problem-solving in Asperger's syndrome. *Journal of Autism and Developmental Disorders, 31,* 461–469.

Charlop, M.H., & Milstein, J.P. (1989). Teaching autistic children conversational speech using video modeling. *Journal of Applied Behavior Analysis, 22,* 275–285.

Charlop-Christy, M.H., & Daneshvar, S. (2003). Using video modeling to teach perspective taking to children with autism. *Journal of Positive Behavior Interventions, 5(1),* 12–21.

Charlop-Christy, M.H., Le, L., & Freeman, K.A. (2000). A comparison of video modeling with in vivo modeling for teaching children with autism. *Journal of Autism and Developmental Disorders, 30,* 537–552.

Crozier, S., & Tincani, M. (2007) Effects of Social Stories on prosocial behavior of preschool children with autism spectrum disorders. *Journal of Autism and Developmental Disorders, 37,* 1803–1814.

Dawson, G., Toth, K., Abbott, R., Osterling, J., Munson, J., Estes, A., …Liaw, J. (2004). Early social attention impairments in autism: Social orienting, joint attention, and attention to distress. *Developmental Psychology, 40(2),* 271–283.

Delano, M., & Snell, M.E. (2006). The effects of Social Stories on the social engagement of children with autism. *Journal of Positive Behavior Intervention, 8,* 29–42.

Dodd, S., Hupp, S.D.A., Jewell, J.D., & Krohn, E. (2008.) Using parents and siblings during a Social Story intervention for two children diagnosed with PDD-NOS. *Journal of Developmental and Physical Disabilities, 20,* 217–229.

Dunn, M. (2006). *S.O.S.: Social skills in our schools: A social skills program for children with pervasive developmental disorders, including high functioning autism and Asperger syndrome, and their typical peers.* Overland Park, KS: Autism Asperger Publishing.

Gagnon, E. (2001). *Power Cards: Using special interests to motivate children and youth with Asperger syndrome and autism.* Overland Park, KS: Autism Asperger Publishing.

Goddard, L., Howlin, P., Dritschel, B., & Patel, T. (2007). Autobiographical memory and social problem-solving in Asperger syndrome. *Journal of Autism and Developmental Disorders, 37,* 291–300.

Gray, C. (1993). *The original Social Story book.* Arlington, TX: Future Education.

Gray, C. (1994). *The new Social Story Book.* Arlington, TX: Future Education.

Gray, C.A. (1995). Teaching children with autism to "read" social situations. In K.A. Quill (Ed.), *Teaching children with autism: Strategies to enhance communication and socialization* (pp. 219–242). Albany, NY: Delmar.

Gray, C. (2000). *The new Social Story handbook* [Illustrated edition]. Arlington, TX: Future Horizons.

Gray C. (2008). *What are Social Stories?* Retrieved from http://www.thegraycenter. org/social-stories/what-are-social-stories

Haring, T., Kennedy, C., Adams, M., & Pitts-Conway, V. (1987). Teaching generalization of purchasing skills across community settings to autistic youth using videotape modeling. *Journal of Applied Behavior Analysis, 20,* 89–96.

Ingersoll, B., & Schreibman, L. (2006). Teaching reciprocal imitation skills to young children with autism using a naturalistic behavioral approach: Effects on language, pretend play, and joint attention. *Journal of Autism and Developmental Disorders, 36,* 487–505.

Kasari, C., Freeman, S., & Paparella, T. (2006). Joint attention and symbolic play in young children with autism: A randomized controlled intervention study. *Journal of Child Psychology and Psychiatry, 47*(6), 611–620.

Kasari, C., Paparella, T., Freeman, S., & Jahromi, L.B. (2008). Language outcome in autism: Randomized comparison of joint attention and play interventions. *Journal of Consulting and Clinical Psychology, 76*(1), 125–137.

Keeling, K., Smith Myles, B., Gagnon, E., & Simpson, R.L. (2003). Using the Power Card strategy to teach sportsmanship skills to a child with autism. *Focus on Autism and Other Developmental Disabilities, 18,* 105–111.

Krantz, P.J., MacDuff, G.S., Wadstrom, O., & McClannahan, L.E. (1991). Using video with developmentally disabled learners. In P.W. Dowrick (Ed.), *Practical guide to video in the behavioral sciences* (pp. 256–266) New York, NY: Wiley.

Krantz, P.J., & McClannahan, L.E. (1993). Teaching children with autism to initiate to peers: Effects of a script-fading procedure. *Journal of Applied Behavior Analysis, 26,* 121–132.

Krantz, P.J., & McClannahan, L.E. (1998). Social interaction skills for children with autism: A script-fading procedure for beginning readers. *Journal of Applied Behavior Analysis, 31,* 191–202.

Leaf, R., & McEachin, J. (1999). *A work in progress: Behavior management strategies and a curriculum for intensive behavioral treatment of autism.* New York, NY: DRL Books.

LeBlanc, L.A., Coates, A.M., Daneshvar, S., Charlop-Christy, M.H., Morris, C., & Lancaster, B.M. (2003). Using video modeling and reinforcement to teach perspective-taking skills to children with autism. *Journal of Applied Behavior Analysis, 36,* 253–257.

Lovaas, O.I. (1981). *Teaching developmentally disabled children: The ME book.* Baltimore, MD: University Park Press.

Maurice, C., Green, G., & Foxx, R. (Eds.). (2001). *Making a difference: Behavioral intervention for autism.* Austin, TX: PRO-ED.

Maurice, X., Green, X., & Luce, S. (1996) Behavioral intervention for young children with autism: A manual for parents and professionals. Austin, TX: PRO-ED.

McGinnis, E., & Goldstein, A.P. (1990). *Skillstreaming.* Champaign, IL: Research Press.

Mesibov, G.B., Adams, L.W., & Klinger, L.G. (1997) *Autism: Understanding the disorder.* New York, NY: Plenum.

Morales, M., Mundy, P., Delgado, C.E.F., Yale, M., Messinger, D., Neal, R., et al. (2000). Responding to joint attention across the 6- through 24-month age period and early language acquisition. *Journal of Applied Developmental Psychology, 21*(3), 283–298.

More, C. (2008). Digital stories targeting social skills for children with disabilities: Multidimensional learning. *Intervention in School and Clinic, 43,* 168–177.

Mundy, P., Block, J., Vaughan Van Hecke, A., Delgado, C., Venezia Parlade, M., & Pomares, Y. (2007). Individual differences and the development of infant joint attention. *Child Development, 78*(3), 938–954.

Mundy, P., & Crawson, M. (1997). Joint attention and early social communication implications for research on intervention with autism. *Journal of Autism and Developmental Disorders, 27,* 653–676.

Ozonoff, S., & Miller, J.N. (1995). Teaching theory of mind: A new approach to social skills training for individuals with autism. *Journal of Autism and Developmental Disorders, 25*(4), 415–433.

Rao, P.A., Beidel, D.C., & Murray, M.J. (2008). Social skills interventions for children with Asperger's syndrome or high-functioning autism: A review and recommendations. *Journal of Autism and Developmental Disorders, 38*(2), 353–361.

Rehfeldt, R.A., Dillen, J.E., Ziomek, M.M., & Kowalchuk, R.K. (2007). Assessing relational learning deficits in perspective-taking in children with high-functioning autism spectrum disorder. *Psychological Record, 57*(1), 23–48.

Reynhout, G., & Carter, M. (2006). Social Stories for children with disabilities. *Journal of Autism and Developmental Disorders, 36,* 445–469.

Richardson, R.C. (1996). *Connecting with others: Lessons for teaching social and emotional competence.* Champaign, IL: Research Press.

Sansosti, F.J., & Powell-Smith, K.A. (2008). Using computer-presented Social Stories and video models to increase the social communication skills of children with high-functioning autism spectrum disorders. *Journal of Positive Behavior Interventions, 10,* 162–178.

Sansosti, F.J., Powell-Smith, K.A., & Kincaid, D. (2004). A research synthesis of Social Story interventions for children with autism spectrum disorders. *Focus on Autism and Developmental Disorders, 19,* 194–204.

Sheinkopf, S.J., Mundy, P., Claussen, A.H., & Willoughby, J. (2004). Infant joint attention skill and preschool behavioral outcomes in at-risk children. *Development and Psychopathology, 16,* 273–291.

Sherer, M., Pierce, K.L., Parades, S., Kisacky, K.L., Ingersoll, B., & Schreibman, L. (2001). Enhancing conversation skills in children with autism via video technology: Which is better, "self" or "other" as a model? *Behavior Modification, 25,* 140–158.

Shure, M.B. (2001a). *I can problem solve* [Kindergarten and primary grades]. Champaign, IL: Research Press.

Shure, M.B. (2001b). *I can problem solve* [Intermediate elementary grades]. Champaign, IL: Research Press.

Shure, M.B. (2004). *I can problem solve* [Preschool]. Champaign, IL: Research Press.

Snell, M.E., & Brown, F. (2000). *Instruction of students with severe handicaps.* Upper Saddle River, NJ: Prentice Hall.

Stevenson, C.L., Krantz, P.J., & McClannahan, L.E. (2000). Social interaction skills for children with autism: A script-fading procedure for nonreaders. *Behavioral Interventions, 15*(1), 1–20.

Sundberg, M.L., & Partington, J.W. (1998). *Teaching language to children with autism or other developmental disabilities.* Pleasant Hill, CA: Behavior Analysts.

Sundberg, M.L., & Partington, J.W. (1999). The need for both discrete trial and natural environment training for children with autism. In P.M. Ghezzi, W.L. Williams, & J.E. Carr (Eds.), *Autism: Behavior analytic approaches* (pp. 139–156). Reno, NV: Context Press.

Swaggart, B.L., Gagnon, E., Bock, S.J., Earles, T.L., Quinn, C., Myles, B.S., … Simpson, R.L. (1995). Using Social Stories to teach social and behavioral skills to children with autism. *Focus on Autistic Behavior, 10,* 1–16.

Taylor, B.A. (2001). Teaching peer social skills to children with autism. In C. Maurice, G. Green, & R. Foxx (Eds.), *Making a difference: Behavioral intervention for autism* (pp. 83–96). Austin, TX: PRO-ED.

Taylor, B.A., & Jasper, S. (2001). Teaching programs to increase peer interaction. In C. Maurice, G. Green, & R. Foxx (Eds.), *Making a difference: Behavioral intervention for autism* (pp. 97–162). Austin, TX: PRO-ED.

Taylor, B.A., & McDonough, K. (1996). Selecting teaching programs. In C. Maurice, G. Green, & R. Luce (Eds.), *Behavioral interventions for children with autism* (pp. 63–180). Austin, TX: PRO-ED.

Taylor, M., & Carlson, S.M. (1997). The relation between individual differences in fantasy and theory of mind. *Child Development, 68*(3), 436–455.

Thiemann, K.S., & Goldstein, H. (2001). Social Stories, written text cues, and video feedback: Effects on social communication of children with autism. *Journal of Applied Behavior Analysis, 34,* 425–446.

Watkins, L.T., Sprafkin, J.N., & Krolikowski, D.M. (1993.) Using videotaped lessons to facilitate the development of manual sign skills in students with mental retardation. *Augmentative and Alternative Communication, 9,* 177–183.

Weiss, M.J., & Harris, S.L. (2001). *Reaching out, joining in: Teaching social skills to young children with autism.* Bethesda, MD: Woodbine House.

Whalen, C., & Schreibman, L. (2003). Joint attention training for children using behavior modification procedures. *Journal of Child Psychiatry, 44,* 456–468.

4

Interpreting the Efficacy Research on Group-Delivered Social Skills Intervention for Children with Autism Spectrum Disorders

Kathleen Koenig

Group intervention that promotes social skills development in children with autism spectrum disorders (ASDs) is widespread in community and school settings. Intervention to address impairments in social reciprocity skills is clearly needed, and significant resources are being invested in this type of intervention. Numerous social skills curricula are commercially available, designed by expert clinicians and educators (Aspy & Grossman, 2008; Baker, 2003; Bellini, 2006; Dunn, 2005; Garcia, 2005). These curricula are valuable resources for both professionals and parents. However, the evidence base for group-delivered social skills intervention is not particularly strong (Koenig, De Los Reyes, Cicchetti, Scahill, & Klin, 2009; White, Koenig, & Scahill, 2007). Thus, although a child may enjoy a group experience in which the focus is on learning socialization skills, it is not clear how effective such groups are for helping a child change his or her behavior or whether these newly learned skills will generalize to other contexts. In this regard, greater evidence of the efficacy of this type of intervention is needed.

A problem that arises in the investigation of group-based social skills intervention is that the *nature of the problem*—impairment in social reciprocity skills—presents unique challenges for designing and testing intervention. The *format for intervention* (group therapy) also requires careful consideration when designing efficacy studies. Finally, the *measurement of gains* in social reciprocity skills is a particularly complex challenge.

Given these issues, the conventional guidelines for establishing the evidence base for an intervention may not necessarily be the best fit for this particular problem and intervention. At the very least, it is worthwhile to consider these guidelines in the light of the unique problems that impaired

53

social reciprocity in children with ASDs presents and the particular challenges that measuring group intervention entail. In this way, scientists can be confident that the paradigm for examining efficacy fits well with the problem under study.

In this chapter, the paradigm for examining the evidence base of intervention is described as well as the historical roots and underlying assumptions that guided this paradigm. Next, the evidence base for group-delivered social skills training for school-age children with ASDs is examined in the context of this paradigm, and the difficulties with the fit between the research problem and this paradigm are explored. Finally, thoughts regarding clinical practice and future research are presented.

A FRAMEWORK FOR EVALUATING
THE EVIDENCE BASE OF THE INTERVENTIONS

Stepping back from the evaluation of group-delivered intervention to promote social skills in children with ASDs, it is useful to consider how the guidelines for evaluating the evidence base of psychological interventions have been developed. The model for evaluating the evidence base of a particular intervention, with the aim of promoting clinical practice grounded in science, was initially developed to examine medical treatments for a particular illness. In 1897, Fibiger conducted the first randomized clinical trial (RCT) to determine whether diphtheria was responsive to serum treatment (Hróbjartsson, Gøtzsche, & Gluud, 1998). A second well-known example of using an RCT design was a 1948 investigation of streptomycin for treating tuberculosis (Concato, Shah, & Horwitz, 2000). Subsequent clinical trials published since the 1950s demonstrated the strengths of conducting rigorous, controlled research and the importance of considering random error and bias. The fields of medicine and public health developed guidelines to determine to what degree treatments were evidence based, including the Evidence-Based Medicine Working Group and the Preventive Services Task Force (Concato et al., 2000; Sackett, Richardson, Rosenberg, & Harris, 1997). It is important to highlight that although these guidelines were devised to deal with a myriad of medical and public health problems, the systematic examination of evidentiary support for treatments originated from very early work conducted to eradicate infectious disease. In this regard, the *nature of the problem* was likely pertinent in determining how to measure the efficacy of treatment.

Turning to the evaluation of intervention for psychological problems, one should keep in mind that although the investigators who were designing and testing an intervention probably had a sophisticated understanding of the problem being studied, the need to define the problem operationally and measure change accurately—as a prerequisite for examining the efficacy of the intervention—required adopting a very basic view of the problem. With this in mind, at least six factors were most likely *assumed* when researchers designed the construct for study and worked to design an operational definition for the research. These factors would be the following:

1. The problem could be isolated within the individual (or unit of) treatment.
2. The problem was more similar than different in those for whom the intervention was designed.
3. The problem looked the same in most contexts.
4. The problem manifested itself in ways that suggested what was driving the problem and what logical solutions might be indicated.
5. The problem had a discrete beginning and end.
6. The problem could be eradicated to nearly the same degree in all individuals.

When investigators consider physical illnesses originating from infection, injury, environmental conditions, or biological vulnerabilities, these assumptions will generally (but not always) be met. *For considerations of developmental disorders, this may be much less true.* So those who test intervention to remediate features of a developmental disorder must consider to what degree the problem under study conforms to the assumptions. In fact, the characteristics of developmental disorders *do not* conform to those assumptions, so it is possible that the design of research to establish the efficacy of an intervention should be quite different from what is currently considered the gold standard. Further, an additional question remains: What degree of variation within the disability influences the validity of the evaluation of the intervention?

The American Psychological Association (APA) convened the Task Force on Psychological Intervention Guidelines and the Task Force on the Promotion and Dissemination of Psychological Procedures to establish parameters for determining the evidence base for psychological intervention (Chambless & Hollen, 1998). These committees identified a number of psychological interventions that were empirically validated (Chambless & Ollendick, 2001). There were, and continue to be, objections to using such stringent criteria. Refer to Chambless and Ollendick (2001) for a detailed discussion of these issues.

In an effort to bring some order to the field of psychosocial intervention research in ASDs, the National Institute of Mental Health (NIMH) convened a working group to examine the evidence base of existing intervention (Lord et al., 2005). This working group, which included expert scientists in the field, devised a set of guidelines similar to those established by the APA task force. Furthermore, they highlighted the methodological challenges related to measuring symptomatology and outcome, the lack of group designs comparing intervention, and the dearth of longitudinal studies (Lord et al., 2005; Smith et al., 2007). The activities of the working group were timely and critical because there are numerous purported interventions available to address the core symptoms of ASDs, but many have absolutely no scientific foundation. Furthermore, some medical treatments expose children to disease or even death (Offit, 2008).

The guidelines developed by the working group require that techniques and strategies be devised to remediate particular skill impairments, precisely described in a treatment procedure and tested using group designs with varying levels of controls (see Table 4.1). Indeed, several strategies have been tested in this manner, providing additional guidance for practitioners. However, several problems arise when applying this template for evaluating *social skills intervention delivered in a group format*, which is the topic of this chapter.

RESEARCH ON TEACHING SOCIAL SKILLS TO CHILDREN WITH AUTISM SPECTRUM DISORDERS

In a review of social skills intervention for children with autism, Matson, Matson, and Rivet (2007) describe case studies and case series that represent more than 90% of the available literature. The sample size for most of these studies was three to four children; multiple-baseline designs were

Table 4.1.   NIMH trial guidelines

Quality indicators in clinical trials on psychosocial interventions for individuals with ASD
1. Random assignment of participants to intervention and control groups
2. Manuals for all groups
3. A recruitment plan to obtain a representative sample
4. Clearly stated inclusion and exclusion criteria
5. Careful characterization of participants at entry into the study (e.g., diagnosis, symptom severity, and level of functioning)
6. Systematic monitoring of intervention fidelity
7. Clear rationale for the choice of outcome measures and, especially in studies of comprehensive intervention packages, inclusion of measures that assess core features of autism such as reciprocal social interaction
8. Use of outcome measures collected blind to intervention group
9. Appropriate statistical analysis of differences between groups after intervention, effect size and clinical significance of differences, and variables that may influence outcomes (i.e., mediators and moderators)

From Smith, T., et al. (2007). Designing research studies on psychosocial interventions in autism. *Journal of Autism and Developmental Disorders, 37*, 354–366. Journal of autism and developmental disorders by SPRINGER NEW YORK LLC. Reproduced with permission of SPRINGER NEW YORK LLC in the format use in a book/textbook via Copyright Clearance Center.

most frequently employed. Matson et al. acknowledged that various operational definitions are used in the literature. However, they chose to define social skills as "interpersonal responses with specific operational definitions that allow the child to adapt to the environment through verbal and nonverbal communication" (2007, p. 683). For most of the studies reviewed, little rationale for choosing one skill or set of skills rather than another was provided. The targets were behaviors thought to be either aberrant or absent in children with ASDs, for example, poor eye contact, initiating conversation, maintaining conversation, or reducing atypical behavior. The dominant theoretical orientation for teaching was social learning theory. Strategies for teaching new skills included modeling and reinforcement, peer-mediated intervention, reinforcement schedules and activities, and using scripts and Social Stories. It is not surprising that these strategies would be employed given the robust literature on the efficacy of using behavioral strategies for teaching skills of all sorts to children with ASDs. Thus, it is reasonable to believe that a wide variety of skills needed for competent social interaction can be taught, if the skill is defined discretely and the strategy for intervention is systematic and promotes generalization.

In contrast to the large literature base using single-subject, case series, or small samples to test intervention approaches for teaching discrete skills, the evaluation of social skills curricula and the evaluation of group-delivered intervention are not common (Matson et al., 2007; Rao, Beidel, & Murray, 2008; White et al., 2007). White et al. (2007) identified 14 studies that examined the efficacy of group-delivered social skills intervention for school-age children with ASDs. The sample size ranged from 4 to 20 children; 5 studies employed a control or comparison group; none of the studies used random assignment to experimental or control group. Outcome measurement included self-report, parent or teacher report, direct observation, or a combination of these methods. These studies are difficult to synthesize in terms of understanding their practical implications because so many different skills and procedures were used; in addition, despite including only school-age children with ASDs, the population under study was exceedingly heterogeneous. In the largest study to date, Koenig et al. (2010) conducted an RCT of a group social skills intervention that included 43 children with ASDs between the ages of 8 and 11 years. The children were assessed using state-of-the-art diagnostic instruments and clinical observations; then they attended a 16-week group intervention designed to promote social initiation behavior and social responsiveness in peer interaction. The curriculum was manualized, and fidelity to the curriculum was assessed as well.

Outcomes were assessed through ratings conducted by a clinician blind to the treatment status (experimental condition versus control) and parent report based on the Social Competence Inventory (SCI; Rydell, Hadekull, & Bohlin, 1997). Although blinded ratings showed global improvement in the children's social reciprocity behavior, the SCI showed improvement in the index designated a priori as likely to change but not to the level of statistical significance conventionally accepted as meaningful. The inconsistent and statistically nonsignificant results obtained in this investigation are consistent with the results of prior reviews of group-delivered intervention (Rao et al., 2008; White et al., 2007); the evidence for the efficacy of this intervention is inconclusive (Koenig et al., 2009).

With regard to the lack of consistency in outcome, the heterogeneity within the study samples and the methodological differences are likely sources of inconsistency (Koenig et al., 2009; Lord et al., 2005). Accordingly, if inconsistency in outcome is related to a lack of knowledge regarding strategies that work well for teaching skills, then the obvious course is to design and test new strategies (Koenig et al., 2009). If inconsistency can be attributed to error variance, then greater rigor in research design, execution, and data analysis are required (Koenig et al., 2009). These explanations for the conflicting evidence have been explored to some degree (Lord et al., 2005; Smith et al., 2007). Nevertheless, it may also be true that the particular problem under study—*impaired social reciprocity*—is sufficiently complex that an evaluation of intervention for this problem requires a modified approach.

CHALLENGES IN INTERPRETING THE EXTANT LITERATURE

With regard to identifying the difficulties associated with interpreting the group intervention literature, one must recognize the complexity of the psychological construct of social reciprocity and the complexity of the impairment in social reciprocity associated with ASDs. The chronic and pervasive nature of ASDs also requires outcome measurements that consider the impact of growth and development as well as the impact of the intervention itself. Finally, intervention delivered in a group format imposes additional restrictions on the research design and particularly data analyses.

Impaired Social Reciprocity in Autism Spectrum Disorders

Social impairment in ASDs is *qualitatively* different from that encountered in other childhood psychiatric disorders (Rao et al., 2008). Koenig et al. noted, "An affected child presents with an intricate set of interpersonal difficulties based not just on current functional limitations but also on the paucity of a rich historical knowledge regarding relationships and their complexities" (2009, p. 1164). The impairment is complicated by multiple factors, including a child's level of cognitive functioning, the presence of behavioral rigidity, the presence of anxiety or other comorbid conditions, the degree of receptive and expressive language impairment, and the degree and the severity of stereotypic or repetitive behaviors (Volkmar, Paul, Klin, & Cohen,

2005). Features of social functioning deemed affected include the following: impaired ability to identify faces and facial expressions (Schultz & Robins, 2005), impaired understanding of the nuances of verbal and nonverbal communication and the pragmatics of communication (Tager-Flusberg, Paul, & Lord, 2003), poor interpretation of contextual elements of the social environment (Klin, 2000), poor ability to regulate affect (Dawson, Hill, Spencer, Gilbert, & Watson, 1990), poor insight into the emotional components of relationships (Hobson, 2003), the lack of ability to take the perspective of the other (Baron-Cohen, Tager-Flusberg, & Cohen, 2000), and poor ability to self-monitor behavior (Koegel & Koegel, 1995). Furthermore, a hallmark of effective social functioning noticeably absent in pervasive developmental disorders is the *fluid application* of one's knowledge and behavior to reciprocal interaction with others (Klin, Jones, Schultz, & Volkmar, 2003). This requires a sense of timing and rapid recognition of what is emotionally salient in a particular context—two elements of social interaction that are not well understood. Moreover, a lack of motivation to learn these skills is a frequent but not inevitable component of the clinical picture (Chevallier, Kohls, Troiani, Brodkin, & Schultz, in press; Koegel & Koegel, 1995). In summary, the complexity of the clinical picture, given the multiple components that may contribute to the impairment, and the fact that competency in each component exists along a continuum, makes designing intervention inordinately complicated. Evaluation of the evidentiary support for intervention is just as complex as well.

The Measurement of Change Following Intervention

The process of conceptualizing change and identifying beneficial outcomes as a result of intervention is challenging for most psychological constructs (De Los Reyes & Kazdin, 2008). This becomes evident when reviewing the outcome of intervention for any number of conditions; inconsistent results in outcome assessments are consistently noted (Achenbach, 2006; De Los Reyes & Kazdin, 2006). A significant source of variation is that *multidimensional psychological constructs* present unique challenges for intervention, intervention research, and outcome evaluation (De Los Reyes & Kazdin, 2006). Understanding this issue is particularly important when considering evaluation of the evidence base for intervention aimed at the core symptoms of ASDs.

De Los Reyes and Kazdin (2006) illustrated that measurement of the same construct with the same instrument among intervention studies can result in different outcomes (significant versus nonsignificant), and measures of the same construct within and among studies using different instruments may also result in widely different outcomes. Varying outcomes are likely to occur when the target of psychosocial intervention is a *complex and multidimensional construct.* Furthermore, a *range of possible changes* may occur as a result of intervention (De Los Reyes & Kazdin, 2006). With regard to social skills intervention in children with ASDs, the essential point is that the complex, multidimensional construct of social reciprocity is a *dynamic entity* that is buffeted by myriad diverse factors at different times and in different contexts. This entity cannot be treated as an unmoving, static target for intervention. Moreover, the change associated with intervention will be variable and involve multiple influences.

When considering impaired social reciprocity as a target for intervention, the complexity of the construct must be acknowledged, as well as the likelihood that postintervention changes will be *variable*, not uniform. Delay and deviance in social reciprocity skills, which are central characteristics of ASDs, take varied forms across time and reflect the dynamic nature of development. Predictive models and outcome measurement must incorporate estimates of growth as well as stable and time-specific effects (Curran & Bollan, 2001). Accordingly, outcome cannot be measured as a singular, fixed entity.

These complexities have major implications for designing and evaluating group-delivered intervention to remediate problems associated with impaired social reciprocity. For example, the common practice of choosing a primary outcome measure for a study necessarily reduces the target of intervention to a single dimension, in the sense that the outcome is limited to one source or one method of measurement. Although the demand that intervention research select a primary outcome measure forces researchers to specify, a priori, an indicator representing the extent to which an evaluated intervention changes a target behavior, a laudable objective, there are limitations to this methodological strategy. The approach can mislead investigators and consumers to the false assumption that a single indicator can entirely capture change in the targeted construct. Specifically, investigators cannot capitalize on the utility of inconsistent information for informing whether and how intervention works (De Los Reyes & Kazdin, 2008).

An additional point with regard to study design is that estimates of effect size for the calculation of sample size depend on the particular aspect of the construct under study, as well as the direction and the magnitude of change predicted as a result of the intervention (i.e., the possible *range of changes* that may occur). By examining these factors systematically, a person can begin to tease out not only whether an intervention is effective but also when, where, and for whom. Estimated effect sizes need not be uniform because disparate skills compose the broad construct of social reciprocity. Furthermore, conventional assessments of the magnitude of effects may not be useful because these conventionally accepted values have been established based on medical research (Lipsey & Wilson, 1993).

Attending to and interpreting inconsistent findings when examining group intervention to promote social skills in children with pervasive developmental disorders also involve a consideration of the unique nature of this problem. The outcome of an intervention might change any one or a combination of these factors (in a positive or a negative direction), although the magnitude of the effect will vary based on the particular factors that are the focus of the intervention, as well as the measures used to gauge improvement (and their varying sources). For example, behavior improvement with regard to reducing unusual repetitive motor movements (an improvement in terms of increasing socially acceptable behavior) may coincide with an increase in the level of anxiety experienced by a child. Increased awareness of internal emotional states might lead to impulsive responses in social situations. In summary, changes in behavior in a particular domain may improve or complicate social interaction overall. These kinds of trade-offs with regard to the benefit of the intervention must be considered on a child-by-child basis.

An additional point is that the expectation of uniform improvement in a complex psychological construct, such as social reciprocity, following intervention is extremely problematic (De Los Reyes & Kazdin, 2006). Scientists, as peer reviewers, may base their evaluation of a study on the assumption that if an intervention is truly effective, all indices used to measure outcome will move in an expected, positive direction, and inconsistency among outcome measures can be attributed to error variance or a lack of efficacy of the intervention (Smith et al., 2007). The expectation of uniform improvement across measures and studies in response to intervention is consistent with the way clinical trials are evaluated, particularly in psychopharmacology research (Lipsey & Wilson, 1993; Wang & Bakhai, 2006). Nonetheless, when evaluating group-delivered social skills intervention, the premise of uniform improvement on all measures needs examination given the complexity of the problem.

Considering psychosocial intervention in general, reports from different informants regarding a child's emotional or behavior difficulties are most often *not* highly correlated (Achenbach, 2006; De Los Reyes & Kazdin, 2005). In this regard, variability is due to the perspective of the informant, his or her perception of the child's difficulties, and the context within which the informant observes the child (Kraemer et al., 2003; Wakschlag et al., 2008). Furthermore, the difference between cross-informant reliability and interrater reliability is pertinent. Cross-informant correlation reflects the ratings of behavior based on varying perspectives, contexts, and roles vis-à-vis the child. In contrast, interrater reliability represents correlations based on informant ratings of concurrent observed behavior (Achenbach, 2006). Researchers and consumers must be careful not to assume that the

measurement of social reciprocity skills in diverse settings will yield consistent results.

In ASDs, differences in behavior and performance depending on context are the rule, not the exception. A lack of generalization is a major issue
for interventionists. As such, seeking to reconcile disparate points of view
regarding a child's social behavior in an attempt to get a consistent picture
seems to be somewhat counterproductive. Rather than working to eradicate, reduce, or partition the factors contributing to variability in outcome,
it may be more productive to both seek to understand these differences and
consider that they represent different realities, all of which may have some
validity in a particular context (Kraemer et al., 2003). Stated another way,
variability in outcomes may represent different expressions of intervention
effect (or lack thereof), depending on the context in which the intervention effects were observed, the contexts in which social reciprocity skills
are expressed, or both.

The inevitability of variable outcomes directly affects the choice of outcome measures. Again, choosing a primary outcome measure—a standard
practice in clinical trials—is commonly employed based on a plan to use
group comparisons for examining change because of the intervention, rather
than selecting data analysis strategies that match the complexity of the measurement problem (Gueorguieva & Krystal, 2004; Jacobson & Truax, 1991).
With regard to intervention to remediate impairments in social reciprocity,
De Los Reyes and Kazdin note, "It is difficult to argue that adequate examination of such complex constructs can be captured with a single indicator"
(2006, p. 556). Specificity regarding the estimated effect of an intervention
on different aspects of the impairment requires using multiple indicators of
change. Several data analytic strategies are available to model the kind of
intraindividual, dynamic variability associated with social growth and development as the result of intervention (Boker, 2001). Furthermore, the assumption that the same indicator measures the same construct at different
time points in development can be tested (Sayer & Cumsille, 2001). For
example, a questionnaire assessing social initiation behavior may not tap the
same construct of this behavior at age 7 versus age 17. Appropriate social
initiation behavior is quite different at these two developmental time points,
and the influence of latent factors or error may not be consistent. These
issues complicate the analysis of longitudinal data with straightforward statistical models that treat data from two time points as representing the same
construct.

Analyzing Data Derived
from Group-Delivered Intervention

Yet another complexity in measuring change in social reciprocity is that
the analysis of outcome data obtained from intervention delivered in a

group format requires that the impact of participation in a *particular* group be considered as a random variable. This adds another layer of complexity to the analysis of intervention effects. Baldwin, Murray, and Shadish (2005) identified significant difficulties with data analysis related to *group intervention* for psychological and psychiatric problems in research studies purported to support the efficacy of intervention. After reanalyzing the data and incorporating estimated intragroup correlations, less than 50% of the studies analyzed showed statistically significant effects, yielding 20 interventions for psychological disorders that no longer could be considered evidence based according to APA guidelines (Baldwin et al., 2005). Intragroup correlation must be considered in the design of social skills intervention studies for children with ASDs delivered in a group format, which will considerably influence research designs.

CHALLENGES FOR ASSESSING
THE EFFICACY OF GROUP SOCIAL SKILLS INTERVENTION

The complexities of designing outcome studies for group delivered intervention need not discourage clinicians or researchers from considering the problem. Ultimately, the field requires firm evidence of efficacy to justify training clinicians and funding these programs, despite the challenges the process entails. From a clinical point of view, whether a practitioner uses an existing curriculum or pulls together a variety of strategies from different sources, the recommended practice is to systematically and rigorously evaluate effectiveness for each individual child, much like a study based on a sample of one. Rather than aiming to teach social skills on a broad level, clinicians should assess the needs of each child participating in a group intervention and construct a specific plan with measurable goals and objectives. The interval for measurement and the method of measurement should be specified a priori, and every effort should be made to obtain data from multiple sources. In this way, each child's plan for intervention is customized, based on his or her specific profile of social reciprocity impairments as well as associated problems or difficult behaviors.

Although the goals for each child can be tailored to individual learning needs, this does not mean that group leaders must devise individual activities for each child within the group; rather, group leaders should maintain a focus on the specific objectives for each child as social activities are planned and carried out during group therapy. Ultimately, newly learned skills must be smoothly integrated into ongoing interaction with peers and adults, and the most opportune time to teach and reinforce these skills is as they are practiced in vivo. This does not preclude taking some group time to explicitly teach a specific skill to a particular child, and it helps a child practice new skills in a natural context. Furthermore, group members can be engaged in supporting new learning and skill building in their peers. The requirement that all group members provide mentoring to one another encourages group members to observe others' behavior and respond to it, rather than to focus solely on their own experiences in the group.

This approach to conducting group-based social skills intervention for children with ASDs may appear to be quite labor intensive, and it is. However, the alternative, often, is to conduct a series of preplanned skill sessions (e.g., making eye contact, greeting others, recognizing facial expressions) with the aim of somehow making an impact on a child who may or may not have impairments in those skills. This seems akin to throwing a dart in the direction of a wall and hoping to hit a 1-inch target.

RECOMMENDATIONS FOR FUTURE RESEARCH

This chapter may give the reader the impression that conducting research on the efficacy of social skills intervention delivered in a group therapy format is impossible. There is no doubt that it presents multiple challenges not associated with intervention for a clear-cut behavioral symptom (e.g., aggressive behavior), but rigorous, sophisticated research is possible. Koenig et al. (2009) constructed a model for conceptualizing the impairment in social responding in ASD.

As investigators consider each construct, component skills necessary for competency in each domain (e.g., social perception) must be identified and reduced to the smallest possible constituent parts. Specific strategies can be tested to identify effective methods for teaching these skills; effective strategies can be combined to develop intervention to address a particular construct. Some might argue that group-delivered social skills curricula are composed in this way. However, established strategies for intervention are often included along with popular strategies with a minimal evidence base (e.g., Social Stories). Furthermore, a means of evaluating a child's competency with regard to a discrete skill as well as the integration of that skill with other related skills and the appropriate performance of the skill in diverse social contexts is not typically included in extant social skills curricula. This seems to be a critical gap that can be addressed through research. In fact, ample evidence supporting the use of particular strategies to improve discrete skills exists, and the task is really to bring this wide-ranging evidence base together in a conceptually coherent way. The model offered here provides the first step toward that objective.

REFERENCES

Achenbach, T. (2006). As others see us: Clinical and research implications of cross-informant correlations for psychopathology. *Current Directions in Psychological Science, 15*(2), 94–98.

Aspy, R., & Grossman, B. (2008). *Designing comprehensive interventions for individuals with high-functioning autism and Asperger syndrome: The Ziggurat model.* Overland Park, KS: Autism Asperger Publishing.

Baker, J. (2003). *Social skills training for children and adolescents with Asperger syndrome and social-communications problems.* Overland Park, KS: Autism Asperger Publishing.

Baldwin, S., Murray, D., & Shadish, W. (2005). Empirically supported treatments or type I errors? Problems with the analysis of data from group-administered treatments. *Journal of Consulting and Clinical Psychology, 73,* 924–935.

Baron-Cohen, S., Tager-Flusberg, H., & Cohen, D. (2000). *Understanding other minds: Perspectives from cognitive neuroscience.* New York, NY: Oxford University Press.

Bellini, S. (2006). *Building social relationships: A systematic approach to teaching social interaction skills to children and adolescents with autism spectrum disorders.* Overland Park, KS: Autism Asperger Publishing.

Boker, S. (2001). Differential structural equation modeling of intraindividual variability. In L.M. Collins & A.G. Sayer (Eds.), *New methods for the analysis of change* (pp. 3–28). Washington, DC: American Psychological Association.

Chambless, D., & Hollen, S. (1998). Defining empirically supported therapies. *Journal of Consulting and Clinical Psychology, 66*(1), 7–18.

Chambless, D.L., & Ollendick, T.H. (2001). Empirically supported psychological interventions: Controversies and evidence. *Annual Review of Psychology, 52,* 685–716.

Chevallier, C., Kohls, G., Troiani, V., Brodkin, E., & Schultz, R.T. (in press). The Social motivation theory of autism. *Trends in Cognitive Sciences.*

Concato, J., Shah, N., & Horwitz, R. (2000). Randomized, controlled trials, observational studies, and the hierarchy of research designs. *New England Journal of Medicine, 342*(25), 1887–1892.

Curran, P., & Bollan, K. (2001). The best of both worlds: Combining autoregressive and latent curve models. In L.M. Collins & A.G. Sayer (Eds.), *New methods for the analysis of change* (pp. 105–136). Washington, DC: American Psychological Association.

Dawson, G., Hill, D., Spencer, A., Gilbert, L., & Watson, L. (1990). Affective exchanges between young autistic children and their mothers. *Journal of Abnormal Child Psychology, 18* (3), 335–345.

De Los Reyes, A., & Kazdin, A. (2005). Informant "discrepancies" in the assessment of childhood psychopathology: A critical review, theoretical framework, and recommendations for further study. *Psychological Bulletin, 131*(4), 483–509.

De Los Reyes, A., & Kazdin, A. (2006). Conceptualizing changes in behavior in intervention research: The range of possible changes model. *Psychological Review, 113,* 554–583.

De Los Reyes, A., & Kazdin, A. (2008). When the evidence says, "Yes, no, and maybe so": Attending to and interpreting inconsistent findings among evidence-based interventions. *Current Directions in Psychological Science, 17* (1), 47–51.

Dunn, M. (2005). *S.O.S. social skills in our schools: A social skills program for children with pervasive developmental disorders, including high-functioning autism and Asperger syndrome, and their typical peers.* Overland Park, KS: Autism Asperger Publishing.

Garcia, M.W. (2005). *Think social! A social thinking curriculum for school-age students for teaching social thinking and related skills to students with high-functioning autism, PDD-NOS, Asperger syndrome, nonverbal learning disability, ADHD.* Overland Park, KS: Autism Asperger Publishing.

Gueorguieva, R., & Krystal, J. (2004). Move over ANOVA: Progress in analyzing repeated-measures data and its reflection in the *Archives of General Psychiatry. Archives of General Psychiatry, 61,* 310–317.

Hobson, P. (2003). Autism and emotion. In F. Volkmar, R. Paul, A. Klin, & D. Cohen (Eds.), *Handbook of autism and pervasive developmental disorders, Vol. 1: Diagnosis, development, neurobiology, and behavior* (3rd ed., pp. 406–422). Hoboken, NJ: Wiley.

Hróbjartsson, A., Gøtzsche, P., & Gluud, C. (1998). The controlled clinical trial turns 100 years: Fibiger's trial of serum treatment of diphtheria. *British Medical Journal, 317,* 1243–1245.

Jacobson, N., & Truax, P. (1991). Clinical significance: A statistical approach to defining meaningful change in psychotherapy research. *Journal of Consulting and Clinical Psychology, 59*(1), 12–19.

Klin, A. (2000). Attributing social meaning to ambiguous visual stimuli in higher-functioning autism and Asperger syndrome: The social attribution task. *Journal of Child Psychology and Psychiatry, 41*(7), 831–846.

Klin, A., Jones, W., Schultz, R., & Volkmar, F. (2003). The enactive mind, or from actions to cognition: Lessons from autism. *Philosophical Transactions of the Royal Society of London Series B—Biological Sciences, 358*(1430), 345–360.

Koegel, L., & Koegel, R. (1995). *Current issues in autism: Learning and cognition in autism.* New York, NY: Plenum Press.

Koenig, K., De Los Reyes, A., Cicchetti, D., Scahill, L., & Klin, A. (2009). Group intervention to promote social skills in school-age children with pervasive developmental disorders: Reconsidering efficacy. *Journal of Autism and Developmental Disorders, 39*(8), 1163–1172.

Koenig, K., White, S., Pachler, M., Lau, M.L, Pachler, M., Klin, A., & Scahill, L. (2010). Promoting social skill development in children with pervasive developmental disorders: A feasibility and efficacy study. *Journal of Autism and Developmental Disorders, 40*(10), 1209–1218.

Kraemer, H., Measelle, J., Ablow, J., Essex, M., Boyce, W., & Kupfer, D. (2003). A new approach to integrating data from multiple informants in psychiatric assessment and research: Mixing and matching contexts and perspectives. *American Journal of Psychiatry, 160,* 1566–1577.

Lipsey, M., & Wilson, D. (1993). The efficacy of psychological, educational and behavioral treatments: Confirmation from meta-analysis. *American Psychologist, 48,* 1181–1209.

Lord, C., Wagner, A., Rogers, S., Szatmari, P., Aman, M., Charman, T.,…Yoder, P. (2005). Challenges in evaluating psychological interventions for autistic spectrum disorders. *Journal of Autism and Developmental Disorders, 14,* 395–404.

Matson, J., Matson, M., & Rivit, T. (2007). Social skills treatments for children with autism spectrum disorders: An overview. *Behavior Modification, 31*(5), 682–707.

Offit, P. (2008). *Autism's false prophets: Bad science, risky medicine, and the search for a cure.* New York, NY: Columbia University Press.

Rao, P., Beidel, D., & Murray, M. (2008). Social skills interventions for children with Asperger's syndrome or high-functioning autism: A review and recommendations. *Journal of Autism and Developmental Disorders, 38*, 353–361.

Rydell, A., Hadekull, B., & Bohlin, G. (1997). Measurement of two social competence aspects in middle childhood. *Developmental Psychology, 33*, 824–833.

Sackett, D., Richardson, W., Rosenberg, W., & Harris, R. (1997). *Evidence-based medicine.* New York, NY: Churchill Livingston.

Sayer, A., & Cumsille, P. (2001). Second-order latent growth models. In L.M. Collins & A.G. Sayer (Eds.), *New methods for the analysis of change* (pp. 177–200). Washington, DC: American Psychological Association.

Schultz, R., & Robins, D. (2005). Functional neuroimaging studies of autism spectrum disorders. In F. Volkmar, R. Paul, A. Klin, & D. Cohen (Eds.), *Handbook of autism and pervasive developmental disorders, Vol. 1: Diagnosis, development, neurobiology, and behavior* (3rd ed., pp. 515–533). Hoboken, NJ: Wiley.

Smith, T., Scahill, L., Dawson, G., Guthrie, D., Lord, C., Odom, S.,…Wagner, A. (2007). Designing research studies on psychosocial interventions in autism. *Journal of Autism and Developmental Disorders, 37*, 354–366.

Tager-Flusberg, H., Paul, R., & Lord, C. (2003). Language and communication in autism. In F. Volkmar, R. Paul, A. Klin, & D. Cohen (Eds.), *Handbook of autism and pervasive developmental disorders, Vol. 1: Diagnosis, development, neurobiology, and behavior* (3rd ed., pp. 335–364). Hoboken, NJ: Wiley.

Volkmar, F., Paul, R., Klin, A., & Cohen, D. (2005). *Handbook of autism and pervasive developmental disorders.* New York, NY: Wiley.

Wakschlag, L., Briggs-Gowan, M., Hill, C., Danis, B., Leventhal, B., Keenan, K.,… Carter, A.S. (2008). Observational assessment of preschool disruptive behavior. Part I: Reliability of the Disruptive Behavior Diagnostic Observation Schedule (DB-DOS). *Journal of the American Academy of Child and Adolescent Psychiatry, 47*(6), 622–631.

Wang, D., & Bakhai, A. (2006). *Clinical trials: A practical guide to design, analysis, and reporting.* London, UK: Remedica.

White, S., Koenig, K., & Scahill, L. (2007). Social skills development in children with autism spectrum disorders: A review of the intervention research. *Journal of Autism and Developmental Disorders, 37*(10), 1858–1868.

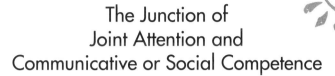

The Junction of Joint Attention and Communicative or Social Competence

Joanne Gerenser

Infants begin responding to and engaging in social interactions with others within the first 6 months of life. This human capacity for coordinating social attention is called joint attention (Bakeman & Adamson, 1984; Mundy et al., 2007). Joint attention is defined as two people actively sharing attention about an object or an event and also monitoring each other's attention to that object or event (Jones & Carr, 2004). Research has indicated that impairments in joint attention may be some of the earliest signs of an autism spectrum disorder (ASD; Charman, 1988; Dawson, Meltzoff, Osterling, Rinaldi, & Brown, 1998). In addition, joint attention skills seem to be highly correlated with outcome measures in the areas of communication and social competence (Carpenter, Nagel, & Tomasello, 1998; Mundy, Sigman, & Kasari, 1990).

To achieve communicative competence, an individual must become both linguistically and pragmatically competent. Linguistic competence requires an internalized functional knowledge of the elements and the structure of the language. This includes having functional knowledge of phonology (the sound system), syntax (grammar), and the lexicon (vocabulary). Pragmatic communicative competence is an understanding of how a language is used in communicative situations to achieve a purpose (Hoffman-Hicks, 1992).

Social competence is far more complicated to define. In fact, it has been said that the definitions of social competence are as plentiful as the number of researchers examining it (Rubin & Rose-Krasnor, 1992). A simple definition of social competence is a combination of adaptive behavior and social skills. More specifically, such competence involves three broad skill areas: an ability to express interest in others and positive emotions, an ability to integrate one's own behavior with that of another in a dynamic flow of social interaction, and an ability to regulate attention and emotional reactivity (Vaughan Van Hecke et al., 2007). These dimensions of behavior greatly overlap with the behaviors required for joint attention. To demonstrate true joint attention, one first must have an interest in others, be able to integrate his or her own behavior with the behavior of others, and regulate attention and affect.

JOINT ATTENTION AND TYPICAL DEVELOPMENT

Joint attention is often described as consisting of two different components. The first component is responding to joint attention from others, which is an ability to follow the direction of gaze or the point of another person to an object, an event, or an activity. The second component is initiating joint attention, which is an ability to use the direction of gaze or the point to direct the attention of others (Mundy et al., 2007). For example, when a young child hears or sees an activity, points to the activity and looks at a person nearby, and then points back at the activity, he or she is initiating joint attention.

Consistent developmental milestones are usually achieved as joint attention develops. By 3 months of age, infants can discriminate triadic from nontriadic contexts (Striano & Stahl, 2005). This means that they are already sensitive to cues from a social partner that are necessary for later engagement in joint attention. In addition, gaze following is very clearly established, and infants are able to perceive adult eye movement and act on changes of eye movement alone (Hood, Willen, & Driver, 1998). By 5 months of age, an infant's cuing of an object by adult gaze significantly enhances object processing. In other words, infants attend to and process objects that are cued through adult eye gaze more significantly than other objects in their environment. This enhanced processing has been documented via behavioral preferential looking paradigms as well as by using event-related potentials (Parise, Reid, Stets, & Striano, 2008). Study results indicate that 5-month-old infants allocate more attention to objects that have been previously cued by adults visually within interactions.

Pointing is clearly established by 9 months of age. It is still unclear, however, whether infants are actually using the point in the true sense of joint attention or are simply marking their own attention rather than focusing the attention of others (Carpenter et al., 1998). By 12 months of age, however, it is clear that pointing is being used to get the attention of or to request something in the environment because it is also accompanied with gaze alteration (Bates, 1979).

There is no question that joint attention plays a critical role in language development (Mundy & Gomes, 1998; Sigman & Kasari, 1995). Early vocabulary and language skills are learned during joint attention routines (Baldwin, 1993). One of the biggest obstacles to early word learning is the problem of infinite possibilities (Quine, 1960). After hearing a novel word, a young child must rapidly map that word onto the appropriate corresponding object, action, or event in the environment—and do so with ease. This happens even though there may be hundreds of other objects, actions, or events that can serve as distracters for the child. The behaviors developed during joint attention allow the young word learner to cue into the correct referent. The ability to follow a person's gaze or point and then integrate that information is referred to as a knowledge-based constraint (Baldwin & Tomasello, 1998; Woodward, 2003). These nonverbal cues provide the necessary information for the young word learner to determine the appropriate referent in the environment. That is, the cues help constrain the possible data sets that a child must consider when mapping the novel word on the referent. Children are significantly more likely to map a word onto a novel referent when following an adult gaze or point (Baldwin, 1993). In the language acquisition literature, this process of word learning is called fast mapping (Dollaghan, 1985).

More than 30 years ago, Carey and Bartlett (1978) first described fast mapping as having two components: a reference component (or skill) and a memory component. The reference skill involves the ability to establish a reference between a novel word and an object and is developed during early joint attention routines. The memory component requires a young word learner to remember the word long enough to recognize it when it is subsequently reintroduced.

Joint attention plays a critical and a pivotal role in developing social competence. Early intentional use of eye contact marks the beginning of social cognition (Brooks & Meltzoff, 2005). The period between 9 and 12 months of age has been described as the social cognitive revolution (Tomasello, 1995). It has been suggested that the child's overt behaviors demonstrated within joint attention, such as looking where others look or following the gaze of another, may actually be precursors to more covert social behaviors seen in childhood, such as following the abstract theme of a conversation in a classroom (Mundy & Sigman, 2006).

Mundy and colleagues have described multiple processes involved in the development of joint attention that ultimately contribute to social competence development (Mundy et al., 2007; Vaughan Van Hecke et al., 2007). One important variable is the degree to which sharing an experience with another person is rewarding (Dawson, 2002). This is described as social motivation. The intentional use of eye contact and gestures, most notably pointing, is another important variable (Carpenter, Pennington, & Rogers, 2001; Woodward, 2003). It has been suggested that these processes may be influenced by several executive functions (Mundy, 2003). Specifically, the aspects of executive attention that regulate inhibitory control, the disengagement of attention, and self-awareness or self-monitoring may be involved (Landry & Bryson, 2004; Mundy, Card, & Fox, 2000; Mundy & Newel, 2007; Nichols, Fox, & Mundy,

2005). Mundy et al. (2007) comprehensively overviewed the theories of joint attention, language competence, and social competence.

JOINT ATTENTION AND AUTISM SPECTRUM DISORDERS

Impairments in early joint attention behaviors are often the earliest manifestations of an ASD. Observations of joint attention skills alone may be sufficient for discriminating up to 80%–90% of young children diagnosed with ASDs from other young children with developmental delays (Doehring, Benaroya, Klaiman, & Scuceimarri, 1995; Lewy & Dawson, 1992). For many years, the behavioral profiles of infants and toddlers with autism were somewhat unclear because the autism diagnosis was not made until the child was 3 or even 4 years old. Parents were then asked to recall development that occurred 2–3 years earlier. Unfortunately, there are many problems with relying solely on parent recall for information about behaviors present in early development. Recall is prone to errors and distortions. One major problem is that parents are asked to recall their child's early behaviors after an autism diagnosis is given. This could inadvertently bias a parent toward reporting behaviors consistent with the diagnosis (Zwaigenbaum et al., 2007). An alternative retrospective format involves the analysis of videotapes made by parents (Baranek, 1999; Osterling & Dawson, 1994). This method has significant strengths relative to the interview format because it allows for the direct observation of behaviors in natural settings by unbiased observers. Zwaigenbaum et al. (2007) pointed out, however, that even this format has several potential problems. The first is that parents videotape their children to preserve memories, not document behavior. In many cases, if a child does not behave as expected, the parent may re-record. Frequently, the quality as well as the content of videotapes varies considerably across families, making any type of standardization almost impossible (Baranek, 1999).

One important new strategy involves prospective studies of at-risk infants, including infants born with specific medical conditions or genetic anomalies associated with autism, infants identified during general early population screenings, and infants with older siblings with autism (Landa & Garrett-Mayer, 2006; Zwaigenbaum et al., 2007). Collectively, through retrospective and prospective studies, differences in joint attention behaviors, including a lack of a social smile, a failure to respond to name, and a lack of appropriate social orienting, have been found in infants with ASDs as young as 8–12 months of age (Baranek, 1999; Landa & Garrett-Mayer, 2006; Osterling & Dawson, 1994; Werner, Dawson, Osterling, & Dinno, 2000; Zwaigenbaum et al., 2007). In addition, impairments in declarative and referential looking as well as pointing are common in the early development of children later diagnosed with autism (Baron-Cohen, 1995;

Leekam, Lopez, & Moore, 2000). When a child is 2 years old, behaviors are more overt and may include limited or no use of gestures, a clear preference for nonsocial stimuli relative to social stimuli, and simply ignoring people (Charman et al., 1998; Osterling & Dawson, 1994).

Joint attention behaviors account for the variability in language outcomes in learners with autism (Landry & Loveland, 1988; Sigman & Ruskin, 1999). Specifically, joint attention behaviors are significant predictors of language (Luyster, Kadlee, Connolly, Carter, & Tager-Flusberg, 2008). In numerous studies, children with joint attention behaviors at the baseline demonstrated more rapid vocabulary growth and better general language scores than children who did not demonstrate joint attention behaviors at the beginning of the research (Carpenter et al., 1998; Smith, Mirenda, & Zaidman-Zait, 2007; Thurm, Lord, Lee, & Newschaffer, 2007).

A deficit in the development of early joint attention behaviors would interfere with the ability to follow a speaker's gaze, which, in turn, would limit the ability to establish reference in the presence of new words. The ability to establish reference is the first and most essential step in the word learning process of fast mapping. Baron-Cohen, Baldwin, and Crowson (1997) were the first to demonstrate difficulty with word learning in children with autism because of impairments in following a speaker's gaze. In their study, they exposed children to a series of single trial, rapid word learning tests. Specifically, the children were required to follow the speaker's gaze to figure out which of two novel objects was being labeled. In the follow-in condition, the experimenter labeled the object that the child was already looking at. In the discrepant labeling condition, the experimenter labeled the object that the child was not looking at. After a delay, the child was given a retention task to see how many words he or she could accurately remember, given the novel objects. The children with autism performed similarly to two control groups (children who are typically developing and children with intellectual disabilities) in the follow-in condition. Significant differences, however, were noted in the discrepant labeling condition, with children with ASDs accurately identifying only 29% of the novel objects, compared with 70% by the group with intellectual disabilities and almost 80% by the group that was typically developing. Of even greater interest is that there were several instances of mapping or associating the word with the incorrect object. This would indicate that the breakdown in fast mapping involved the referencing component more so than the memory component.

Joint attention behaviors, initiation in particular, have been found to account for enhanced social competence outcomes in learners with autism. Sigman and Ruskin (1999) found that initiating joint attention (but not responding to joint attention) predicted higher rates of social initiations in children with autism. A large group of children with autism was followed for 7 years. The children were seen at ages 2, 3, 5, and 9. This work provided an excellent opportunity to track the developmental trajectories of children at risk for autism. One of the key findings was that the level of initiating behaviors in 2-year-olds was predictive of social skills at 9 years of age (Anderson, et al., 2007; Lord et al., 2006).

JOINT ATTENTION AND INTERVENTION

Research has shown that joint attention behaviors can be taught to individuals with autism. Several studies have examined the effects of behavioral, developmental, and mixed approaches to teaching the components of initiating and responding to joint attention. These studies have ranged from single-subject studies (Kasari, Freeman, & Paparella, 2001) to small-group, multiple-baseline studies (Jones, Carr, & Feeley, 2006; Taylor & Hoch, 2008; Whalen & Schreibman, 2003) to a well-designed randomized control study (Kasari et al., 2001). Several important conclusions can be drawn from this intervention research. The first is that the components of joint attention can be taught to children with autism, which in turn, enhances language outcomes when compared with children who were not taught joint attention behaviors. Although the research does not definitively identify one intervention model as being superior to another, it does suggest that using child preferences as well as a component of rapport building with the child may be important (Jones et al., 2006). One strategy that has been identified to promote rapport has been for an individual to pair him- or herself with the child's highly preferred object or activity. In joint attention routines, it has been suggested that any potential social reinforcer for the child (e.g., tickles, blowing in face) be identified. Relying on these shared interactive routines should strengthen the social aspect of the joint attention routine (Jones et al., 2006).

Kasari et al. (2001) found that a behavioral approach alone, without direct instruction in joint attention, did not result in language gains when compared with the joint attention group. They suggested that because the joint attention group received a combination of behavioral and developmental approaches, this might be of importance when working with young children with autism.

In many cases, measures of language development were employed when looking at the outcomes of joint attention studies (Jones et al., 2006; Kasari et al., 2001). Although there were some attempts to include measures of social competence, these results were limited, with little or no long-term follow-up. For example, Jones et al. (2006) attempted to measure changes in social-communicative characteristics, such as spontaneous initiations, happiness, and relationships. To measure these characteristics, mothers (of children who are typically developing) were asked to rate the preintervention and postintervention videotapes of the participants with autism. The raters were blind to the condition shown in the videotapes. The mothers responded to questions such as the following, using a 7-point Likert scale: "How happy does the child appear during the interaction?" and "How interested does the child appear to be in interacting with his or her mother?" In all cases, the mothers rated the children as appearing more interested in interacting, happier, and having a closer relationship with the mother in the postintervention tapes. In all cases, the adults rated the postintervention videotapes as higher on all measures. It was not clear, however, whether the raters perceived these improvements because of actual changes of a child's social competence or simply enhanced interactions within those specific routines. That is, a child's familiarity with the routine may have enhanced the perception of the characteristics being measured.

Several researchers have addressed both initiating and responding to joint attention. They frequently reported that more time was needed to teach initiations, and, in some cases, the learners did not demonstrate improvements in initiating joint attention, despite improvements in responding to joint attention (Taylor & Hoch, 2008). It has been speculated that initiating joint attention and responding to joint attention behaviors may actually demonstrate dissocial paths of development in children with autism (Mundy, Kasari, Sigman, & Ruskin, 1995). That is, initiating and responding to joint attention may demonstrate distinct paths of development. Some evidence to support this concept lies in variances found in initiating and responding to joint attention at different points in development. For example, the frequency of initiating joint attention does not seem to display the type of linear increase with age as evident in responding to joint attention (Mundy et al., 2000).

Initiating and responding to joint attention may also reflect unique and differentiated aspects of executive functioning. Findings from electroencephalogram studies revealed that responding to joint attention might be largely regulated by temporal and parietal systems that involve attention, disengaging, and orienting. In contrast, initiating joint attention may reflect a multifaceted frontal, temporal, and parietal system that involves initiating goal-directed social behavior based on motivational constraints and flexibly switching attention (Mundy et al., 2000; Mundy, Fox, & Card, 2003). Specifically, responding to bids for joint attention may be a more involuntary form of social orienting, whereas initiating joint attention may require more intentional control of social attention (Mundy & Newell, 2007). Inherent in this distinction is the fact that initiating joint attention is far more influenced by social motivation or the relative enthusiasm for social engagement (Mundy & Sigman, 2006).

SUMMARY AND CONCLUSIONS

Children with ASDs have been shown to demonstrate early and pervasive problems with joint attention, language competence, and social competence. The area of social competence most clearly differentiates young children on the autism spectrum from children who are developmentally delayed. More important, it has been shown that practitioners are able to teach joint attention behaviors to young learners with autism and enhance language outcomes in these children. One problem that remains, however, is to demonstrate the efficacy of joint attention instruction on social competence in individuals with ASDs. Many children with autism can be taught to engage in responsive joint attention behaviors but continue to demonstrate significant challenges with initiating joint attention behaviors. One concern is that practitioners may be teaching a rudimentary social responsiveness but not the critical social cognition or the underlying social motivation. Although practitioners may be supporting linguistic development or enhanced language outcomes, they may not be adequately promoting the social or communicative competence that is necessary to be a socially competent individual. It is the experiences that infants have with intentional control of their own social attention coordination acts within initiating joint attention that may provide the unique types of learning opportunities that are necessary for developing social cognition (Mundy et al., 2007).

Important to keep in mind is that social competence probably plays a more significant role in the quality of life and good long-term outcomes than linguistic competence or a person's intelligence quotient (Denham et al., 2001). The inability to develop social competence has been found to be the leading factor in the failure of most adults with ASDs to attain even a minimal level of quality of life in their lives (Howlin, Goode, Hutton, & Rutter, 2004). More specifically, those individuals who fail to achieve some level of social competence are most likely to be unemployed or underemployed, be unable to live independently, and have no quality social relationships (Gutstein & Whitney, 2002).

Although researchers have come a long way in understanding and treating impairments in joint attention in individuals with ASDs, there is still a great deal that is not yet sufficiently explained. For example, it appears that initiating bids for joint attention as an infant has a direct impact on the later development of social competence. Furthermore, enthusiasm for social engagement underlies an infant's bids for joint attention. What is not yet clear is why an infant with autism does not appear to have this enthusiasm for social engagement, and researchers have not fully identified strategies to address it.

Several points should be considered with regard to the challenges that remain. The first point is that social motivation is generally well established in infants who are typically developing by 9–10 months of age (Venezia, Messinger, Thorp, & Mundy, 2004). Intervention for children on the autism spectrum begins at 18–20 months of age, at best, but more frequently well past the child's third birthday. The research done to date on early signs of autism has gone a long way to earlier and earlier identification. Unfortunately, this research has not yet been adequately translated into practice. The majority of children with autism are diagnosed between the ages of 3 and 6 years (Landa, 2008). It appears vital that to improve long-term outcomes for more and more individuals with ASDs, particularly in the area of social competence, practitioners should begin intervention with children as early as possible. In addition, researchers must increase research into therapeutic techniques that will increase social motivation in at-risk infants and toddlers.

Charman (2004) described the early development of children with ASDs with a dynamic systems approach. More specifically, this approach states that early atypical brain development will lead to atypical psychological development, which, in turn, will then lead to later secondary atypical brain development. Given the idea that infants with autism are responding to the environment in atypical ways from very early in life, the earlier this can be detected and modified, the more likely that researchers could then alter the trajectory of secondary atypical brain development.

Another point to consider is the distinction between linguistic competence and pragmatic competence. In many cases, practitioners are able to teach an individual with an ASD to demonstrate linguistic competence. That is, they can teach vocabulary, meaning, and grammar. But they have a difficult time teaching or facilitating the development of pragmatic competence (the appropriate use of language in context). Unfortunately, the lack of pragmatic competence, most notably in social contexts, greatly diminishes the likelihood of social interactions and, ultimately, social competence.

The challenge with teaching an individual with an ASD to initiate social interactions or social conversations lies in the difficulty in establishing or promoting social motivation. It is not difficult to teach a child with autism to ask for a drink (because the underlying motivation of thirst can readily be both recognized and established). Teaching an individual to make a social comment or some other form of social initiation is not as easy. Researchers are still in the early stages of identifying strategies to promote or teach social motivation. Unfortunately, the lack of underlying social motivation to initiate greatly reduces the opportunities for interactions with others. Much is gained from having social interactions, including exposure to novel vocabulary, new concepts, and the possibility of friendship or companionship.

One alternative to consider, in the interim, might be to teach an individual with an ASD to become a competent social responder by building up response rate accuracy and reducing response latency. If an individual frequently ignores the social initiations of others, this will result in less contact and certainly shorter interactions with others. An individual too slow in responding or responding inappropriately will also reduce social contact. On the other hand, if an individual responds appropriately and in a timely manner, the likelihood of follow-up social contact is far greater. It does not really matter who starts a conversation, as long as both parties participate. The key to helping individuals with ASDs become competent social responders lies in building up the necessary contextual vocabulary, fluency in responding, and the skill of reliable responding. Although it is unlikely that becoming a competent social responder will lead to the underlying social motivation to initiate these types of interactions, it will, at least, provide the individual with an ASD much more frequent and longer interactions, thereby exposing him or her to many of the benefits of social interactions.

Some areas of future research that will be critical for enhancing long-term outcomes for children with autism will be to continue to extend the work on early signs of ASDs. The earlier that intervention can begin with this population, the earlier important work can follow. In addition, researchers must extend the research on strategies to teach joint attention behaviors to children with autism. Long-term measures of social competence, however, must be included in the outcome measures of these studies. It may be important to explore the impact of direct instruction in areas that enhance executive functioning behaviors, such as rapidly shifting attention, fluently responding, and inhibiting competing responses on the development of joint attention. This may be particularly relevant given the work of Mundy et al. (2007) on the role of executive functions in the development of joint attention skills that are essential for developing social competence.

Autism is a complex disorder that greatly affects language development and social competence. Impairments in joint attention have been identified as one of the earliest signs of autism. Given the role that joint attention plays in both language development and social competence, it is not surprising that research in this area will have a significant impact on the future of individuals with ASDs. In addition to providing critical insight into earlier and earlier identification, developing effective intervention strategies to promote joint attention in learners with autism will provide the essential skills necessary for them to become both linguistically and socially competent.

REFERENCES

Anderson, D.K., Lord, C., Risi, S., DiLavore, P.S., Schulman, C., Thurm, A.,... Pickles, A. (2007). Patterns of growth in verbal abilities among children with autism spectrum disorders. *Journal of Consulting and Clinical Psychology, 4,* 594–604.

Bakeman, R., & Adamson, L.B. (1984). Coordinating attention to people and objects in mother-infant and peer-infant interaction. *Child Development, 55,* 1278–1289.

Baldwin, D.A. (1993). Infants' ability to consult the speaker for clues to word reference. *Journal of Child Language, 20,* 395–418.

Baldwin, D.A., & Tomasello, M. (1998). Word learning: A window on early pragmatic understanding. In E.V. Clark (Ed.), *Proceedings of the 29th Annual Child Language Research Forum.* Stanford, CA: Center for the Study of Language and Information.

Baranek, G.T. (1999). Autism during infancy: A retrospective video analysis of sensory-motor and social behaviors at 9–12 months of age. *Journal of Autism and Developmental Disorders, 29,* 213–224.

Baron-Cohen, S. (1995). *Mindblindness: An essay on autism and theory of mind.* Cambridge, MA: MIT Press/Bradford.

Baron-Cohen, S., Baldwin, D.A., & Crowson, M. (1997). Do children with autism use the speaker's direction of gaze strategy to crack the code of language? *Child and Development, 68,* 48–57.

Bates, E. (1979). *The emergence of symbols: Cognition and communication in infancy.* New York, NY: Academic Press.

Brooks, R., & Meltzoff, A.N. (2005). The development of gaze following and its relation to language. *Developmental Science, 8,* 535–543.

Carey, S., & Bartlett, E., (1978). Acquiring a single new word. *Proceedings of the Stanford Child Language Conference, 15,* 17–29.

Carpenter, M., Nagel, K., & Tomasello, M. (1998). Social cognition, joint attention, and communicative competence. *Monographs of the Society of Research in Child Development, 36*(4), 1–174.

Carpenter, M., Pennington, B., & Rogers, S. (2001). Understanding of others' intentions in children with autism. *Journal of Autism and Developmental Disorders, 31,* 589–599.

Charman, T. (1988). Specifying the nature and course of the joint attention impairment in autism in the preschool years: Implications for diagnosis and intervention. *Autism, 2,* 61–79.

Charman, T. (2004). Why is joint attention a pivotal skill in autism? In U. Frith & E. Hill (Eds.), *Autism: Mind and brain* (pp. 67–87). New York, NY: Oxford University Press.

Charman, T., Swettenham, J., Baron-Cohen, S., Cox, A., Baird, G., & Drew, A. (1998). An experimental investigation of social-cognitive abilities in infants with autism: Clinical implications. *Infant Mental Health Journal, 19,* 260–275.

Charman, T., Taylor, E., Drew, A., Cockerill, H., Brown, J., & Baird, G. (2005). Outcome at 7 years of children diagnosed with autism at age 2: Predictive validity of assessments conducted at 2 and 3 years of age and pattern of symptom change over time. *Journal of Child Psychology and Psychiatry, 46,* 500 513.

Dawson, G., Meltzoff, A.N., Osterling, J., Rinaldi, J., & Brown, E. (1998). Children with autism fail to orient to naturally occurring social stimuli. *Journal of Autism and Developmental Disorders, 28,* 479–485.

Dawson, G., Munson, J., Estes, A., Osterling, J., McPartland, J., Toth, K., ...Abbott, R. (2002). Neurocognitive function and joint attention ability in young children with autism spectrum disorder versus developmental delay. *Child Development, 73,* 345–358.

Denham, S.A., Mason, T., Caverly, S., Schmidt, M., Hackney, R., Caswell, C., … DeMulder, E. (2001). Preschoolers at play: Co-socializers of emotional and social competence. *International Journal of Behavioral Development, 25,* 290–301.

Doehring, P., Benaroya, S., Klaiman, C., & Scuceimarri, C. (1995). *Using joint attention, play and imitation skill in the differential diagnosis of young children with autism and with developmental disorders.* Paper presented at the Conference of the Society for Research in Child Development, Indianapolis, IN.

Dollaghan, C. (1985). Child meets word: "Fast mapping" in preschool children. *Journal of Speech and Hearing Research, 28,* 449–454.

Gutstein, S.E., & Whitney, T. (2002). Asperger syndrome and the development of social competence. *Focus on Autism and Other Developmental Disabilities, 17,* 161–171.

Hoffman-Hicks, S. (1992). Linguistic and pragmatic competence: Their relationship to overall competence of a language learner. *Pragmatics and Language Learning Monograph Series, 3,* 67–81.

Hood, B.M., Willen, J.D., & Driver, J. (1998). Adult's eyes trigger shifts of visual attention in human infants. *Psychological Science, 9,* 131–134.

Howlin, P., Goode, S., Hutton, J., & Rutter, M. (2004). Adult outcome for children with autism. *Journal of Child Psychology and Psychiatry, 45,* 212–229.

Jones, E.A., & Carr, E.G. (2004). Joint attention and autism: Theory and intervention. *Focus on Autism and Developmental Disabilities, 19,* 13–26.

Jones, E.A., Carr, E.G., & Feeley, K.M. (2006). Multiple effects of joint attention intervention for children with autism. *Behavior Modification, 30,* 782–834.

Kasari, C., Freeman, S.F.N., & Paparella, T. (2001). Early intervention in autism: Joint attention and symbolic play. *International Review of Research in Mental Retardation, 23,* 207–237.

Landa, R. (2008). Diagnosis of autism spectrum disorders in the first three years of life. *Nature Clinical Practice Neurology, 4,* 138–147.

Landa, R., & Garrett-Mayer, E. (2006). Development in infants with autism spectrum disorders: A prospective study. *Journal of Child Psychology and Psychiatry and Allied Disciplines, 47,* 629–638. doi:10.1111/j.1469-7610.2006.01531.x

Landry, R., & Bryson, S. (2004). Impaired disengagement of attention in young children with autism. *Journal of Child Psychology and Psychiatry, 45,* 1115–1122.

Landry, S.H., & Loveland, K.A. (1988). Communication behaviors in autism and developmental language delay. *Journal of Child Psychology and Psychiatry, 29,* 621–634.

Leekam, S.R., Lopez, B., & Moore, C. (2000). Attention and joint attention in preschool children with autism. *Developmental Psychology, 36,* 261–273.

Lewy, A.L., & Dawson, G. (1992). Social stimulation and joint attention in young autistic children. *Journal of Abnormal Child Psychology, 20,* 555–566.

Lord, C., Risi, S., DiLavore, P.S., Shulman, C., Thurm, A., & Pickles, A. (2006). Autism from 2 to 9 years of age. *Archives of General Psychiatry, 63,* 694–701.

Luyster, R., Kadlec, M.B., Connolly, C., Carter, A., & Tager-Flusberg, H. (2008). Language assessment and development in toddlers with autism spectrum disorders. *Journal of Autism and Developmental Disorders, 38,* 1426–1438.

Mundy, P. (2003). The neural basis of social impairments in autism: The role of the dorsal medial-frontal cortex and anterior cingulate system. *Journal of Child Psychology and Psychiatry and Allied Disciplines, 44,* 793–809.

Mundy, P., Block, J., Delgado, C., Pomares, Y., Van Hecke, A.V., & Parlade, M.V. (2007). Individual differences and the development of joint attention in infancy. *Child Development, 78*, 938-954. doi:10.llll/j.1467-8624.2007.0l042.x

Mundy, P., Card, J., & Fox, N. (2000). EEG correlates of the development of infant joint attention skills. *Developmental Psychobiology, 36*, 325–338.

Mundy, P., Fox, N., & Card, J. (2003). Joint attention, EEG coherence and early vocabulary development. *Developmental Science, 6*, 48–54.

Mundy, P., & Gomes, A. (1998). Individual differences in joint attention skill development in the second year. *Infant Behavior and Development, 21*, 469–482.

Mundy, P., Kasari, C., Sigman, M., & Ruskin, E. (1995). Nonverbal communication and early language acquisition in children with Down syndrome and in normally developing children. *Journal of Speech and Hearing Research, 38*, 157–167.

Mundy, P., & Newell, L. (2007). Attention, joint attention, and social cognition. *Current Directions in Psychological Science, 16*, 269–274.

Mundy P., & Sigman, M. (2006). Joint attention, social competence and developmental psychopathology. In D. Cicchetti & D. Cohen (Eds.), *Developmental psychopathology, Vol. 1: Theory and methods* (2nd ed., pp. 293–332). Hoboken, NJ: Wiley.

Mundy, P., Sigman, M., & Kasari, C. (1990). A longitudinal study of joint attention and language development in autistic children. *Journal of Autism and Developmental Disorders, 20*, 115–128.

Nichols, K.E., Fox, N., & Mundy, P. (2005). Joint attention, self-recognition, and neurocognitive functioning. *Infancy, 7*, 35–51.

Osterling, J., & Dawson, G. (1994). Early recognition of children with autism: A study of first birthday home videotapes. *Journal of Autism and Developmental Disorders, 24*, 247–257.

Parise, E., Reid, V.M., Stets, M., & Striano, T. (2008). Direct eye contact influences the neural processing of objects in 5-month-old infants. *Social Neuroscience, 3*, 141–150.

Quine, W.V.O. (1960). *Word and object.* Cambridge, MA: MIT Press.

Rubin, K.H., & Rose-Krasnor, L. (1992). Interpersonal problem solving and social competence in children. In V.B. Van Hasselt & M. Hersen (Eds.), *Handbook of social development* (pp. 283–323). New York, NY: Plenum Press.

Sigman, M., & Kasari, C. (1995). Joint attention across contexts in normal and autistic children. In C. Moore & P.J. Dunham (Eds.), *Joint attention: Its origins and role in development* (pp. 189–203). Mahwah, NJ: Lawrence Erlbaum Associates.

Sigman, M., & Ruskin, E. (1999). Continuity and change in the social competence of children with autism, Down syndrome and developmental delays. *Monographs of the Society for Research in Child Development, 64*, 1–114.

Smith, V., Mirenda, P., & Zaidman-Zait, A. (2007). Predictors of expressive vocabulary growth in children with autism. *Journal of Speech, Language, and Hearing Research, 50*, 149–160.

Striano, T., & Stahl, D. (2005). Sensitivity to triadic attention in early infancy. *Developmental Science, 8*, 333–343.

Taylor, B.A., & Hoch, H. (2008). Teaching children with autism to respond to and initiate bids for joint attention. *Journal of Applied Behavior Analysis, 41*, 377–391.

Thurm, A., Lord, C., Lee, L., & Newschaffer, C. (2007). Predictors of language acquisition in preschool children with autism spectrum disorders. *Journal of Autism and Developmental Disorders, 37,* 1721–1734.

Tomasello, M. (1995). Joint attention as social cognition. In C. Moore & P. Dunham (Eds.), *Joint attention: Its origin and role in development* (pp. 103–130). Hillsdale, NJ: Lawrence Erlbaum Associates.

Vaughan Van Hecke, A., Mundy, P.C., Francoise Acra, C., Block, J.C., Delgado, C.E.F., Parlade, M.V., …Pomares, Y.B. (2007). Infant joint attention, temperament, and social competence in preschool children. *Child Development, 78,* 53–69.

Venezia, M., Messinger, D., Thorp, D., & Mundy, P. (2004). Timing changes: The development of anticipatory smiling. *Infancy, 6,* 397–406.

Werner, E., Dawson, G., Osterling, J., & Dinno, N. (2000). Brief report: Recognition of autism spectrum disorder before one year of age: A retrospective study based on home videotapes. *Journal of Autism and Developmental Disorders, 30,* 157–162.

Whalen, C., & Schreibman, L. (2003). Joint attention training for children with autism using behavior modification procedures. *Journal of Child Psychology and Psychiatry and Allied Disciplines, 44,* 456–468.

Woodward, A.L. (2003). Infants' developing understanding of the link between looker and object. *Developmental Science, 6*(3), 297–311.

Zwaigenbaum, L., Thurm, A., Stone, W., Baranek, G., Bryson, S., Iverson, J., … Sigman, N. (2007). Studying the emergence of autism spectrum disorders in high-risk infants: Methodological and practical issues. *Journal of Autism and Developmental Disabilities, 37,* 466–480.

Building Social Skills and Social Relationships in School Settings

The Role of Schoolwide Positive Behavior Interventions and Supports

Ilene S. Schwartz and Pei-Yu Chen

Members of our research team often begin talks for teachers and parents by saying that "children with autism are children first." This statement underlies the importance of understanding typical development and recommended practices in early childhood education plus being fluent in instructional practices that have demonstrated effectiveness with children with autism spectrum disorders (ASDs). It also summarizes what is known about teaching social skills and facilitating the social relationships of young children with ASDs. See McConnell (2002), National Research Council (2001), and Strain, Schwartz, and Bovery (2007) for comprehensive reviews.

As with all children, those with ASDs benefit from consistent, positive relationships with caregivers; thrive in safe and well-designed environments; engage in reinforcing behaviors; and learn when they are taught with effective instruction. In other words, strategies that are effective in facilitating social relationships in children who are typically developing and children with other developmental disabilities are often effective in facilitating social relationships in children with ASDs—if these strategies are done with adequate intensity, implemented with high fidelity, and presented in an explicit manner. Although practitioners can create school, community, and home environments that facilitate the social interactions of children with ASDs, many of the evidence-based instructional interventions do not generalize across settings and participants (Bellini, Peters, Benner, & Hopf, 2007). Placing a child with an ASD in an environment with children who are typically developing does not increase social interaction unless support and instruction for the child are provided (Myles, Simpson, Ormsbee, & Erickson, 1993; Strain, 1983; Strain et al., 2007). If practitioners want children with ASDs to engage in social interactions with their peers, then they must teach them how to interact across activities, settings, and partners.

The purpose of this chapter is to build a case that the primary focus for children with autism should be social relationships, not social skills. It is not that practitioners, researchers, and family members should not or do not value social skills. Rather, social skills outside the context of meaningful social relationships will not contribute to an increased quality of life. The chapter argues that increased quality of life should be the overarching outcome variable used for evaluating the effectiveness of comprehensive intervention programs for students with ASDs and related disorders (cf. Carr, 2007). The chapter also reviews strategies that have been effective in teaching social skills to children with autism and describes how practitioners can expand these strategies to address the development and the maintenance of social relationships. We then describe how the schoolwide positive behavior interventions and supports (SWPBIS) movement can facilitate the inclusion of social skills instruction and support in schools. Finally, some issues that may create barriers for this work must be addressed as knowledge and experience grows.

Most researchers, parents, teachers, and advocates for students with ASDs agree that having friendships and avoiding peer rejection, bullying, and loneliness are important outcomes for people with autism—in fact, for all people. (Remember, people with ASDs are people first.) The strategies chosen to help students accomplish these outcomes can affect their success in achieving them and can require changes in how practitioners conceptualize the social lives of people with ASDs.

Consider two approaches for facilitating social outcomes. One is a traditional skills-based approach, whereas the other is based on the promotion of social relationships. The more traditional approach may adopt a curriculum such as *Skillstreaming* (McGinnis & Goldstein, 2003) or *Do-Watch-Listen-Say* (Quill, 2000); teach the skills listed in the curriculum and as indicated by related assessments; and then assume that improved social skills will result in increased social interactions, broader social networks, and, ultimately, more friendships.

A different approach to facilitating friendships and social relationships supports the interaction of children with and without disabilities in valued rituals and routines that occur naturally in contexts that they share (Staub, Peck, Gallucci, & Schwartz, 2000). This approach does not focus on the discrete social skills that a child may demonstrate but emphasizes preparing the person as a member of a group or a learning community. This view of promoting social relationships and friendships does not devalue the importance of skills across domains; rather, it emphasizes the importance of accomplishing functions in context rather than in isolation. We adopt this approach in general work and throughout this chapter. Such an approach meshes well with the ideas and practices promoted by SWPBIS, in which all students in a school community are provided with guidelines and supports for facilitating prosocial behavior across the school environment.

SOCIAL SKILLS INTERVENTION FOR CHILDREN WITH AUTISM SPECTRUM DISORDERS AND OTHER DISABILITIES

Although researchers endorse a relationship-focused approach for promoting friendships among students with and without disabilities, the majority of the extant research focuses on a skills-based approach to teaching. Explicit instruction in social skills is one widely used approach to improve the social competence of children with disabilities (Gresham, Sugai, & Horner, 2001; Hwang & Hughes, 2000a; Strain et al., 2007). Some promising social skills training approaches include adult-mediated interventions, peer-mediated strategies, initiation by children with disabilities, and whole-class interventions (Laushey & Heflin, 2000; Weiss & Harris, 2001). Using skills-based social skill instruction does not preclude a more relationship-focused approach to planning for the social development of students with ASDs. Our work is guided by the important contributions of Carr (2007). Practitioners should always consider how the skills being taught might improve the quality of life for students with ASDs and their families.

According to a review conducted by Hwang and Hughes (2000a), adult-mediated social interactive strategies result in positive changes in social and affective behaviors, nonverbal and verbal communication, eye contact, joint attention, and motor imitation for children with autism. Some studies—for example, English, Shafer, Goldstein, and Kaczmarek (1996) and Hwang and Hughes (2000b)—report, however, that students with disabilities often do not generalize social skills across people or settings even though they demonstrate skill acquisition during social skills trainings. Therefore, without direction and adult supports, children with disabilities are more likely to interact with adults, not with other children (English et al., 1996).

In addition to adult-mediated strategies, McConnell (2002) reviewed empirical studies and defined social interventions in five categories: ecological variations/environmental arrangements, collateral skills interventions, child-specific strategies, peer-mediated interventions, and comprehensive interventions. Each intervention strategy is defined in Table 6.1.

Ecological Variations/Environmental Arrangements

As reviewed by DiSalvo and Oswald (2002) and Odom et al. (1999), the effects of environmental arrangements on increasing social interactions among children who are typically developing and children with disabilities

Table 6.1. Definitions of five social skills interventions

Social skills interventions	Definition
Ecological variations/environmental arrangements	Typically developing peers and children with disabilities are placed together without providing training to the typically developing children prior to the intervention.
Collateral skills interventions	Children's social interaction is increased as a function of trainings in other skills, such as play and sociodramatic play.
Child-specific strategies	Social skills are taught directly to children with disabilities, and opportunities are arranged to practice learned skills with typically developing children. These strategies are usually implemented in pulled-out sessions.
Peer-mediated interventions	Peers are considered the best teachers of social competence skills for children with disabilities. Social skill lessons are provided to typically developing peers to help them engage and interact with children with disabilities.
Comprehensive interventions	Social skills lessons are provided to children with and without disabilities. These interventions are a combination of environmental arrangement, peer-mediated, and child-specific interventions.

Source: McConnell, 2002.

depend on the level of adult support and the structure of the activities. For students with autism, the effects of providing structured activities or integrated social playing with children who are typically developing rely on the characteristics of the activity and the group (McConnell, 2002). These findings indicate that ecological variations alone may not result in the desired social behavior change in students with autism but may be used with other social skills interventions (e.g., child-specific interventions) to increase positive social skills for these students.

Collateral Skills Interventions

McConnell (2002) reviewed nine collateral skills intervention studies in which the effects of teaching related skills, such as language or dramatic play, were investigated by measuring their effects on students' social behaviors. The findings indicated the positive effects of using collateral skills interventions to promote social interactions among children with ASDs. Bellini et al. (2007) reported similar findings in a meta-analysis of school-based social skills interventions for children with ASDs. Despite the positive effects of the interventions, McConnell (2002) and Bellini et al. (2007) indicated that the small number of studies and a lack of systematic measurement of generalization were major limitations of this type of intervention.

Child-Specific Interventions

To address the maintenance and the generalization problems demonstrated by many children with ASDs and other disabilities, child-specific interventions were implemented to directly teach social initiation and responding skills to students with disabilities (Bellini et al., 2007; McConnell, 2002; Odom et al., 2003). In addition to comprehensive interventions, child-specific interventions were the most common and widely used strategies to teach social skills to students with ASDs in school settings. Although these interventions are commonly used to teach social skills to students with ASDs, researchers have indicated limitations with child-specific interventions across studies.

According to Bellini et al. (2007), collateral skills, child-specific, and comprehensive interventions were effective in directly promoting social skills in students with ASDs. Child-specific interventions, such as video modeling, Social Stories, and self-monitoring, were also effective in maintaining the acquired social skills of students with ASDs compared with peer-mediated and comprehensive interventions. Although the child-specific interventions demonstrated promising short-term effects in enhancing social initiation and responding by students with ASDs, using these interventions to promote generalization and long-term social relationship change requires additional investigation (McConnell, 2002).

Peer-Mediated Interventions

Peer-mediated interventions require that children who are typically developing apply learned social skills directly to interact with and teach same-age peers with disabilities (Prendeville, Prelock, Unwin, 2006; Strain, 1983; Weiss & Harris, 2001). For example, Laushey and Heflin (2000) used a peer-buddy system to build the social interactions of two kindergartners with ASDs. Before the intervention, peers who were typically developing were taught to stay with, play with, and talk to their partners. During the intervention phase, the trained peers were randomly assigned to interact with a peer with an ASD, and the change of social interactions was recorded as a result of the peer-mediated intervention.

The peer-mediated strategy has been used to enhance social interaction skills of preschool and elementary children with autism across settings (English, Goldstein, Shafer, & Kaczmarek, 1997; Prendeville et al., 2006). The purpose of peer-mediated intervention strategies is to enhance the social behaviors of children with disabilities by teaching peers to initiate interactions, respond to others' social behaviors, and sustain the interactions with children with disabilities (Goldstein, Kaczmarek, Pennington, & Shafer, 1992). Although these interventions have demonstrated impressive and sustained effects on children's participation in social interaction and the quality of the interaction (English et al., 1997; Fantuzzo, Manz, Atkins, & Meyers, 2005; Goldstein et al., 1992; Kamps et al., 2002; Laushey & Heflin, 2000; Odom & Watts, 1991; Odom et al., 1999; Robertson, Green, Alper, Schloss, & Kohler, 2003; Roeyers, 1996; Weiner, 2005), most peer-mediated interventions have been conducted in small groups with limited generalization probes across settings and peers. That is, during peer-mediated interventions, children who are typically developing are taught to interact with one or two children with disabilities during a specific activity, such as free play.

Despite the large and growing number of studies documenting the effects of peer-mediated interventions, only a few studies investigated the extent to which students with ASDs generalize social skills across either activities or untrained peers (e.g., Fantuzzo et al., 2005; Kamps et al., 2002; Laushey & Heflin, 2000; Odom et al., 1999). Moreover, compared with collateral skills, child-specific, and comprehensive interventions, the peer-mediated intervention studies demonstrated the least effects in promoting the generalization of social skills for students with ASDs (Bellini et al., 2007).

Comprehensive Interventions

Compared with peer-mediated interventions, comprehensive strategies apply social skills lessons to children with and without disabilities in structured environments (Odom et al., 1999). Whole-class peer-tutoring strategies that focus on improving academic learning outcomes of children with disabilities are the most common comprehensive interventions in inclusive settings.

Laushey and Heflin (2000) predicted that, by training the entire class, comprehensive strategies could increase interaction among children with and without disabilities and enhance generalization across peers and activities. Some studies—for example, Gonzale-Lopez and Kamps (1997); Hundert and Houghton (1992); Kamps, Barbetta, Leonard, and Delquadri (1994); and Kamps et al. (1992)—investigating the effects of comprehensive interventions on social skills have demonstrated positive outcomes. Others have reported mixed results.

Dion, Fuchs, and Fuchs (2005) found no significant effect on children's social preferences or friendships as a result of whole-class, peer-tutoring interventions. Similarly, Odom et al. (1999) indicated that although the interactions among children with and without disabilities increased after the intervention, comprehensive strategies were often less effective than peer-mediated and child-specific strategies and resulted in negative sociometric ratings for children with disabilities. Odom et al. found this result surprising "because this intervention appeared to be more intense than any of the other interventions" (1999, p. 89). They also suggested that the intervention required teachers to do too much and thus resulted in less effective outcomes.

Various social skills interventions and strategies have shown convincing short-term effects in changing the social behaviors of students with ASDs or other disabilities. The long-term effects of these social skills interventions, however, are limited in helping students with ASDs build and maintain positive social relationships (Bellini et al., 2007; McConnell, 2002). The limitation of the existing social skills interventions might result from a lack of a schoolwide or communitywide infrastructure to sustain the intervention and new social behaviors. Hence, Fixsen, Blase, Horner, and Sugai (2009) proposed to switch the research paradigm from providing child-specific interventions to fostering macroenvironmental changes in schools and communities. Their focus is to support sustainable interventions across macrosystems, mesosystems, and microsystems that would promote better learning outcomes for each student.

SOCIAL SKILLS INSTRUCTION IN SCHOOL

It is important to discuss who "owns" the social skills domain in public schooling. Unlike academic skills, communication skills, and even motor skills, the domain of social skills does not align clearly with any of the roles, professions, or activities in most public schools. In addition, social skills are not measured by the high-stakes tests used by most states and are often ignored by statewide and districtwide curricula and educational benchmarks. When social skills are addressed in these formats, they tend to focus on issues of classroom behavior (e.g., students can work independently) rather than peer interaction (e.g., a student can successfully join a group of peers in an unstructured activity).

If social skills are to be taught effectively in school, they must move beyond an item on selected individualized education programs that are conceptualized, taught, and evaluated differently for every child with a social skills goal. They must be reconceptualized as a core component of the curriculum for every student (Siperstein & Favazza, 2008). Social skills must be viewed as just as essential to school success as prime academic subjects. The ideas of forming and maintaining relationships must be seen to be as central to school success as reading fluently, writing coherently, and understanding mathematical principles. Such an emphasis on social skills will happen only when parents and educators realize that all children benefit from systematic social skills instruction.

SCHOOLWIDE POSITIVE BEHAVIOR INTERVENTIONS AND SUPPORTS

For students with ASDs to have an effective and supportive school environment, they must attend a school that supports all learners across all domains.

SWPBIS is an approach that systematically addresses the need to create school environments that support all students. It focuses on both the system and individual levels to sustain long-term behavior and relationship changes for students with and without disabilities, including students with ASDs. In the 2000s, the effects of SWPBIS have been widely examined by rigorous research, and this intervention model has been successfully applied in school settings to prevent challenging behaviors and promote the academic performance of school-age children (Horner & Sugai, 2007; Horner et al., 2009).

The social development of students, however, is not yet a major outcome measure of SWPBIS, and it has not been widely discussed for children with disabilities. The following subsections survey the history and the structure of SWPBIS and address ways this approach can integrate social skills and relationship development for students with ASDs.

Overview

The philosophy and the characteristics of SWPBIS are derived from the fields of applied behavior analysis (ABA) and positive behavior interventions and supports (PBIS) (Dunlap, Carr, Horner, Zarcone, & Schwartz, 2008). Developed in the late 1960s, ABA implemented behavioral principles, such as systematic reinforcement, extinction, or punishment, to address socially significant behaviors. Teachers, parents, and advocates of students with ASDs and other disabilities quickly embraced strategies, such as discrete trial training, that were developed by behavior analysts. By the mid 1970s, ABA, then called behavior modification, was endorsed by the National Society of Autistic Children (later renamed the Autism Society of America) as the effective teaching approach for students with ASDs. In the past 4 decades, the ABA approach has been viewed as an evidence-based practice to effectively teach or manage the behaviors of individual students with disabilities, including students with ASDs.

In the 1980s, a group of ABA researchers proposed using nonaversive strategies to address the challenging behaviors of students with disabilities. This change was initiated in response to concerns about using aversive interventions, such as electric shock and restraint, which many people believed violated the human rights and the dignity of students with disabilities. In addition to using nonaversive strategies to address challenging behaviors, researchers supported directly teaching alternative skills to students with disabilities in an attempt to prevent the occurrence of challenging behavior (Horner et al., 1990; Koegel, Koegel, & Dunlap, 1996). This paradigm shift was driven by research that demonstrated the communicative functions of challenging behaviors (Carr & Durand, 1985; Dunlap et al., 2008). The pairing of nonaversive strategies as the first level of intervention and directly teaching adaptive skills to students with disabilities became known as PBIS.

PBIS differs from ABA in its philosophy and goals, but the intervention strategies and the techniques applied to teach students with disabilities are directly derived from ABA. Rather than focusing on short-term behavior changes, PBIS focuses on promoting the quality of life of students with disabilities; proactively addressing challenging behaviors across natural contexts; and looking beyond immediate environments that trigger challenging behaviors to macroenvironmental factors, such as groups, classrooms, school systems, and communities, even when it requires practitioners and researchers to use strategies that are not behavior analytic (Carr, 2007; Carr et al., 2002; Dunlap et al., 2008). PBIS emphasizes that students with disabilities are students first who have strengths and preferences rather than simply a collection of skill deficits. Students with disabilities are expected to learn and apply adaptive skills in natural environments, such as schools, families, and communities, so that they can build positive social relationships and improve the quality of their lives. PBIS interventions move beyond learning specific behaviors and toward emphasizing such valued life outcomes as positive social relationships, health care, and leisure activities.

For students with disabilities, including ASDs, successful life outcomes refer to not only acquiring academic achievement and functional skills but also building and maintaining social relationships with families and friends. Achieving positive learning outcomes for these students requires close collaboration among individuals across school, family, and community environments (Koegel et al., 1996).

In the 1980s, most individuals with disabilities were placed in isolated institutions or segregated classrooms and were often not considered part of their communities. For students with disabilities, the role of public schools changed drastically as a result of the normalization and inclusion movements and the amendment of the Individuals with Disabilities Education Act in 1997. From 1995 to 2005, the share of school-age children with disabilities spending 80% or more of their school days in a general classroom increased from 45% to 52% (National Center for Education Statistics, 2007). This finding indicates the trend of educating students with disabilities in natural environments and with their peers who are typically developing.

Educating students with disabilities in general school settings, however, also means increasing the educational needs of students with disabilities that teachers and peers must address. Without appropriate interventions or structures in place, physical proximity certainly will not facilitate and might actually hinder the development of positive social relationships among students with disabilities and their peers who are typically developing. According to Little (2002), as reported by their mothers, 94% of school-age children with Asperger syndrome experienced bullying from both peers and their siblings.

To increase the access of children with disabilities to their peers who are typically developing, schools must support positive learning environments and foster the adaptive, cognitive, and social skills acquisition of school-age children with disabilities. PBIS, however, does not provide an intervention structure to foster systemwide change in school settings.

In 1996, Walker et al. applied PBIS concepts, including nonaversive interventions and directly teaching appropriate alternative behaviors, to a three-tiered prevention model in school settings—SWPBIS. Their goal was to use a public health approach to create a safe learning environment for all students, moving beyond the remediation of challenging behaviors to the prevention of even minor discipline problems in school. This approach was inclusive; rather than targeting students who demonstrated challenging behavior or qualified for special education only, it addressed all students, all teachers, and all members of the school community. The underlying assumption of this new approach was that including all members of the school community would make the interventions more effective and sustainable.

Intervention Model

SWPBIS, as proposed by Walker et al. (1996) and in common with PBIS, draws from ABA to teach appropriate behaviors. It focuses on changing the school system at different levels and providing different levels of behavioral and social supports to all children and staff to create sustainable system change (Sprague & Horner, 2006). This emphasis on systems change grew out of repeated attempts to influence teacher and child behavior from the bottom up. Specifically, the SWPBIS intervention model includes primary intervention (i.e., universal or schoolwide intervention) that targets all students at school, secondary intervention (i.e., individualized or small-group interventions) that involves students at risk for developing chronic problem behavior patterns, and tertiary intervention (i.e., wraparound or comprehensive interventions) that addresses the needs of students with chronic or life-course persistent challenging behaviors (Carr et al., 2002; Lewis & Sugai, 1999). The three-tiered model organizes intervention strategies in a hierarchical order to address mild to severe challenging behaviors.

Primary Intervention

Primary intervention provides support to the whole school population (Lannie & McCurdy, 2007). The purpose of the primary intervention is to prevent new cases of challenging behaviors or special education referrals by setting up schoolwide rules, directly teaching appropriate behaviors, and altering physical arrangements for all students. Examples of altering physical arrangements include posting around the school behavioral expectations as visual reminders and assigning school staff to common areas to remind and reinforce students' appropriate behaviors.

After school staff set up a supportive physical environment, they define specific schoolwide behavioral expectations and teach them directly to all students. First, staff members introduce behavioral expectations to all students. Those in intermediate grade levels or higher could be involved in generating the rationale for learning and performing the behaviors to enhance their ownership of the schoolwide expectations. Next, students are taught and practice the behaviors in real settings, such as in the lunchroom and hallways, using specific examples and nonexamples of the target behaviors. After practicing the behavioral expectations, students receive feedback from peers, staff, and teachers, and the behaviors are also reinforced through a schoolwide reward system (Turnbull et al., 2002). For example, students who perform the expected behavior of being respectful are recognized by teachers and staff and receive a "Certified Mr./Ms. Polite" award during a school rally. This process not only promotes positive interactions among students and teachers but also enhances the feeling of belonging for students with disabilities. These primary interventions systematically teach the social behaviors needed to create safe school environments that support the inclusion of children with ASDs.

In the 2000s, the effects of primary intervention have been validated across studies to address the needs and the challenging behaviors of 80% of the total school population. Fifteen percent of the students who do not respond to primary interventions are referred to targeted secondary intervention (National Technical Assistance Center on Positive Behavioral Interventions and Supports, 2012).

Secondary Intervention

Secondary intervention is applied for students considered at higher risk of developing chronic or serious problem behavior without appropriate interventions (Baker, 2005; McCurdy, Kunsch, & Reibstein, 2007; Scott & Shearer-Lingo, 2002). The secondary intervention applies more intensive behavior management strategies to a small group of at-risk students, with the content and the format of the intervention often varying based on students' behavior patterns. For some students, staff and teachers could simply provide frequent feedback as prompts and reinforcement for students and track their behavioral performance across time. Other students might participate in social skills groups or academic tutoring as part of the secondary intervention.

Regardless of the format of the intervention, secondary intervention is defined by the following characteristics: provides continuously available services and rapid access for target students, requires low teacher efforts, is implemented by all school staff, implements interventions consistent with school expectations, applies flexible interventions based on assessment, conducts functional assessment, provides students with choices to participate in the intervention, devotes adequate school resources, and continuously monitors students' progress (National Technical Assistance Center on Positive Behavioral Interventions and Supports, 2012). Researchers have also discussed components that influence the effects of secondary intervention, such as providing systematic feedback, building connection with key adults at school, or providing ample practice opportunities to increase social and academic competence (Baker, 2005; Hawken & O'Neill, 2006; Korb, 2006; Scott & Shearer-Lingo, 2002). The wide range of secondary intervention components demonstrates the comprehensive focus of SWPBIS in not only academic performance but also social development and competence of students.

Among the 15% of the school population who receive secondary intervention, some students exhibit chronic problem behaviors that might not respond to the targeted intervention. These students—about 5% of all students—will be referred to student support teams formed by teachers, administrators, and related services professionals in each school for more intensive tertiary interventions (National Technical Assistance Center on Positive Behavioral Interventions and Supports, 2012).

Tertiary Intervention

Tertiary intervention is a more intensive and individualized preventive approach for students who still show a pattern of problem behaviors after receiving primary and secondary interventions. Tertiary intervention aims to decrease students' problem behaviors and increase their adaptive skills by providing individualized behavioral intervention plans based on the results of a functional behavioral assessment. A functional behavioral assessment gathers information to understand the interaction between a student's challenging behaviors and the ways the behaviors might be triggered and maintained by specific environmental factors. The process and result of a functional behavioral assessment will provide information to guide an individualized behavioral intervention plan. That is, after identifying interaction patterns among the challenging behaviors and the environmental factors, educational professionals can generate an individualized behavioral intervention plan to address challenging behaviors by not only changing environments but also teaching appropriate alternative behaviors.

In the 2000s, the effects of applying SWPBIS in creating safer learning environments and promoting academic achievement have been documented across more than 50 studies (Horner & Sugai, 2007). The majority of these studies, however, document observable behavior changes in students who are typically developing. Therefore, the effects of integrating students with disabilities in SWPBIS to enhance their relationships with peers and teachers require additional investigation. The following section discusses how the SWPBIS structure would shape the social development of students with ASDs and how to integrate effective social skills intervention strategies into the SWPBIS framework for students with ASDs to develop long-term social relationships.

SCHOOLWIDE POSITIVE BEHAVIOR INTERVENTIONS AND SUPPORTS AND SOCIAL RELATION-SHIPS OF STUDENTS WITH AUTISM SPECTRUM DISORDERS

For teachers and all school-age children, the SWPBIS philosophy of applying nonaversive interventions has changed the traditional methods of addressing challenging behaviors, such as suspension and expulsion. Using aversive interventions to address challenging behaviors has limited long-term effects in decreasing challenging behaviors and might negatively affect the relationship among students and teachers (Koegel et al., 1996). In contrast, applying the SWPBIS approach has demonstrated effectiveness in helping students achieve social acceptability (Horner et al., 2009).

In addition to targeting students' challenging behaviors, the three-tiered SWPBIS model focuses on explicitly teaching and reinforcing students' appropriate behaviors. Instead of reacting to students' challenging behaviors through punishment, the SWPBIS model encourages administrators, teachers, and staff to adapt proactive strategies by setting up supportive environments and directly teaching and reinforcing acceptable behaviors. These strategies encourage positive interactions among teachers and students, improve student-teacher relationships, and—in the long run—might improve peer relationships among students. SWPBIS has the potential to change the school atmosphere and set the stage for the successful inclusion of students with ASDs into general education environments.

The three-tiered SWPBIS structure also fosters the generalization of social behaviors among students with and without disabilities across such microenvironments as classrooms, small groups, and school lunchrooms. All students might be taught schoolwide behavioral expectations during school rallies or in their classrooms as part of the SWPBIS primary intervention. Depending on their educational needs, students with disabilities and students who are at risk for developing challenging behaviors might be taught more intensive interventions through the SWPBIS secondary and tertiary interventions. Regardless of the location and the intensity of the interventions, teachers and school staff reinforce the appropriate behaviors of all students when the target behavioral expectations are met. For students with ASDs, the SWPBIS structure is necessary to promote the generalization of appropriate behaviors within school settings.

At the same time, SWPBIS interventions might not be sufficient to spontaneously address the needs of students with ASDs. The SWPBIS intervention tiers allow for different approaches to integrate evidence-based interventions for students with ASDs. To foster positive peer relationships through primary intervention, for example, students with ASDs who are learning behavioral expectations should be involved in schoolwide or whole-class instruction with their peers who are typically developing. Comprehensive social skills intervention can help integrate students with ASDs in group instruction, and this approach was validated in the 2000s (McConnell, 2002). Child-specific intervention strategies, such as video modeling, choice making, and self-monitoring, can also be incorporated into SWPBIS. For example, teachers can include video modeling or physical modeling to provide examples and nonexamples of the expected behaviors during the instruction process. Teachers can also provide students with ASDs choices to practice examples or nonexamples of the target behavior, pick one expected behavior from three to five schoolwide expectations to practice, or choose a student to practice the behaviors together. Self-monitoring strategies can also be integrated into the practice procedure for students with ASDs and other students by listing every step of performing an expected behavior. Students with ASDs can self-monitor their performances by going through the checklist. The key to incorporating the evidence-based social skills interventions into SWPBIS primary interventions is to increase the opportunities for students with ASDs to access their peers who are typically developing during natural instruction time.

Students who do not respond to primary interventions are considered at higher risk to develop chronic challenging behaviors that are associated with lower academic ability, weaker social skills, and negative relationships with teachers and peers. Secondary interventions that can meet these challenges include check and connect, the behavior education program, social skills groups, academic tutoring, and behavioral interventions (Hawken & O'Neill, 2006; Korb, 2006; Lane, Gresham, & O'Shaughnessy, 2002).

Developed by Hawken and O'Neill (2006), the behavior education program focuses on decreasing challenging behaviors and school dropouts by building positive adult-student relationships. When they arrive at school, students who are at risk for developing chronic challenging behaviors check in with a mentor or a coach, such as a school counselor, a special education teacher, or a secretary. The mentor reviews the schoolwide behavioral expectations with the students and helps them establish behavioral goals for that school day. The expectations and the goals are listed on a progress monitoring card that the students carry with them throughout the day and that teachers use to rate students' behaviors in class. At the end of the school day, the students check out with the mentor by showing the card and reviewing performance. Students meeting daily behavior goals receive reinforcers, such as items from the school treasure chest. The success of this intervention was documented for students with and without disabilities in the 2000s, and it has been found to help at-risk students build bonding relationships with mentors and mobilize effective social skills integration strategies (Fairbanks, Sugai, Guardino, & Lathrop, 2007; McCurdy et al., 2007; Sinclair, Christenson, & Thurlow, 2005).

Such strategies are consistent with the evidence-based social skills interventions for students with ASDs (e.g., using visual cues and self-monitoring strategies). The check-in and check-out interventions can be easily adapted to address the individual needs of students with ASDs, including the behavioral expectations listed on the progress monitoring card and the frequency of providing behavioral feedback and reinforcements for positive behaviors. The overall structure and process of implementing the check-in and check-out interventions, however, should remain consistent to avoid discriminating students with ASDs from other students.

Another secondary intervention, social skills groups, directly teaches appropriate social skills to replace the challenging behaviors of at-risk students. The effects of providing social skills training for students with ASDs and other disabilities have been documented in the past 2 decades (Bellini et al., 2007; Gresham, Van, & Cook, 2006; Lo, Loe, & Cartledge, 2002; McConnell, 2002). Pull-out social skills groups, consisting of either students with disabilities or students both with and without disabilities, attempt to build social skills and social relationships and prevent challenging behaviors. One question that teachers and education professionals encounter with the pull-out groups is how to involve peers and adults outside the groups to promote the generalization of social skills.

Other secondary intervention programs, such as academic tutoring, do not directly address social variables to decrease the occurrence of challenging behaviors, but they can create opportunities for students with ASDs to build positive relationships with peers. For example, when providing academic tutoring to at-risk students, high-functioning students with ASDs or students with Asperger syndrome can be assigned as peer tutors to help and demonstrate their strengths to other students. Being a peer tutor may increase the social status of students with ASDs and thus decrease the experiences of peer rejection and peer victimization in the long run (Craig, Pepler, Connolly, & Henderson, 2001; Rodkin & Hodges, 2003).

Tertiary intervention of SWPBIS is highly individualized based on students' needs and behaviors. The ultimate goal of providing intensive social skills training is to teach appropriate alternative skills for students to interact positively in school, family, and community settings (National Technical Assistance Center on Positive Behavioral Interventions and Supports, 2012).

The process of conducting a functional behavioral assessment and developing individualized behavioral intervention plans is explored in O'Neill et al. (1997) and Umbreit, Ferro, Liaupsin, and Lane (2007).

Educators, parents, and advocates often assume that students with ASDs require tertiary interventions. This view embraces interventions that are isolated and specialized looking. In reality, practitioners do not know that "more is better" for children with ASDs. There appears to be a threshold of service intensity that must be met—the National Research Council puts this threshold at 25 hours per week—but practitioners do not know what those 25 hours should consist of and whether increasing the hours provides added value. Practitioners have strong evidence to support the use of behavior analysis with young children with autism (Reichow & Wolery, 2009; Rogers & Vismara, 2008). Practitioners do not know, however, if 25 hours of discrete trial training is as effective as 25 hours of incidental teaching or Pivotal Response Training or time spent in a program such as Project DATA at the University of Washington, which blends approaches to meet the individual needs of students (Schwartz, Sandall, McBride, & Boulware, 2004). Practitioners know that for students with ASDs, the generalization and the maintenance of skills are major concerns (Bellini et al., 2007). Therefore, the next section of this chapter reviews program characteristics that are related to robust behavior change as well as its maintenance and generalization.

CHARACTERISTICS AFFECTING INTERVENTION EFFICACY

Knowing what to teach and understanding effective teaching strategies are important, but several other variables affect interventions for students with ASDs. Without understanding and controlling for these variables, the most elegant and well-designed intervention may be ineffective. These variables should be considered in determining the overall efficacy of any intervention. They are especially important when considering social skills instruction and address the documented difficulty in achieving the generalization and the maintenance of these skills (e.g., Bellini et al., 2007; McConnell, 2002; Strain et al., 2007).

Fidelity of Implementation

The first variable, fidelity of implementation, refers to the integrity with which the intervention is implemented. Billingsley, White, and Munson (1980) referred to this concept as procedural reliability—whether the intervention is implemented correctly and delivered in the way that it is intended. Bellg et al. called the variable treatment fidelity and defined it as "the methodological strategies used to monitor and enhance the reliability and validity of behavioral interventions" (2004, p. 443). Without carefully examining the integrity of an intervention, implementers and researchers may make incorrect assumptions about the data and elevate irrelevant factors to explain outcomes (Yeaton & Sechrest, 1981).

Although this issue is discussed broadly in the fields of health promotion and clinical psychology, there is relatively little discussion of this important topic in special education (Bellg et al., 2004; Peterson, Homer, & Wonderlich, 1982). Attention to the fidelity of interventions could improve the integrity of research on social skills and the quality of services that children receive in schools and the community. Attention to treatment fidelity could also improve the consistency of social skills interventions for children with ASDs and be an important tool in teacher preparation and program evaluation.

Functionality of Behavioral Targets

The quality of the behavioral targets selected for intervention will affect the outcomes of the intervention. Functional target behaviors are more likely to be generalized and maintained across time. Functional skills are behaviors that increase students' independence and enable them to access preferred materials, activities, and routines in normalized environments (Brown et al., 1979). Functional social skills enable students to improve the breadth of their social networks and the quality of their social relationships. To be functional, learning objectives should focus on teaching students to participate in a variety of social settings, with a variety of social partners, around a variety of topics. Functional skills might include interacting with age-appropriate materials that are interesting to others, initiating and responding to peers and other partners, and joining a play activity. These skills are pivotal to progress in social interactions because they increase children's access to other interesting and normalizing activities (Koegel & Koegel, 2006). In other words, some skills and behaviors are keystone behaviors that serve as a bridge to more efficient and effective learning (Wolery, 1991).

Dosage

Dosage is the amount or the intensity of an intervention. A multidimensional concept, dosage includes the number of intervention sessions, the length of each session, and the percentage of time a child is engaged during an intervention session. Complex issues govern the determination and the delivery of adequate dosage of an intervention, especially one designed to facilitate social relationships. These include the child's participation in and engagement with the intervention, the frequency of the intervention, and the opportunities to practice the skills targeted in the intervention. In fact, there are no recommendations about the specific dosage children should receive on peer-related social skills and social interaction. A commonsense guideline suggests that children with ASDs should receive explicit instruction on social interaction every day, with appropriate social partners and numerous opportunities to practice appropriate social interaction embedded across all environments in which they spend time. The only way to determine whether a child with an ASD is receiving an appropriate dose of intervention and support to develop social relationships is to continuously measure outcomes. If a child is making progress, the appropriate dosage is assumed.

Strategies Promoting Generalization and Maintenance

Generalization is the ability to use newly acquired skills across settings, materials, and people; maintenance is the ability to use new skills across time. Some scholars suggest that generalization and maintenance are stages of learning (Wolery, Sugai, & Bailey, 1988), and most would agree that learners must generalize and maintain skills before they can truly be integrated into their repertoire and improve the quality of their lives. Difficulty with generalization and maintenance is often cited as a defining characteristic of ASDs and has been explored in important studies. (See Chandler, Lubeck, & Fowler, 1992; McConnell, 2002; and Schwartz, Davis, McLaughlin, & Rosenberg, 2009, for pertinent reviews.) Teachers, parents, and researchers have used many effective strategies to teach skills to children with ASDs in isolation; the challenge is how to teach skills in a manner that promotes their use in everyday situations when they are most appropriate.

Social Validity

Montrose Wolf (1978) introduced social validity in his seminal article in the *Journal of Applied Behavior Analysis.* Social validity asks consumers of a behavioral or an educational intervention to rate the acceptability of the intervention. The purpose of asking people who use the intervention what they think about it is to assess whether the intervention is addressing the behaviors that the consumers think are important in a manner that the consumers think are acceptable and sustainable. According to Wolf, social validity should be assessed across three components of an intervention: goals, procedures, and the outcome.

Social validity is not intended to assess the effectiveness of an intervention; it determines the acceptability of an intervention after its effectiveness has been ascertained using validated research methods (Schwartz & Baer, 1991). Understanding the social validity of an intervention is an important step in understanding what interventions practitioners are likely to maintain and implement with high fidelity.

Although the concept of social validity is well accepted, it has not been widely reported in the literature. Even when reported, social validity assessments are usually relegated to judging the acceptability of an intervention or a behavior change rather than setting the agenda for one. The following study is a notable exception. Thieman and Goldstein (2001) examined the effectiveness of Social Stories, written text cues, and video feedback on increasing interaction among students with and without ASDs. They used a panel of 13 raters (7 general education teachers and 6 graduate students in speech and language) to assess the quality and the quantity of behavior change. After watching preintervention and postintervention video segments, all 13 raters reported improvement in the social communication skills of the students with ASDs and improvements in the social behavior of the children who are typically developing directed toward their peers with ASDs.

Garfinkle and Schwartz (2002) demonstrated another interesting use of social validity data. Using a more traditional social validity tool—a postintervention teacher survey—they were interested in assessing the sustainability of an intervention from the teachers' point of view. The survey combined open-ended and closed questions about the acceptability of the intervention, the likelihood of the intervention being used again, and any related behavioral changes observed by the teachers. Every teacher was extremely positive, stating that he or she would use the intervention again. In their responses to open-ended questions, the teachers described behavior changes that were similar to those demonstrated by the quantitative data (before the teachers actually saw the data) and described how they would continue to implement the intervention after the experimenters left the environment.

FUTURE DIRECTIONS

Functional skills that help children with ASDs develop and maintain social relationships are among the most important behaviors that children with ASDs learn during their early schooling. Although researchers have many validated strategies for teaching social skills to children with ASDs (e.g., prompting, reinforcing, modeling) and good programmatic inquiry on peer-mediated techniques and group-oriented contingencies, they still have much to learn about implementing strategies to produce skills that can be sustained and generalized. As the number of children with ASDs continues to increase and more of these children participate in inclusive child care, recreation, and community settings, it is necessary for researchers to develop a better understanding of the characteristics of interventions that contribute to their high-fidelity use by teachers, parents, and child care providers in a wide variety of settings. This means that as research moves ahead, researchers do not need to ask whether children with ASDs can acquire social skills; they can. Rather, they must study issues such as treatment fidelity, the functionality of behavioral targets, dosage, and social validity to determine how communities that support children with ASDs can help them develop and generalize skills that are so important in their everyday lives.

REFERENCES

Baker, C.K. (2005). The PBS triangle: Does it fit as a heuristic? A reflection on the first international conference on positive behavior support. *Journal of Positive Behavior Interventions, 7,* 120–123.

Bellg, A.J., Borrelli, B., Resnick, B., Hecht, B., Minicucci, J., Ory, M.,…Czajkowski, S. (2004). Enhancing treatment fidelity in health behavior change studies: Best practices and recommendations from the NIH Behavior Change Consortium. *Health Psychology, 23,* 443–451.

Bellini, S., Peters, J.K., Benner, L., & Hopf, A. (2007). A meta-analysis of school-based social skills interventions for children with autism spectrum disorders. *Remedial and Special Education, 28,* 153–162.

Billingsley, F., White, O.R., & Munson, R. (1980). Procedural reliability: A rationale and an example. *Behavioral Assessment, 2,* 229–241.

Brown, L., Branston, M.B., Hamre-Nietupski, S., Pumpian, I., Certo, N., & Grunewald, L. (1979). A strategy for developing chronological-age-appropriate and functional curricular content for severely handicapped adolescents and young adults. *Journal of Special Education, 13,* 81–90.

Carr, E.G. (2007). The expanding vision of positive behavior support: Research perspectives on happiness, helpfulness, hopefulness. *Journal of Positive Behavior Interventions, 9,* 3–14.

Carr, E.G., Dunlap, G., Horner, R.H., Koegel, R.L., Turnbull, A.P., Sailor, W., …Fox, L. (2002). Positive behavior support: Evolution of an applied science. *Journal of Positive Behavior Interventions, 4,* 4–16.

Carr, E.G., & Durand, V.M. (1985). Reducing behavior problems through functional communication training. *Journal of Applied Behavior Analysis, 18,* 111–126.

Chandler, L., Lubeck, R., & Fowler, S.A. (1992). Generalization and maintenance of preschool children's social skills: A critical review and analysis. *Journal of Applied Behavior Analysis, 25,* 415–428.

Craig, W.M., Pepler, D.J., Connolly, J., & Henderson, K. (2001). Towards a developmental perspective on victimization. In J. Juvonen & S. Graham (Eds.), *Peer harassment in school: The plight of the vulnerable and victimized* (pp. 242–262). New York, NY: Guilford Press.

Dion, E., Fuchs, D., & Fuchs, L.S. (2005). Differential effects of peer-assisted learning strategies on students' social preference and friendship making. *Behavioral Disorders, 30,* 421–429.

DiSalvo, C.A., & Oswald, D.P. (2002). Peer-mediated interventions to increase the social interaction of children with autism: Consideration of peer expectancies. *Focus on Autism and Other Developmental Disabilities, 17,* 198–207.

Dunlap, G., Carr, E.G., Horner, R.H., Zarcone, J.R., & Schwartz, I. (2008). Positive behavior support and applied behavior analysis: A familial alliance. *Behavior Modification, 32*, 682–698.

English, K., Goldstein, H., Shafer, K., & Kaczmarek, L. (1997). Promoting interactions among preschoolers with and without disabilities: Effects of a buddy skills-training program. *Exceptional Children, 63*, 229–243.

English, K., Shafer, K., Goldstein, H., & Kaczmarek, L. (1996). "Buddy skills" for preschoolers. *Teaching Exceptional Children, 28*, 62–66.

Fairbanks, S., Sugai, G., Guardino, D., & Lathrop, M. (2007). Response to intervention: Examining classroom behavior support in second grade. *Exceptional Children, 73*, 288–310.

Fantuzzo, J., Manz, P., Atkins, M., & Meyers, R. (2005). Peer-mediated treatment of socially withdrawn maltreated preschool children: Cultivating natural community resources. *Journal of Clinical Child and Adolescent Psychology, 34*, 320–325.

Fixsen, D.L., Blase, K.A., Horner, R.H., & Sugai, G. (2009). Scaling up evidence-based practices in education. *State Implementation & Scaling-up of Evidence-Based Practices web site.* Retrieved from http://sisep.fpg.unc.edu

Garfinkle, A.N., & Schwartz, I.S. (2002). Peer imitation: Increasing social interactions in children with autism and other developmental disabilities in inclusive preschool classrooms. *Topics in Early Childhood Special Education, 22*, 26–38.

Goldstein, H., Kaczmarek, L., Pennington, R., & Shafer, K. (1992). Peer-mediated intervention: Attending to, commenting on, and acknowledging the behavior of preschoolers with autism. *Journal of Applied Behavior Analysis, 25*, 289–305.

Gonzale-Lopez, A., & Kamps, D.M. (1997). Social skills training to increase social interactions between children with autism and their typical peers. *Focus on Autism and Other Developmental Disabilities, 12*, 2–14.

Gresham, F.M., Sugai, G., & Horner, R.H. (2001). Interpreting outcomes of social skills training for students with high-incidence disabilities. *Exceptional Children, 67*, 331–344.

Gresham, F.M., Van, M.B., & Cook, C.R. (2006). Social skills training for teaching replacement behaviors: Remediating acquisition deficits in at-risk students. *Behavioral Disorders, 31*, 363–377.

Hawken, L.S., & O'Neill, R.E. (2006). Including students with severe disabilities in all levels of school-wide positive behavior support. *Research and Practice for Persons with Severe Disabilities, 31*, 46–53.

Horner, R.H., Dunlap, G., Koegel, R.L., Carr, E.G., Sailor, W., Anderson, J., …O'Neill, R.E. (1990). Toward a technology of "nonaversive" behavioral support. *Journal of the Association for Persons with Severe Handicaps, 15*, 125–132.

Horner, R.H., & Sugai, G. (2007). Is school-wide positive behavior support an evidence-based practice? A research summary. *OSEP Center on Positive Behavioral Interventions and Supports web site.* Retrieved from http://www.pbis.org/research/default.aspx

Horner, R.H., Sugai, G., Smolkowski, K., Eber, L., Nakasato, J., Todd, A.W., & Esperanza, J. (2009). A randomized, wait-list controlled effectiveness trial assessing school-wide positive behavior support in elementary schools. *Journal of Positive Behavior Interventions, 11*, 133–144.

Hundert, J., & Houghton, A. (1992). Promoting social interaction of children with disabilities in integrated preschools: A failure to generalize. *Exceptional Children, 58*, 311–320.

Hwang, B., & Hughes, C. (2000a). The effects of social interactive training on early social communicative skills of children with autism. *Journal of Autism and Developmental Disorders, 30*, 331–343.

Hwang, B., & Hughes, C. (2000b). Increasing early social-communicative skills of preverbal preschool children with autism through social interactive training. *The Association for Persons with Severe Handicaps, 25*, 18–28.

Kamps, D.M., Barbetta, P.M., Leonard, B.R., & Delquadri, J. (1994). Classwide peer tutoring: An integration strategy to improve reading skills and promote peer interactions among students with autism. *Journal of Applied Behavior Analysis, 27*, 49–61.

Kamps, D.M., Leonard, B.R., Vermon, S., Dugan, E.P., Delquadri, J.C., Greshon, B.,…Folk, L. (1992). Teaching social skills to students with autism to increase peer interactions in an integrated first-grade classroom. *Journal of Applied Behavior Analysis, 25*, 281–288.

Kamps, D., Royer, J., Dugan, E., Kravits, T., Gonzalez-Lopez, A., Garcia, J.,… Kane, L.G. (2002). Peer training to facilitate social interaction for elementary students with autism and their peers. *Exceptional Children, 68*, 173–187.

Koegel, R.L., & Koegel, L.K. (2006). *Pivotal Response Treatments for autism: Communication, social, and academic development.* Baltimore, MD: Paul H. Brookes Publishing Co.

Koegel, L., Koegel, R., & Dunlap, G. (1996). *Positive behavioral support: Including people with difficult behavior in the community.* Baltimore, MD: Paul H. Brookes Publishing Co.

Korb, D. (2006). Responding to problem behavior in school: The behavior education program [Review of the book *The Autism Encyclopedia*]. *Journal of Developmental & Behavioral Pediatrics, 27*, 418–419.

Lane, K.L., Gresham, F.M., & O'Shaughnessy, T.E. (2002). Serving students with or at risk for emotional and behavior disorders: Future challenges. *Education and Treatment of Children, 25*, 507–521.

Lannie, A.L., & McCurdy, B.L. (2007). Preventing disruptive behavior in the urban classroom: Effects of the good behavior game on student and teacher behavior. *Education and Treatment of Children, 30*, 85–98.

Laushey, K.M., & Heflin, L.J. (2000). Enhancing social skills of kindergarten children with autism through the training of multiple peers as tutors. *Journal of Autism and Developmental Disorders, 30*, 183–193.

Lewis, T.J., & Sugai, G. (1999). Effective behavior support: A systems approach to proactive schoolwide management. *Focus on Exceptional Children, 31*, 1–24.

Little, L. (2002). Middle-class mothers' perceptions of peer and sibling victimization among children with Asperger's syndrome and nonverbal learning disorders. *Issues in Comprehensive Pediatric Nursing, 25*, 43–57.

Lo, Y., Loe, S.A., & Cartledge, G. (2002). The effects of social skills instruction on the social behaviors of students at risk for emotional or behavioral disorders. *Behavioral Disorders, 27*, 371–385.

McConnell, S.R. (2002). Interventions to facilitate social interaction for young children with autism: Review of available research and recommendations for educational intervention and future research. *Journal of Autism and Developmental Disorders, 32,* 351–372.

McCurdy, B.L., Kunsch, C., & Reibstein, S. (2007). Secondary prevention in the urban school: Implementing the behavior education program. *Preventing School Failure, 51,* 12–19.

McGinnis, E., & Goldstein, A.P. (2003). *Skillstreaming in early childhood: Program forms: New strategies and perspectives for teaching prosocial skills.* Champaign, IL: Research Press.

Myles, B.S., Simpson, R.L., Ormsbee, C.K., & Erickson, C. (1993). Integrating preschool children with autism with their normally developing peers: Research findings and best practice recommendations. *Focus on Autistic Behavior, 8,* 1–18.

National Center for Education Statistics. (2007). *School Crime Supplement to the National Crime Victimization Survey (SCS/NCVS).* Retrieved from http://nces .ed.gov/programs/crime/surveys.asp

National Research Council. (2001). *Educating children with autism.* Washington, DC: National Academy Press.

National Technical Assistance Center on Positive Behavioral Interventions and Supports. (2012). Retrieved from http://www.pbis.org

Odom, S.L., Brown, W.H., Frey, T., Karasu, N., Smith-Canter, L.L., & Strain, P.S. (2003). Evidence-based practices for young children with autism: Contributions for single-subject design research. *Focus on Autism and Other Developmental Disabilities, 18,* 166–175.

Odom, S.L., McConnell, S.R., McEvoy, M.A., Peterson, C., Ostrosky, M., Chandler, L.K.,...Favazza, P.C. (1999). Relative effects of interventions supporting the social competence of young children with disabilities. *Topics in Early Childhood Special Education, 19,* 75–91.

Odom, S.L., & Watts, E. (1991). Reducing teacher prompts in peer-mediated interventions for young children with autism. *Journal of Special Education, 25,* 26–43.

O'Neill, R., Horner, R., Albin, R., Sprague, J., Storey, K., & Newton, J. (1997). *Functional assessment and program development for problem behavior: A practical handbook* (2nd ed.). Pacific Grove, CA: Brooks/Cole.

Peterson, L., Homer, A.L., & Wonderlich, S.A. (1982). The integrity of independent variables in behavior analysis. *Journal of Applied Behavior Analysis, 15,* 477–492.

Prendeville, J., Prelock, P., & Unwin, G. (2006). Peer play interventions to support the social competence of children with autism spectrum disorders. *Seminars in Speech and Language, 27,* 32–46.

Quill, L.A. (2000). *Do-Watch-Listen-Say: Social and communication intervention for children with autism.* Baltimore, MD: Paul H. Brookes Publishing Co.

Reichow, B., & Wolery, M. (2009). Comprehensive synthesis of early intensive behavioral interventions for young children with autism based on the UCLA Young Autism Project model. *Journal of Autism and Developmental Disorders, 39,* 23–41.

Robertson, J., Green, K., Alper, S., Schloss, P., & Kohler, F. (2003). Using a peer-mediated intervention to facilitate children's participation in inclusive childcare activities. *Education and Treatment of Children, 26,* 182–197.

Rodkin, P.C., & Hodges, E.V.E. (2003). Bullies and victims in the peer ecology: Four questions for psychologists and school professionals. *School Psychology Review, 32*, 384–400.

Roeyers, H. (1996). The influence of nonhandicapped peers on the social interactions of children with a pervasive developmental disorder. *Journal of Autism and Developmental Disorders, 26*, 303–320.

Rogers, S.J., & Vismara, L.A. (2008). Evidence-based comprehensive treatments for early autism. *Journal of Clinical Child and Adolescent Psychology, 37*, 8–38.

Schwartz, I.S., & Baer, D.M. (1991). Social-validity assessments: Is current practice state-of-the-art? *Journal of Applied Behavior Analysis, 24*, 189–204.

Schwartz, I.S., Davis, C.A., McLaughlin, A., & Rosenberg, N. (2009). Generalization in school settings: Strategies for planning and teaching. In C. Whalen (Ed.), *Real life, real progress for children with autism spectrum disorders: Strategies for successful generalization in natural environments* (pp. 195–212). Baltimore, MD: Paul H. Brookes Publishing Co.

Schwartz, I.S., Sandall, S.R., McBride, B.J., & Boulware, G.L. (2004). Project DATA (developmentally appropriate treatment for autism): An inclusive, school-based approach to educating children with autism. *Topics in Early Childhood Special Education, 24*, 156–168.

Scott, T.M., & Shearer-Lingo, A. (2002). The effects of reading fluency instruction on the academic and behavioral success of middle school students in a self-contained EBD classroom. *Preventing School Failure, 46*, 167–173.

Sinclair, M.F., Christenson, S.L., & Thurlow, M.L. (2005). Promoting school completion of urban secondary youth with emotional or behavioral disabilities. *Exceptional Children, 71*, 465–482.

Siperstein, G.N., & Favazza, P.C. (2007). Placing children "at promise": Future directions for promoting social competence. In W.H. Brown, S.L. Odom, & S.R. McConnell (Eds.), *Social competence of young children: Risk, disability, and intervention* (pp. 321–332). Baltimore, MD: Paul H. Brookes Publishing Co.

Sprague, J.R., & Horner, R.H. (2006). Schoolwide positive behavioral supports. In S.R. Jimerson & M.J. Furlong (Eds.), *Handbook of school violence and school safety* (pp. 413–427). Mahwah, NJ: Lawrence Erlbaum Associates.

Staub, D., Peck, C.A., Gallucci, C., & Schwartz, I.S. (2000). Peer relationships. In M. Snell & F. Brown (Eds.), *Instruction of students with severe disabilities* (pp. 381–408). Upper Saddle River, NJ: Merrill.

Strain, P.S. (1983). Generalization of autistic children's social behavior change: Effects of developmentally integrated and segregated settings. *Analysis & Intervention in Developmental Disabilities, 3*, 23–34.

Strain, P.S., Schwartz, I.S., & Bovery, E.H. (2007). Social skills intervention for young children with autism: Programmatic research findings and implementation issues. In W.H. Brown, S.L. Odom, & S.R. McConnell (Eds.), *Social competence of young children: Risk, disability, and intervention* (pp. 253–272). Baltimore, MD: Paul H. Brookes Publishing Co.

Thiemann, K.S., & Goldstein, H. (2001). Social Stories, written text cues, and video feedback: Effects on social communication of children with autism. *Journal of Applied Behavior Analysis, 34*, 425–446.

Turnbull, A., Edmonson, H., Griggs, P., Wickham, D., Sailor, W., Freeman, R.,... Warren, J. (2002). A blueprint for schoolwide positive behavior support: Full implementation of three components. *Exceptional Children, 68*, 377–402.

Umbreit, J., Ferro, J., Liaupsin, C., & Lane, K. (2007). *Functional behavioral assessment and function-based intervention: An effective, practical approach.* Columbus, OH: Pearson Prentice Hall.

Walker, H.M., Horner, R.H., Sugai, G., Bullis, M., Sprague, J.R., Bricker, D., ... Kaufman, M.J. (1996). Integrated approaches to preventing antisocial behavior patterns among school-age children and youth. *Journal of Emotional and Behavioral Disorders, 4*, 194–209.

Weiner, J.S. (2005). Peer-mediated conversational repair in students with moderate and severe disabilities. *Research and Practice for Persons with Severe Disabilities, 30*, 26–37.

Weiss, M.J., & Harris, S.L. (2001). Teaching social skills to people with autism. *Behavior Modification, 25*, 785–802.

Wolery, M. (1991). Instruction in early childhood special education: "Seeing through a glass darkly...knowing in part." *Exceptional Children, 58*, 127–135.

Wolery, M., Sugai, G., & Bailey, D.B. (1988). *Effective teaching: Principles and procedures of applied behavior analysis with exceptional students.* Boston, MA: Allyn & Bacon.

Wolf, M.M. (1978). Social validity: The case for subjective measurement or how applied behavior analysis is finding its heart. *Journal of Applied Behavior Analysis, 11*, 203–214.

Yeaton, W.H., & Sechrest, L. (1981). Critical dimensions in the choice and maintenance of successful treatments: Strength, integrity, and effectiveness. *Journal of Consulting and Clinical Psychology, 49*, 156–167.

Pivotal Response Treatment and the Development of Social Competence

Daniel Openden

Although interventions for autism spectrum disorders (ASDs) have long focused on teaching social skills, only more recently has the field started to consider the importance of social competence. Social competence is an evolving concept that is broadly defined in the literature (Bierman & Welsh, 2000; Fisher & Meyer, 2002; Spence, 2003; Spence & Donovan, 1998; Stichter, Randolph, & Gage, 2007). Generally, social competence refers to the integration of social, emotional, and cognitive skills and behaviors that individuals need for successful social adaptation. The skills and the behaviors required to demonstrate social competence vary with the age of the individual, cultural expectations, and the demands of a particular social situation. Socially competent individuals do not rely on only individual skills or discretely taught behaviors; rather, they are flexible, can read social cues, and can adjust their behavior to the social expectations of the environment. In doing so, socially competent individuals may have an easier time navigating the social world, developing meaningful friendships, and getting a job. Essentially, an individual's social competence is likely to significantly influence quality of life.

The literature has primarily focused on teaching children with ASDs social skills as individual target behaviors, the underlying assumption of which is that the more skills a person has, the more socially competent he or she will be. However, Bellini, Peters, Benner, and Hopf (2007) conducted a meta-analysis of social skills interventions; their results are mixed, and they discovered that many interventions lack efficacy. Many social skills programs have focused on teaching social "rules" so that individuals with ASDs know how to behave under specified conditions. For many individuals with ASDs, this is a very effective teaching strategy, but even though they can learn to perform a given social skill under these conditions, generalization of the skill may often be lacking, particularly in natural settings. The nuances of social behavior are so great that it would seem insurmountable to teach the rules of every social situation, not to mention the related social skills necessary to navigate that situation. Ideally, it may be better to focus on pivotal skills and behaviors that produce widespread generalization across several behaviors and environments.

Pivotal Response Treatment (PRT) is a comprehensive and naturalistic behavioral approach for children with ASDs (Koegel & Koegel, 2006, 2012; National Research Council, 2001) that may be particularly useful for improving social competence. Based on the science of applied behavior analysis (ABA), PRT does not primarily focus on improving individual target behaviors (which is the focus of most traditional ABA approaches); rather, PRT targets pivotal areas underlying the core symptoms of autism that, when changed, produce generalized improvements across many behaviors. To date, the literature has identified four pivotal areas for intervention: motivation, responsivity to multiple cues, self-management, and self-initiations (Koegel, Openden, Fredeen, & Koegel, 2006).

There is an interesting analogy between targeting individual social skills and discrete behaviors versus social competence and pivotal areas, respectively. Traditional ABA approaches and social skills interventions focus more on teaching individual target behaviors, whereas social competence and PRT address broader areas for intervention in autism. The purpose of this chapter, then, is to show how a focus on pivotal areas in PRT may lead to improvements in developing social competence in individuals with ASDs, to discuss how PRT has been translated into effective and accessible practice, and to identify unanswered questions and research priorities related to PRT.

PIVOTAL RESPONSE
TREATMENT: AN EVIDENCE-BASED APPROACH

More than 20 years of empirical evidence support the efficacy and the effectiveness of PRT for children with ASDs. The first iteration of PRT was the Natural Language Paradigm (NLP), which was designed to systematically incorporate parameters of natural language interactions into an ABA program that would improve generalization and the maintenance of treatment gains. In two seminal studies, compared with an analog behavioral intervention, NLP demonstrated more rapid and generalized improvements in prompted, deferred, and spontaneous speech (Koegel, Koegel, & Surratt, 1992; Koegel, O'Dell, & Koegel, 1987). Interestingly, in a critical review of eight published studies, Delprato (2001) indicated that naturalistic behavioral approaches were more effective at improving language than traditional discrete trial training (DTT) interventions. Furthermore, Koegel, Koegel, and Surratt (1992), showed collateral decreases in problem behavior, the first

PRT-based study to demonstrate generalized improvement in an untargeted behavior. As more studies began showing this effect, NLP became PRT to more directly reference the broader targets and effects of the intervention.

Following these early studies, researchers from various laboratories began demonstrating that PRT was an efficacious approach for improving many different behaviors (Koegel, Koegel, & Brookman, 2003; Koegel, Koegel, Vernon, & Brookman-Frazee, 2010). Improvements have been documented in positive affect (Koegel, Bimbela, & Schreibman, 1996; Schreibman, Kaneko, & Koegel, 1991), social skills and peer interactions (Harper, Symon, & Frea, 2008; Pierce & Schreibman, 1995, 1997), play skills (Gillett & LeBlanc, 2007; Stahmer, 1995; Thorp, Stahmer, & Schreibman, 1995), speech intelligibility (Koegel, Camarata, Koegel, Ben-Tall, & Smith, 1998), question asking (Koegel, Camarata, Valdez-Manchaca, & Koegel, 1998; Koegel, Carter, & Koegel, 2003; Koegel, Koegel, Shoshan, & McNerney, 1999), adaptive behavior (Baker-Ericzén, Stahmer, & Burns, 2007), and joint attention (Bruinsma, 2005; Bruinsma, Koegel, & Koegel, 2004; Fredeen, 2005; Vismara & Lyons, 2007).

Several reviews and reports have also identified PRT as an evidence-based practice. For instance, the National Research Council (2001) released a report reviewing research for educating young children with autism and included PRT among its list of comprehensive programs. Simpson (2005) and Simpson et al. (2005) reviewed more than 30 interventions for ASDs and categorized them into one of four categories: scientifically based practice, promising practice, limited supporting information for practice, and not recommended. PRT was one of only four interventions identified as a scientifically based practice. Similarly, the National Autism Center released its National Standards Report to provide "comprehensive information about the level of scientific evidence that exists in support of the many educational and behavioral treatments currently available" (2009, p. 1); PRT was identified as 1 of 11 established interventions.

PIVOTAL RESPONSE TREATMENT AND THE DEVELOPMENT OF SOCIAL COMPETENCE

Although there is both substantial empirical support and accumulating evidence supporting the efficacy and effectiveness of PRT, the relationship between PRT and social competence development has rarely been discussed. One explanation for this may be that specific measures of social competence have not been employed in studies in which PRT was implemented. However, there are four ways in which the data relate to the development of social competence, which suggests that incorporating social competence measures into PRT studies may be an important area for future research.

Early Emergence of Pivotal Response
Treatment from Traditional Discrete Trial Training

PRT emerged from traditional DTT, and both are interventions for children with ASDs based on the science of ABA. Two PRT researchers, Robert L. Koegel and Laura Schreibman, were graduate students of O. Ivar Lovaas and share early publications on DTT for autism (Lovaas, Koegel, Simmons, & Long, 1973; Lovaas, Schreibman, & Koegel, 1974; Lovaas, Varni, Koegel, & Lorsch, 1977; Russo, Koegel, & Lovaas, 1978; Varni, Lovaas, Koegel, & Everett, 1979). Essentially, NLP attempted to improve traditional discrete trial methodology for teaching language and address concerns with generalization and maintenance of treatment gains while simultaneously improving spontaneous speech.

NLP primarily focused on teaching language in a more naturalistic context that more closely resembled the way typically developing children learn to produce speech. The first goal of NLP, then, was to bring responding under the control of natural environmental stimuli, allowing children to better interact with and learn from real-world environments.

Typically developing children become socially competent adults through the shaping of social behaviors learned from an early age in the real world, much of which is language based (Hart & Risley, 1989, 1992, 1995). Although children with ASDs can certainly be taught to use language in analog environments, the more social aspects of language and social communication may be missed—or at least not shaped as well as if language were learned in the natural environment. Learning speech in NLP, then, may help children with ASDs be better able to learn and produce the social aspects of communication, which may in turn lead to improved social competence.

A second goal of NLP was to improve generalization and maintenance of skills taught during intervention. Although data indicated that many children with ASDs made great progress within traditional DTT programs, some did not maintain skills over time, whereas others failed to generalize across settings or people (Gresham & MacMillan, 1998; Lovaas et al., 1973). Thus, NLP shifted from arbitrary reinforcers in traditional DTT programs to natural reinforcers that were directly and functionally related to a child's communication, producing better generalization and maintenance of treatment gains (Koegel et al., 1987; Koegel, Koegel, et al., 1992). These improvements, particularly those in generalizing newly learned skills, relate directly to social competence: Individuals better able to not only maintain but also generalize social communication skills across environments and with different people tend to be more socially competent than those whose skills are limited to specific settings or with only particular individuals. Furthermore, the ability to generalize skills may increase opportunities for developing social relationships, participating more fully in the community, and getting a job, thereby enhancing an individual's quality of life (Openden, Whalen, Cernich, & Vaupel, 2009).

In addition to improving generalization, incorporating natural reinforcers also put the focus of the intervention squarely on functional, social communication. Although many children in traditional DTT programs were learning a variety of skills, the requirement to use language was often for the purpose of labeling or identifying objects or pictures. Having language becomes meaningful, though, when children are able to use it to communicate within a social context (e.g., between parent and child, with teachers and peers). By moving away from arbitrary reinforcers that were not functional to the interaction in favor of natural reinforcers that were directly related to a child's interest and communicative response, NLP emphasized the social function of language. Indeed, the ability to use communication across social contexts may be central to the development of social competence.

A third goal of NLP was to address prompt dependency by improving spontaneous speech. Another possible explanation for problems with generalization and maintenance in traditional DTT programs was that responding was often taught and remained under stimulus control of verbal prompts to produce language. That is, some children with ASDs did not speak unless they were instructed to do so by a therapist, thus limiting their ability to learn to interact with others. By improving spontaneous speech, children with ASDs may be better able to generalize interactions with additional communicative partners. Furthermore, the ability to not only respond to but also initiate language is likely critical to the development of social competence.

Finally, NLP produced collateral decreases in problem behaviors. Many traditional DTT programs often began with compliance training to gain instructional control and reduce behaviors that interfered with learning, particularly for children with ASDs who entered treatment with high rates of problem behavior. In a seminal study on language and problem behavior, Koegel, Koegel, et al. (1992) compared occurrences of problem behavior during language training taught using an analog behavioral approach (i.e., DTT) versus NLP using a repeated reversals design. In all three children studied, lower rates of problem behavior occurred in the NLP conditions. Of primary importance is that language—not problem behavior—was targeted during intervention, thus documenting a collateral improvement in an untargeted behavior in NLP. Consequently, the name of the intervention began to transition from NLP to PRT as researchers increasingly began to identify and document collateral changes in other untargeted behaviors (Koegel, Openden, et al., 2006).

Although being socially competent likely implies the absence of problem behavior, it is important to note that the collateral reduction of problem behavior occurs within the natural environment and thus comes under the control of natural environmental stimuli (as discussed earlier). Thus, learning within the natural environment, where children with ASDs are more frequently exposed to social stimuli, can be maximized with respect to the amount of time (i.e., hours of intervention) and learning opportunities (i.e., communicative exchanges and interactions). Furthermore, by targeting pivotal areas of responding, it is likely that, in addition to social communication, many other behaviors are exposed to, learned, and appropriately shaped by the natural environment.

Core Intervention Components for Implementing Pivotal Response Treatment

Implementing PRT requires, at a minimum, three critical intervention components: early intervention, intervention in natural environments, and parent training. Although the many unanswered questions in autism have led to widespread disagreement on several issues, there is general agreement about the importance of early identification and intervention. Providing intervention for children with autism when they are young may lead to more substantial developmental gains (Dawson & Osterling, 1997; Kasari, 2002; Koegel, Openden, et al., 2006; Lovaas, 1987; McGee, Daly, & Jacobs, 1994; National Research Council, 2001; Strain & Cordisco, 1994). In the PRT model, intervention begins as early as possible and during the earliest stages of brain development to maximize outcomes. Although many skills for children with ASDs must be taught within an intervention program, subtle social behaviors are often the most difficult to teach. When children are engaged in meaningful intervention within social contexts from an early age, appropriate social behaviors may be learned more incidentally, and, as children get older, these skills may not need to be taught directly. Developing social competence may be as much about practice as it is about specific social skills. Thus, by implementing PRT with young children, the number of opportunities to teach, learn, shape, and reinforce appropriate social behavior increases dramatically, improving the likelihood that children with ASDs can become socially competent adults.

Second, as a naturalistic behavioral intervention, PRT is implemented primarily in home, school, and community settings. As discussed earlier, generalization and the maintenance of gains has long been a concern for children with autism as well as an important intervention outcome (Gresham & MacMillan, 1998). Thus, an increased focus on delivering interventions in natural contexts has emerged, wherein generalization is built directly into the intervention (National Research Council, 2001; Openden et al., 2009). Indeed, problems with generalization may have more to do with the teaching and the environments in which interventions are delivered than with the child. Thus, PRT does not remove children with

ASDs from the typical settings in which practitioners ultimately want the target behaviors to occur. Rather, intervention is delivered and embedded within real-world environments. If practitioners want children with ASDs to grow up to become socially competent individuals, then they must regularly expose them to natural environmental stimulation and implement interventions in social contexts so that social behaviors can be more easily learned, maintained, and generalized.

Finally, parent training is central to the PRT model because parents are often considered primary intervention agents. Research has shown that parents can learn to effectively implement intervention for children with autism (Brookman-Frazee, Vismara, Drahota, Stahmer, & Openden, 2009; Koegel, Symon, & Koegel, 2002; Laski, Charlop, & Schreibman, 1988; McGee, Morrier, & Daly, 1999; Meadan, Ostrosky, Zaghlawan, & Yu, 2009; Openden, 2005; Symon, 2005). Intervention typically begins early and in the child's natural environment (i.e., the home), where children spend the majority of their time interacting with their parents. Because reciprocal, natural interactions between a caregiver and a child greatly influence child development (Wetherby & Prizant, 2000), it is critical that parents not only are involved in the treatment of their children but also learn to implement intervention procedures with fidelity. By doing so, interventions are systematically implemented within a context that closely resembles the ways typically developing children learn (i.e., through early and repeated interactions with their parents), which yields increased opportunities for learning appropriate social behaviors.

Parent training also likely improves both the quantity and the intensity of treatment because interventions can be delivered throughout a child's waking hours and are not solely dependent on a highly qualified therapist. Although studies and reports have differed with respect to the recommended number of intervention hours (Kasari, 2002; Lovaas, 1987; National Research Council, 2001; Sheinkopf & Siegel, 1998), children with ASDs should be engaged in meaningful learning opportunities for as much of the day as possible. Thus, training parents to implement PRT may increase the number of hours of intervention and, more important, improve treatment intensity. In addition, embedding interventions during typical, everyday parent–child interactions across all environments (e.g., home, grocery store, park, restaurants) may also drive the development of social competence.

As researchers in the field increasingly begin to view ASDs from a lifespan perspective, we have become more aware of the numerous life changes that families face. For instance, teachers change from year to year, therapists turn over, and families relocate. Parents who receive training in PRT may be better prepared to coordinate with and/or provide training for other caregivers and professionals, thereby increasing the spread of the effect of the intervention (Symon, 2005). Such coordination of care allows for more consistency in the implementation of interventions and supports learning the skills necessary for children with ASDs to become socially competent adults.

Implementing Pivotal Response Treatment within Social Skills Interventions

PRT has also been used as the primary intervention for directly teaching social skills. Although PRT is generally implemented within the context of play-based interactions, particularly for young children, Stahmer (1999) and colleagues have used PRT to target appropriate play skills in children with ASDs, including object play (Stahmer, Ingersoll, & Carter, 2003), symbolic play (Stahmer 1995; Stahmer & Schreibman, 1992), and socio-dramatic play (Thorp et al., 1995). Play skills are critical for early language and social development (Siller & Sigman, 2002, 2008) and likely relate to the development of prosocial behaviors and social competence.

Several PRT studies have evaluated peer-implemented interventions in which typically developing peers learn to use PRT with children with ASDs. Pierce and Schreibman (1995) taught typically developing peers to implement PRT strategies in the classroom and found that children with autism maintained longer interactions, initiated play and conversations, and increased engagement in language and joint attention behaviors. A later study documented improvements in collateral language and play behaviors that were maintained 3 months after intervention ended (Pierce & Schreibman, 1997). Outside the classroom, Harper et al. (2008) taught typically developing peers to implement PRT during recess activities and found increases in social initiations and turn taking. Baker, Koegel, and Koegel (1998) employed the obsessive interests of children with autism as the motivational variable for improving social interaction with peers on the playground. For instance, typically developing peers were taught to play a tag game on a giant outline of the United States for a child who perseverated on maps. Dramatic increases in the percentage of social interactions were found and maintained during follow-up. Perhaps more important, the children with autism generalized social interactions during other play activities with peers. In a related study implemented with siblings, similar results were demonstrated when incorporating the thematic ritualistic activities of children with autism into typical games (Baker, 2000).

Other studies have used cooperative arrangements to provide training in PRT for both typically developing peers and children with ASDs. Cooperative arrangements require mutually reinforcing activities to ensure that peers also receive reinforcement and maintain interactions with children with ASDs. For instance, Koegel, Fredeen, and Koegel (2003) trained parents to implement PRT to facilitate social interaction between

two sibling dyads during cooperative play. In addition to increased reciprocal interactions, both children with autism generalized social interactions
with untrained peers. Klein (2007) trained paraprofessionals to use PRT
and cooperative arrangements to facilitate social interactions among children with autism and their typically developing peers on the playground
during recess. After paraprofessionals were trained to implement intervention procedures with fidelity and could generalize teaching to untrained
activities, the reciprocal social behavior of the children increased rapidly.
Similar work has also been done with paraprofessionals working at an inclusive summer camp to facilitate social interactions among all children
(Brookman et al., 2003; Koegel, Klein, et al., 2006).

PRT and cooperative arrangements have also been used during play
dates among children with ASDs and their typically developing peers
(Koegel, Werner, Vismara, & Koegel, 2005). Many children with ASDs
are not invited to play dates; some children with ASDs are invited to play
dates, but the play date rarely ends positively, meaning children with ASDs
may be missing critical opportunities to interact with peers and develop the
skills associated with social competence. Again, improvements were found
in reciprocal social interactions among children with ASDs and their peers.
Furthermore, the data showed an increase in play-date invitations from
peers, perhaps indicating increases in the peers' desire to spend additional
time with children with autism. Clearly, interacting successfully with peers
is paramount to becoming socially competent.

As a pivotal area, self-management has also demonstrated improvements in social behaviors, including generalized changes in untargeted social
behaviors (Koegel & Frea, 1993; Koegel, Harrower, & Koegel, 1999; Koegel,
Koegel, Hurley, & Frea, 1992). Boettcher (2004) used self-management
to teach social conversation skills, skills that are often overlooked yet essential for developing social competence. Although children with ASDs
have been taught to respond with on-topic comments, many do not initiate questions during social conversation. For instance, when Boettcher
presented one participant with a leading statement such as "I saw a great
movie last night," the child frequently directed the conversation back to his
perseverative interest and responded with "Do you like elevators?" rather
than asking about the movie. Thus, children were taught to ask appropriate, on-topic questions that were related to the other person's interests
(e.g., "What movie did you see?" or "Who went with you to the movies?").
Data indicated that self-management was an efficacious intervention for
teaching these social conversation skills, and the skills were maintained and
generalized to new settings with new conversation partners (e.g., untrained
adults or typically developing peers). Part of being a socially competent individual includes showing an interest in others during conversation through
initiating questions even when the topic may not be immediately reinforcing.

Collateral Improvements in Untargeted Social Behaviors

Although increases in targeted social communication and social skills are critical for children with ASDs, collateral improvements in untargeted social behaviors may have the most impact for social competence development. By focusing on pivotal areas of responding, these behaviors are not taught directly; rather, they are generalized behaviors that emerge naturally and as a result of the intervention. Thus, many studies demonstrating the efficacy of PRT have documented improvements in both targeted and untargeted behaviors (Koegel, Openden, et al., 2006).

Collateral improvements in positive affect—a measure of happiness, interest, and enthusiasm—that occur as PRT is implemented have been demonstrated across several studies. Schreibman et al. (1991) compared the affect of parents who were trained in PRT versus those who were trained in an analog behavioral intervention. The results indicated that parents in the PRT condition exhibited significantly more positive affect, suggesting that natural parent–child interactions may be more pleasant for parents to implement. Significant differences were also found in a similar study that compared affect during family interactions at dinnertime (R. Koegel et al., 1996). If parents appear happier when interacting with their child, they may engage their child more often, increasing the intensity of intervention during activities that would not typically be thought of as therapy time (e.g., dinnertime).

Improvements in positive affect have also been reported during intensive parent-training programs (R. Koegel et al., 2002; Tran, 2008) and group parent-training programs (Openden, 2005). For instance, Openden (2005) trained groups of 7–10 parents to implement PRT with fidelity and found a significant difference in the number of times the parents smiled before and after the training. Although it is noteworthy that parents seemed to be enjoying the interactions with their children more after they received training in PRT, the increase in parent smiling may be important for a child's development of social competence because children with autism may have difficulty appreciating the affect that is intrinsic to social interactions (Weiss & Harris, 2001). If children are engaged in motivating, enjoyable interactions with their parents paired with increased opportunities to observe their parents smiling, children with autism may have an easier time relating to the intrinsic rewards of social interaction.

Collateral improvements in positive affect in children with ASDs suggest that they may indeed be enjoying the interaction. Koegel and Frea (1993) used the pivotal area of self-management to target social communication skills in two adolescent boys with autism and found generalized improvements in facial expression and affect. As discussed earlier, R. Koegel et al. (2005) used PRT during play dates to improve reciprocal social interactions and also documented collateral improvements in positive affect for not only the children with autism but also their typically developing peers.

Improvements in child affect have also been demonstrated with younger children. Brookman-Frazee (2004) compared two models of parent training—clinician directed and parent/clinician partnership—while teaching parents to implement PRT with their children. Decreased parent stress and increased parent confidence were observed in the parent–clinician partnership model. Furthermore, in addition to increases in child responsiveness and engagement, improvements in child affect were also observed. Koegel, Vernon, and Koegel (2009) evaluated whether embedding social interactions into natural reinforcers, delivered as PRT was implemented to improve language, would lead to increased levels of child-initiated social behaviors. Embedded social reinforcers produced collateral improvements in child-initiated social engagement during communication, nonverbal dyadic orienting, and general child affect. Improvements in child affect likely indicate that the children in these studies were enjoying the interactions, meaning they may be less avoidant of and more likely to engage in social interactions that in turn may help them become more socially competent individuals.

Among the many important skills and behaviors that relate to social competence development is initiating joint attention. Researchers have come to understand the critical importance of joint attention and its relationship to later language and social development (Bruinsma et al., 2004; Mundy, 1995; Mundy & Crowson, 1997; Mundy & Sigman, 1989; Mundy, Sigman, & Kasari, 1990, 1993, 1994; Tomasello, 1998; Tomasello & Farrar, 1986). Thus, several interventions have directly targeted improvements in joint attention (Dawson et al., 2010; Gulsrud, Kasari, Freeman, & Paparella, 2007; Ingersoll, Dvortcsak, Whalen, & Sikora, 2005; Jones, Carr, & Feeley, 2006; Kasari, Freeman, Paparella, 2006; Kasari, Paparella, Freeman, & Jahromi, 2008; Rocha, Schreibman, & Stahmer, 2007; Whalen & Schreibman, 2003).

Collateral improvements in child initiation of joint attention, though, have also been documented in PRT. Bruinsma (2005) taught parents of young, nonverbal children with autism (children had fewer than 10 functional words at baseline) to implement PRT to improve expressive language. Increases in joint attention—specifically, eye gaze alternation to share enjoyment—were documented as a collateral effect of PRT. Furthermore, this increase generalized to another familiar adult and the Early Social Communication Scales (ESCS; Mundy et al., 2003; Seibert, Hogan, & Mundy, 1982) following intervention. Vismara and Lyons (2007) implemented PRT in conjunction with the perseverative interests of young nonverbal children with autism. Collateral improvements in joint attention initiations for social sharing were demonstrated with both highly preferred and less preferred stimuli. Finally, Fredeen (2005) implemented PRT with elementary school–age children with autism to increase the quantity and the quality of initiations toward typically developing peers. Joint attention initiations increased as a collateral effect of PRT and generalized to untrained peers at postintervention and follow-up.

TRANSLATION INTO EFFECTIVE AND ACCESSIBLE PRACTICE

Although extensive data support the efficacy of the model, PRT may not be as widely implemented as other behavioral approaches. With the continuing rise in the incidence of ASDs to 1 in 88 children (Centers for Disease Control and Prevention, 2012), the need to translate efficacious interventions into effective and accessible practices has become even more urgent. In addition to the publication of training manuals (Koegel, Koegel, Bruinsma, Brookman, & Fredeen, 2003; R. Koegel et al., 1989) and a book that covers communication, social, and academic development (Koegel & Koegel, 2006), translational research studies have demonstrated the effective dissemination of PRT.

With the increasing prevalence of autism has come a shortage of highly trained professionals to meet the growing demand for effective services. Thus, in addition to improving treatment intensity, parent training may also be an important methodology for broadly disseminating interventions. That is, the number of children reached could be substantially increased if highly trained professionals spent less time working directly with children in favor of training parents to implement interventions. In addition to maximizing impact, this approach may be a more cost-effective way to disseminate effective services for children with ASDs, who require extensive costs during their lifetimes (Ganz, 2007; Jacobson & Mulick, 2000; Jacobson, Mulick, & Green, 1998).

R. Koegel et al. (2002) provided a weeklong intensive parent-training session in PRT for parents who lived geographically distant from an intervention center (e.g., rural or remote areas). Parents were brought to a university campus and received 25 hours of training on how to implement the motivational procedures of PRT for improving social communication with their child. Data indicated improvements in parents' correct implementation of PRT and affect as well as in the child's expressive language. More important, parents generalized their newly learned skills at home and maintained them across time. These data suggest that parents could be effective interventionists and could produce improvements in their children without more frequent visits from highly trained professionals. Furthermore, in a replication study, Symon (2005) assessed the spread of effect of parent training by asking parents to train other significant caregivers in PRT (e.g., spouse, grandparent) after they returned home. The results indicated that parents were able to successfully train others, and child gains in social communication and appropriate behaviors improved with other caregivers. Thus, parents can learn to not only implement PRT correctly but also train others who regularly interact with their child, further expanding the number of families who receive effective services.

As briefly discussed earlier, Openden (2005) assessed whether groups of parents could be trained together to implement PRT within a randomized clinical trial. Parents, most residing in rural or remote areas, participated in groups of 7–10 in a 4-day workshop in the motivational procedures of PRT for improving social communication. Following 1 day of didactic instruction, parents returned home and videotaped their implementation of PRT with their child. Each day, every parent in the group presented his or her videotape and received feedback from the workshop presenter (as well as other parents in the group). The results showed significant differences between the treatment group and the control group on the fidelity of implementation of PRT, parent affect, and child social communication. These data suggest that group parent training may be an effective mechanism for broader dissemination of PRT.

The training model employed in Openden (2005) may also be useful for training groups of parents and professionals to correctly implement PRT, thereby improving the coordination of care and wraparound support as well as increasing the number of families affected. Bryson et al. (2007) trained teams of parents and intervention providers to implement PRT as part of a provincewide dissemination project in Nova Scotia, Canada. The teams included a minimum of one or both parents, a one-to-one interventionist, and a clinical supervisor, and they were trained in three different locations. Furthermore, clinical supervisors received an additional train-the-trainer training to disseminate the model in other areas around the province. One-year outcome data on the first cohort of children showed significant improvements in expressive and receptive language and behavior problems (Smith et al., 2010). These data have important implications for large-scale dissemination, implementation, and accessible effective service delivery for children with ASDs.

UNANSWERED QUESTIONS AND RESEARCH PRIORITIES

Although a substantial research base supports PRT, several important questions remain unanswered and may be considered research priorities. First, further translational research is necessary to make PRT accessible to more families with children with ASDs. Developing a comprehensive curriculum—including the scope and the sequence of what is to be taught during a child's lifetime—that could be tested for efficacy and effectiveness may be a critical step toward more widespread implementation. One of the major benefits of many behavioral programs is that they are often clearly laid out so that teachers and/or therapists can easily develop and implement an appropriate program. With respect to the individual differences in children, adolescents, and adults with ASDs, the need for the individualization of treatment, and the desire to maintain a high level of teaching creativity, developing such a curriculum will likely be challenging and require ongoing testing and refinement. Koegel, Openden, et al. (2006) laid out the structure for a PRT curriculum that may be used as a framework for future development.

Another way to increase implementation is to conduct more research on PRT in schools, particularly in inclusive general education classrooms. Although early intervention targets in inclusive school settings have been identified (Koegel, Koegel, Frea, & Fredeen, 2001) and a few studies have evaluated PRT interventions either in the classroom (Koegel, Harrower, & Koegel, 1999; Koegel, Koegel, Frea, & Green-Hopkins, 2003) or with academic tasks (Koegel, Singh, & Koegel, 2010; Koegel, Tran, Mossman, & Koegel, 2006), most of the research supporting PRT has been conducted in home, clinical, and community settings. Almost all children with ASDs will attend schools, making understanding of how best to train teachers to correctly implement PRT in inclusive general education classrooms essential.

A second research priority is to improve researchers' understanding of individual response to treatment. Although PRT appears to be effective for many children with ASDs, individual differences within the disorder imply that it is unlikely that any one intervention will be efficacious for all individuals with ASDs. Sherer and Schreibman (2005) analyzed archival data to investigate how a child's characteristics may be associated with different outcomes with PRT and developed two distinct behavioral profiles for responders and nonresponders. These profiles were then used to correctly predict which children would demonstrate positive changes (responders) and those who would not exhibit improvements (nonresponders). Additional research in this area is critical to improving the identification of phenotypes that can be matched to interventions most likely to produce positive outcomes, thereby maximizing the impact of early intervention.

Researchers may also begin to better understand response to treatment if intervention studies more carefully define participant characteristics, including the use of standardized diagnostic assessments. Many published treatment studies in autism merely indicate that participants met the criteria for autism consistent with the *Diagnostic and Statistical Manual of Mental Disorders, Fourth Edition* (American Psychiatric Association, 1994) or were diagnosed by an outside, independent agency. This information tells us very little about the characteristics of an individual with an ASD, which limits understanding of response to treatment. If research participants are more carefully described across studies using gold standard diagnostic assessments, practitioners may be better able to identify profiles of children that may predict response to PRT.

Similarly, more research should be done to improve response to treatment for those who do not respond to PRT. For instance, Koegel, Shirotova, and Koegel (2009a, 2009b) used individualized orienting cues to facilitate first-word acquisition in children who failed to respond to PRT in the past and found increased correct responding to verbal models and subsequent word use. By modifying existing PRT instructional methods, it is plausible that even the most challenging children with ASDs may be able to respond to treatment.

Finally, future research should evaluate the efficacy of PRT with very young children as well as adolescents and adults with ASDs. Similar to many interventions, PRT has been primarily developed and evaluated with children from about 2 years old through the elementary school years. As practitioners begin identifying children at 18, 14, or even 12 months, it is likely that the associated interventions will look different from those implemented with 2- and 3-year-olds. For instance, the Denver model has been adapted and evaluated as the early start Denver model for younger children with autism (Dawson et al., 2010; Rogers & Dawson, 2009). Although there is considerable overlap with the early start Denver model, similar efforts should be developed and tested for PRT.

The increase in the incidence of children with ASDs and the inevitable transition of these children into adulthood indicate that future research should assess the effects of PRT with older populations. LeBlanc, Geiger, Sautter, and Sidener (2007) used NLP to increase vocalizations of older adults with cognitive impairments. Although the participants in this study were not diagnosed with autism, they were between the ages of 54 and 57, had fairly significant impairments, and had limited verbal communication, implying that these procedures may also be efficacious with adolescents and adults with autism. Of central importance for this population is a focus on the functional skills and outcomes that are most likely to improve the quality of life. For many adolescents and adults with ASDs, quality of life is most threatened by poor social skills and interactions, often with community members, peers, romantic interests, and employers. However, Koegel (2007) suggested that social development in high-functioning autism and Asperger syndrome, once thought to be relatively unchangeable, may be mediated through interventions that improve motivation, self-management, and initiations—all pivotal areas. Although several interventions that incorporate PRT may indeed be effective for this population (Koegel & LaZebnik, 2009), future research should specifically select older participants to evaluate the potential benefits of PRT on the communicative, social, adaptive, behavioral, vocational, and life skills that most significantly affect quality of life for adolescents and adults living with ASDs.

REFERENCES

American Psychiatric Association. (1994). *Diagnostic and statistical manual of mental disorders* (4th ed.). Washington, DC: Author.

Baker, M.J. (2000). Incorporating the thematic ritualistic behaviors of children with autism into games. *Journal of Positive Behavior Interventions, 2,* 66–84.

Baker, M.J., Koegel, R.L., & Koegel, L.K. (1998). Increasing the social behaviors of young children with autism using their obsessive behaviors. *Journal of the Association for Persons with Severe Handicaps, 23,* 300–308.

Baker-Ericzén, M.J., Stahmer, A.C., & Burns, A. (2007). Child demographics associated with outcomes in a community-based Pivotal Response Training program. *Journal of Positive Behavior Interventions, 9,* 52–60.

Bellini, S., Peters, J.K., Benner, L., & Hopf, A. (2007). A meta-analysis of school-based social skills interventions for children with autism spectrum disorders. *Remedial and Special Education, 28,* 153–162.

Bierman, K., & Welsh, J.A. (2000). Assessing social dysfunction: The contributions of laboratory and performance-based measures. *Journal of Clinical Child Psychology, 29,* 526–539.

Boettcher, M.A. (2004). *Teaching social conversation skills to children with autism through self-management: An analysis of treatment gains and meaningful outcomes* (Unpublished doctoral dissertation). University of California, Santa Barbara.

Brookman, L., Boettcher, M., Klein, E., Openden, D., Koegel, R.L., & Koegel, L.K. (2003). Facilitating social interactions in a community summer camp setting for children with autism. *Journal of Positive Behavior Interventions, 5,* 249–252.

Brookman-Frazee, L. (2004). Using parent/clinician partnerships in parent education programs for children with autism. *Journal of Positive Behavior Interventions, 6,* 195–213.

Brookman-Frazee, L., Vismara, L., Drahota, A., Stahmer, A., & Openden, D. (2009). Parent training interventions for children with autism spectrum disorders. In J. Matson (Ed.), *Applied behavior analysis for children with autism spectrum disorders: A handbook* (pp. 237–257). New York, NY: Springer.

Bruinsma, Y.E.M. (2005). *Increases in the joint attention behavior of eye gaze alternation to share enjoyment as a collateral effect of Pivotal Response Treatment for three children with autism* (Unpublished doctoral dissertation). University of California, Santa Barbara.

Bruinsma, Y., Koegel, R.L., & Koegel, L.K. (2004). Joint attention and children with autism: A review of the literature. *Mental Retardation and Developmental Disabilities Research Reviews, 10,* 169–175.

Bryson, S.E., Koegel, L.K., Koegel, R.L., Openden, D., Smith, I.M., & Nefdt, N. (2007). Large scale dissemination and community implementation of Pivotal Response Treatment: Program description and preliminary data. *Research and Practice for Persons with Severe Disabilities, 32,* 142–153.

Centers for Disease Control and Prevention. (2012). Prevalence of autism spectrum disorders: Autism and developmental disabilities monitoring network, 14 sites, United States, 2008. *Morbidity and Mortality Weekly Report 2012, 61,* 1–19.

Dawson, G., & Osterling, J. (1997). Early intervention in autism. In M.J. Guralnick (Ed.), *The effectiveness of early intervention* (pp. 307–326). Baltimore, MD: Paul H. Brookes Publishing Co.

Dawson, G., Rogers, S., Munson, J., Smith, M., Winter, J., Greenson, J., …Varley, J. (2010). Randomized, controlled trial of an intervention for toddlers with autism: The early start Denver model. *Pediatrics, 125,* e17–e23.

Delprato, D.J. (2001). Comparisons of discrete-trial and normalized behavioral language intervention for young children with autism. *Journal of Autism and Developmental Disorders, 31,* 315–325.

Fisher, M., & Meyer, L.H. (2002). Development and social competence after two years for students enrolled in inclusive and self-contained educational programs. *Research and Practice for Persons with Severe Disabilities, 27,* 165–174.

Fredeen, R.M. (2005). *Increasing initiations towards peers in children with autism using Pivotal Response Training and collateral gains in quality of initiations* (Unpublished doctoral dissertation). University of California, Santa Barbara.

Ganz, M.L. (2007). The lifetime distribution of the incremental societal costs of autism. *Archives of Pediatric & Adolescent Medicine, 161,* 343–349.

Gillett, J.N., & LeBlanc, L.A. (2007). Parent-implemented natural language paradigm to increase language and play in children with autism. *Research in Autism Spectrum Disorders, 1,* 247–255.

Gresham, F.M., & MacMillan, D.L. (1998). Early intervention project: Can its claims be substantiated and its effects replicated? *Journal of Autism and Developmental Disorders, 28,* 5–13.

Gulsrud, A.C., Kasari, C., Freeman, S., & Paparella, T. (2007). Children with autism's response to novel stimuli while participating in interventions targeting joint attention or symbolic play skills, *Autism, 11,* 535–546.

Harper, C.B., Symon, J.B.G., & Frea, W.D. (2008). Recess is time-in: Using peers to improve social skills of children with autism. *Journal of Autism and Developmental Disorders, 38,* 815–826.

Hart, B., & Risley, T.R. (1989). The longitudinal study of interactive systems. *Education and Treatment of Children, 12,* 347–358.

Hart, B., & Risley, T.R. (1992). American parenting of language-learning children: Persisting differences in family-child interactions observed in natural home environments. *Developmental Psychology, 28,* 1096–1105.

Hart, B., & Risley, T.R. (1995). *Meaningful differences in the everyday experience of young American children.* Baltimore, MD: Paul H. Brookes Publishing Co.

Ingersoll, B., Dvortcsak, A., Whalen, C., & Sikora, D. (2005). The effects of a developmental, social-pragmatic language intervention on rate of expressive language production in young children with autistic spectrum disorders. *Focus on Autism and Other Developmental Disabilities, 20,* 213–222.

Jacobson, J.W., & Mulick, J.A. (2000). System and cost research issues in treatments for people with autistic disorders. *Journal of Autism and Developmental Disorders, 30,* 585–593.

Jacobson, J.W., Mulick, J.A., & Green, G. (1998). Cost-benefit estimates for early intensive behavioral intervention for young children with autism—general model and single state case. *Behavioral Interventions, 13,* 201–226.

Jones, E.A., Carr, E.G., & Feeley, K.M. (2006). Multiple effects of joint attention intervention for children with autism. *Behavior Modification, 30,* 782–834.

Kasari, C. (2002). Assessing change in early intervention programs for children with autism. *Journal of Autism and Developmental Disorders, 32,* 447–461.

Kasari, C., Freeman, S., & Paparella, T. (2006). Joint attention and symbolic play in young children with autism: A randomized controlled intervention study. *Journal of Child Psychology and Psychiatry, 47,* 611–620.

Kasari, C., Paparella, T., Freeman, S., & Jahromi, L.B. (2008). Language outcome in autism: Randomized comparison of joint attention and play interventions. *Journal of Consulting and Clinical Psychology, 76,* 125–137.

Klein, E. (2007). *Training paraprofessionals to facilitate social interactions between children with autism and their typically developing peers* (Unpublished doctoral dissertation). University of California, Santa Barbara

Koegel, L.K., Camarata, S.M., Valdez-Manchaca, M., & Koegel, R.L. (1998). Setting generalization of question-asking by children with autism. *American Journal on Mental Retardation, 102,* 346–357.

Koegel, L.K., Harrower, J.K., & Koegel, R.L. (1999). Support for children with developmental disabilities in full inclusion classrooms through self-management. *Journal of Positive Behavior Interventions, 1,* 26–34.

Koegel, L.K., Koegel, R.L., Frea, W.D., & Fredeen, R.M. (2001). Identifying early intervention targets for children with autism in inclusive school settings. *Behavior Modification, 25,* 745–761.

Koegel, L.K., Koegel, R.L., Frea, W., & Green-Hopkins, I. (2003). Priming as a method of coordinating educational services for students with autism. *Language, Speech, and Hearing Services in Schools, 34,* 228–235.

Koegel, L.K., Koegel, R.L., Hurley, C., & Frea, W.D. (1992). Improving social skills and disruptive behavior in children with autism through self-management. *Journal of Applied Behavior Analysis, 25,* 341–353.

Koegel, L.K., Koegel, R.L., Shoshan, Y., & McNerney, E. (1999). Pivotal response intervention II: Preliminary long-term outcomes data. *Journal of the Association for Persons with Severe Handicaps, 24,* 186–198.

Koegel, L.K., & LaZebnik, C. (2009). *Growing up on the spectrum: A guide to life, love, and learning for teens and young adults with autism and Asperger's.* New York, NY: Viking Penguin.

Koegel, L.K., Singh, A.K., & Koegel, R.L. (2010). Improving motivation for academics in children with autism. *Journal of Autism and Developmental Disorders, 40,* 1057–1066.

Koegel, R.L. (2007). Social development in individuals with high functioning autism and Asperger disorder. *Research and Practice for Persons with Severe Disabilities, 32,* 140–141.

Koegel, R.L., Bimbela, A., & Schreibman, L. (1996). Collateral effects of parent training on family interactions. *Journal of Autism and Developmental Disorders, 26,* 347–359.

Koegel, R.L., Camarata, S.M., Koegel, L.K., Ben-Tall, A., & Smith, A.E. (1998). Increasing speech intelligibility in children with autism. *Journal of Autism and Developmental Disorders, 28*, 241–251.

Koegel, R.L., Carter, C.M., & Koegel, L.K. (2003). Teaching children with autism self-initiations as a pivotal response. *Topics in Language Disorders, 23*, 134–145.

Koegel, R.L., & Frea, W.D. (1993). Treatment of social behavior in autism through the modification of pivotal social skills. *Journal of Applied Behavior Analysis, 26*, 369–377.

Koegel, R.L., Fredeen, R.M., & Koegel, L.K. (2003, February). Increasing initiations in children with autism across interactions. Paper presented at the California Association for Behavior Analysis Annual Conference, Burlingame, CA.

Koegel, R.L., Klein, E.F., Koegel, L.K., Boettcher, M.A., Brookman-Frazee, L., & Openden, D. (2006). Working with paraprofessionals to improve socialization in inclusive settings. In R.L. Koegel & L.K. Koegel (Eds.), *Pivotal Response Treatments for autism: Communication, social, and academic development* (pp. 189–198). Baltimore, MD: Paul H. Brookes Publishing Co.

Koegel, R.L., & Koegel, L.K. (2006). *Pivotal Response Treatments for autism: Communication, social, and academic development.* Baltimore, MD: Paul H. Brookes Publishing Co.

Koegel, R.L., & Koegel, L.K. (2012). *The PRT pocket guide: Pivotal Response Treatment for autism spectrum disorders.* Baltimore, MD: Paul H. Brookes Publishing Co.

Koegel, R.L., Koegel, L.K., & Brookman, (2003). Empirically supported pivotal response interventions for children with autism. In A.E. Kazdin & J.R. Weisz (Eds.), *Evidence-based psychotherapies for children and adolescents* (pp. 341–357). New York, NY: Guilford Press.

Koegel, R.L., Koegel, L.K., Bruinsma, Y., Brookman, L., & Fredeen, R.M. (2003). *Teaching first words to children with autism and communication delays using Pivotal Response Training.* Santa Barbara: University of California.

Koegel, R.L., Koegel, L.K., & Surratt, A. (1992). Language intervention and disruptive behavior in preschool children with autism. *Journal of Autism and Developmental Disorders, 22*, 141–153.

Koegel, R.L., Koegel, L.K., Vernon, T., and Brookman-Frazee, L. (2010). Empirically supported Pivotal Response Treatment for children with autism spectrum disorders. In J.R. Weisz & A.E. Kazdin (Eds.), *Evidence-based psychotherapies for children and adolescents* (2nd ed., pp. 327–344). New York, NY: Guilford Press.

Koegel, R.L., O'Dell, M.C., & Koegel, L.K. (1987). A natural language teaching paradigm for nonverbal autistic children. *Journal of Autism and Developmental Disorders, 17*, 187–199.

Koegel, R.L., Openden, D., Fredeen, R.M., & Koegel, L.K. (2006). The basics of Pivotal Response Treatment. In R.L. Koegel & L.K. Koegel (Eds.), *Pivotal Response Treatments for autism: Communication, social, and academic development* (pp. 3–30). Baltimore, MD: Paul H. Brookes Publishing Co.

Koegel, R.L., Schreibman, L., Good, A., Cerniglia, L., Murphy, C., & Koegel, L.K. (1989). *How to teach pivotal behaviors to children with autism: A training manual.* Santa Barbara/San Diego: University of California.

Koegel, R.L., Shirotova, L., & Koegel, L.K. (2009a). Antecedent stimulus control: Using orienting cues to facilitate first-word acquisition for nonresponders with autism. *The Behavior Analyst, 32,* 281–284.

Koegel, R.L., Shirotova, L., & Koegel, L.K. (2009b). Brief report: Using individualized orienting cues to facilitate first-word acquisition in non-responders with autism. *Journal of Autism and Developmental Disorders, 39,* 1587–1592.

Koegel, R.L., Symon, J.B., & Koegel, L.K. (2002). Parent education for families of children with autism living in geographically distant areas. *Journal of Positive Behavior Interventions, 4,* 88–103.

Koegel, R.L., Tran, Q., Mossman, A., & Koegel, L.K. (1996). Incorporating motivational procedures to improve homework performance. In R. Koegel & L. Koegel (Eds.), *Pivotal Response Treatments for autism: Communication, social, and academic development* (pp. 81–91). Baltimore, MD: Paul H. Brookes Publishing Co.

Koegel, R.L., Vernon, T.W., & Koegel, L.K. (2009). Improving social initiations in young children with autism using reinforcers with embedded social interactions. *Journal of Autism and Developmental Disorders, 39,* 1240–1251.

Koegel, R.L., Werner, G.A., Vismara, L.A., & Koegel, L.K. (2005). The effectiveness of contextually supported play date interactions between children with autism and typically developing peers. *Research and Practice for Persons with Severe Disabilities, 30,* 93–102.

Laski, K.E., Charlop, M.H., & Schreibman, L. (1988). Training parents to use the natural language paradigm to increase their autistic children's speech. *Journal of Applied Behavior Analysis, 21,* 391–400.

LeBlanc, L.A., Geiger, K.B., Sautter, T.M., & Sidener, T.M. (2007). Using the natural language paradigm (NLP) to increase vocalizations of older adults with cognitive impairments. *Research in Developmental Disabilities, 28,* 437–444.

Lovaas, O.I. (1987). Behavioral treatment and normal educational and intellectual functioning in young autistic children. *Journal of Consulting and Clinical Psychology, 55,* 3–9.

Lovaas, O.I., Koegel, R.L., Simmons, J.Q., & Long, J.S. (1973). Some generalization and follow-up measures on autistic children in behavior therapy. *Journal of Applied Behavior Analysis, 6,* 131–166.

Lovaas, O.I., Schreibman, L., & Koegel, R.L. (1974). A behavior modification approach to the treatment of autistic children. *Journal of Autism and Developmental Disorders, 4,* 111–129.

Lovaas, O.I., Varni, J.W., Koegel, R.L., & Lorsch, N. (1977). Some observations on the nonextinguishability of children's speech. *Child Development, 48,* 1121–1127.

McGee, G.G., Daly, T., & Jacobs, H.A. (1994). The Walden Preschool. In S.L. Harris & J.S. Handleman (Eds.), *Preschool education programs for children with autism* (pp. 127–162). Austin, TX: PRO-ED.

McGee, G.G., Morrier, M.J., & Daly, T. (1999). An incidental teaching approach to early intervention for toddlers with autism. *Journal of the Association for Persons with Severe Handicaps, 24,* 133–146.

Meadan, H., Ostrosky, M.M., Zaghlawan, H.Y., & Yu, S.Y. (2009). Promoting the social and communicative behavior of young children with autism spectrum disorders: A review of parent-implemented intervention studies. *Topics in Early Childhood Special Education, 29,* 90–104.

Mundy, P. (1995). Joint attention and social emotional approach behavior in children with autism. *Development and Psychopathology, 7*, 63–82.

Mundy, P., & Crowson, M. (1997). Joint attention and early communication: Implications for intervention with autism. *Journal of Autism and Developmental Disorders, 6*, 653–676.

Mundy, P., Delgado, C., Block, J., Venezia, M., Hogan, A., & Seibert, J. (2003). *A manual for the abridged Early Social Communication Scales (ESCS)*. Coral Gables, FL: University of Miami, Department of Psychology.

Mundy, P., & Sigman, M. (1989). The theoretical implications of joint-attention deficits in autism. *Development and Psychology , 1*, 173–183.

Mundy, P., Sigman, M., & Kasari, C. (1990). A longitudinal study of joint attention and language development in autistic children. *Journal of Autism and Developmental Disorders, 20*, 115–128.

Mundy, P., Sigman, M., & Kasari, C. (1993). The theory of mind and joint attention deficits in autism. In S. Baron-Cohen, H. Tager-Flusberg, & D.J. Cohen (Eds.), *Understanding other minds: Perspectives from autism* (pp. 181–203). Oxford, UK: Oxford University Press.

Mundy, P., Sigman, M., & Kasari, C. (1994). Joint attention, developmental level, and symptom presentation in young children with autism. *Development and Psychopathology, 6*, 389–401.

National Autism Center. (2009). *National standards report*. Randolph, MA: Author.

National Research Council. (2001). *Educating children with autism*. Washington, DC: National Academy Press.

Openden, D. (2005). *Pivotal Response Treatment for multiple families of children with autism: Effects of a 4-day group parent education workshop* (Unpublished doctoral dissertation). University of California, Santa Barbara.

Openden, D., Whalen, C., Cernich, S., & Vaupel, M. (2009). Generalization and autism spectrum disorders. In C. Whalen (Ed.), *Real life, real progress for children with autism: Strategies for successful generalization in natural environments* (pp. 1–18). Baltimore, MD: Paul H. Brookes Publishing Co.

Pierce, K., & Schreibman, L. (1995). Increasing complex social behaviors in children with autism: Effects of peer-implemented Pivotal Response Training. *Journal of Applied Behavior Analysis, 28*, 285–295.

Pierce, K., & Schreibman, L. (1997). Multiple peer use of Pivotal Response Training to increase social behaviors of classmates with autism: Results from trained and untrained peers. *Journal of Applied Behavior Analysis, 30*, 157–160.

Rocha, M.L., Schreibman, L., & Stahmer, A.C. (2007). Effectiveness of training parents to teach joint attention in children with autism. *Journal of Early Intervention, 2*, 154–172.

Rogers, S., & Dawson, G. (2009). Randomized, controlled trial of an intervention for toddlers with autism: The early start Denver model. *Pediatrics, 125*, 17–23.

Russo, D.C., Koegel, R.L., & Lovaas, O.I. (1978). A comparison of human and automated instruction of autistic children. *Journal of Abnormal Child Psychology, 6*, 189–201.

Schreibman, L., Kaneko, W.M., & Koegel, R.L. (1991). Positive affect of parents of autistic children: A comparison across two teaching techniques. *Behavior Therapy, 22*, 479–490.

Seibert, J.M., Hogan, A.E., & Mundy, P.C. (1982). Assessing interactional competencies: The Early Social-Communication Scales. *Infant Mental Health Journal, 3*, 244–258.

Sheinkopf, S.J., & Siegel, B. (1998). Home-based behavioral treatment of young children with autism. *Journal of Autism and Developmental Disorders, 28*, 15–23.

Sherer, M.R., & Schreibman, L. (2005). Individual behavioral profiles and predictors of treatment effectiveness for children with autism. *Journal of Consulting and Clinical Psychology, 73*, 525–538.

Siller, M., & Sigman, M. (2002). The behaviors of parents of children with autism predict the subsequent development of their children's communication. *Journal of Autism and Developmental Disorders, 32*, 77–89.

Siller, M., & Sigman, M. (2008). Modeling longitudinal change in the language abilities of children with autism: Parent behaviors and child characteristics as predictors of change. *Developmental Psychology, 44*, 1691–1704.

Simpson, R.L. (2005). Evidence-based practices for students with autism spectrum disorders. *Focus on Autism and Other Developmental Disorders, 20*, 140–149.

Simpson, R.L., de Boer-Ott, S.R., Griswold, D.E., Myles, B.S., Byrd, S.E., Ganz, J.B.,...Adams, L.G. (2005). *Autism spectrum disorders: Interventions and treatments for children and youth.* Thousand Oaks, CA: Corwin Press.

Smith, I.M., Koegel, R.L., Koegel, L.K., Openden, D., Fossum, K.L., & Bryson, S.E. (2010). Effectiveness of a novel community-based early intervention model for children with autistic spectrum disorder. *American Journal on Intellectual and Developmental Disabilities, 115*, 504–523.

Spence, S.H. (2003). Social skills training with children and young people: Theory, evidence, and practice. *Child & Adolescent Mental Health, 8*, 84–96.

Spence, S.H., & Donovan, C. (1998). Interpersonal problems. In P.J. Graham (Ed.), *Cognitive behaviour therapy for children and families* (pp. 217–245). New York, NY: Cambridge University Press.

Stahmer, A.C. (1995). Teaching symbolic play skills to children with autism using Pivotal Response Training. *Journal of Autism and Developmental Disorders, 25*, 123–141.

Stahmer, A.C. (1999). Using Pivotal Response Training to facilitate appropriate play in children with autistic spectrum disorders. *Child Language Teaching and Therapy, 15*, 29–40.

Stahmer, A.C., Ingersoll, B., & Carter, C. (2003). Behavioral approaches to promoting play. *Autism, 7*, 401–413.

Stahmer, A.C., & Schreibman, L. (1992). Teaching children with autism appropriate play in unsupervised environments using a self-management treatment package. *Journal of Applied Behavior Analysis, 25*, 447–459.

Stichter, J.P., Randolph, J., & Gage, N. (2007). A review of recommended social competency programs for students with autism spectrum disorders. *Exceptionality, 15*, 219–232.

Strain, P., & Cordisco, L. (1994). LEAP Preschool. In S.L. Harris & J.S. Handleman (Eds.), *Preschool education programs for children with autism* (pp. 225–244). Austin, TX: PRO-ED.

Symon, J.B. (2005). Expanding interventions for children with autism: Parents as trainers. *Journal of Positive Behavior Interventions, 7*, 159–173.

Thorp, D., Stahmer, A.C., & Schreibman, L. (1995). Effects of sociodramatic play training on children with autism. *Journal of Autism and Developmental Disorders, 25*, 265–282.

Tomasello, M. (1998). Intending that others jointly attend. *Pragmatics & Cognition, 6,* 229–243.

Tomasello, M., & Farrar, M.J. (1986). Joint attention and early language. *Child Development, 57,* 1454–1463.

Tran, Q.H. (2008). *Using a self-assessment procedure to improve parent implementation of intervention for children with autism* (Unpublished doctoral dissertation). University of California, Santa Barbara.

Varni, J.W., Lovaas, O.I., Koegel, R.L., & Everett, N.L. (1979). An analysis of observational learning in autistic and normal children. *Journal of Abnormal Child Psychology, 7,* 31–43.

Vismara, L.A., & Lyons, G.L. (2007). Using perseverative interests to elicit joint attention behaviors in young children with autism: Theoretical and clinical implications for understanding motivation. *Journal of Positive Behavior Interventions, 9,* 214–228.

Weiss, M.J., & Harris, S.L. (2001). Teaching social skills to people with autism. *Behavior Modification, 25,* 785–802.

Wetherby, A., & Prizant, B.M. (2000). *Autism spectrum disorders: A transactional developmental perspective.* Baltimore, MD: Paul H. Brookes Publishing Co.

Whalen, C., & Schreibman, L. (2003). Joint attention training for children with autism using behavior modification procedures. *Journal of Child Psychology and Psychiatry, 44,* 456–468.

The Development
of Self-Help Skills
in Children with Autism

Stephen R. Anderson

A diagnosis of autism typically is determined by using a diagnostic instrument or a checklist specifically designed to assess the core symptoms of the disorder: qualitative impairments in social interaction and communication and restricted and stereotyped patterns of behavior (American Psychiatric Association, 1994). The diagnostic process often includes a careful interview of the parents of the child who might have autism (Rutter, LeCouteur, & Lord, 2003) and/or a direct observation of the child conducted by an experienced professional (e.g., Lord, Rutter, DiLavore, & Risi, 2003). In addition to a diagnostic scale, an intelligence assessment helps a practitioner to better understand the complexity of the child's disorder and may assist in planning and placement decisions.

It also has been suggested that an adaptive skills assessment may help to more accurately differentiate a diagnosis of autism from other developmental concerns, such as intellectual disability without autism (Rodrique, Morgan, & Geffken, 1991), and may be useful in educational planning. Adaptive behavior represents practical skills that enable children to function in their everyday lives (American Association on Mental Retardation, 2002). Instruments that assess adaptive skills typically emphasize communication, community self-sufficiency, socialization, behavior, and activities of daily living (ADLs).

This chapter focuses on ADLs for children with autism, specifically the development of self-help skills (e.g., dressing, toileting, eating, personal hygiene). It begins by arguing that there is a link between self help skills development and general quality-of-life issues for individuals with autism. Subsequent sections of the chapter summarize the effects of early intensive behavioral intervention on self-help skills development, discuss ways to conduct a meaningful assessment, and describe the unique developmental profile for children with autism and the implications for instruction. The chapter concludes with general strategies for teaching self-help skills and summarizes areas for future research.

SELF-HELP SKILLS AND QUALITY OF LIFE

The absence of self-help skills may have long-term effects on many aspects of an individual's life. Parents and teachers do not spend a lot of time talking about impairments in self-help skills until individuals reach school age. Even then, there seems to be very little emphasis on teaching self-help skills until early adolescence when impairments in these areas start to be more visible relative to same-age peers and greater importance is placed on self-sufficiency.

For a child at a very young age, no one seems to notice that a parent or a teacher helps with most self-help activities. Furthermore, it is sometimes easier to help a child complete a task than it is to instruct, prompt, and help a child learn the skill. In one study, 25 families living with a child with autism were interviewed. They reported that many of the children with autism needed extra maternal attention in feeding, toileting, and dressing relative to same-age peers (O'Moore, 1978). However, self-help skills development is important to an individual's self-esteem, independence, and ability to integrate into a community. As children develop self-care skills, such as dressing, eating, toileting, and toothbrushing, their ability to live and function independently across multiple environments increases and enhances the opportunities for additional learning (Heward, 2009). The presence or the absence of self-help skills greatly influences the supports an individual will need for school, work, and community environments.

It has often been suggested that individuals with disabilities may have fewer choices and less self-determination than individuals without disabilities. Factors such as age and the levels of adaptive and maladaptive behavior may also be associated with quality of life and self-determination (Felce & Emerson, 2001). Vine and Hamilton (2005) examined the individual characteristics associated with community integration for 37 individuals with developmental disabilities. The scores on daily-living scales were found to correlate with objective aspects of quality of life, such as community access, daily routines, and choice opportunities.

EARLY INTENSIVE
BEHAVIORAL INTERVENTION AND SELF-HELP SKILLS

The early intervention field is becoming increasingly more successful at helping many individuals with autism overcome severe developmental challenges and live more normal lives. Growing scientific evidence suggests that if practitioners start instruction at an early age, use instructional methods that are scientifically demonstrated to be effective, and provide enough hours, many children with autism make substantial gains (Howard, Sparkman, Cohen, Green, & Stanislaw, 2005; Lovaas, 1987; Remington et al., 2007; Sallows & Graupner, 2005; Smith, Eikeseth, Klevstrand, & Lovaas, 1997; Smith, Groen, & Wynn, 2000). Collectively, the approach used in these studies is called early intensive behavioral intervention (EIBI) and is part of a larger area of research and practice called applied behavior analysis (ABA). Basic and applied research under the rubric of behavioral treatment or ABA has been used for several decades, and researchers have documented ABA's effectiveness for building a wide range of important skills and reducing problem behavior in individuals with autism (Green, 1996). The principles and the methods of ABA have been described in detail in textbooks dedicated to the topic (Alberto & Troutman, 2009; Cooper, Heron, & Heward, 2007). Other resources provide detailed descriptions of using ABA methods to teach self-help skills to individuals with severe disabilities (e.g., Anderson, Jablonski, Thomeer, & Madaus Knapp, 2007; Baker et al., 1997; Snell & Brown, 2006).

Studies using EIBI often report the results for standardized instruments assessing progress in a variety of developmental areas (e.g., intelligence, adaptive behavior, communication). Several authors have reported adaptive behavior results after a period of intervention (Anderson, Avery, DiPietro, Edwards, & Christian, 1987; Birnbrauer & Leach, 1993; Howard et al., 2005; Lovaas, 1987; Smith et al., 1997). Only a few studies report a specific subtest score for self-help skills and/or are able to compare preintervention and postintervention scores against a control group. Sallows and Graupner (2005) demonstrated significant gains for children with autism who participated in EIBI. Whereas socialization and communication improved on the Vineland Adaptive Behavior Scales (Sparrow, Balla, & Cicchetti, 2005), there was no significant change in ADLs (which include self-help skills).

Howard et al. (2005) compared the effects of three approaches on preschool children with autism. Individualized education program (IEP) or individualized family service plan (IFSP) teams (with input from parents) dictated group placement, with some children receiving EIBI (the treatment group), and two other groups receiving a combination of the treatments (the control groups). Some children received EIBI (the treatment group), and two other groups received a combination of the treatment approaches (the control groups). The results indicated that the children who participated in EIBI had statistically more significant improvements in self-help skills development than children in either control group. Given that the participants in the EIBI studies were typically under the age of 5 years and demonstrated impairments in most areas of development, it is not surprising that self-help skills were not the primary focus of the intervention. Nevertheless, future research should answer questions about the generalized benefit of EIBI to self-help skills development and whether there is a need to specifically focus on teaching skills as part of the intervention efforts.

THE ASSESSMENT OF SELF-HELP SKILLS

Instruments that measure adaptive behavior are not unique to children with autism and are widely used with a broad range of individuals having or presumed to have developmental disabilities. Some of the most commonly used instruments are in Table 8.1. These instruments consist of a series of questions answered by a teacher, a parent, or another person familiar with the child. These tools emphasize somewhat different areas of adaptive functioning but generally elicit information about a child's development in the areas of socialization, communication, community, and ADLs (including self-help skills). They are widely used to help make a diagnosis and establish entitlement to services (Klin, Saulner, Tsatsanis, & Volkmar, 2005) and may help differentiate children with autism from children with disabilities that do not include autism (Rodrique et al., 1991).

The Vineland Adaptive Behavior Scales, for example, assess independence in the domains of communication, ADLs, socialization, motor skills, and behavior. ADLs aggregate a large group of behaviors, including self-help skills (e.g., toothbrushing, bathing, hair care), functional domestic skills (e.g., completing chores, setting the table), and community skills (e.g., understanding money, looking both ways before crossing the street). Unfortunately, these instruments do not have the breadth and the depth needed to provide specific recommendations for curriculum planning. Thus, they are useful for identifying broad areas of strengths and weaknesses but may not lead to the identification of specific areas of intervention. Other assessment tools (Coster et al., 1998; Haley et al., 1998) measure across multiple domains but include more detail in the self-help area and can assess the level of caregiver assistance and adaptations that may be required (see Table 8.1).

In the end, a meaningful assessment will consist of many different ways of gathering information, including interviews with parents and team members and direct observation of the child. Simple checklists, such as the Self-Help Skills Inventory (Anderson et al., 2007) may also be useful for program and curriculum planning. This inventory instructs the rater to indicate not only whether a skill is present or absent (e.g., cuts with a knife) but also the level of independence and whether the skill is age appropriate. The inventory also instructs the rater to indicate whether the skill is essential to the child at that moment in time (i.e., its absence prevents him or her from participating in school, community, or work opportunities). This approach helps to prioritize what to teach first, given myriad items that may not have reached a level of independence that is age appropriate.

THE UNIQUE PROFILE OF CHILDREN WITH AUTISM

It has been suggested that the developmental profile for children with autism often differs from that of individuals with developmental dis-

Table 8.1. Instruments for measuring adaptive skills development

Instrument	Research team	Age group
Vineland Adaptive Behavior Scales	Sparrow, Balla, and Cicchetti (2005)	3–21 years
AAMR Adaptive Behavior Scale, 2nd Edition (ABS-2)	Lambert, Nihira, and Leland (1993)	Residential/Community Edition, 18 years and older; School Edition, 3–16 years
Scales of Independent Behavior, Revised	Bruininks, Woodcock, Weatherman, and Hill (1996)	Birth to 80 years
Adaptive Behavior Assessment System, 2nd Edition (ABAS-II)	Harrison and Oakland (2003)	Birth to 89 years
School Function Assessment	Coster, Deeney, Haltiwanger, and Haley (1998)	Kindergarten to grade 6
Pediatric Evaluation of Disability Inventory	Haley, Coster, Ludlow, Haltiwanger, and Andrellos (1998)	6 months to 7 years

abilities without autism, and a gap exists for children with autism between intellectual functioning and adaptive functioning (Carter, Gillham, Sparrow, & Volkmar, 1996). Burack and Volkmar (1992) reported that high-functioning individuals displayed greater unevenness among developmental domains than high-functioning children who were not autistic; this finding was even more significant for low-functioning children with autism. Within the autism spectrum, the children with lower IQ scores displayed more scatter (strengths in one developmental domain and impairments in another) than the high-IQ peers. Gillham, Carter, Volkmar, and Sparrow (2000) also found that autistic children displayed poorer adaptive skills (including ADLs) and significantly more maladaptive behaviors than a comparison group of individuals with developmental delays without autism. This was true even when the analysis controlled for differences in mental age. Matson, Mayville, Lott, Bielecki, and Logan (2003) reported that individuals with autism or pervasive developmental disorders, when compared with individuals with a psychotic disorder or behavior problems with similar intellectual disabilities, tended to have lower social and adaptive skills. Jacobson and Ackerman (1990) reported differences in ADLs for individuals with autism relative to individuals with intellectual disabilities. Their findings indicated that the skills of young children with autism were more developed than those of children with intellectual disabilities, but these differences were reversed in their adolescent years. Many individuals with Asperger syndrome have been shown to have moderately low levels in most adaptive skills, including ADLs, in spite of their advanced vocabulary and normal IQ scores (Lee & Park, 2007).

A few studies report little or no difference in ADLs relative to individuals with developmental disabilities other than autism. Loveland and Kelley (1991) reported differences in the socialization domain for children with autism when compared with children with Down syndrome, but they did not find significant differences in communication and ADLs. VanMeter, Fein, Morris, Waterhouse, and Allen (1997) examined the pattern of social skills, communication skills, and ADLs for children with autism relative to control groups of children with intellectual disabilities and children without disabilities. Children with autism had more gaps in their developmental sequences of communication and socialization (within domains) when compared with children with and without intellectual disabilities, but the area of ADLs had less scatter. The authors argued that ADLs may be more consistent in children with autism because the tasks are more concrete and teachable than skills in communication and socialization.

In summary, research appears to indicate that children with autism, including children with Asperger syndrome, often present impairments in the development of ADLs relative to children who are typically developing. Most studies also show that children with autism have greater scatter and delay in ADLs relative to control groups with developmental disabilities other than autism; however, the results are not consistent across all studies. Clarifying this issue may be more than just an academic exercise. A better understanding of the unique profile of children with autism may strengthen the argument for increasing the focus on assessment and instruction of ADLs/self-help skills and may help to pinpoint the specific characteristics of children with autism that affect normal development and challenge effective instruction.

CORE FEATURES AND IMPLICATIONS FOR INSTRUCTION

One of the challenges in writing about autism spectrum disorders (ASDs) is to avoid statements and recommendations that suggest that people with ASDs are a homogeneous group of individuals. At one end of the autism spectrum are individuals with a diagnosis of autism and intellectual disabilities. It is estimated that 75% of the individuals with autism fit into this category (American Psychiatric Association, 1994). At the other end are individuals with high-functioning autism and Asperger syndrome who often have IQ scores within the normal range. Children with ASDs also present a broad range of individual differences in communication and interests. Communication can range from no speech to pragmatic speech disorders. A restricted range of interests and repetitive mannerisms can present as motor stereotypes (e.g., rocking) to an extreme fascination with a specific topic (e.g., Shakespeare's character Macbeth). It is fairly safe to assume that different profiles of communication and social and intellectual impairments may result in different developmental outcomes in ADLs and may present different challenges for teaching new skills. Impairments in attention, imitation, observational learning, and symbolic play are very likely to affect a child's learning and the instructor's choice of instructional strategies. Likewise, behavioral issues, such as an interest in consistent routines, stereotypical behavior, and aggression, may present unique challenges to instruction and learning.

Imitation and Observational Learning

There is little research to explain how children who are typically developing learn self-help skills. Children appear to learn largely from their parents' coaching, demonstration, and frequent reminders. Simply showing and telling seems to be enough for most children who are typically developing. Even the small numbers of children who develop problems (e.g., chronic bed-wetting) eventually improve as they mature physically and respond to social consequences.

A skill observed early in children who are typically developing is the ability to imitate the behavior of their parents. Young children often spend a great deal of time engaged in behavior that mimics their parents and siblings. By imitation, children learn a variety of basic and complex skills within a short period of time. Very early in life, children engage in pretend self-help activities, such as toothbrushing or brushing their hair. Whether it is the reward of matching or the praise they receive from parents and teachers, the motivation to imitate seems to be present very early. Many children with autism do not learn to imitate naturally, and their play is described as less developed than that of other children, including those with developmental concerns other than autism (Lifter, Sulzer-Azaroff, Anderson, & Cowdery, 1993). It has also been reported that many children with autism are not likely to learn by simply observing their parents or listening to instructions from their parents (Varni, Lovaas, Koegel, & Everett, 1979).

Although imitation is a highly useful way to learn (planned or natural), there is no evidence that its absence predicts failure in the development of daily-life skills. It means that instructors must find another way to teach and for children to learn. Many children with autism will require an approach that relies heavily on breaking the target skills into very small steps and directly teaching the skill one step at a time—often accompanied by direct physical prompts for the desired responses that later must be faded.

Communication

Communication, particularly the ability to understand, process, and integrate information, is important for typical development. Once again, many children with autism experience significant delays in both understanding and producing speech. As a result, methods that rely on verbal instructions and explanations may not work very well. In some cases, however, children with autism may become unusually reliant on communication from adults and fail to gain a sufficient level of independence. For example, they are able to dress themselves but only when the parent verbally prompts each step (e.g., "Now put on your shirt").

Adherence to Rituals and Routines

Another characteristic of children with ASDs is a restricted and stereotyped range of interests. This can present itself as an inflexible adherence to specific routines, stereotypic mannerisms (e.g., hand flapping), or preoccupation with certain facts (e.g., baseball statistics). Children with significant nonfunctional verbal and body and hand mannerisms sometimes are the most challenging because these behaviors may interfere with getting and sustaining the child's attention. It also appears that some children use self-stimulatory behavior to help avoid tasks that may seem too challenging.

Sensory and Motor Issues

Finally, there are a variety of sensory and motor concerns that may interfere with learning self-help skills. These issues may be present at a very early age for some children who are typically developing but rarely persist beyond the first 3 or 4 years of life. In contrast, children with autism may have ongoing sensory and motor issues, such as an extreme sensitivity to the texture of toothpaste, or a struggle with the fine motor skills needed for buttoning.

GENERAL STRATEGIES FOR DECIDING WHAT TO TEACH

Experts have reported that learning in children who are typically developing has a natural ebb and flow; it is not always fluid and uninterrupted (Bloom & Tinker, 2001). Therefore, at any given time, two children of the same age may have distinctively different developmental profiles, but both are considered within the normal range of acceptable growth. However, children with autism may have even more irregular or scattered developmental profiles within and across domains. These differences are beyond the natural ebb and flow of development and create a significant challenge for instructors to decide what to teach and when.

A small number of studies that did not focus on ADLs have shown that children with autism are more likely to learn and generalize a skill when it is within the child's ability, as defined by a normal developmental sequence. For example, researchers who have studied language and play development (Dyer, Santarcangelo, & Luce, 1987; Lifter et al., 1993) have reported that children with autism are more likely to acquire play skills based on each child's level of functioning within known developmental sequences. Although similar studies have not examined developmental readiness in the acquisition of self-help skills, whenever possible, it is reasonable to consider teaching things in developmental sequence. This emphasis on developmental readiness should be moderated somewhat by an additional consideration of what is functional for an individual to learn at a given time (Anderson et al., 2007). That is, given the numerous things that must be taught, the instructor should consider what skill or cluster of skills an individual with autism needs to more fully integrate and participate in at home, school, and work.

Teaching Core Readiness Skills

Anderson et al. (2007) suggested that there may be a core set of behaviors that is important for learning self-help skills, including paying attention to an activity for a sustained period of time (5–10 minutes), responding to one's name, following simple instructions, and imitating the actions of others. These areas form a set of skills that are often the initial targets of early intensive behavioral interventions (Taylor & McDonough, 1996). Although, it has not been empirically demonstrated that severe impairments in these areas are predictive of failure to learn ADLs, it is reasonable to assume that if impairments exist, instructional strategies would have to be adjusted and include a greater reliance on physical prompts and nonverbal cues.

Instructional Strategies

In the last 25 years of research, instructional strategies have emerged for teaching self-help skills. Although many of these studies were done in residential settings with individuals described as having intellectual disabilities, some likely had ASDs as well. The general approach for teaching self-help skills has included various combinations of behaviorally based principles, including stimulus control procedures, chaining and task analysis, shaping and prompting, reinforcement, and stimulus transfer and generalization.

Stimulus Control Procedures

Learning involves understanding how to respond to specific stimuli. Stimuli that signal the availability of a reinforcer for a particular response are called discriminative stimuli (Cooper et al., 2007). One of the first questions to consider when beginning instruction is as follows: What stimuli should control the learner's behavior? In the case of self-help skills, the desire is to avoid a child learning a skill that remains under the control of the teacher's or a parent's instructions, prompts, and cues. For example, the stimuli that control washing hands should be the presence of noticeably dirty hands or a learned sequence such as washing hands before eating. For a preschool child, a verbal instruction from the teacher or a parent to wash one's hands before eating is normal. When a prompt is still necessary when the individual reaches adolescence or young adulthood, it is no longer normal.

The challenge is to teach using unnatural, supplementary prompts only to the extent that they are absolutely necessary for learning and then fade and transfer them quickly to a natural stimulus—a process often referred to as the transfer of stimulus control. For example, at first, a parent must verbally instruct his or her child to get out of bed and get dressed in the morning. Eventually, control is transferred when the child is taught to respond to an alarm clock. Therefore, identifying and incorporating natural stimuli (i.e., those that encourage and support independent responding) and choosing natural times and places to conduct instruction and promote greater independence and generalization (Farlow & Snell, 2006).

Chaining and Task Analysis

A *behavior chain* is a sequence of discrete responses that make up more complex behavior. Each step in the chain serves as a conditioned reinforcer for the response that produced it and is a discriminative stimulus for the next response in the chain (Cooper et al., 2007). This is an important part of teaching children with developmental disabilities, including autism, because it simplifies complex behaviors into a series of steps for learning. Each step in the chain can lead to a presentation of positive reinforcement and can be combined into a longer series of responses to form more complex behaviors. Examples of chaining are plentiful, such as chaining together simple steps to form the skill of putting on a T-shirt. Once learned, this simple skill can be combined with all other articles of clothing to form the act of dressing (an even longer chain). And, of course, the chain can be expanded to form even more complex behaviors, such as getting ready for school (dressing, eating, and toothbrushing).

The job of breaking down complex behaviors into a series of teachable steps is called *task analysis* (Horner & Keilitz, 1975). The number of steps can range from 4 or 5 steps to 30 or more steps. The number of steps is determined by the age and the beginning level of ability of the learner. It is not uncommon that task analyses will need to be modified (e.g., additional steps added) during teaching if it appears that specific steps are still too complex for a learner. The common methods for determining a task analysis are to observe a competent individual perform the task, seek examples in published materials, or perform the task oneself and delineate the steps.

As an example, Table 8.2 shows a 5-step program and a 9-step program for teaching a child to put on his or her socks.

After the task analysis has been determined, the instructor can choose among three chaining methods for teaching the target skill: forward chaining, whole-task chaining, and backward chaining. In a *forward chaining* approach, the sequence of skills is taught in the naturally occurring order. Referring to Table 8.2, the instructor begins by teaching Step 1; after it has been achieved using predetermined criteria, Step 2 is added to Step 1 and so forth until every step has been taught. In a *backward chaining* approach, the instructor completes every step for the learner except for the final step in the chain. The learner is given the opportunity to finish the last step, and reinforcement is delivered. After achieving a preset criterion, the next-to-the last step is added, and the learner must demonstrate both steps to a predetermined criterion. One step at a time is added in reverse order until every step has been learned. A third approach is called *whole-task chaining*. This approach may be particularly useful if there is evidence that the learner can complete some of the steps prior to initiating instruction. In this approach, the learner is given the opportunity to complete each step of the chain independently, but if he or she is unable to do so, a physical prompt is provided.

Shaping and Prompting

Shaping is a process that involves gradually reinforcing more similar approximations of the desired behavior. It may be a useful tool for teaching some self-help skills, such as gradually reinforcing longer streams of urination in the toilet to help a child learn to empty his or her bladder

Table 8.2. A task analysis for putting on socks

Step	5-Step plan	Step	9-Step plan
1	Pick up socks one at a time.	1	Sit on floor with socks near feet.
2	Insert thumbs and pull sock over toes.	2	Pick up one sock.
3	Pull sock over heel.	3	Insert thumbs on each side of sock opening.
4	Pull sock up over ankle.	4	Bend knee and push foot into opening of sock.
5	Repeat with other sock.	5	Grab remaining loose fabric and pull over toes completely.
		6	Insert thumbs on each side of sock opening.
		7	Pull opening of sock over heel.
		8	Pull sock up completely over ankle.
		9	Repeat with other sock.

completely or reinforcing a child for consuming progressively larger portions of a nonpreferred food. However, it is not uncommon that the desired behavior occurs too infrequently (or not at all) to provide enough opportunities for shaping to work. Therefore, the instructor often must rely on *prompting* to occasion the behavior so that it can be reinforced.

There are three basic ways to prompt desired behavior: verbal prompts, modeling, and physical guidance. *Verbal prompts* involve specific instructions (e.g., "Get dressed") to help a child begin or continue a target task. Verbal prompts can also be subtler, such as statements of encouragement ("You are doing a good job; keep going"). Although these kinds of statements may be necessary, they also may be very difficult to fade, and the learner may actually wait for the instructor's words. It is as if the verbal prompts become part of the chain of steps. *Modeling* involves demonstrating the desired behavior as a child observes. It may be effective for learners who can imitate and who have some of the component skills prior to instruction. For example, Matson, Taras, Sevin, Love, and Fridley (1990) used modeling as one component of an approach to teach a variety of self-help skills to three children with autism. *Physical guidance* prompts are often used with children with severe disabilities. Physical guidance may involve the instructor fully guiding a learner or partial prompts such as touching a learner's elbow to encourage picking up a toothbrush.

Although very effective for teaching new skills and maximizing instructional time, prompts present a risk that a learner may become dependent on them and not begin to respond to the most natural and relevant stimuli (Green, 2001). Thus, the instructor must consider the best approach that will minimize the risk of prompt dependence. The first advice is to not introduce prompts at all if they are not necessary for a child to learn. But when prompts are necessary, they should be faded quickly and systematically.

Wolery and Gast (1984) described four procedures for fading supplementary prompts after a skill is learned and transferring stimulus control to natural stimuli: most-to-least prompting, least-to-most prompting, graduated guidance, and time delay. The *most-to-least prompting* approach is probably the most widely used. When most-to-least prompting is applied, the instructor provides physical guidance at the level where a child is likely to correctly perform the task. Across trials or sessions, the instructor slowly reduces the amount of help as a child begins to independently perform a task (e.g., reducing the amount of effort needed to guide a child). The key is to fade slowly enough that the child makes very few errors. This approach is particularly useful for learners who have few or none of the component skills and with tasks that have a series of discrete responses (e.g., toothbrushing, dressing).

In a *least-to-most prompting* strategy, the instructor begins by giving a learner an opportunity to perform a task with a natural stimulus. Prompts are then added, if needed, from less to more assistance until a learner responds. The key is to try and use prompts that are most similar to the natural cue or direct an individual to observe a natural cue (e.g., an alarm clock signaling that it is time to get up and get dressed; food and a fork to signal eating using utensils).

Another prompting strategy is *graduated guidance* (Foxx & Azrin, 1973). With graduated guidance, the physical assistance that a trainer provides is continuously adjusted, depending on a child's performance. Assistance can be faded by applying less pressure or by fading the position or the type of prompt (e.g., moving from a learner's hand to his or her elbow). Unlike the most-to-least strategy, a child is allowed to perform the steps independently almost from the very beginning.

The *time delay* procedure is an approach in which the prompt is gradually and systematically delayed after the natural stimulus is presented. In a progressive time delay procedure, the amount of time between presenting the natural stimuli and the prompt is increased in very short increments (usually 1 second) across trials. For example, an instructor may present a tissue as a natural stimulus to wipe one's nose before presenting either a verbal or a physical prompt. A second type of time delay is called a constant time delay procedure. In this approach, the prompt is delayed for a specific number of seconds (e.g., 5 seconds) after the natural stimulus is presented but before a prompt is provided. There are very few examples in the literature of the use of time delay to teach ADLs (Snell, 1982).

Other Stimulus Transfer and Prompt-Fading Strategies

A variety of creative visual and tactile strategies have been employed to minimize dependence on adults and maximize the strengths of children with autism. For example, pictures, activity schedules, and videotape have all been reported as useful strategies. Quill (2000) argued that visually cued instruction may compensate for a child's difficulty with responding to social and language information and uses a child's strength in visual processing. Visually cued instruction in the form of activity schedules (MacDuff, Krantz, & McClannahan, 1993; McClannahan and Krantz, 1999) and video modeling (Charlop-Christy, Le, & Freeman, 2000) has been used to teach a variety of skills and holds great promise for teaching self-help skills, although it is largely untested. In one study, Pierce and Schreibman (1994) taught a variety of ADLs to children with autism with pictures to show the individual steps. The results indicated that the children successfully increased engagement in ADLs and that inappropriate behavior decreased. Tactile prompts, such as using a beeper's vibrating function, have also been used to cue learners to respond without an adult verbal or physical prompt (Taylor & Levin, 1998).

Reinforcement

Although studies indicate the use of reinforcement (e.g., praise, edibles) to teach skills, the precise manner in which reinforcement is delivered is not described in much detail (Matson et al., 1990; Richman, Reiss, Bauman, & Bailey, 1984). Forward, backward, and whole-task chain procedures involve a fairly complex system of using and fading reinforcement. For example, the delivery of edible or other tangible reinforcement for individual steps can be disruptive to the flow of the steps, yet waiting until the end could result in a child's failure to connect the receipt of a reinforcement with the demonstration of a step much earlier in the chain. This problem can be reduced by delivering praise after each successfully completed step (less likely to disrupt the flow) and then providing the tangible reinforcement (e.g., hugs, food) after every step is completed. The instructor must quickly begin to fade praise to reduce the risk of a child becoming dependent on feedback after each step. At this point, relevant research provides very little guidance on the best ways to use and fade reinforcement when teaching self-help skills.

Generalization Strategies

The ability to generalize is often stated as a problem for children with autism (Lovaas & Schreibman, 1971; National Research Council, 2001). A skill may be learned in one very specific set of conditions, but a child may then fail to generalize across stimuli different from those present during instruction (e.g., the materials, people, setting). During instruction, some teachers impose conditions that minimize distractions and provide multiple opportunities for learning. This simplification of the context appears to help some children learn, but it may restrict the degree of generalization to the natural context. The challenge is to balance the need for simplification with the requirement to help a child generalize.

Across many years, a technology for encouraging greater generalization without having to directly teach everything the child should know has emerged (Stokes & Baer, 1977, Stokes & Osnes, 1988). Baer (1999) indicated that the first step is to clearly identify what is to be learned and where, when, and how it will be used. For example, a child who is learning to wash his or her hands must learn to use a variety of faucets (e.g., single lever, separate hot and cold, automated sensor) in a variety of settings (e.g., school, home, community). With this information known, the instructor must plan his or her approach to maximize generalization. Some specific strategies for enhancing generalization include teaching in the most natural context whenever possible, using common physical stimuli in both the training and the natural context, teaching lots of examples of the concepts to be learned, reinforcing unprompted generalizations, and fading extrinsic reinforcement. (See Stokes & Osnes, 1988, for a complete description of methods.) The point to be emphasized is that ensuring generalization must be a thoughtful, planned, and active process.

Stokes, Cameron, Dorsey, and Fleming (2004) provided one example of actively programming for generalization to teach self-help skills. Using chaining and task analysis methods, three adults with intellectual disabilities (one also was diagnosed with autism) were taught to wipe themselves after a bowel movement. After the skill was learned, the researchers identified the environments where the skill would be performed (e.g., family home, vocational setting, two community settings) and the stimulus conditions that the participants would need to respond to (e.g., various toilet paper dispensers). Each individual was given a single training session under each condition. Follow-up data indicated that the skills were generalized and maintained in a 9-month period.

TEACHING BASIC SKILLS FOR ACTIVITIES FOR DAILY LIVING

Teaching basic dressing, bathing, eating, and personal hygiene skills closely aligns with the instructional strategies discussed thus far (e.g., stimulus control, chaining, task analysis). Complex skills (e.g., getting ready for school) are broken into smaller sets of skills (e.g., dressing, toothbrushing) that are broken into even smaller units for instruction (e.g., putting on underwear). Many studies of teaching self-help skills were done in the 1970s and 1980s involving individuals with intellectual disabilities (although some of these studies included individuals with autism). Surprisingly, very few studies have been reported in the last 15 years. Although learning to independently dress, bathe, and engage in other personal hygiene activities is important, the professional literature provides limited guidance on how to teach specific skills. Table 8.3 is a summary of self-help skills that have been successfully taught, as reported in the literature. In each study, an intervention package that included a task analysis with chaining, shaping, prompting, and reinforcement procedures was employed. Unfortunately, the literature tells us very little about which specific elements of each package were important (cf. Walls, Crist, Sienicki, & Grant, 1981), and very few studies have addressed the issue of generalization and maintenance (cf. Matson et al., 1990; Richman et al., 1984; Stokes et al., 2004).

The Special Case of Eating Disorders

Food selectivity and/or refusal are fairly common among children with developmental disabilities, including autism. Individuals who present with these behaviors have a higher risk of malnutrition and associated health problems. Fortunately, there is a strong body of literature relevant to these concerns. For example, the *Journal of Applied Behavior Analysis* has published

Table 8.3. Examples of self-help skills taught and reported in the literature

Research team(s)	Self-help skill target
O'Brien and Azrin (1972)	Eating with a spoon
Horner and Keilitz (1975); and Kissel, Whitman, and Reid (1983)	Brushing teeth
Azrin, Schaeffer, and Wesolowski (1976); Martin, Kehoe, Bird, Jensen, and Darbyshire (1971); and Pierce and Schreibman (1994)	Dressing
Nutter and Reid (1978)	Clothing selection
Matson, Ollendick, and Adkins (1980)	Mealtime behaviors (e.g., using spoon, chewing, using a napkin)
Kissel, Whitman, and Reid (1983)	Combing hair and washing hands
Richman, Reiss, Bauman, and Bailey (1984)	Menstrual care
Matson, Taras, Sevin, Love, and Fridley (1990)	Tying shoes; brushing teeth; combing hair; drinking; eating with a spoon; and putting on a shirt, pants, and socks
Stokes, Cameron, Dorsey, and Fleming (2004)	Personal hygiene

more than 30 studies addressing food refusal, expulsion, and consumption or packing (holding food in mouth); most of these studies include children.

Successful intensive feeding interventions have been based on various hypotheses that include medical issues, oral and sensory impairments, and learned behaviors. Of course, a thorough medical exam is critical prior to behavioral interventions to rule out a biophysical cause. Piazza et al. (2003) also argued that conducting a functional behavioral assessment prior to intervention is important to better understand the functional characteristics of the behavior and to develop interventions that are highly specific to the identified functions.

One approach to increasing food consumption has been to provide access to preferred foods to a child contingent on consuming nonpreferred foods (Luiselli, Evans, & Boyce, 1985; Riordan, Iwata, Finney, Wohl, & Stanley, 1984). Riordan et al. (1984) provided social praise and access to preferred foods to increase food consumption for three children with eating disorders and used praise, access to toys, and physical guidance to reinforce food consumption in a fourth child. Piazza, Patel, Gulotta, Sevin, and Layer (2003) compared three conditions: positive reinforcement alone, escape extinction procedure alone, and positive reinforcement plus escape extinction in treating four children with feeding disorders. In their study, positive reinforcement alone was insufficient to increase consumption, but when positive reinforcement was combined with escape extinction procedures, benefits were demonstrated.

Two escape extinction procedures that have been reported in the literature are presenting and re-presenting the food and physical guidance. Several studies (Ahearn, Kerwin, Eicher, Shantz, & Swearingin, 1996; Coe et al., 1997; Girolami, Boscoe, & Roscoe, 2007; Sevin, Gulotta, Sierp, Rosica, & Miller, 2002) have shown that presenting and re-presenting food until it is consumed has been an effective approach. In this procedure, the food remains on a spoon positioned at the mouth until a child opens his or her mouth and allows food to be placed inside. If a bite is expelled, the instructor catches the food and re-presents it. If the food is accepted, social praise and access to preferred materials are given. In physical guidance, the food is positioned at the mouth; if a child does not display acceptance, the instructor provides gentle pressure to the jaw until the child opens his or her mouth and accepts the food. If the food is expelled, the food is caught and re-presented (Patel, Piazza, Santana, & Volkert, 2002). Ahearn et al. (1996) demonstrated that both methods work, but physical guidance procedures were associated with fewer behavior problems related to shorter meal durations and were preferred by parents.

Regardless of the approach used, several studies have incorporated methods to gradually increase bolus sizes and add texture (Coe et al. 1997; Gulotta, Piazza, Patel, & Layer, 2005; Munk & Repp, 1994). Patel et al. (2002) investigated the food type and the texture that were hypothesized to affect the expulsions of a 3-year-old child with a feeding disorder. The researchers systematically varied the presence or the absence of meat and the texture of the food. The child was more likely to expel food that included meat, although when meat was presented as a 100% puree, it was consumed. This suggests selectivity by both the type of food and the texture. Munk and Repp (1994) manipulated the type and the texture of food for five individuals with severe intellectual disabilities and feeding disorders. A behavioral assessment indicated that the feeding problems fell into one of four categories: total refusal, type of food selectivity, texture selectivity, or both type and texture selectivity.

Toileting Training

Independent toileting is one of the most important skills associated with an individual's opportunity for full community integration. However, it may be a challenging skill to teach because complete independence is possible only if a child understands the connection between a physical feeling of a full bladder or a bowel and the need to use the toilet. It has been reported that children typically learn to toilet around the age of 30 months to 3 years old; by age 5, nearly 85% of children have complete bladder and bowel control (Latham, 1990). Dalrymple and Ruble (1992) surveyed 100 parents of people with autism with a mean age of 19.5 years. The results indicated that lower cognitive and language levels were correlated with the age of achieving bowel and urine control. The study also indicated that individuals in their sample took, on average, an additional 1.6 years to achieve urine control and 2.1 years to be fully bowel trained.

Many parenting books (cf. Eisenberg, Murkoff, & Hathaway, 1994) recommend an approach for children who are typically developing that relies heavily on a child's strong motivation to be more independent. Toileting begins when a child initiates some actions on his or her own (e.g., spontaneously sits on the toilet). After a child has shown some interest or readiness, a parent encourages the child to use the toilet when he or she shows signs that he or she should go to the bathroom. When a child successfully uses the toilet, the parents praise their child, and eventually the child begins to communicate his or her need to use the bathroom. Although some children with autism may learn this way, the approach assumes that a child is interested, highly motivated, and eager to please parents and teachers. But this depiction does not correctly describe most children with autism. As a result, toilet training for children with autism typically involves a planned, highly structured approach that includes a consideration of the child's readiness, data collection and analysis, and a highly systematic approach to instruction.

Readiness and Data Collection

Manuals and textbooks relevant to teaching children with disabilities typically refer to age (at least 2 years) and a consistent pattern of elimination (bowel and urine) as an indication of the readiness for toilet training (Baker et al.,1997; Farlow & Snell, 2006). Based on their survey findings, Dalrymple and Ruble (1992) suggested waiting until children with ASDs are 4 years old to begin urine training and 4.5 years old to begin bowel training. Determining a consistent pattern of toileting (a sign of physical readiness) is determined by carefully collecting data on the frequency and the time of the day of the urine or bowel elimination. These data also serve as a baseline against which a child's progress can be evaluated during training. Most professionals suggest about a 2-week assessment period (e.g., Blacher et al., 1997).

Schedule Training

There are two systematic methods for conducting toilet training: schedule training and intensive training. Schedule training consists of scheduled opportunities for toileting based on an assessment of a child's elimination patterns, dry-pants inspections (Foxx & Azrin, 1973), reinforcement when a child eliminates in the toilet, and gradually extending the length of time between scheduled opportunities for toileting. Once a child is toileting consistently on a schedule, the instructor looks for subtle signs that a child needs to use the toilet (e.g., physical signs of discomfort) and prompts the child to use the toilet. Prompts are gradually faded, and the child is encouraged to use words, pictures, or signs to communicate the need to toilet. Gradually, the instructor fades the prompts to use the toilet and help the child complete the bathroom routine (e.g., fading prompts for clothing, sitting, flushing). Variations on schedule training may occur and include increasing fluids, providing a consequence for accidents, and using a device that signals that an accident has occurred. It is typically recommended that children do not wear diapers during schedule training because of evidence that links diapers with an increase in accidents (Tarbox, Williams, & Friman, 2004). For some children with autism, schedule training may be helpful but will not result in a consistent use of the toilet without accidents. Therefore, a more intensive approach has been suggested for these individuals.

Intensive Training Programs

Azrin and Foxx (1971) and Foxx and Azrin (1973) described toilet training procedures that used a dedicated time and place for training, a frequent schedule of opportunities for toileting (every 30 minutes), increased fluid intake, dry-pants inspections, detecting eliminations with a signaling device, the systematic use of graduated guidance and prompt fading, and positive reinforcement of correct toileting. Verbal reprimands for accidents, overcorrection, and positive practice procedures were also incorporated. With some variations, this approach has been the standard for intensive training since Azrin and Foxx's pioneering work. Modifications of the Foxx and Azrin approach have typically involved changes to the manner in which accidents are corrected (Cicero & Pfadt, 2002; Smith, 1979). When an accident occurred, Foxx and Azrin (1973) described using a brief cleanliness training procedure (later expanded to full cleanliness training) that involved a verbal reprimand ("No, you wet your pants") and requiring that a learner clean up traces of urine on the floor and/or the chair. It also included a positive practice component that involved a learner walking rapidly to the toilet, lowering his or her pants, sitting on the toilet for a few seconds, rising, pulling up his or her pants, and repeating this procedure several times. Cicero and Pfadt (2002) successfully toilet trained three individuals with autism using a modified correction procedure. As soon as the instructor noticed the start of an accident, he or she immediately approached the learner and delivered a statement to startle the learner and stop the flow of urine. Simultaneous with this verbalization, the learner was prompted to the toilet and encouraged to reinitiate the urine flow. If the urine flow was reinitiated, the learner was reinforced with praise and a tangible reinforcement.

Signal-Detection Devices

Several studies have demonstrated the benefits of using a signal-detection device in the toilet or in a child's underpants (Azrin & Foxx, 1971; Azrin, Bugle, & O'Brien, 1971; Vermandel, Weyler, Wachter, & Wyndaele, 2008). The device gives an auditory signal when it detects small amounts of moisture. The signal helps a child recognize the flow of urine or bowel and signals the adult to quickly help the learner to the toilet.

SUMMARY

With the increasing emphasis on community integration for individuals with autism, it is becoming more important that parents and teachers focus on skills that promote personal independence. Developing independence in the completion of ADLs, including self-help, is particularly important for improving the quality of life for individuals with autism and is the responsibility of parents, school personnel, and caregivers. The Individuals with Disabilities Education Improvement Act (U.S. Department of Education, 2004) mandates that all children with disabilities receive a coordinated set of transition services that includes, when appropriate, the acquisition of daily living skills.

Research in EIBI shows considerable promise for helping many children with autism to integrate into mainstream school and community settings with few or no supplemental supports. But there are many other children who continue to demonstrate significant delays even as they enter adulthood. The good news is that there is a body of studies demonstrating the benefits of applying ABA principles (e.g., shaping, task analysis, chaining, reinforcement) to teach a broad range of adaptive skills.

LIMITATIONS AND FUTURE RESEARCH

Despite the significant research base, many questions remain unanswered relevant to the development of ADLs in individuals with autism. First, there are inconsistent reports regarding the development of ADLs in children with autism when compared with children without autism who have developmental disabilities. Although the majority of studies suggest that children with autism show a unique developmental profile, a few studies show little or no difference in the area of ADLs. A better understanding of the developmental profile of children with autism, including considering variables such as cognitive and social functioning, may help to develop more successful strategies for instruction that consider the strengths and the weaknesses associated with the disorder. For example, is it important to assess and teach core readiness skills (e.g., imitation and instruction following) prior to intervention? Will interventions that minimize an instructor's use of language by using pictures, video modeling, or activity schedules be more effective?

Most of the research conducted in the area of instruction has been done using within-subject designs. Future research should include randomized control group designs (or comparison wait-list groups) to demonstrate the benefits of intervention and compare various approaches to instruction (e.g., stimulus transfer procedures). Similar studies are needed for evaluating toilet training procedures and the methods to increase food consumption and variety. This line of research would also allow a long-term assessment of intervention effects on such outcomes as placement and the cost of care (cf. Jacobson, Mulick, & Green, 1998). A positive cost-benefit analysis could have a significant influence on funding for additional research, model demonstration projects, and evidence-based practice.

The literature provides a wide range of methods to teach self-help skills but offers very little specificity as to which method or combination of methods works best for which children. Stimulus transfer procedures, shaping, reinforcement, and prompting are described in various intervention packages, but there is little or no evaluation of the individual components. The applied literature has not addressed issues such as what stimulus control and prompting strategies are most effective (e.g., graduated guidance, most to least); practitioners do not know much about the precision of reinforcement delivery and error correction. In addition, evaluating outcomes based on factors such as cognitive functioning, communication, sensory, and behavioral issues would help to differentiate what methods work best with which learner developmental profile. Finally, given the huge emphasis on community integration, future research needs to document the generalized benefits of instruction in ADLs and identify effective strategies for ensuring generalization and maintenance.

REFERENCES

Ahearn, W.H., Kerwin, M.E., Eicher, P.S., Shantz, J., & Swearingin, W. (1996). An alternating treatments comparison of two intensive interventions for food refusal. *Journal of Applied Behavior Analysis, 29,* 321–332.

Alberto, P.A., & Troutman, A.C. (2009). *Applied behavior analysis for teachers* (7th ed.). Upper Saddle River, NJ: Prentice Hall.

American Association on Mental Retardation. (2002). *Mental retardation: Definition, classification and systems of support* (10th ed.). Washington, DC: Author.

American Psychiatric Association. (1994). *Diagnostic and statistical manual of mental disorders* (4th ed.). Washington, DC: Author.

Anderson, S.R., Avery, D.L., DiPietro, E.K., Edwards, G.L., and Christian, W.P. (1987). Intensive home-based early intervention with autistic children. *Education and Treatment of Children, 10,* 352–366.

Anderson, S.R., Jablonski, A.L., Thomeer, M.L., & Madaus Knapp, V. (2007). *Self-help skills for people with autism: A systematic teaching approach.* Bethesda, MD: Woodbine House.

Azrin, N.H., Bugle, C., & O'Brien, F. (1971). Behavioral engineering: Two apparatuses for toilet training retarded children. *Journal of Applied Behavior Analysis, 4,* 249–253.

Azrin, N.H., & Foxx, R.M. (1971). A rapid method of toilet training the institutionalized retarded. *Journal of Applied Behavior Analysis, 4,* 89–99.

Azrin, N.H., Schaeffer, R.M., & Wesolowski, M.D. (1976). A rapid method of teaching profoundly retarded persons to dress. *Mental Retardation, 14,* 29–33.

Baer, D.M. (1999). *How to plan for generalization.* Austin, TX: PRO-ED.

Baker, B.L., & Brightman, A.J. with Blacher, J.B., Heifetz, L.J., Hinshaw, S.P., & Murphy, D.M. (1997). *Steps to independence: Teaching everyday skills to children with special needs* (3rd ed.). Baltimore, MD: Paul H. Brookes Publishing Co.

Birnbrauer, J.S., & Leach, D.J. (1993). The Murdock early intervention program after 2 years. *Behaviour Change, 10,* 63–74.

Bloom, L. & Tinker, E. (2001). The intentionality model and language acquisition: Engagement, effort, and the essential tension. *Monographs of the Society for Research in Child Development, 66* (4, Serial No. 267).

Bruininks, R.H., Woodcock, R.W., Weatherman, R.R., & Hill, B.K. (1996). *Scales of Independent Behavior—Revised (SIB-R).* Rolling Meadows, IL: Riverside Publishing.

Burack, J.A., & Volkmar, F.R. (1992). Development of low- and high-functioning autistic children. *Journal of Child Psychology and Psychiatry, 33,* 607–616.

Carter, A.S., Gillham, J.E., Sparrow, S.S., & Volkmar, F.R. (1996). Adaptive behavior in autism. *Mental Retardation, 5,* 945–960.

Charlop-Christy, M.H., Le, L., & Freeman, K.A. (2000). A comparison of video modeling with in vivo modeling for teaching children with autism. *Journal of Autism and Developmental Disabilities, 30,* 537–552.

Cicero, F.R., & Pfadt, A. (2002). Investigation of a reinforcement-based toilet training procedure for children with autism. *Research in Developmental Disabilities, 23,* 319–331.

Coe, D.A., Babbitt, R.L., Williams, K.E., Hajimihalis, C., Snyder, A.M., Ballard, C., & Efron, L.A. (1997). Use of extinction and reinforcement to increase food consumption and reduce expulsion. *Journal of Applied Behavior Analysis, 30,* 581–583.

Cooper, J.O., Heron, T.E., & Heward, W.L. (2007). *Applied behavior analysis* (2nd ed.). Upper Saddle River, NJ: Merrill Prentice Hall.

Coster, W., Deeney, T., Haltiwanger, J., & Haley, S. (1998). *School Function Assessment.* San Antonio, TX: The Psychological Corporation.

Dalrymple, N.J., & Ruble, L.A. (1992). Toilet training and behaviors of people with autism: Parent views. *Journal of Autism and Developmental Disorders, 22,* 265–275.

Dyer, K., Santarcangelo, S., & Luce, S.C. (1987). Developmental influences in teaching language forms to individuals with developmental disabilities. *Journal of Speech and Hearing Disorders, 42,* 335–347.

Eisenberg, A., Murkoff, H.E., & Hathaway, S.E. (1994). *What to expect in the toddler years.* New York, NY: Workman Publishing.

Farlow, L.J., & Snell, M.E. (2006). Teaching self-care skills. In M.E. Snell & F. Brown (Eds.), *Instruction for students with severe disabilities* (6th ed.). Upper Saddle River, NJ: Pearson.

Felce, D., & Emerson, E. (2001). Living with support in a home in the community: Predictors of behavioral development and household and community activity. *Mental Retardation and Developmental Disabilities Research Reviews, 7,* 75–83.

Foxx, R.M., & Azrin, N.H. (1973). *Toilet training persons with developmental disabilities: A rapid program for day and nighttime independent toileting.* Harrisburg, PA: Help Services Press.

Gillham, J.E., Carter, A.S., Volkmar, F.R., & Sparrow, S.S. (2000). Toward a developmental operational definition of autism. *Journal of Autism and Developmental Disorders, 30,* 269–278.

Girolami, P.A., Boscoe, J.H., & Roscoe, N. (2007). Decreasing expulsions by a child with a feeding disorder: Using a brush to present and represent food. *Journal of Applied Behavior Analysis, 40,* 749–753.

Green, G. (1996). Early behavioral intervention for autism. In C. Maurice, G. Green, S. Luce (Eds.), *Behavioral intervention for young children with autism* (pp. 29–44). Austin, TX: PRO-ED.

Green, G. (2001). Behavior analytic instruction for learners with autism: Advances in stimulus control technology. *Focus on Autism and Other Developmental Disabilities, 16,* 72–85.

Gulotta, C.S., Piazza, C.C., Patel, M.R., & Layer, S.A. (2005). Using food redistribution to reduce packing in children with severe food refusal. *Journal of Applied Behavior Analysis, 38,* 39–50.

Haley, S.M., Coster, W.J., Ludlow, L.H., Haltiwanger, J.T., & Andrellos, P. (1998). *Pediatric Evaluation of Disability Inventory.* Boston, MA: Boston University Center for Rehabilitation Effectiveness.

Harrison, P.L., & Oakland, T. (2003). Adaptive behavior assessment system (2nd ed.). San Antonio, TX: The Psychological Corporation.

Heward, W.L. (2009). *Exceptional children: An introduction to special education* (9th ed.). Upper Saddle River, NJ: Pearson Education.

Horner, R.D., & Keilitz, I. (1975). Training mentally retarded adolescents to brush their teeth. *Journal of Applied Behavior Analysis, 8,* 301–309.

Howard, J.S., Sparkman, C.R., Cohen, H.G., Green, G., & Stanislaw, H. (2005). A comparison of intensive behavior analytic and eclectic treatments for young children with autism. *Research in Developmental Disabilities, 26,* 359–383.

Jacobson, J.W., & Ackerman, L.J. (1990). Differences in adaptive functioning among people with autism or mental retardation. *Journal of Autism and Developmental Disorders, 20,* 205–219.

Jacobson, J.W., Mulick, J.A., & Green, G. (1998). Cost-benefit estimates for early intensive behavioral intervention for young children with autism: General model and single state case. *Behavioral Interventions, 13,* 201–226.

Klin, A., Saulner, C., Tsatsanis, K., & Volkmar, F.R. (2005). Clinical evaluation in autism spectrum disorders: Psychological assessment within a transdisciplinary framework. In F.R. Volkmar, P. Rhea, A. Klin, & D. Cohen (Eds.), *Handbook of autism and pervasive developmental disorders (Vol. 2): Assessment, interventions and policy* (pp. 772–798). Hoboken, NJ: Wiley.

Lambert, N., Nihira, K., & Leland, H. (1993). *AAMR Adaptive Behavior Scales* (2nd ed.). Los Angeles, CA: Western Psychological Services.

Latham, G.I. (1990). *The power of positive parenting.* North Logan, UT: P&T Ink.

Lee, H.J., & Park, H.R. (2007). An integrated literature review on the adaptive behavior of individuals with Aspergers syndrome. *Remedial and Special Education, 28,* 132–139.

Lifter, K., Sulzer-Azaroff, B., Anderson, S.R., & Cowdery, G.E. (1993). Teaching play activities to preschool children with disabilities: The importance of developmental considerations. *Journal of Early Intervention, 17,* 139–159.

Lord, C., Rutter, M., DiLavore, P., & Risi, S. (2003). *Autism diagnostic observation schedule.* Los Angeles, CA: Western Psychological Services.

Lovaas, O.I. (1987). Behavioral treatment and normal educational and intellectual functioning in young autistic children. *Journal of Clinical and Consulting Psychology, 55,* 3–9.

Lovaas, O.I., & Schreibman, L. (1971). Stimulus overselectivity of autistic children in a two stimulus situation. *Behavior Research and Therapy, 9,* 305–310.

Loveland, K.A., & Kelley, M.L. (1991). Development of adaptive behavior in preschoolers with autism or Down syndrome. *American Journal on Mental Retardation, 96,* 13–20.

Luiselli, J.K., Evans, T.P., & Boyce, D.A. (1985). Contingency management of food selectivity and oppositional eating in a multiply handicapped child. *Journal of Clinical Child Psychology, 14,* 153 -156.

MacDuff, G.S., Krantz, P.J., & McClannahan, L.E. (1993). Teaching children with autism to use photographic activity schedules: Maintenance and generalization of complex response chains. *Journal of Applied Behavior Analysis, 26,* 89–97.

Martin, G.L., Kehoe, B., Bird, E., Jensen, V., & Darbyshire, M. (1971). Operant conditioning in dressing behavior of severely retarded girls. *Mental Retardation, 9,* 27–31.

Matson, J.L., Mayville, E.A., Lott, J.D., Bielecki, J., & Logan, R. (2003). A comparison of social and adaptive functioning in persons with psychosis, autism and severe or profound mental retardation. *Journal of Developmental and Physical Disabilities, 15,* 57–65.

Matson, J.L., Taras, M.E., Sevin, J.A., Love, S.R., & Fridley, D. (1990). Teaching self-help skills to autistic and mentally retarded children. *Research in Developmental Disabilities, 11,* 361–378.

McClannahan, L., & Krantz, P. (1999). *Activity schedules for children with autism: Teaching independent behavior.* Bethesda, MD: Woodbine House.

Munk, D.D., & Repp, A.C. (1994). Behavioral assessment of feeding problems of individuals with severe disabilities. *Journal of Applied Behavior Analysis, 27,* 241–250.

National Research Council (2001). *Educating children with autism.* National Research Council: Washington, D.C.

Nutter, N.A., & Reid, D.H. (1978). Teaching retarded woman a clothing selection skill using community norms. *Journal of Applied Behavior Analysis, 11,* 475–487.

O'Brien, F., & Azrin, N.H. (1972). Developing proper mealtime behaviors of the institutionalized retarded. *Journal of Applied Behavior Analysis, 5,* 389–399.

O'Moore, M. (1978). Living with autism. *The Irish Journal of Psychology, 1*, 33–52.

Patel, M.R., Piazza, C.C., Santana, C.M., & Volkert, V.M. (2002). An evaluation of food type and texture in the treatment of a feeding problem. *Journal of Applied Behavior Analysis, 35*, 183–186.

Piazza, C.C., Fisher, W.W., Brown, K.A., Shore, B.A., Patel, M.R., Katz, R.M.,… Blakely-Smith, A. (2003). Functional analysis of inappropriate mealtime behaviors, *Journal of Applied Behavior Analysis, 36*, 187–204.

Piazza, C.C., Patel, M.R., Gulotta, C.S., Sevin, B.M., & Layer, S.A. (2003). On the relative contributions of positive reinforcement and escape extinction in the treatment of food refusal. *Journal of Applied Behavior Analysis, 36*, 309–324.

Pierce, K.L., & Schreibman, L. (1994). Teaching daily living skills to children with autism in unsupervised settings through pictorial self-management. *Journal of Applied Behavior Analysis, 27*, 471–481.

Quill, K.A. (2000). *Do-Watch-Listen-Say: Social and communication intervention for children with autism.* Baltimore, MD: Paul H. Brookes Publishing Co.

Remington, B., Hastings, R.P., Kovshoff, H., Espinosa, F.D., Jahr, E., Brown, T., …Ward, N. (2007). Early intensive behavioral intervention: Outcomes for children with autism and their parents after two years. *American Journal of Mental Retardation, 112*, 418–438.

Richman, G.S., Reiss, M.L., Bauman, K.E., & Bailey, J.S. (1984). Teaching menstrual care to mentally retarded women: Acquisition, generalization, and maintenance. *Journal of Applied Behavior Analysis, 17*, 441–451.

Riordan, M.M., Iwata, B., Finney, J.W., Wohl, M.K., & Stanley, A.E. (1984). Behavioral assessment and treatment of chronic food refusal in handicapped children. *Journal of Applied Behavior Analysis, 17*, 327–341.

Rodrique, J.R., Morgan, S.B., & Geffken, G.R. (1991). A comparative evaluation of adaptive behavior in children and adolescents with autism, Down syndrome, and normal development. *Journal of Autism and Developmental Disorders, 21*, 187–196.

Rutter, M., LeCouteur, A., & Lord, C. (2003). *Autism diagnostic interview—Revised.* Los Angeles, CA: Western Psychological Services.

Sallows, G.O., & Graupner, T.D. (2005). Intensive behavioral treatment for children with autism: Four-year outcome and predictions. *American Journal on Mental Retardation, 110*, 417–438.

Sevin, B.M., Gulotta, C.S., Sierp, B.J., Rosica, L.A., & Miller, L.J. (2002). Analysis of response covariation among multiple topographies of food refusal. *Journal of Applied Behavior Analysis, 35*, 65–68.

Smith, P. (1979). A comparison of different methods of toilet training the mentally retarded. *Behavior Research and Therapy, 17*, 33–43.

Smith, T., Eikeseth, S., Klevstrand, M., & Lovaas, O.I. (1997). Intensive behavioral treatment for preschoolers with severe mental retardation and pervasive developmental disorder. *American Journal on Mental Retardation, 102*, 238–249.

Smith, T., Groen A.D., & Wynn, J.W. (2000). Randomized trial of intensive early intervention for children with pervasive developmental disorder. *American Journal on Mental Retardation, 105*, 269–285.

Snell, M.E. (1982). Analysis of time delay procedures in teaching daily living skills to retarded adults. *Analysis and Intervention in Developmental Disabilities, 2*, 139–155.

Snell, M.E., & Brown, F. (2006). *Instruction of students with severe disabilities* (6th ed). Upper Saddle River, NJ: Pearson–Merrill Prentice Hall.

Sparrow, S.S., Balla, D., & Cicchetti, D.V. (2005). *Vineland Adaptive Behavior Scales* (2nd ed.). San Antonio, TX: Pearson Education.

Stokes, J.V., Cameron, M., Dorsey, M.F., & Fleming, E. (2004). Task analysis, correspondence training, and general case instruction for teaching personal hygiene skills. *Behavioral Interventions, 19*, 121–135.

Stokes, T.F., & Baer, D.M. (1977). An implicit technology of generalization. *Journal of Applied Behavior Analysis, 10*, 349–367.

Stokes, T.F., & Osnes, P.G. (1988). The developing applied technology of generalization and maintenance. In R.H. Horner, G. Dunlap, & R.L. Koegel (Eds.), *Generalization and maintenance: Life-style changes in applied settings* (pp. 5–19). Baltimore, MD: Paul H. Brookes Publishing Co.

Tarbox, R.S.F., Williams, W.L., & Friman, P.C. (2004). Extended diaper wearing: Effects on continence in and out of the diaper. *Journal of Applied Behavior Analysis, 37*, 97–100.

Taylor, B.A., & Levin, L. (1998). Teaching a student with autism to make verbal initiations: Effects of a "tactile prompt." *Journal of Applied Behavior Analysis, 31*, 651–654.

Taylor, B.A., & McDonough, K.A. (1996). Selecting teaching programs. In C. Maurice and G. Green, & S.C. Luce (Eds.), *Behavioral intervention for young children with autism: Manual for parents and professionals* (pp. 63–177). Austin, TX: PRO-ED.

U.S. Department of Education. (2004). *Individuals with Disabilities Education Improvement Act.* Washington, DC: Author.

VanMeter, L., Fein, D., Morris, R., Waterhouse, L., & Allen, D. (1997). Delay versus deviance in autistic social behavior. *Journal of Autism and Developmental Disorders, 27*, 557–569.

Varni, J.W., Lovaas, O.I., Koegel, R.L., & Everett, N.L. (1979). An analysis of observational learning in autistic and normal children. *Journal of Abnormal Child Psychology, 7*, 31–43.

Vermandel, A., Weyler, J., Wachter, S.D., Wyndaele, J.J. (2008). Toilet training of healthy young toddlers: A randomized trial between a daytime wetting alarm and timed potty training. *Journal of Developmental and Behavioral Pediatrics, 29*, 191–196.

Vine, X.K.L., & Hamilton, D.I. (2005). Individual characteristics associated with community integration of adults with intellectual disability. *Journal of Intellectual and Developmental Disability, 30*, 171–175.

Walls, R.T., Crist, K., Sienicki, D.A., & Grant, L. (1981). Prompting sequences in teaching independent living skills. *Mental Retardation, 19*, 243–246.

Wolery, M., & Gast, D.L. (1984). Effective and efficient procedures for the transfer of stimulus control. *Topics in Early Childhood Special Education, 4*, 52–77.

Adaptive Behavior in Adolescents and Adults with Autism Spectrum Disorders

Ongoing Research and Future Implications

Peter F. Gerhardt, Jessica Zawacki, and Gloria Satriale

INTRODUCTION

In general, adaptive behavior constitutes those skills and abilities that allow a person to function independently in his or her environment. Adaptive behavior is very important; it has been argued that outcomes for adults with autism spectrum disorders (ASDs) can, in part, be seen as a function of adaptive behavior competencies (Mazefsky, Williams, & Minshew, 2008). Thus, it is not an overstatement to say that adaptive behavior competencies will get people through times of no academic skills better than academic skills will get people through times of no adaptive behavior competencies.

Heward (2005) describes adaptive behavior as being that cohort of skills that allows each individual to meet standards of personal independence as expected for his or her age and social group. Adaptive behavior also refers to the ability of those without disabilities (i.e., neurotypicals) to meet current and future environmental demands. Heward notes that adaptive behavior changes according to a person's cultural expectations and environment. As such, adaptive behavior is, quite simply, everything we do that is not purely academic in nature.

Using this definition, adaptive behavior can be understood as being referenced to normative standards of behavior, but it is also reflective of the individualized demands associated with where a person lives and what a person does or is expected to do. In other words, although a cohort of adaptive skills is common to most individuals across most environments (e.g., dressing), there are various combinations and permutations of these skills that require a degree of individualization (e.g., dressing for a particular climate) or are relevant only to a particular condition (e.g., women do not need to learn to shave their faces, whereas men generally do not need to learn to shave their legs or underarms). In practice, adaptive behavior is a much more complex concept than merely functional skills and represents a difficult yet critical instructional challenge for individuals with ASDs.

Unfortunately, beyond basic functional skills or activities of daily living (ADLs), adaptive behavior has little attention in the ASD literature. This can partly be understood as a function of the diagnostic criteria for ASDs. ASDs are diagnosed via a triad of impairments in the areas of communication and social skills and the presence of idiosyncratic or repetitive behavior (American Psychiatric Association, 2000). Although communication and social skills are established components of adaptive behavior, they might be best understood as necessary but not sufficient conditions for adequate adaptive responding. The second edition of the Vineland Adaptive Behavior Scales (VABS-II; Sparrow, Cicchetti, & Balla, 2005), for example, includes assessments in the areas of gross and fine motor skills; personal, domestic, and community daily-living skills; play/leisure skills; and coping skills, with a secondary assessment of problematic behavior. By attending to only those impairments defined in the diagnostic criteria, an entire repertoire of skills—particularly those required for success beyond the classroom—is seemingly ignored. For adolescents across the spectrum, this omission often represents a significant impediment to life outside the classroom, postgraduation opportunities for employment and community inclusion, and a positive quality of life.

MEASURING ADAPTIVE BEHAVIOR

The measurement systems associated with adaptive behavior provide a valid and a reliable representation of the skills that individuals with ASDs need in the areas of communication, socialization, and independent living. Standardized measures can also be useful as an adjunct in the diagnostic process because they can provide age-referenced information relevant to personal functioning (Kenworthy, Case, Harms, Martin, & Wallace, 2010). The significant advantages in using standardized measures include the ease with which the measures may be completed, observations covering large periods of time, and collected data that directly relate to concrete observable behavior (Kraijer, 2000).

The second edition of the Adaptive Behavior Assessment System (ABAS-II; Harrison & Oakland, 2003) provides a complete assessment of adaptive skills broken down into conceptual, social, and practical behaviors. The ABAS-II is applicable from birth to 89 years of age and addresses the skill areas of communication, community use, functional academics, school/home living, health and safety, leisure, self-care, self-direction, social, and work. The Scales of Independent Behavior (SIB-R; Bruininks, Woodcock, Calherman, & Hill, 1996) address both problem behavior and adaptive behavior across the settings of school, home, employment, and community. VABS-II (Sparrow et al., 2005) includes domains of communication, daily living, motor skills, and socialization with an optional maladaptive behavior index. Although primarily descriptive in nature (i.e., where a person is at a certain point in time), these systems are also useful in identifying impairments in adaptive behavior to develop appropriate and effective interventions.

ADAPTIVE BEHAVIOR AND AUTISM SPECTRUM DISORDERS

Investigating adaptive behavior competencies between individuals with ASDs and age-matched peers with developmental delays (not ASDs), researchers have demonstrated that individuals with ASDs show more and greater impairments than age-matched peers with nonspecific developmental delays (Kenworthy et al., 2010; Rodrigue, Morgan, & Geffken, 1991). Additional research (Kanne et al., 2011) has demonstrated that children with ASDs do not acquire adaptive skills at a rate consistent with their age or cognitive development. In measuring adaptive behavior across time, it appears that regardless of the cognitive level, adaptive functioning either becomes stable or decreases with age (Gabriels, Ivers, Hill, Agnew, & McNeil, 2007; Williams et al., 2006). Individuals with ASDs also have less of an increase in adaptive skills across time (Gabriels et al., 2007).

There appears to be a general consensus in the literature that adaptive behavior impairments are prevalent in ASDs. In fact, research indicates that individuals with ASDs tend to have greater impairments in adaptive behavior compared with other skill areas, including basic communication (Anderson, Oti, Lord, & Welch, 2009; Liss et al., 2001). Although studies vary in the degree of impairment found across adaptive domains, a consistent if unsurprising finding is that the most significant impairments are in the area of social skills (Bolte & Poustka, 2002; Kenworthy et al., 2010; Liss et al., 2001; Rodrigue et al., 1991). This relatively greater impairment in social skills exists even in the framework of overall impaired adaptive functioning (Kenworthy et al., 2010). Across the spectrum, studies vary in the degree of impairment found in the areas of communication and daily living within an overall reduction in adaptive responding. Because adaptive behavior consists of the skills necessary to independently function across environments, it has been linked to positive outcomes for adults with ASDs (Paul et al., 2004). A growing understanding of the central importance of adaptive behavior has recently led both researchers and clinicians to consider adaptive behavior in assessing the ability of individuals to live on their own versus needing parent or professional supervision and care (Liss et al., 2001; Matson, Rivet, Fodstad, Dempsey, & Boisjoli, 2009).

Studies vary drastically in their estimates of the relationship between adaptive behavior and cognition (IQ), ranging from a near perfect relationship to no relationship (Reschly, Myers, & Hartel, 2002). Collective sample research suggests that individuals with ASDs, on average, show higher general cognitive functioning than overall adaptive behavior level. In subdividing individuals as being either higher functioning (i.e., IQ > 70) or lower functioning (i.e., IQ < 70), the adaptive behavior level and general cognitive functioning differ in a much greater magnitude for those who are higher functioning than for those who are lower functioning (Bolte & Poustka, 2002). In other words, for individuals with a comorbid intellectual disability, adaptive responding is similarly affected. For individuals without such comorbidity, there is greater variability in adaptive responding despite greater intellectual competencies.

The levels of cognitive and adaptive functioning are considered important predictors of outcomes for individuals with ASDs (Bolte & Poustka, 2002). The adaptive behavior level has a strong influence over lifestyle outcomes, and those with more severe disabilities lead more restricted lives (Felce, Perry, Lowe, & Jones, 2011). The daily-living skills domain of adaptive behavior is most closely related to better outcomes for individuals with autism. The implications of this include devising intervention programs centered on adaptive behavior to promote independence in adulthood (Farley et al., 2009).

ADAPTIVE BEHAVIOR
INTERVENTION WITH OLDER INDIVIDUALS

Not surprisingly, the majority of the studies focusing on teaching adaptive skills typically involve individuals with ASDs who are low functioning (Tsatsanis, Saulnier, Sparrow, & Cicchetti, 2011) due to the intensity of need and the ease with which certain individual skills can be targeted and taught. Skills such as toileting, dressing, feeding, and self-care, to name a few, have been addressed in the literature (Matson, Hattier, & Belva, 2012). However, these studies represent a necessary but overly narrow view of adaptive behavior as a collection of individual skills rather than an integrated repertoire of skills applicable across environments.

There is a move to investigate adaptive behavior in a more context-based and, therefore, more applicable way. For example, Hoch, Taylor, and Rodriguez (2009) taught three adolescents with autism to address being lost by using a cell phone and seeking assistance from a nearby adult. Ghuman, Cataldo, Beck, and Slifer (2004) successfully tested a protocol to instruct individuals with ASDs to independently swallow pills of different sizes, thereby promoting compliance and reducing distress. Pitetti, Rendoff, Grover, and Beets (2007) addressed the issue of weight management by developing a systematic and preferred treadmill walking program for adolescents with severe autism. Green, Reid, Rollyson, and Passante (2005) investigated ways to reduce resistance and indexes of unhappiness in three women with profound multiple disabilities. Although this later study did not focus on autism, it demonstrates that happiness, which is a desirable outcome of adaptive behavior competencies, is a definable, measurable, viable, and important goal.

Significant gaps, however, remain in understanding adaptive behavior interventions for older individuals. As noted by Letso (see Chapter 1), there is little to no research in the critical areas of shaving, menstrual care, street crossing, health care, sexuality, safety, and accessing transportation. In addition, there continues to be a significant need for research in such diverse areas as safe and independent travel training, employment, personal hygiene, public restroom use, college life, aging, leisure, emotional regulation, personal advocacy, and clothes shopping.

COMPONENTS OF EFFECTIVE INTERVENTION

Although research on specific target skills or skill competencies may be limited, a variety of evidence-based interventions may be used to provide adaptive behavior interventions. Among these are using preference assessments to determine effective reinforcement, prompting, task analysis, shaping, chaining, self-monitoring, schedule training, stimulus control procedures, fading, and systematic desensitization. In addition, if the goal of such interventions is the generalized use of a skill in the environment in which its use is intended, numerous instructional parameters must be taken into account, including context inclusive of production, social, and navigation skills; intensity; efficiency; and value.

Adaptive Behavior and Context

In the provision of adaptive behavior interventions, a primary consideration is that instruction must be provided where the behavior is most likely to be displayed. There is ample documentation that individuals with ASDs are not proficient at generalizing skills to new environments or maintaining them across time (Simpson & Otten, 2005). Because the classroom cannot permanently be the primary environment for effective adaptive behavior instruction, instruction must be targeted toward the skills necessary for succeeding in the environments in which the individuals will spend the rest of their lives (e.g., neighborhoods, communities of faith, home, jobs). For example, teaching purchasing or money concepts in the isolated context of a classroom may have little, if any, influence on an individual's ability to use money in exchange for desired goods at the supermarket. Being able to differentiate count by value, although a potentially usable skill, is a significantly different skill from using money to purchase a candy bar. As individuals begin to age out of educational entitlements, specific attention must be given to the context of instruction, whether it is the classroom, the home, or the community. Figure 9.1 illustrates this concept.

Adaptive behavior in context is, unfortunately, a highly complex set of interrelated competencies across at least three domains: production (motor) skills, navigation skills, and social skills. Production skills are those motor skills that actually constitute task completion and are separate from context. Hammering a nail would be a production skill because it is basically the same skill independent of context. Production skills tend to be the most clearly defined skills and usually are the easiest component skills to teach. Navigation skills are those skills that enable an individual to independently respond to environmental cues to initiate skills; shift between tasks; and access community resources, activities, and supports. In the example of hammering a nail, navigation skills might include recognizing the need to hammer, retrieving the correct nail from the bin, hammering in the correct location, and so forth. Navigation skills tend to vary in instructional difficulty from very easy to very difficult as a function of context. Lastly, social skills are those skills that enable a person to navigate the interpersonal environment in a way that is socially acceptable and allows a person to access positive reinforcement while avoiding undesirable consequences. In this example, social skills might include asking for help or more materials, making sure the environment is safe, telling someone the nail has been successfully hammered, or compli-

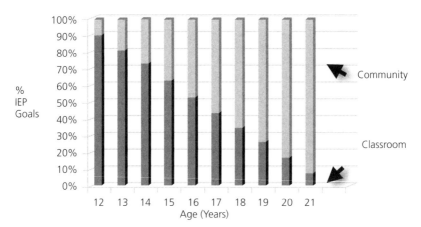

Figure 9.1.   As an individual ages out of his or her educational entitlements, the individualized education program (IEP) needs to reflect this change by shifting from classroom-based (academic) goals to more adaptive community-based goals.

menting coworkers on their nailing prowess. Social skills, almost by definition, tend to be the hardest component skills to teach. Another example of this complexity can be found in Table 9.1.

Adaptive Behavior and Intensity

As students age out of elementary school, there is a tendency for direct instruction to diminish somewhat in the rate of presentation (i.e., intensity). For skill acquisition, individuals with ASDs often require numerous, sometimes repetitive, opportunities to respond (or discrete trials). Unfortunately, the onset of young adolescence in the classroom often brings with it a lessening of instructional intensity that may then be associated with a decreased rate of skill acquisition. As an example, consider a 5-year-old child with ASD who requires 1,000 opportunities to respond (i.e., 50 sets of 20 trials each) to be able to expressively and receptively identify all 64 colors in the crayon box and generalize this new acquired skill across all teachers and all environments. (Note: This is not an extreme number of opportunities because, in fact, 1,000 trials can easily be presented over the course of 1 week if so required.)

Now take the same child at age 15 with the goal of independently buying lunch at a fast-food restaurant. If the child is provided only one trial (i.e., opportunity to respond) per week, (which is typical of most school programs), more than 15 years would be needed to provide this person with the 1,000 trials previously required to learn a relatively simple discrimination skill (color identification). On the other hand, if the instructional intensity was increased so that the person was provided with one opportunity to respond per day, it is reasonable to assume that such desirable skills could be mastered in significantly less time, primarily as a function of the increase

Table 9.1.   Production, social, and navigation skills when using an elevator

Production	Social	Navigation
		Locate elevator
Press correct button	Wait (correct distance)	
	When door opens, wait for others to leave	
		Enter elevator
		Turn around
Press correct button or	Ask for button to be pressed	
		Adopt appropriate distance from others
Monitor floor(s)		
		Exit elevator at correct floor
		Proceed to destination

in instructional intensity. The effective acquisition of adaptive skills may be less a function of individual learning ability than a function of insufficient instructional intensity provided in the natural context.

Adaptive Behavior and Efficiency

Directly related to both skill generalization and maintenance is the response effort, which can be understood as the response efficiency. Response efficiency is the ease (i.e., the amount of effort) with which a task—desirable or not—can be effectively completed. Some simple examples of high-response efficiency versus low-response efficiency in accomplishing a task are presented in Table 9.2.

On a more complex level, response efficiency can be understood as the effort required by an individual to acquire a skill that he or she might not find inherently important, although practitioners consider it important. An example would be cell phone use. There are many ways and reasons to use a cell phone, so consider the following four teaching options:

1. Teaching to initiate calling, dial numbers from memory, or look up numbers in the relevant directory: For a very able individual, this might be a very efficient strategy for normal cell phone use.
2. Teaching to dial by finding a familiar face or icon in the phone's contact directory: This is a simpler strategy, but it may restrict the ability to call new people. For some, however, this might be the most efficient.
3. Teaching to dial by pressing a single face or icon, out of a small number of such faces or icons, on a phone's home screen: This greatly simplified strategy allows phone contact with a few designated individuals only. To some, this may also be the most efficient option.
4. Teaching to simply keep the phone with the person to allow for answering the phone and, as appropriate, monitoring with a global positioning system: This involves fewer options but may be the most efficient option if cell phone use is primarily a community safety skill.

In all four cases, the individual is using a cell phone in a manner in which it is intended. Some individuals with ASDs may see little functional utility in acquiring the skill outlined in Steps 3 and 4, but the high response efficiency associated with each may make them more easily acquired.

Adaptive Behavior and Value

Value simply refers to the extent to which the individual in question finds a skill to be of personal value. For example, absent an awareness of the social prohibition against body odor, instruction in the use of deodorant may have

Table 9.2. High-efficiency versus low-efficiency tasks

Goal	High efficiency	Low efficiency
Cleaning the floor	Using a commercially available duster	Sweeping or mopping
Washing the dishes	Using packets of dishwasher detergent	Measuring, pouring, and then cleaning up spilled dishwasher detergent
Purchasing a preferred item	Using a credit card or a gift card	Using cash
Having an appropriate physical appearance	Purchasing a wrinkle-free shirt	Getting out the iron, ironing board, and ironing
Following a schedule	Using an iPod app	Using a laminated and velcroed picture schedule
Eating healthy foods	Microwaving a healthy meal for dinner	Cooking a healthy meal from scratch for dinner

little value to an individual. However, to the same individual, instruction on how to prepare a tray of brownies may have significant value. Skills that are of great value (i.e., highly preferred skills or skills that have significant functional utility) to an individual tend to be skills that, once acquired, are maintained over time with little additional intervention. Conversely, skills that are of little value generally require significant instructional intensity during both the skill acquisition and maintenance phases. Any effective and appropriate program of intervention must combine both high-value and low-value targets in such a way as to support engagement, competence, maintenance, enjoyment, and personal safety.

DISCUSSION AND RECOMMENDATIONS

Adaptive behavior is a complex and generally interrelated set of skills that allows an individual to successfully live, work, and recreate in his or her community. Adaptive behavior, as an instructional domain, is more complex than many academic subjects taught and requires direct, intense, and systematic instruction if the skills are to be acquired in a timely manner, generalized across environments, and maintained across time. Adaptive behavior is so central to adult life that it would not be an understatement to say that good adaptive behavior skills will get a person through times of no academic skills better than good academic skills will get a person through times of no adaptive behavior. Unfortunately, beyond instruction in a few basic functional skills, adaptive behavior has received little attention in the literature. These skills, with a few notable exceptions, tend to be taught in isolation with little (if any) attention to the complexity of adaptive behavior repertoires in the natural environment. Greater attention to adaptive behavior is important on more than an individual level. More than 85% of adults with autism still live with their siblings, parents, or another relative, and more than 88,000 adults are already on waiting lists for residential housing (Donvan & Zucker, 2010). Assuming that the majority of these individuals lack a functional set of adaptive skills, the burden on parents, relatives, and other caregivers is greater than it might otherwise be.

As the field continues to demonstrate progress toward the goal of providing individuals with ASDs the skills required to live a competent and socially valued adult life, the following recommendations are offered:

- There must be general agreement that an "appropriate" education consists of more than just academic competences or functional skills. An appropriate education is defined as one that, through evidence-based interventions, provides the individual with the greatest potential for success outside the classroom.
- There must be broader recognition as to the complexity of adaptive behavior as an instructional domain for individuals with ASDs. Adaptive behavior as an instructional domain is as complex as, for example, inferential calculus, but it has far greater applicability. As such, adaptive behavior instruction does not represent a lessening of curricular difficulty and complexity when compared with academic instruction.
- Community-based instruction in adaptive skills must be provided with sufficient intensity (i.e., opportunities to respond) to promote skills acquisition in a reasonable amount of time. Community-based instruction must be differentiated from field trips that, in practice, are not considered as significant opportunities for instruction.
- Research must address best practices in developing adaptive behavior skills across the life span. Instructional parameters such as context, intensity, efficiency, and value must be systematically investigated.

REFERENCES

American Psychiatric Association. (2000). *Diagnostic and statistical manual of mental disorders* (4th ed., text rev.). Washington, DC: Author.

Anderson, D.K., Oti, R.S., Lord, C., & Welch, K. (2009). Patterns of growth in adaptive social abilities among children with autism spectrum disorders. *Journal of Abnormal Child Psychology, 37,* 1019–1034.

Bolte, S., & Poustka, F. (2002). The relation between general cognitive level and adaptive behavior domains in individuals with autism with and without co-morbid mental retardation. *Child Psychiatry and Human Development, 33*(2), 165–172.

Bruininks, R., Woodcock, R.W., Calherman, R., & Hill, B. (1996). *Scales of Independent Behavior—Revised.* Park Allen, TX: DLM Teaching Resources.

Donvan, J., & Zucker, C. (2010). Autism's first child. *The Atlantic,* 2–12.

Farley, M.A., McMahon, W.M., Fombonne, E., Jenson, W.R., Miller, J., Gardner, M.,…Coon, H. (2009). Twenty-year outcome for individuals with autism and average or near-average cognitive abilities. *Autism Research, 2*, 109–118.

Felce, D., Perry, J., Lowe, K., & Jones, E. (2011). The impact of autism or severe challenging behaviour on lifestyle outcome in community housing. *Journal of Applied Research in Intellectual Disabilities, 24*, 95–104.

Gabriels, R.L., Ivers, B., Hill, D.E., Agnew, J.A., & McNeil, J. (2007). Stability of adaptive behaviors in middle-school children with autism spectrum disorders. *Research in Autism Spectrum Disorders, 1*, 291–303.

Ghuman, J.K., Cataldo, M.D., Beck, M.H., & Slifer, K.J. (2004). Behavioral training for pill-swallowing difficulties in young children with autistic disorder. *Journal of Child and Adolescent Psychopharmacology, 14*(4), 601–611.

Green, C.W., Reid, D.H., Rollyson, J.H., & Passante, S.C. (2005). An enriched teaching program for reducing resistance and indices of unhappiness among individuals with profound multiple disabilities. *Journal of Applied Behavior Analysis, 38*(2), 221–233.

Harrison, P.L., & Oakland, T. (2003) *Adaptive Behavior Assessment System* (2nd ed.). San Antonio, TX: The Psychological Corporation.

Heward, W.I., (2005). *Exceptional children: An introduction to special education.* Upper Saddle River, NJ: Prentice Hall.

Hoch, H., Taylor, B.A., & Rodriguez, A. (2009). Teaching teenagers with autism to answer cell phones and seek assistance when lost. *Behavior Analysis in Practice, 2*(1), 14–20.

Kanne, S.M., Gerber, A.J., Quirmbach, L.M., Sparrow, S.S., Cicchetti, D.V., & Saulnier, C.A. (2011). The role of adaptive behavior in autism spectrum disorders: Implications for functional outcome. *Journal of Autism and Developmental Disorders, 41*, 1007–1018.

Kenworthy, L., Case, L., Harms, M.B., Martin, A., & Wallace, G.L. (2010). Adaptive behavior ratings correlate with symptomatology and IQ among individuals with high-functioning autism spectrum disorders. *Journal of Autism and Developmental Disorders, 40*, 416–423.

Kraijer, D. (2000). Review of adaptive behavior studies in mentally retarded persons with autism/pervasive developmental disorder. *Journal of Autism and Developmental Disorders, 30*(1), 39–47.

Liss, M., Harel, B., Fein, D., Allen, D., Dunn, M., Feinstein, C.,…Rapin, I. (2001). Predictors and correlates of adaptive functioning in children with developmental disorders. *Journal of Autism and Developmental Disorders, 31*(2), 219–230.

Matson, J.L., Hattier, M.A., & Belva, B. (2012). Treating adaptive living skills of persons with autism using applied behavior analysis: A review. *Research in Autism Spectrum Disorders, 6*(1), 271–276.

Matson, J.L., Rivet, T.T., Fodstad, J.C., Dempsey, T., & Boisjoli, J.A. (2009). Examination of adaptive behavior differences in adults with autism spectrum disorders and intellectual disability. *Research in Developmental Disabilities, 30*, 1317–1325.

Mazefsky, C.A., Williams, D.L., & Minshew, N.J. (2008). Variability in adaptive behavior in autism: Evidence for the importance of family history. *Journal of Abnormal Child Psychology, 36*(4), 591–599.

Paul, R., Miles, S., Cicchetti, D., Sparrow, S., Klin, A., Volkmar, F.,…Booker, S. (2004). Adaptive behavior in autism and pervasive developmental disorder-not otherwise specified: Microanalysis of scores on the Vineland Adaptive Behavior Scales. *Journal of Autism and Developmental Disorders, 34*(2), 223–228.

Pitetti, K.H., Rendoff, A.D., Grover, T., & Beets, M.W. (2007). The efficacy of a 9-month treadmill walking program on the exercise capacity and weight reduction for adolescents with severe autism. *Journal of Autism and Developmental Disorders, 37*(6), 997–1006.

Reschly, D.J., Myers, T.G., & Hartel, C.R. (2002). Mental retardation: Determining eligibility for social security benefits. In D.J. Reschly, T.G. Myers, & C.R. Hartel (Eds.), *Mental retardation: Determining eligibility for social security benefits* (pp. 1–14). Washington, DC: National Academy Press.

Rodrigue, J.R., Morgan, S.B., & Geffken, G.R. (1991). A comparative evaluation of adaptive behavior in children and adolescents with autism, Down syndrome, and normal development. *Journal of Autism and Developmental Disorders, 21*(2), 187–196.

Simpson, R., & Otten, K. (2005). Structuring behavior management strategies and building social competence. In D. Zager (Ed.), *Autism spectrum disorders: Identification, education, and treatment* (3rd ed., pp. 367–394). Mahwah, NJ: Lawrence Erlbaum Associates.

Sparrow, S.S., Cicchetti, D.V., & Balla, D.A., (2005). *Vineland Adaptive Behavior Scales* (2nd ed.). Circle Pines, MN: American Guidance Service.

Tsatsanis, K.D., Saulnier, C., Sparrow, S.S., & Cicchetti, D.V. (2011). The role of adaptive behavior in evidence-based practices for ASD: Translating intervention into functional success. In B. Reichow, P. Doehring, D.V. Cicchetti, & F.R. Volkmar (Eds.), *Evidence-based practices and treatments for children with autism* (pp. 297–308). New York, NY: Springer.

Williams, S.K., Scahill, L., Vitiello, B., Aman, M.G., Arnold, L.E., McDougle, C.J.,…Sparrow, S. (2006). Risperidone and adaptive behavior in children with autism. *American Academy of Child and Adolescent Psychiatry, 45*(4), 431–439.

10

Peer Acceptance, Social Engagement, and Friendship

Critical Social Goals for Children with Autism Spectrum Disorders

Connie Kasari, Jill Locke, Eric Ishijima, and Mark Kretzmann

For the majority of children with an autism spectrum disorder (ASD), friendships are notably absent. Yet having a friend is often their most desired goal. Several studies have highlighted the difficulty of friendship development for children with ASDs. In a follow-up study of children with autism as adults, more than one half of these adults reported no friends or even acquaintances (Howlin, Goode, Hutton, & Rutter, 2004). When parents were asked about their children's friendships, they often reported desired friendships rather than actual ones (Bauminger & Kasari, 2000), and one half of the parents reported no peer relations at all for adolescents and adults with autism (Orsmond, Krauss, & Seltzer, 2004). When children report having a best friend, more than 80% of these friendships in elementary school are not reciprocated (Chamberlain, Kasari, & Rotheram-Fuller, 2007). Finally, school inclusion with typically developing peers has sometimes been associated with more friendships (Bauminger et al., 2008) or making little difference in increasing friendships (Orsmond et al., 2004).

Although this situation appears quite discouraging, it should be noted that nearly one half of children with autism *do have friends* according to previous reports. In longitudinal studies of children with ASDs, there are typically a small number of individuals with good outcomes. For example, Szatmari, Bryson, Boyle, Streiner, and Duku (2003) examined the adult outcomes of 20 individuals with ASDs. Several of these adults were living independently and were successfully employed. More promising, 4 individuals had close relationships, with 1 married and 3 who dated regularly. Similarly, Cederlund, Hagberg, Billstedt, Gillberg, and Gillberg (2008) found that about one fourth of individuals with Asperger syndrome had a close or a long relationship, with a good social outcome. Individuals with classic autism did much worse in terms of optimal outcome, with only 2 out of 70 reporting any friendship relationships. From these data, individuals with Asperger

171

syndrome have a higher probability of being engaged in relationships than individuals with autism, thus highlighting the contribution individual differences can play in relating to others.

Practitioners may be able to learn about facilitating positive outcomes in individuals with ASDs by studying those individuals who have had good outcomes. Unfortunately, to date there are too few studies focused on positive outcomes. More often, studies document factors associated with good outcomes for children who are typically developing and relationship issues that are common for children with ASDs. Considering what researchers know about children with and without ASDs, they examine factors that contribute to an individual's development of positive peer relationships and the ways in which these relationships have been fostered for children with ASDs. These factors include the self-perception of peer relationships by an individual with an ASD, the acceptance by peers in natural settings of the child with an ASD, and general experiences with peers.

FACTORS ASSOCIATED WITH PEER RELATIONSHIPS

Self-Perceptions of Peer Relationships

Children with ASDs range in their understandings of peer relationships, and these understandings change with development. At very young ages, children with ASDs may be less aware of their social position among peers and their feelings about friendships. Chamberlain et al. (2007) found that most 7- to 9-year-old children with or without autism were not lonely at school. These data differ from those in studies of older, high-functioning children who often report more loneliness compared with other children of the same age (Bauminger & Kasari, 2000; Locke, Ishijima, Kasari, & London, 2010; White & Roberson-Nay, 2009), suggesting that there are developmental changes in children's understanding or feelings of loneliness. Loneliness may also be associated with other issues that affect friendship development. White and Roberson-Nay (2009) have found that 7- to 14-year-old children who reported more loneliness also reported higher levels of social anxiety. Although loneliness is a negative feeling, recognizing loneliness in oneself suggests that social desire is present. Moreover, mild levels of loneliness (without high levels of social anxiety) could serve as a motivating factor to seek out friendships.

Although older individuals report not having friends, younger children often identify friendships. In five studies, researchers found that the majority of children with autism could identify their top three friends, including a best friend (Bauminger & Kasari, 2000; Chamberlain et al., 2007; Kasari, Locke, Gulsrud, & Rotheram-Fuller, 2011; Kasari, Rotheram-

Fuller, Locke, & Gulsrud, 2012; Rotheram-Fuller, Kasari, Chamberlain, & Locke, 2010). Researchers also found that children with ASDs older than 9 years of age report more loneliness than their peers, suggesting that the presence of a friend does not lessen the feelings of loneliness (Bauminger & Kasari, 2000). Why does having a good friend not lessen the negative feelings associated with loneliness? Two likely reasons are the possibility that the friendship is not truly reciprocated and/or the friendship is of poor quality.

Reciprocity may be harder to achieve if the friend whom a child with autism selects is a mismatch in terms of similar characteristics or interests. For example, parents reported that the friend chosen by their child with an ASD was unusual, such as being the child's tutor or step-parent (Bauminger & Kasari, 2000). Another reason is that children with autism often report the quality of their friendships as poorer compared with other children of the same age. They often report less companion-ship, security, and helpfulness in their relationships with friends. Quality appears poorer whether comparison children are matched on cognitive ability, gender, and age (Bauminger & Kasari, 2000) or are matched on gender from the same class (Chamberlain et al., 2007). It may be that even though children with ASDs identify a friend, the benefits from the friendship may not be realized because of their own perceptions of that friendship—in terms of the child he or she identifies as a friend and how the child feels about the friendship.

Perceptions also extend to how socially involved children with ASDs see themselves. Again, reports have been conflicting, sometimes report-ing that children with ASDs see themselves as more socially involved than their peers see them (Chamberlain et al., 2007) or less involved than their parents see them (Bauminger & Kasari, 2000). In Bauminger and Kasari, mothers acknowledged that children reported on a desired relationship rather than an actual relationship—for example, "He says that Joe is his best friend, but Joe ignores him most of the time" (2000, p. 451). Mothers also reported that most interactions with friends took place at school, with their children rarely initiating play with their neighbors or asking for play dates (Bauminger & Kasari, 2000).

True reciprocity in friendship relationships can be a challenge for children with ASDs and may relate to the lower quality of friendships that they report. Children with ASDs more often nominate children as top friends who do not reciprocate the friendship nomination; in other words, the nominated child does not see the child with an ASD as one of the nominated child's top friends. In a study of high-functioning children with ASDs in general education classrooms, friendship nominations of children with ASDs were reciprocated about one third of the time compared with the friendship nominations of children who were typically developing that were reciprocated 60% of the time (Chamberlain et al., 2007). These practitioners found very similar findings in a peer relationship study in inclusive classrooms in which the friend nominations of first- to fifth-grade children with ASDs were reciprocated approximately 20% of the time. The children who were typically developing (matched to the child with an ASD on class and gender) received reciprocated nominations approximately 80% of the time (Kasari et al., 2011).

It is possible that the concept of a friend is not well developed in children with ASDs. Lee and Hobson (1998) noted that children are less likely to view themselves in relation to others. Thus, they may less often see themselves as a friend or consider themselves in terms of their relationships with others. These self-perceptions (or lack of self-understandings) likely contribute to their feelings of friendship quality, loneliness, and reciprocity in their relationships with peers.

Peer Acceptance of a Child with an Autism Spectrum Disorder

Peers are not always as accepting of children with ASDs as they are of other children. Swaim and Morgan (2001) showed third- and sixth-grade children video clips of a typically developing 12-year-old boy who in one clip acted normal and in the other acted "autistic." Sometimes the boy was given a label of autism, but other times he was not. Children rated the boy in the video acting "autistic" less favorably regardless of whether they had a label for his behavior. Indeed, an explanation for his behavior did not seem to affect their opinions of the boy.

Actual experiences with children with ASDs may result in more positive views. A study of second- and third-grade children in inclusive classrooms found that children with ASDs were connected to the other children in the class as reported by classmates (Chamberlain et al., 2007). They were not isolated, but they tended to be peripheral to most networks of children in the class. In other words, they were often connected to groups of children by just one or two children. Although not as centrally connected as many children in the class, children with autism were still within the mix of the class. In this study, data on active rejections of children were not collected; thus, it is not known whether these children were more rejected than other children in the class.

Some studies find that children with ASDs are more rejected than other children in their classes (Church, Alisanski, & Amanullah, 2000), and there are qualitative reports that children with ASDs are frequently targeted for harassment or bullying (Humphrey & Lewis, 2008). Future studies should examine the issue of rejection and isolation more closely across time as these issues may surface more with older children or in the context of less cohesive and supportive classrooms.

Peer Experiences

Friendships develop from repeated experiences with peers in which shared interests and mutual caring can develop. Children learn about relationships through both positive and negative interactions. Although too much conflict in peer relationships can cause distress to a child, some conflict is important in helping a child negotiate and share in interactions and learn what acceptable behavior is with peers.

One issue for children with autism is the reduced number of experiences they have with peers, thus limiting the amount of time they are engaged with their peers and the number of opportunities they have to learn from these interactions. Even in the presence of other children, children with autism may not fully benefit from this exposure. On playgrounds filled with children, the child with an ASD may be isolated or playing alone; it is not uncommon to find the child with an ASD running the periphery of the yard. At times, other children may be playing in the same area and even in the same activity, but the child with autism will make few attempts to engage with another child or respond when bids from another child are made to him or her (Sigman & Ruskin, 1999). The children with ASDs appear to distance themselves from interactions and not take advantage of the social opportunities around them. This may explain the finding that children in inclusive settings may not develop friendships despite a great deal of exposure to typically developing children and presumably good social models (Orsmond et al., 2004).

Without direct intervention (some facilitation between children who are typically developing and children with ASDs), the child with an ASD may be just as isolated in an inclusive environment as in any other environment. The chapter now considers solutions for encouraging engagement, peer acceptance, and friendships for children with ASDs.

EMPIRICAL RESEARCH ON
PRACTICES IN SOCIAL SKILLS INTERVENTIONS

Despite the peer interaction difficulties of children with autism, parents prefer mainstreaming and/or inclusion of their children (Kasari, Freeman, Bauminger, & Alkin, 1999). There are some data suggesting that children with ASDs (particularly high-functioning children) are more attracted to interactions with peers who are typically developing (Bauminger, Shulman, & Agam, 2003) and more engaged if these peers are available on the playground (Sigman & Ruskin, 1999). However, inclusion alone appears to have little effect on increased social skills and friendships (Kasari et al., 2011; Orsmond et al., 2004). Some facilitation of peers and the child with an ASD is necessary, but the manner in which interventions are delivered varies. In this section, we consider three common interventions: having a shadow teacher, peer-mediated interventions, and social skills groups.

Classroom Aide or Shadow Teacher

A common adjunctive intervention in inclusion is the assignment of a one-to-one aide or shadow teacher for a child with an ASD. The aide may be assigned to an individual child or the classroom as a whole (Giangreco & Broer, 2005). The role of the shadow teacher varies depending on the child he or she is assigned to, the supervision of the aide, and the classroom culture. Some shadow teachers are responsible for all of the instruction of a child with an ASD; others are directed by the head teacher and may help the entire classroom rather than targeting only the child with an ASD, and still others are directed by outside agencies. There is great variability in how these assistants work. There also are few outcome data for this type of intervention, and some data suggest that the one-to-one aide may not be effective for facilitating better social interactions for children with ASDs (Giangreco & Broer, 2005; Humphrey & Lewis, 2008).

Although the one-to-one aide is often supervised by more experienced individuals, a study of paraprofessionals in the school setting suggested that they make their own instructional decisions about 70% of the time and receive only about 7% of the teacher's time in supervision (Giangreco & Broer, 2005). Nearly one half of these paraprofessionals believe the child they are assigned to sees them as their primary friend. Children themselves question whether the adult who is there to support them marks them in the eyes of their classmates, ultimately interfering with friendship development (Humphrey & Lewis, 2008).

In a 2012 study, researchers compared a one-to-one adult-to-child intervention (target-child intervention) versus a peer-mediated intervention on the social relationships of children with ASDs in inclusive classrooms. Children were randomized to one of these two interventions, a combination of the two, or to the practice-as-usual group (inclusion only). Although the target child intervention was individualized for the needs of the child and carried out by an expert interventionist with close supervision, this short-term targeted intervention yielded no significant differences between the target child condition and practice-as-usual (inclusion) on classmates' acceptance of the child with an ASD (Kasari et al., 2012). Thus, the assignment of an aide for facilitating social interactions should be carefully evaluated. Future researchers may want to examine the effects of various models of aide assignments on the social inclusion of children with ASDs.

Peer-Mediated Interventions

Mainstream classrooms offer an ideal context to use typically developing peers as social models, encouraging the generalization and the maintenance of skills from interventions that are often not achieved when using an adult as the interventionist (Carr & Darcy, 1990; Kamps, Potucek, Lopez, Kravits, & Kemmerer, 1997; Kroger, Schultz, & Newsom, 2007; Roeyers, 1996; Shearer, Kohler, Buchan, & McCullough, 1996). In a 2012 intervention for high-functioning children with ASDs in inclusive classrooms, the target child intervention, in which an adult worked one on one with the child, was no more effective than inclusion alone. In contrast, interventions that taught peers how to engage children on the playground had a positive effect on the whole-class acceptance of children with ASDs (Kasari et al., 2012).

Three early qualitative reviews of the social interaction literature suggest that although peer-mediated interventions appear effective, most have been conducted with preschool-age children with autism in specialized settings, where the approaches were behavioral in nature and involved single-subject designs (Goldstein, 2000; McConnell, 2002; Rogers, 2000). Few researchers have replicated an intervention approach across multiple studies, so only a handful of children may have received any one type of intervention. The findings support positive effects on teaching children who are typically developing to engage with children with ASDs. Children with ASDs improve in responding to others but struggle to spontaneously initiate interactions and/or maintain initiations across time. A general concern is the amount of prompting and oversight that is necessary to maintain these attempts by peers or by the target child.

A goal is to increase the amount of time children are engaged in play routines with their peers without significant support by adults. Adult scaffolding must be used judiciously and then systematically faded as soon as possible. More opportunities to develop shared interests increase the potential for friendship development, not just peer contact. Interventions that focus specifically on authentic engagement between children with ASDs and their classmates are promising but are untested using rigorous designs (i.e., randomized control trials; Wolfberg & Schuler, 1993).

Another promising intervention focuses on facilitated play dates. Play dates usually occur in a child's home or in the community and have the potential for also facilitating friendships (Frankel & Myatt, 2003, 2007; Koegel, Werner, Vismara, & Koegel, 2005). In a single-subject design, Koegel et al. (2005) used contextually supported play-date interactions to help children with ASD become more engaged with their classmates at school. Two children with ASDs were observed at school as isolated on their playgrounds. The researchers intervened with each child, using play dates at home with and without adult support. When the researchers supported the child with autism and his or her playmate from school in activities that were socially motivating to both children, engagement increased; more invitations and friendships developed as time progressed. These data are similar to Wolfberg and Schuler's (1993) data on integrated playgroups at school, in which adult facilitation of motivating social activities between children is set up with systematic fading of the adult to increase engagement and potential friendships.

Play dates at home are easier to implement with young children and are more difficult to arrange for adolescents, especially with the potential stigma of adult support. However, Frankel and colleagues used a parent-mediated friendship development program for high-functioning school-age children and teenagers (Frankel & Myatt, 2003, 2007; Laugeson, Frankel, Mogil, & Dillon, 2009). In this program, parents learn how to help their children host a play date, and children with ASDs learn social manners, especially how to be a good host to increase their number of play-date opportunities. The results indicated significant positive effects for children who received intervention compared with children in the control group. Thus, facilitated play dates with systematic adult support programs may help increase positive peer contact and potential friendships.

Social Skills Groups

A common social skills intervention for children with ASDs is to attend an organized group in which social skills are systematically taught. Group social skills programs are typically implemented outside school settings, such as in clinics with children who do not attend the same schools or programs. The social skills curricula in these programs have familiar elements (e.g., greetings, making eye contact, initiating conversations), but a uniformly accepted set of curricular skills appears to be lacking (Rao, Beidel, & Murray, 2008). Comparing across studies is difficult given the differences in social skills content and outcome measures. Two reviews of social skills programs (Rao et al., 2008; White, Koenig, & Scahill, 2007) noted a particular concern in the lack of tests of generalization. Studies that have tested for generalization find limited effects for group social skills programs. Changes can be made on the particular skills taught within the group setting, but there is little carryover into new settings or with new partners.

There are likely several reasons for this state of affairs. One is that most studies intervene with children in nonschool settings, such as a clinic or a program away from where they will need to practice their social skills (Ozonoff & Miller, 1995; Tse, Strulovitch, Tagalakis, Meng, & Fombonne, 2007). Another is that the skills that are taught may not be the actual skills needed in everyday interactions at school (Bellini, Peters, Benner, & Hopf, 2007). In other words, polite manners (e.g., shaking hands, making eye contact) may be useful when introduced to an adult but may be less typical when trying to enter a game or a conversation on the playground. Few studies target the skills that are specific and idiosyncratic for a particular child (Bellini et al., 2007).

Although skills learned in the social skills group at the clinic may not generalize to school settings, they may benefit friendship development. Friendships are known to develop among individuals who share similar characteristics and have similar interests (Farmer & Farmer, 1996). Thus, the social group context may result in friendships for members of the group. Some issues for future studies to consider are whether effectiveness of the social group context is enhanced by including children from the same school in the mix of the group and whether friendships that may develop as a result of the group can be sustained in a more consistent context, such as school.

EVALUATING THE EFFECTIVENESS
OF SOCIAL SKILLS INTERVENTIONS

Individuals other than those targeted for intervention often evaluate social skills interventions. Thus, a parent or a teacher measures and/or reports on the effects. There are rare reports by the children themselves; depending on who is delivering the interventions, the reporter may or may not be knowledgeable or may be biased in his or her viewpoint. For example, if interventions are delivered by teachers or parents and they are asked to report on children's social skills, they risk being biased in their estimates of change. Similarly, teachers or parents may be asked to report on children's social behavior at school, but neither parents nor teachers may be present on the playground or have knowledge of children's social relationships. In this case, the adults are not informed reporters.

Children can also report on their relationships, although they often are not asked to do so. Several studies have indicated that children with autism identify friends in their classes, although these are less often reciprocated compared with other children in their classes (Chamberlain et al., 2007). They also report more loneliness at older (not younger) ages, and they report poorer quality friendships (Bauminger & Kasari, 2000; Chamberlain et al., 2007). These child-reported measures may be useful outcomes of a social skills intervention. Do children feel less lonely after receiving a social skills intervention? Are friendships reciprocated at higher levels? Is quality improved in friendship relationships after intervention?

Social network methods yield several measures of children's social relationships at school. When children are asked who hangs out with whom on the playground (Cairns & Cairns, 1994), social network maps can be generated that allow a researcher to determine how connected the target child with an ASD is to his or her classmates. This served as the primary outcome measure in the Kasari 2012 randomized controlled intervention trial. As shown in Figure 10.1, E5 is a second-grade child with an ASD who is isolated prior to beginning the intervention (Time 1). No child nominated this child to a group of children, and E5 did not nominate himself or herself to a group. By collecting information from every child in the class, the strength or the centrality of children's networks can be determined. Some children are isolated, others are peripheral to groups (being only minimally connected to one or more children in the class), and some are popular and well connected to a group of children. The child in Figure 10.1 who is isolated at Time 1 becomes connected to a group after a social skills intervention of only 12 sessions. At Time 3, at a 12-week follow-up assessment, the child continues to be connected to a group of children in his or her class. In this case, the intervention appears to have been effective for increasing the child's social connections in class, as reported by the children themselves.

Social network measures yield a great deal of information on all children in the class and can help researchers identify children in need of intervention from the perspective of the peer group. These measures also provide information on how well accepted children are within their class. Using the network measure by Cairns and Cairns (1994), children are asked to list their top three friends and circle their best friend. This information from classmates yields information on reciprocity. If child

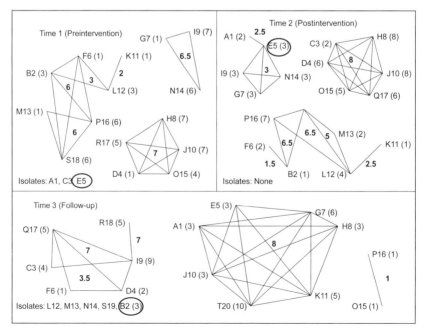

Figure 10.1. Social network centrality. (Key: Letter/Number = Individual student; (Number) = Peer nominations; ———— = Social connections.)

A puts child B down as a top friend, but child B does not put child A down as a top friend, then they do not have friendship reciprocity. Reciprocity is another measure that could improve as the result of an intervention if in fact child A and child B are well suited to be playmates.

SUMMARY AND CONCLUSIONS

There is little evidence that children improve in their social acceptance and involvement in peer relationships without some type of intervention. The typical model is inclusion itself. Although parents prefer inclusion for their children with disabilities, particularly for the potential development of friendships, inclusion alone does not help in this regard (Chamberlain et al., 2007; Kasari et al., 1999; Kasari et al., 2012).

Several factors contribute to children's difficulties with peer relationships. Children with ASDs often have little confidence in their own social abilities. Knott, Dunlop, and Mackay (2006) reported that children with high-functioning autism or Asperger syndrome rate themselves far below their peers in social skills and social competence, such as the ability to develop a close friendship. Even when children do report having a friend (or friends), the quality of these friendships is lower than those of peers, and despite having a friend, children with autism report feeling greater loneliness at school (Bauminger & Kasari, 2000). Others also perceive children to be poorly connected to their classmates. Children with autism are more likely to be peripheral to peer groups in their classrooms and report fewer reciprocal friendships (Chamberlain et al., 2007; Kasari et al., 2011). Finally, children with autism have fewer experiences with peers. Even in the presence of their classmates, they are observed as isolated or uninvolved (Kasari et al., 2011; Kasari et al., 2012).

Social skills interventions have shown some positive outcomes in children's knowledge of social skills, but these tend to be poorly generalized and maintained. Peer- and parent-mediated approaches evidence better child outcomes than social skills groups composed of only children with ASDs and curricula that use a standard discrete skills approach. However, outcome measures do not always yield informative changes. Thus, parents and teachers may either have a biased perspective because they were actively involved in the intervention or be uninformed because they are asked to report on areas they have not observed and have little knowledge about. Rarely have children been asked about their own perspectives. Future studies would benefit from multimodal assessments and multiple informants. The future relies on well-designed studies that dismantle some of the active elements of the interventions.

In addition to scientifically rigorous studies of effects, practitioners also need better understandings of positive outcome cases. Some children are able to achieve positive peer relationships and friendships (Cederlund et al., 2008; Szatmari et al., 2003). Thus, there is an important place for descriptive studies that highlight positive practices and outcomes among individuals with ASDs. Future studies are needed that focus on children's experiences in real-life settings and developmental changes in these experiences.

REFERENCES

Bauminger, N., & Kasari, C. (2000). Loneliness and friendships in high-functioning children with autism. *Child Development, 71,* 447–456.

Bauminger, N., Shulman, C., & Agam, G. (2003). Peer interaction and loneliness in high-functioning children with autism. *Journal of Autism and Developmental Disorders, 33,* 489–507.

Bauminger, N., Solomon, M., Aviezer, A., Heung, K., Gazit, L., Brown, J., & Rogers, S.J. (2008). Children with autism and their friends: A multidimensional study of friendship in high-functioning autism spectrum disorder. *Journal of Abnormal Child Psychology, 36*(2), 135–150.

Bellini, S., Peters, J.K., Benner, L., & Hopf, A. (2007). A meta-analysis of school-based social skills interventions for children with autism spectrum disorders. *Remedial and Special Education, 28,* 153–162.

Cairns, R.B., & Cairns, B.D. (1994). *Lifelines and risks: Pathways of youth in our time.* New York, NY: Cambridge University Press.

Carr, E.G., & Darcy, M. (1990). Setting generality of peer modeling in children with autism. *Journal of Autism and Developmental Disorders, 20,* 45–59.

Cederlund, M., Hagberg, B., Billstedt E., Gillberg, I.C., & Gillberg, C. (2008). Asperger syndrome and autism: A comparative longitudinal follow-up study more than 5 years after original diagnosis. *Journal of Autism and Developmental Disorders, 38,* 72–85.

Chamberlain, B., Kasari, C., & Rotheram-Fuller, E. (2007). Involvement or isolation? The social networks of children with autism in regular classrooms. *Journal of Autism and Developmental Disorders, 37*(2), 230–242.

Church, C., Alisanski, S., & Amanullah, S. (2000). The social, behavioral, and academic experiences of children with Asperger syndrome. *Focus on Autism and Other Developmental Disabilities, 15*(1), 12–20.

Farmer, T.W., & Farmer, E.M.Z. (1996). Social relationships of students with exceptionalities in mainstream classrooms: Social networks and homophily. *Exceptional Children, 62*(5), 431–450.

Frankel, F., & Myatt, R. (2003). *Children's friendship training.* New York, NY: Brunner-Routledge.

Frankel, F., & Myatt, R. (2007). Parent-assisted friendship training for children with autism spectrum disorders: Effects associated with psychotropic medication. *Child Psychiatry and Human Development, 37*(4), 337–346.

Giangreco, M., & Broer, S. (2005). Questionable utilization of paraprofessionals in inclusive schools: Are we addressing symptoms or causes? *Focus on Autism and Other Developmental Disabilities, 20,* 10–25.

Goldstein, H. (2000). *Communication intervention for children with autism: A review of treatment efficacy.* Paper prepared for the Committee on Educational Interventions for Children with Autism, National Research Council, Washington, DC.

Howlin, P., Goode, S., Hutton, J., & Rutter, M. (2004). Adult outcome for children with autism. *Journal of Child Psychology and Psychiatry, 45*, 212–229.

Humphrey, N., & Lewis, S. (2008). Make me normal: The views and experiences of pupils on the autistic spectrum in mainstream secondary schools. *Autism, 12*, 1362–1363.

Kamps, D.M., Potucek, J., Lopez, A., Kravits, T., & Kemmerer, K. (1997). The use of peer networks across multiple settings to improve social interaction for students with autism. *Journal of Behavioral Education, 7*, 335–357.

Kasari, C., Freeman, S., Bauminger, N., & Alkin, M. (1999). Parental perceptions of inclusion: Effects of autism and Down syndrome. *Journal of Autism and Developmental Disorders, 29*, 297–305.

Kasari, C., Locke, J., Gulsrud, A., & Rotheram-Fuller, E. (2011). Social networks and friendships at school: Comparing children with and without autism. *Journal of Autism and Developmental Disorders, 41*, 533–544.

Kasari, C., Rotheram-Fuller, E., Locke, J., & Gulsrud, A. (2012). Making the connection: Randomized controlled trial of social skills at school for children with autism. *Journal of Child Psychology and Psychiatry, 53*(4), 431–439.

Knott, F., Dunlop, A., & Mackay, T. (2006). Living with ASD. *Autism, 10*, 609–617.

Koegel, R.L., Werner, G.A., Vismara, L.A., & Koegel, L.K. (2005). The effectiveness of contextually supported play date interactions between children with autism and typically developing peers. *Research and Practice for Persons with Severe Disabilities, 30*, 93–102.

Kroeger, K.A., Schultz, J.R., & Newsom, C. (2007). A comparison of two group-delivered social skills programs for young children with autism. *Journal of Autism and Developmental Disorders, 37*(5), 808–817.

Laugeson, L., Frankel, F., Mogil, C., & Dillon, A. (2009). Parent-assisted social skills training to improve friendships in teens with autism spectrum disorders. *Journal of Autism and Developmental Disorders, 39*(4), 596–606.

Lee, A., & Hobson, R.P. (1998). On developing self-concepts: A controlled study of children and adolescents with autism. *Journal of Child Psychology and Psychiatry and Applied Disciplines, 39*, 1131–1144.

Locke, J., Ishijima, E., Kasari, C., & London, N. (2010). Loneliness, friendship quality, and the social networks of adolescents with high-functioning autism in an inclusive school setting. *Journal of Research in Special Educational Needs, 10*, 74–81.

McConnell, S.R. (2002). Interventions to facilitate social interaction for young children with autism: Review of available research and recommendations for educational intervention and future research. *Journal of Autism and Developmental Disorders, 32*, 351–372.

Orsmond, G.I., Krauss, M.W., & Seltzer, M.M. (2004). Peer relationships and social and recreational activities among adolescents and adults with autism. *Journal of Autism and Developmental Disorders, 34*(3), 245–256.

Ozonoff, S., & Miller, J.N. (1995). Teaching theory of mind: A new approach to social skills training for individuals with autism. *Journal of Autism and Developmental Disorders, 25*, 415–433.

Rao, P.A., Beidel, D.C., & Murray, M.J. (2008). Social skills interventions for children with Asperger's syndrome or high-functioning autism: A review and recommendations. *Journal of Autism and Developmental Disorders, 38*(2), 353–361.

Roeyers, H. (1996). The influence of nonhandicapped peers on the social interactions of children with a pervasive developmental disorder. *Journal of Autism and Developmental Disorders, 26,* 303–320.

Rogers, S. (2000). Interventions that facilitate socialization in children. *Journal of Autism and Developmental Disorders, 30,* 399–409.

Rotheram-Fuller, E., Kasari, C., Chamberlain, B., & Locke, J. (2010). Grade related changes in the social inclusion of children with autism in general education classrooms. *Journal of Child Psychology and Psychiatry, 51,* 1227–1234.

Shearer, D.D., Kohler, F., Buchan, K., & McCullough, K. (1996). Promoting independent interactions between preschoolers with autism and their nondisabled peers: An analysis of self-monitoring. *Early Education and Development, 7,* 205–220.

Sigman, M., & Ruskin, E. (1999). Continuity and change in the social competence of children with autism, Down syndrome, and developmental delays. *Monographs of the Society for Research in Child Development, 64*(1), v–114.

Swaim, K.F., & Morgan, S.B. (2001). Children's attitudes and behavioral intentions toward a peer with autistic behaviors: Does a brief educational intervention have an effect? *Journal of Autism and Developmental Disorders, 31*(2), 195–205.

Szatmari, P., Bryson, S.E., Boyle, M.H., Streiner, D.L., & Duku, E. (2003). Predictors of outcome among high functioning children with autism and Asperger syndrome. *Journal of Child Psychology and Psychiatry, 44,* 520–528.

Tse, J., Strulovitch, J., Tagalakis, V., Meng, L., & Fombonne, E. (2007). Social skills training for adolescents with Asperger syndrome and high-functioning autism. *Journal of Autism and Developmental Disorders, 37,* 1960–1968.

White, S., Koenig, K., & Scahill, L. (2007). Social skills development in children with autism spectrum disorders: A review of the intervention research. *Journal of Autism and Developmental Disorders, 37*(10), 1858–1868.

White, S., & Roberson-Nay, R. (2009). Anxiety, social deficits, and loneliness in youth with autism spectrum disorders. *Journal of Autism and Developmental Disorders, 39*(7), 1006–1013.

Wolfberg, P.J., & Schuler, A.L. (1993). Integrated play groups: A model for promoting the social and cognitive dimensions of play in children with autism. *Journal of Autism and Developmental Disorders, 23,* 467–489.

Impact of Psychopharmacology on Adaptive and Social Responding in Learners with Autism Spectrum Disorders

Roy Sanders

The use of pharmacologic interventions for autism spectrum disorders (ASDs) is not well researched, although there is a growing body of research related to certain compounds and interventions for specific symptoms or clusters of symptoms (e.g., the studies that have grown out of the Research Units on Pediatric Psychopharmacology [RUPP]). As with all pharmacologic interventions, there are risks and benefits associated with their use. Why would practitioners consider prescribing a pharmacologic agent for a person with an ASD? Practitioners generally do not prescribe a pharmacologic agent because it would somehow "cure" or "fix" the ASD, but pharmacologic agents may be able to help manage some of the maladaptive symptoms associated with ASDs.

By managing maladaptive symptoms, people with an ASD may be able to be more comfortable, be engaged socially as they would like to be, and not be hurtful to themselves or others. Of course, the range of symptoms someone on the spectrum experiences varies greatly, and the kinds of interventions that might be appropriate in one situation would not be appropriate in another.

Pharmacologic interventions might be best considered as a therapeutic tool, and they ultimately allow other, more specific interventions, such as applied behavior analysis (ABA), to have as great an impact as possible in improving the life of an individual with an ASD. An analogy would be crutches, a brace, or a cast that may be used in orthopedic situations that allow for healing to the point that physical therapy can help bring as wide and satisfying a range of rehabilitation as possible.

The symptoms that can sometimes be helped or diminished with pharmacologic interventions include but are not limited to the following: anxiety, irritability, aggression, inattention, hyperactivity, perseveration, sleep disturbance, maladaptive eating behaviors, and problems with mood and rigidity. Craig Erickson and others from the Department of Psychiatry at the Indiana University School of Medicine wrote a very informative review of some of the placebo-controlled studies, looking at the effects of psychopharmacologic intervention in children with some of these symptoms (Erickson et al., 2007).

REVIEW OF RELEVANT RESEARCH

Symptoms of Inattention and Arousal Regulation in Autism Spectrum Disorders

Looking at medications that are used to treat problems with inattention and hyperactivity in individuals with a diagnosis of pervasive developmental disorder, studies with relatively small numbers have shown that methylphenidate, clonidine, and atomoxetine all showed benefits greater than placebo (Erickson et al., 2007). These agents can be helpful in decreasing some of the problems with arousal regulation and inattention. They are, however, not as helpful with decreasing arousal or hyperactivity and improving attention in children with ASDs as they are in children who receive these medications for attention-deficit/hyperactivity disorder.

These medications are able to improve social function by allowing more time for interaction between the person with an ASD and his or her peers. The medications can also assist in improving learning by allowing for increased attention to learning the tasks being presented, including social learning. Additionally, medications may help children with ASD decrease some of the intensity of their perseverations and fixations. A decrease in the intensity of these symptoms can lead to improved social interaction with children who are typically developing.

However, in my clinical experience, these medications are often not as effective in helping children with ASDs as they are for children with other difficulties associated with arousal regulation and inattention. Children with ASDs are often more likely to experience irritability with these medications, have difficulties with appetite and sleep disturbance, and have extreme mood rebounds and even increased aggression. Because of these risks, it is extremely important to carefully monitor children with ASDs when using these medications. It is also important to let parents and teachers know that the efficacy of these medications for children with ASDs may be much less than the adults expect. A child may not be able to tolerate the medications, and it is essential to look at other ways of helping a child with his or her symptoms.

Symptoms of Aggression and Irritability in Autism Spectrum Disorders

Other symptoms that significantly impair the quality of adaptive and social behavior in a child with an ASD are those that include problems with aggression toward others, aggression toward self, and irritability. Several studies across 3 decades involving between 30 and 100 individuals have shown that so-called high potency neuroleptics, such as haloperidol and risperidone, have been more effective than placebo in helping to decrease behaviors associated with these symptoms. One such study is from the RUPP Network (McCracken et al., 2002). Subsequently, the Food and Drug Administration approved risperidone for treating these symptoms in individuals with ASDs.

In addition to haloperidol and risperidone, many other psychopharmacologic agents have been used to decrease the symptoms of aggression and irritability. Although there have been no extensive studies with these other compounds and few, if any, placebo-controlled trials, some of these agents sometimes appear to be helpful clinically. Physicians in the clinical practice at the Marcus Autism Center in Atlanta work closely with board-certified behavioral analysts to track symptom and behavioral changes that may be associated with the medication use.

In addition to risperidone, other neuroleptic or antipsychotic medications that are used to help with the symptoms include other second-generation antipsychotic medications: quetiapine, aripiprazole, ziprasidone, olanzapine, and clozapine. Each medication, including risperidone, can have serious side effects associated with use. Some of the side effects are irreversible and even life threatening. The most common side effect is weight gain, although this is somewhat less prevalent with ziprasidone. This can be a particularly difficult side effect to manage given the eating problems many individuals with ASDs experience and the association with the development of the so-called metabolic syndrome. Metabolic syndrome is the name for a group of risk factors that increase risk for heart disease and other health problems, such as diabetes and stroke. These risk factors include a large waistline, a high triglyceride level, a low HDL cholesterol level, high blood pressure, and a high fasting blood glucose level.

There are recent studies showing favorable results of aripiprazole's effects on behavior in ASDs (Owen et al., 2009; Curran, 2011). There are other small studies that involve other second-generation antipsychotic medications, including a study by Kemner, Willemsen-Swinkels, DeJonge, Tuynman-Qua, and Van Engeland (2002) in which 25 children in an open-label trial of olanzapine had some improvement noted. Hardan, Jou, and Handen (2005) looked retrospectively at quetiapine. Malone, Cater,

Sheikh, Choudhury, and Delaney (2001) engaged in a very small open-label trial of ziprasidone involving 12 adolescents.

Other classes of psychopharmacologic agents that are also used to help with symptoms of aggression and irritability include the anticonvulsants. Although clinically these medications are occasionally helpful in children with ASDs experiencing aggressive symptoms and irritability, very little research supports their use. A study by Hollander et al. (2006) of 13 children with ASDs using valproate and a study by Belsito, Law, Kirk, Landa, and Zimmerman (2001) of 28 children in a placebo double-blind trial with lamotrigine both found no difference in symptoms or change in social interaction.

Additional psychopharmacologic agents that have been used to help with aggression and irritability include antihypertensive alpha-adrenergic agonists (quanfacine and clonidine) and beta-blockers (propranolol). Also, benzodiazepines and other anxiolytics are used because there is a clinical view that decreasing anxious responses to the environment might assist in decreasing aggressive responses. Hormonal therapies are also sometimes implemented, especially if there is a variation in mood with menstrual cycles or a strong sexual aggression component to behaviors. These most often include various estrogen or progesterone preparations. Although there is no significant research that supports the uses of any of these classes of medication in the treatment of symptoms in people with ASDs, they are used. There is some research (Kalachnik, Hanzel, Sevenich, & Harder, 2003; Pary, 1991) associated with using these medications in people with intellectual disabilities, but these studies are also very limited in both numbers and scope.

Symptoms of Repetitive/Perseverative and Stereotypic Behaviors in Autism Spectrum Disorders

The core difficulties experienced by people with ASDs also include the symptoms of repetitive or perseverative behaviors and stereotypies. Several individuals have considered these symptoms across time and possible psychopharmacologic interventions. Relatively well-designed placebo-controlled studies have included studies of serotonergically acting agents, such as clomipramine, fluvoxamine, and fluoxetine (Erickson et al., 2007).

These medications have generally been found to be at least somewhat more effective than placebo in helping with but not controlling these often extremely debilitating symptoms. Placebo-controlled trials include Gordon, State, Nelson, Hamburger, and Rapoport (1993) and Remington, Sloman, Konstantareas, Parker, and Gow (2001), who studied clomipramine, a tricyclic antidepressant with significant serotonergic activity. The results of these studies showed a positive response to the medication or no difference, respectively, with small numbers of participants. McDougle et al. (1996) and Sugie, Sugie, and Fukuda (2005) examined fluvoxamine and found that in at least these two studies, this agent was more helpful than placebo. In separate studies, Buchsbaum et al. (2001) and Hollander et al. (2005) found fluoxetine to be more effective than placebo at decreasing these symptoms.

Several other serotonergically acting agents have been prescribed in children with ASDs to see whether the agents are helpful, but the previous medications have the best study records. Clinicians also often use sertraline, citalopram, escitalopram, and paroxetine, but none of these have significant research showing efficacy.

With these serotonergically acting medications, clinicians must be careful that the symptoms of aggression or irritability are not exacerbated. Generally, however, these medications are well tolerated and exhibit few side effects in people diagnosed with ASDs; they simply are not always very helpful, yet there is often a great deal of expectation that they will be more helpful.

Perseveration, rigidity, and stereotypy are the symptoms that generally must be addressed with specific behavioral interventions geared to decreasing these often nonproductive behaviors and replacing them with more productive and ultimately satisfying behaviors for the child with an ASD. The behaviors associated with these symptoms can often be the most challenging socially. Perseveration, whether on a string, a toy, or other more complex matter, is often the issue that identifies children with an ASD, especially those who are higher functioning, as "odd" or "weird." Using behavioral interventions to decrease these behaviors increases the chances for social interaction and frees the children with an ASD for more learning opportunities. Generally, because these behaviors are also coupled with rigidity, decreasing them across time also helps with a general level of adaptivity in learning and other social environments.

General Symptoms of Social Impairment in Autism Spectrum Disorders

Very few studies have looked specifically at social impairment in people diagnosed with ASDs. Of the placebo-controlled studies that have been completed, only a study of the antibiotic D-cycloserine has shown any particular promise compared with a placebo (Posey et al., 2004), but this was a very small and time-limited study. Of course, every medication discussed previously and many others are often used to help with the core symptoms of ASDs that affect social and adaptive functioning.

Other medications that have been studied include a few that are typically used in the treatment of dementia, including the anticholinesterase inhibitors donepezil (Chez et al., 2003) and galantamine (Nicolson, Craven-Thuss, & Smith, 2006). The N-Methyl-D-aspartate antagonist amantadine (King et al., 2001) and memantine (Owley et al., 2006) have also been studied in small studies, looking at improving social impairment and general cognition.

In addition, research related to the core symptoms of ASD is looking at antibiotics such as vancomycin (Sandler et al., 2000), minocycline (an ongoing, multisite study funded by the National Institute of Mental Health), and D-cycloserine (Posey et al., 2004). Researchers have also considered hormonal therapies, including oxytocin, a hormone thought to be very important in bonding behavior in mammals (Hollander et al., 2003), and vitamin therapies, including vitamin C (Dolske, Spollen, McKay, Lanchanshire, & Tolbert, 1993) and cyanocobalamine (James et al., 2004). Also, an immunosuppressant/antibiotic rampamycin (Ehninger et al., 2008) has shown promise in reversing learning impairments in a mouse model of tuberous sclerosis, which is a rare genetic disorder often associated with ASD symptoms.

USING THESE FINDINGS IN CLINICAL PRACTICE

The challenges of taking the research related to medications and symptoms associated with ASDs and putting it into clinical practice are many, but two are primary.

First, not all ASDs are the same. ASD symptoms are the final common pathway of many different etiologic factors. Without completely understanding the etiology of a particular presentation of an ASD, practitioners cannot definitively know what medication or combination of medications may or may not be helpful. A medication may be helpful in one ASD, but it would not necessarily be helpful in another presentation of an ASD resulting from a completely different etiology.

These concerns about etiology are related to the second issue. Most, if not all, of the research being conducted in medication trials with individuals diagnosed with ASDs does not take into consideration etiologic factors. Such factors are not addressed, and even more broadly phenotypic differences in presentation are not considered. With the studies previously discussed related to medication trials and symptom control in people with ASDs, the numbers are all very small, and the criteria for study inclusion are broad and consistent with diagnostic criteria but nothing more specific. Researchers are neither generally teasing out the participants in a study to look at groups of individuals with a known etiology (although the field is still in the early stages of identifying potential etiologies) nor teasing out specific phenotypes and enrolling those groups of individuals in clinical trials specific to that phenotype.

With these concerns, most of the research trials with medications are somewhat suspect. The research can perhaps generally report what may or may not be helpful, but it says little more. Each time a doctor sees a person with an ASD, he or she must start once again from the beginning to determine what might be the best medication adjunct for that particular person at that particular time.

TOWARD A RECOMMENDED PRACTICE MODEL

Given the state of research related to medication trials in groups of individuals with ASDs, what would be a recommended practice model for determining what medication, if any, and what dose might be appropriate for any individual presenting with debilitating symptoms related to an ASD?

The Marcus Autism Center in Atlanta, Georgia, for example, has developed a model of admission to its day program for significantly impaired individuals to look at the efficacy or the lack of efficacy of a particular medication for a specific individual based on the target behaviors. Data are collected, and the data assist in determining what course to take with medication. This method of analyzing medication efficacy is labor intensive and time consuming, but it does allow for a specific medication regimen tailored to each individual. More broadly, data are now collected at home and at school to judge the effects of medication on specifically targeted behaviors.

Another example is provided by The Learning Tree group homes and schools for individuals with ASDs and other developmental disabilities located at several sites in Alabama and Florida, which similarly collect data related to specific medication trials and changes. These are shared in monthly meetings with the psychiatrist, who then makes decisions related to these psychiatric medications based on the data presented for that individual. In this way, each individual participates in his or her own medication research trial, and the best regimen for that individual is determined.

Using these models, the research outlined earlier in more general studies with people with ASDs with mixed etiologies and phenotypes becomes a general guide for what might work, but it is not definitive in what will work and should not be viewed in that way.

RECOMMENDATIONS FOR FUTURE RESEARCH

In determining the course of future research, phenotypes should be considered in medication trials. Trying to tease out specific groups of individuals with ASDs who clearly meet the diagnostic criteria for ASD and the criteria for a specific phenotype, if not etiology, will go a long way in helping determine the most appropriate medications for a specific individual or group of individuals diagnosed with ASDs. Of course, genetic research will help to continue to define the parameters for medication trials, and as the field's researchers become more knowledgeable of the genetic determinants of specific phenotypes, then more specific and helpful medication trials can be crafted. Ultimately, however, each individual diagnosed with an ASD must be considered just that—an individual; nothing will replace the kind of individual research related to medications and a specific person.

REFERENCES

Belsito, K.M., Law, P.A., Kirk, K.S., Landa, R.J., & Zimmerman, A.W. (2001). Lamotrigine therapy or autistic disorder: A randomized double-blind, placebo-controlled trial. *Journal of Autism and Developmental Disorders, 31*(2), 175–181.

Buchsbaum, M.S., Hollander, E., Haznedar, M.M., Tang, C., Spiegel-Cohen, J., Wei, T-C.,…Mosovich, S. (2001). Effect of fluoxetine on regional cerebral metabolism in autistic spectrum disorders: A pilot study. *International Journal of Neuropsychopharmacology, 4*(2), 119–125.

Chez, M.G., Buchanon, T.M., Becker, M., Kessler, J., Aimonovitch, M.C., & Mrazek, S.R. (2003). Donepezil hydrochloride: A double-blind study in autistic children. *Journal of Pediatric Neurology, 13*(3), 197–204.

Curran, M.P. (2011). Aripiprazole: In the treatment of irritability associated with autistic disorder in pediatric patients. *Pediatric Drugs. 13*(3), 197–204.

Dolske, M.C., Spollen, J., McKay, S., Lanchanshire, E., & Tolbert, L. (1993). A preliminary trial of ascorbic acid as supplemental therapy for autism. *Progress in Neuro-Psychopharmacology and Biological Psychiatry, 17*, 765–774.

Ehninger, D., Han, S., Shilyansky, C., Zhou, Y., Li, W., Kwiatkowski, D.J.,…Silva, A.J.(2008). Reversal of learning deficits in a Tsc2+/– mouse model of tuberous sclerosis. *Nature Medicine, 14*(8), 843–848.

Erickson, C.A., Posey, D.J., Stigler, K.A., Mullett, J., Katschke, A.R., & McDougle, C.J. (2007). A retrospective study of memantine in children and adolescents with pervasive developmental disorders. *Psychopharmacology, 191*, 141–147.

Gordon, C.T., State, C., Nelson, J., Hamburger, S.D., & Rapoport, J.L. (1993). A double-blind comparison of clomipramine, desipramine, and placebo in the treatment of autistic disorder. *Archives of General Psychiatry, 50*(6), 441–447.

Hardan, A., Jou, R., & Handen, B. (2005). Retrospective study of quetiapine in children and adolescents with pervasive developmental disorders. *Journal of Autism and Developmental Disorders, 35*, 387–391.

Hollander, E., Novotny, S., Hanratty, M., Yaffe, R., DeCaria, C.M., Aronowitz, B.R.,…Mosovich, S. (2003). Oxytocin infusion reduces repetitive behaviors in adults with autistic and Asperger's disorders. *Neuropsychopharmacology, 28*, 193–198.

Hollander, E., Phillips, A., Chaplin, W., Zagursky, K., Novotny, S., Wasserman, S.,… Iyengar, R. (2005). A placebo controlled crossover trial of liquid fluoxetine on repetitive behaviors in childhood and adolescent autism. *Neuropsychopharmacology, 30*(3), 582–589.

Hollander, E., Soorya, L., Wasserman, S., Esposito, K., Chaplin, W., & Anagnostou, E. (2006). Divalproex sodium vs. placebo in the treatment of repetitive behaviours in autism spectrum disorder. *International Journal of Neuropsychopharmacology, 9,* 209–213.

James, S.J., Cutler, P., Melnyk, S., Jernigan, S., Janak, L., Gaylor, D.W.,… Neubrander, J.A. (2004). Metabolic biomarkers of increased oxidative stress and methylation capacity in children with autism. *American Journal of Clinical Nutrition, 80,* 1611–1617.

Kalachnik, J.E., Hanzel, T.E., Sevenich, R., & Harder S.R. (2003). Brief report: Clonazepam behavioral side effects with an individual with mental retardation. *Journal of Autism and Developmental Disorders, 33*(3), 349–354.

Kemner, C., Willemsen-Swinkels, S., DeJonge, M., Tuynman-Qua, H., & Van Engeland, H. (2002). Open-label study of olanzapine in children with pervasive developmental disorder. *Journal of Clinical Psychopharmacology, 22,* 455–460.

King, B.H., Wright, D.M., Handen, B.L., Sikitch, L., Zimmerman, A.W., McMahon, W.,…Cook, E.H. Jr. (2001). Double-blind, placebo-controlled study of amantadine hydrochloride in the treatment of children with autistic disorder. *Journal of the American Academy of Child & Adolescent Psychiatry, 40*(6), 658–665.

Malone, R., Cater, J., Sheikh, R., Choudhury, M., & Delaney, M. (2001). Olanzapine versus haloperidol in children with autistic disorder: An open pilot study. *Journal of the American Academy of Child & Adolescent Psychiatry, 40,* 887–894.

McCracken, J.T., McGough, J., Shah, B., Cronin, P., Hong, D., Aman, M.G.,… McMahon, D.(2002). Risperidone in children with autism and serious behavioral problems. *New England Journal of Medicine, 347*(5), 314–321.

McDougle, C.J., Naylor, S.T., Cohen, D.J., Volkmar, F.R., Heninger, G.R., & Price, L.H. (1996). A double-blind, placebo-controlled study of fluvoxamine in adults with autistic disorder. *Archives of General Psychiatry, 53*(11), 1001–1008.

Nicolson, R., Craven-Thuss, B., & Smith, J. (2006). A prospective, open-label trial of galantamine in autistic disorder. *Journal of Child and Adolescent Psychopharmacology, 16*(5), 621–629.

Owen, R., Sikich L., Marcus, R.N., Corey-Lisle, P., Manos, G., McQuade, R.D.,… Findling, R.L. (2009). Aripiprazole in the treatment of irritability in children and adolescents with autistic disorder. *Pediatrics, 124*(6), 1533–1540.

Owley, T., Salt, J., Guter, S., Grieve, A., Walton, L., Ayuyao, N.,…Cooke, E.H., Jr. (2006). A prospective, open-label trial of memantine in the treatment of cognitive, behavioral, and memory dysfunction in pervasive developmental disorders. *Journal of Child and Adolescent Psychopharmacology, 16*(5), 517–524.

Pary, R. (1991). Side effects during lithium treatment for psychiatric disorders in adults with mental retardation. *American Journal of Mental Retardation, 96*(3), 269-273.

Posey, D.J., Kem, D.L., Swiezy, N.B., Sweeten, T.L., Wiegand, R.E., & McDougle, C.J. (2004). A pilot study of D-cycloserine in subjects with autistic disorder. *American Journal of Psychiatry, 161*(11), 2115–2117.

Remington, G., Sloman, L., Konstantareas, M., Parker, K., & Gow, R.. (2001). Clomipramine versus haloperidol in the treatment of autistic disorder: A double-blind, placebo-controlled, crossover study. *Journal of Clinical Psychopharmacology, 4,* 440–444.

Research Unit on Pediatric Psychopharmacology Autism Network (RUPP). (2002). Risperidone in children with autism and serious behavioral problems. *New England Journal of Medicine 347*(5), 314–321.

Sandler, R.H., Finegold, S.M., Bolte, E.R., Buchanan, C.P., Maxwell, A.P., Väisäsnen, M.L.,…Wexler, H.M (2000). Short-term benefit from oral vancomycin treatment of regressive-onset autism. *Journal of Child Neurology, 15*, 429–435.

Sugie, Y., Sugie, H., & Fukuda, T. (2005). Clinical efficacy of fluvoxamine and functional polymorphism in a serotonin transporter gene on childhood autism. *Journal of Autism and Developmental Disorders, 35*(3), 377–385.

Pseudoscience in Social Skills Research and Interventions

Thomas Zane

Pseudoscientific interventions in autism are those that have no research evidence of effectiveness. The proponents of such interventions use scientific-sounding jargon, refer to scientific findings, and provide weak evidence of effectiveness, yet they do not use research designs or controls for potentially confounding variables. Those promoting pseudoscience in autism often make appeals to consumers without first submitting the findings to professional and scientific communities for review. The danger of pseudoscience is that consumers will be misled, waste time and money, and realize little or no benefit. Professionals and consumers should strive to adhere to the basic principles of scientific skepticism and valid research design to guard against the adoption of pseudoscientific (fad) interventions and ensure the application of scientifically proven therapies.

The No Child Left Behind Act of 2001 (PL 107-110) established the requirement that educators may use only those methods that have evidence of effectiveness (i.e., evidence-based practices [EBPs]). For the first time, the law openly addressed the need for scientifically validated interventions in the classroom. The goal was to enhance learning by implementing strategies already proven to be effective, not waste time by teaching with methods that had no history of effectiveness.

Although there is general agreement that educational practice should be based on quality research evidence, some disagreement remains as to what exactly constitutes such evidence. Several standards exist that are used as empirical criteria for EBPs. For example, a task force created by the American Psychological Association (Chambless et al., 1998) included factors such as similar positive effects (of an intervention) demonstrated by multiple researchers; the clear specification of intervention details in program manuals; and several replication studies, using within-subject designs, involving a total of 10 or more people. The New York State Department of Health (1999) published what it considered to be evidence of quality research, including

Thanks to Suzanne Letso for cowriting the section on Relationship Development Intervention (RDI).

195

multiple studies performed by multiple investigators and using experimental designs and controls for bias. Newsom and Hovanitz (2005) proposed several complementary standards, including the reliability of measurement, the use of experimental designs, the use of controls for internal and external validity confounds, the identification of independent and dependent variables, and operational definitions of terms.

Unfortunately, although federal law encourages the use of empirically derived interventions, the spirit of the law has not permeated completely into the education of children with autism. The increasing incidence of autism in the past several years has been followed by an increase in the number of interventions available for this disorder. To illustrate, Green et al. (2006) conducted an Internet survey of parents with children with autism and identified approximately 100 different therapies reportedly being used. Although there is general agreement in the autism field that interventions must have quality evidence of effectiveness (e.g., Zane, Davis, & Rosswurm, 2008), a great discrepancy exists among the interventions on this issue. Metz, Mulick, and Butter (2005) have called autism a "fad magnet" because of the plethora of interventions of unproven effectiveness. Many of these methods are portrayed as being grounded in valid scientific principles and procedures when they are not. Such pseudoscientific interventions are labeled as fads.

PSEUDOSCIENCE DEFINED

Pseudoscience is a way of investigating the world that seems to (but does not really) adhere to basic scientific methodology. Jacobson, Foxx, and Mulick (2005) provided a general description of pseudoscientific interventions; they described these interventions as those that are quickly adopted and used extensively by many people but eventually abandoned because they result in failure. The pseudoscientific approach describes a phenomenon (such as autism) that resembles scientific discourse and thinking but lacks the essential elements of science. In science, for example, findings are published in scholarly professional journals that usually involve a peer-review process to maintain professional standards and research quality. In contrast, pseudoscientists often take their results and information directly to the public without professional review and few standards of quality or evidence. Pseudoscientists will often refer to known scientific principles to appear more scientific and experimental. The practice of science requires the specification of experimental procedures and the replication of results by multiple researchers using traditionally accepted experimental designs. Pseudoscientists, on the other hand, often explain procedures vaguely and have weak operational definitions, which allow little opportunity to verify the protocols or the standards of intervention; use technical jargon (to sound more scientific); and do not use the same level of research quality to study their particular interventions or strategies. Scientific practice dictates that positions are defended by logical argument and an appeal to data and evidence; positions are abandoned when contrary evidence is provided. The practice of pseudoscience, however, tries to argue by appeals to faith and/or testimonials from people who presumably have knowledge or experience about a particular intervention. Claims are made as to the importance of believing in the effectiveness of an intervention or a product. Lastly, scientific practice rarely includes the promotion of strategies and tactics that have ambiguous or no proof. In contrast, proponents of pseudoscience often sell products and services that have little or no proof to support effectiveness. In addition, people who pursue pseudoscience claim that their results cannot be reproduced or verified.

EXAMPLES OF PSEUDOSCIENCE

Examples of pseudoscience claims in treating autism abound. Proponents have claimed that hyperbaric oxygen chambers can significantly improve or even cure autism (Rossignol & Small, 2006). Hyperbaric oxygen therapy makes promises in two areas: the therapy can cure physical anomalies and improve impairments in autism (e.g., increase intelligence, decrease behavioral excesses, improve language). The therapy meets the criteria for a pseudoscientific intervention because these claims of improving symptoms have no scientific verification at this time (e.g., Lerman et al., 2008). In addition, although hyperbaric oxygen therapy has some roots in medicine (a scientific profession) and technical jargon is used, the actual procedures are not fully described. For example, there is little information in the literature about what the person actually does during a therapy session (or "dive" as it is called).

Another example of a pseudoscientific intervention in the field of autism is craniosacral therapy (Upledger Institute, 2008). This therapy involves the physical manipulation of the spine to change the flow of cerebrospinal fluid (Ferreri, 2002). By changing the flow, afflictions and problems are allegedly reduced or eliminated. Examples of what purportedly has been positively treated include autism, bed-wetting, posttraumatic stress disorder, and learning disabilities. On the one hand, craniosacral therapy sounds scientific (with its emphasis on the spine and cerebrospinal fluid), has lots of professional and mysterious jargon, and seems logical. On the other hand, it is promoted directly to the public, and few formal assessments have been submitted for professional review. There is no empirical evidence or a well-controlled research study indicating that craniosacral therapy is causally related to any positive change in these conditions (Green, Martin, Bassett, & Kazanjian, 1999).

There are many more pseudoscientific interventions, such as facilitated communication (Jacobson, Mulick, & Schwartz, 1995), auditory integration training (Bettison, 1996), gentle teaching (Barrera & Teodoro, 1990), the association method (Hanson & Zane, 2009), and Irlen lenses (Fletcher & Martinez, 1994). These and many others fit the criteria for pseudoscientific interventions; they use technical jargon, are rarely submitted for experimental analysis, and have little or no research support for effectiveness.

PROBLEMS WITH PSEUDOSCIENCE IN AUTISM

Parents of children with autism are much more likely to select a pseudoscientific intervention than those parents who do not have such a child in their family (Umbarger, 2007). These people are more at risk for adopting fringe therapies than others. Unfortunately, the appeal of pseudoscientific interventions takes one down a dangerous path. When children with autism experience pseudoscientific interventions, there is danger that they will neither progress nor learn or acquire new competencies or skills. The importance of intensive early education for young children with autism is generally accepted (Ramey & Ramey, 1999). If pseudoscientific interventions are used instead of proven methods, these children may not learn as much as they could with proven strategies, thus wasting the important early years of learning opportunities and developmental growth—a significant concern in the realm of social skills and adaptive behavior. Without the use of empirically supported interventions, children are at risk for not learning what they must learn to grow and become more independent.

Another problem with adopting pseudoscientific interventions is their cost. It has been estimated that the lifetime cost of custodial care for individuals with autism who do not receive effective educational services is more than $13 billion per year (Families for Early Autism Treatment, 1996), with projected future costs approaching $400 billion (Autistic Society, 2008). This underscores the importance of using interventions that have proven effectiveness. Pseudoscientific interventions are not yet proven to have evidence of effectiveness and are less likely to affect an individual's improvement, so long-term care costs will remain higher. Actually, there is a double impact of using pseudoscientific interventions—the cost of the particular intervention and the cost of longer-term care because the ineffective intervention failed. As one example, Zane et al. (2008) estimated that the annual cost of sensory integration therapy (SIT) was approximately $16,500 in 2008. This money could have been better spent on interventions with known effectiveness, which would help an individual with autism improve in one or more life areas, thus reducing the need and the cost of long-term care.

REASONS FOR THE APPEAL OF PSEUDOSCIENCE

Because pseudoscientific interventions exist, there must be attractions to them. There are several possible reasons why people adopt them. First, because parents of children with autism (and other developmental disorders) show higher levels of mental health problems, stress, and impaired physical functioning (e.g., Allik, Larsson, & Smeje, 2006; Dumas, Wolf, Fisman, & Culligan, 1991; Schopler, 1999), research and decision making may be carried out with less care. There is so much pressure to help a child right now that it is understandable that caregivers may sometimes choose interventions without carefully considering every relevant factor (such as documented effectiveness; Metz et al., 2005). Parental stress is then compounded when these interventions fail to lead to any significant positive change in the child.

Another reason may be that some professionals are familiar with a particular intervention and have faith that it will work or believe in testimonials (by well-known public figures or even governmental bodies) without any critical analysis of research that may or may not support its use (Katsiyannis & Maag, 2001). For example, craniosacral therapy was honored by the state of Florida for its perceived ability to improve children with autism (Florida Senate, 2002), although there are no well-controlled scientific studies that support its effectiveness (Zane, 2005).

Another factor that may occasion the continued persistence of pseudoscientific interventions is the role of postmodern thought in the culture (Simon, 2006). Modernism assumes that knowledge is determinable by the objective pursuit of scientific inquiry through deduction and observation. In contrast, the postmodern perspective is that no standard of knowledge can be discovered (Sasso, 2001). Knowledge is relative and gained by intuition and experience. Science and the scientific method were discovered and promoted by people, and all people are biased and subjective; thus, the rules of science must be biased and should not be trusted as truth.

Pseudoscience can thrive within this mind-set. Different types of so-called evidence can be considered equally as worthy as more rigorous experimentation. Under postmodernism, each individual's experiences or perceptions can be considered just as legitimate and valid as any other's experiences or perceptions (Goodman, 1992). So, for the marketer of a pseudoscientific intervention, his or her opinion and perspective on the effectiveness of that intervention are as justified as those of the careful researcher who controls for extraneous variables and demonstrates causal relationships. There is no difference in quality of evidence.

A final hypothesis explaining why pseudoscientific interventions continue to proliferate is that too much of society is scientifically illiterate; that is, society is unaware of the rules of science and logic (which leads to the opportunity for postmodern thinking; Sagan, 1996). Sagan argued that people who are uninformed about scientific thinking and analysis are at greater risk for following pseudoscientific and other unproven claims. Sagan noted how people frequently believe in extraterrestrial sightings, astrology, and slick marketers who promise cures for various ailments. He believed that without the ability for critical thinking and analysis, the criteria for what is believable and true are lowered, which increases the likelihood of people believing in pseudoscientific interventions. Sagan concluded, "If it were widely understood that claims to knowledge require adequate evidence before they can be accepted, there would be no room for pseudoscience" (1996, p. 6).

The remainder of this chapter reviews two popular autism social skill and adaptive behavioral interventions that are considered pseudoscientific interventions: SIT and Relationship Development Intervention (RDI).

SENSORY INTEGRATION THERAPY

SIT is a form of therapy frequently used by occupational therapists who believe that aberrant behavior by children with autism (e.g., self-stimulatory and off-task behaviors) is caused by a dysfunctional sensory system (Parham & Mailloux, 1996). Jean Ayers popularized this conceptualization of problem behavior in 1972. She argued that all human behavior requires a brain that is generally functioning without error. To Ayres, brain dysfunction equaled behavioral or developmental dysfunction. Ayres (1979) explained how the environment produces stimulations that the human senses detect; the brain then processes that information and produces overt behavior in response to the sensory processing. Kranowitz (1998) proposed that a disruption in this circuitry results in sensory dysfunction. Problems associated with sensory dysfunction include sensory discrimination, perception problems, visual perceptual problems, and vestibular processing disorders (Parham & Mailloux, 1996).

After sensory dysfunction is identified (through assessments focusing on sensory abilities), occupational and physical therapists use numerous activities to produce sensory input of various kinds (Ayres, 1989). These professionals select activities that relate to the particular sensory dysfunctions identified in an individual person, but different people may not prescribe the same sensory activity for use in the same way for different individuals with autism. The goal of the activities, based on an individual assessment, is to neutralize the sensory dysfunction by producing increased tolerance for particular stimuli or decreased need for a particular sensory stimulation. In other words, the sensory activities are selected to desensitize individuals to certain sensory inputs, regulate internal sensory processing, and integrate the body's response to incoming sensory stimuli (Ayres, 1989).

Based on this approach, numerous sensory activities can be applied, including deep pressure (given through manual manipulation or a device; Grandin, 1992); weighted vests and backpacks (VandenBerg, 2001); and swinging and brushing parts of a person's body, such as the arms or the legs (Stagnitti, Raison, & Ryan, 1999). These activities are implemented singly or in combination across long periods of time (days and weeks).

SIT has all of the characteristics of pseudoscience. It is presented as a scientific body of knowledge with its own terminology and procedures. Technical jargon is used, and known scientific content is referenced. It is presented as using commonly accepted research designs and seems to meet rigorous research criteria.

However, most of the theory and the research fail to meet any test of scientific rigor or logic. Although many occupational therapists publish studies on SIT in journals for occupational therapy, much of the knowledge about SIT and its perceived effectiveness is disseminated by the public, with little critical review of its scientific merit. Furthermore, few studies have attempted to experimentally assess the effectiveness of SIT by using standard quality research controls and designs. In one study, Fertel-Daly, Bedell, and Hinojosa (2001) examined the effect of a weighted vest on five young children with a pervasive developmental disorder. They measured several dependent variables, such as attention to task and the number of distractions exhibited by the children. Using a within-subject reversal design, the experimenters had the children alternate between wearing and not wearing the vest. The results seemed to indicate that all five children showed increased attention when they wore the vests and lower rates of attention in baseline (i.e., no vest) conditions.

Although, on the surface, this study seems to suggest that the improvement in attention was because of the sensory activities, methodological flaws in the study's design lowers the confidence in a causal relationship between SIT and improvement. For example, Fertel-Daly et al. (2001) noted that increased attention after a weekend could have been because the children were in a more calm and structured context (i.e., school) than on the weekend. However, the more serious charges are that Fertel-Daly et al. failed to collect reliability data on the dependent variable and also failed to gather procedural fidelity data. That is, they failed to prove that the data were collected accurately by having another observer count at the same time. In addition, there was no check on whether the administrators of the intervention were actually adhering to the protocol. The lack of these two fundamental criteria of research methodology leads to little confidence that any positive results would result from the SIT methods.

Watling and Dietz (2007) reported that only three studies have been published using Ayres's traditional form of sensory integration with people with autism spectrum disorders (ASDs). Watling and Dietz admitted that this is an insufficient amount of research to support the use of SIT as extensively as it is being used today, which is often a recommended intervention of choice for children with autism.

When compared with standards of quality evidence from the New York State Department of Health (1999), SIT does not pass muster. Although multiple studies have been done by multiple investigators, most of the studies use poor research design (such as test design pre-post), and rarely were there controls for bias and other potentially confounding variables. Similarly, SIT fails to meet the criteria posed by Newsom and Hovanitz (2005). SIT specifically fails to adequately gather data on the reliability of measurement, provides scant controls for internal and external validity standards, uses poor definition and description of the sensory procedures, and fails to measure the accuracy of implementing the sensory protocol. Not surprisingly, SIT also fails to reach the standards set forth by Chambless et al. (1998), including a lack of demonstration of positive effect using well-established research designs across multiple investigators.

In summary, there is a lack of quality research studies that support the causal relationship between positive changes in autistic behavior and the implementation of SIT. (See Smith, Mruzek, & Mozingo, 2005, for a review.) Although professionals are conducting research studies on SIT, the published reports often include poor research design, uncontrolled confounding variables, and/or measurement error. With such experimental errors, there can be little confidence that SIT is the reason for any changes in the symptomatology of children with autism. Until sufficient studies suggest otherwise, SIT must be considered a pseudoscientific intervention.

RELATIONSHIP DEVELOPMENT INTERVENTION

RDI is an intervention developed in the late 1990s and designed primarily for developing social skills in children with autism. Gutstein (2000), the developer of RDI and the founder of the Connections Center where he trains and certifies RDI therapists, hypothesized that the core impairments of autism include a failure to develop flexible collaboration of neural subsystems and competent dynamic systems, with a desire to remain in a static competence. There is limited motivation to develop more complex subsystems. Gutstein deviates from the American Psychiatric Association (2000) definitions of pervasive developmental disorders by suggesting that impairments in communication and behavioral dysfunction are not primary dimensions of the disorder but simply co-occurring conditions with his presumed core impairments.

Gutstein's RDI program is designed so that parents are the primary interventionists. His program contains more than 1,000 learning and behavioral objectives (Connections Center, 2007). The RDI manual (Gutstein

& Sheely, 2002a) lists about 400 different intervention activities that are purportedly designed to teach various social skills.

RDI meets the criteria for pseudoscience. For example, Gutstein described RDI in a way that makes the intervention appear to be deeply connected to science, experimentation, and empiricism. He wrote, "The initial setting for intervention is the equivalent of a laboratory setting…" (2000, p. xx).

In the RDI training manual, Gutstein and Sheely (2002b) published a chart showing 11 fields of scientific study that contribute to RDI, such as developmental psychology, communications theory, cultural anthropology, systems theory, and biopsychosocial models. Gutstein and Sheely used specialized terminology, such as dynamic intelligence, relationship coregulation, and dynamic thinking. As marketers of pseudoscience are wont to do, Gutstein argues the case for RDI before the public, not the scientific community, as evidenced by publishing only one report purportedly testing the effectiveness of RDI (Gutstein, Burgess, & Montfort, 2007). Gutstein markets RDI products, including several books, an assessment instrument, digital videos on the RDI method, beanbag chairs, and T-shirts.

A search of the literature and professional databases resulted in finding only a single published study attempting to evaluate whether RDI was causally related to changes in any measurable variable of ASDs (Gutstein et al., 2007). Prior to this report, Gutstein had a paper accepted in the *Journal of Autism and Developmental Disorders*, but he abruptly withdrew it. In the one published article, Gutstein et al. (2007) conducted a chart review of children who had received RDI and purportedly showed that these children improved on several dependent variables after receiving the RDI intervention. The review concluded that RDI contributed to, and perhaps was the sole contributor to, the children's improvements. However, the review's methodology involved an "AB" experimental design (commonly called a "pre-post test" design; first, a test given prior to the intervention, then another after or during intervention), which is universally recognized to never prove cause and effect (Fraenkel & Wallen, 2003). Gutstein et al. also did not control for potentially confounding variables, and there was no operational definition of key terms. They failed to gather reliability data on the measurement of the key dependent variables and did not present any evidence to confirm what RDI methods were actually used in the study and whether there was procedural fidelity.

In summary, the evidence that RDI is effective in treating aspects of ASDs is not compelling. When measured against the guidelines from the New York State Department of Health (1999), RDI is not documented by multiple studies performed by multiple investigators, does not use acceptable experimental designs, and does not control for bias. RDI failed to correspond with the criteria set forth by Newsom and Hovanitz (2005).

There is no reliability of measurement, there is no appropriate research design, there are no controls for internal and external validity threats and poor description of the independent variable (i.e., the specific RDI procedures), and there is no measurement of procedural fidelity. Lastly, RDI fails to meet the research standards set forth by Chambless et al. (1998). Because multiple investigators have not demonstrated positive effects for RDI, there is a lack of clarity in the intervention protocol, and there is an absence of reliability studies showing similar results. There is little reason to believe that RDI meets any criteria for acceptable research standards, and thus it should be considered a pseudoscientific intervention at this point in time.

RECOMMENDATIONS FOR THE FUTURE

Pseudoscience in treating autism will continue unless there are changes in several areas. People working with individuals with autism should adopt a rigorous scientific perspective when reviewing different interventions that might be considered for use. This scientist-practitioner model (Lerman, 2008) increases the chances that a professional will adhere to high standards of proof when deciding what intervention to use and evaluating its potential impact. Furthermore, these professionals, who would be guided by an empirical approach toward treating autism, must act as models for other professionals who may not be so inclined or who may simply be less informed about the rules of science and evidence.

However, before this modeling can be accomplished, practitioners from various disciplines must agree on the criteria for evidence of effective interventions. This is a significant dilemma because there are disparate criteria for effectiveness or quality research (Detrich, 2008), which could result in the same strategy being classified as evidence-based by one set of criteria but deemed ineffective by another set of criteria. Digennaro-Reed and Reed (2008) discussed in depth the history of the development of criteria for EBPs but pointed out that several versions of empirically derived standards exist for quality evidence. In addition to the standards for what constitutes quality evidence promulgated by the New York State Department of Health (1999), Newsom and Hovanitz (2005), and Chambless et al. (1998), the Council for Exceptional Children (2006) proposed a different model of criteria. This organization proposed three levels of evidence: research-based and recommended evidence, promising practices that may be included, and emerging practices that are limited to informational use. Dietrich (2008) and Drake, Latimer, Leff, McHugo, and Burns (2004) posed additional perspectives on evidence and have argued that a continuum of evidence strength may exist, thus implying that some evidence is stronger than other evidence.

This definitional issue of what exactly constitutes believable evidence is crucially important. As long as professionals continue to differ on what the criteria are for quality evidence, and even differ on what the levels of evidence are, there may continue to be interventions that vary in evidence supporting their effectiveness. This lack of clear criteria will continue to confuse both professionals and consumers. A good example of what happens when there is a lack of agreement for evidence is the report by Gutstein et al. (2007). They published a pseudostudy involving a chart review of children with autism who had received RDI. The methodology of this study employed no type of research design, had no controls for extraneous variables, and no reliability or validity measures, yet many people accept this study as evidence of the effectiveness of this therapeutic approach, as evidenced by an increasing number of people becoming certified as RDI therapists (Letso & Zane, 2008). As long as there is disagreement or a lack of knowledge about what constitutes quality evidence, pseudoscientific interventions will be adopted for use. This is a two-sided problem: How are standard criteria of evidence determined and adopted? How are professionals and consumers given this information?

Producing the scientist-practitioner (Lerman et al., 2008) requires programs that provide training in science and analytic thought. Therefore, it is important to infuse graduate and professional training programs with intensive instruction on how to behave and work to adhere to the rules of science and identify quality evidence and research-based methodologies. An excellent model of such training programs is the Behavior Analysis Certification Board (2008), which promotes the training of the methods of science and analysis and certifies programs that incorporate these topics of training into its programs.

Pseudoscientific interventions continue to flourish in the field of autism. With the increasing incidence of autism, there is a chance that more of these will become available to consumers. However, there are standards of evidence that can be applied to evaluating autism interventions that should permit discrimination among those interventions that have evidence and those that do not. Fundamentally, professionals and consumers will need to solve the dilemma of how to decide whether an intervention is worthy of implementation. For young children with autism, time cannot be wasted on ineffective therapies. Professionals have an obligation to set common standards of evidence that, when applied, will allow for the public identification of pseudoscientific interventions. Only by doing so can consumers have confidence in the quality of the interventions being provided to their children and loved ones.

Members of the public trust that professionals will act in a way that will protect and benefit them. The public assumes that professionals will know what works and what does not work, discarding the latter. The ability to do this requires adherence to skepticism, science, and the rule of objective evidence.

REFERENCES

Allik, H., Larsson, J., & Smeje, H. (2006). Health-related quality of life in parents of school-aged children with Asperger syndrome or high-functioning autism. *Health and Quality of Life Outcomes, 4*(1). doi:10.1186/1477-7525-4-1

American Psychiatric Association (2000). *Diagnostic and statistical manual of mental disorders* (4th ed., text rev.). Washington, DC: Author.

Autistic Society. (2008). *Facts and statistics.* Retrieved from http://www.autisticsociety.org/about-autism/facts-and-statistics.html

Ayres, A.J. (1972). *Sensory integration and learning disorder.* Los Angeles, CA: Western Psychological Services.

Ayres, A.J. (1979). *Sensory integration and the child.* Los Angeles, CA: Western Psychological Services.

Ayres, A.J. (1989). *Sensory integration and Praxis tests manual.* Los Angeles, CA: Western Psychological Services.

Barrera, F.J., & Teodoro, G.M. (1990). Flash bonding or cold fusion? A case analysis of gentle teaching. In A.C. Repp & N.N. Singh (Eds.), *Perspectives on the use of nonaversive and aversive interventions for persons with developmental disabilities* (pp. 199–214). Sycamore, IL: Sycamore.

Behavior Analysis Certification Board. (2008). *Guidelines for responsible conduct for behavior analysis.* Retrieved from http://www.bacb.com

Bettison, S. (1996). The long-term effects of auditory training on children with autism. *Journal of Autism and Developmental Disorders, 26,* 361–374.

Chambless, D.L., Baker, M., Baucom, D.H., Beutler, L.E., Calhoun, K.S., Crits-Christoph, P.,…Woody, S.R. (1998). Update on empirically validated therapies, II. *The Clinical Psychologist, 51,* 3–16.

Connections Center. (2007). *RDI Program 6.0 = RDIos 1.0: Worldwide Center for Excellence in Autism, Making the RDI Program Even Better.* Newsletter, December 14, 2007, pp. 4 & 6.

Council for Exceptional Children, Professional Standards & Practice Committee. (2006, Spring). *CEC evidence-based professional practices proposal.* Retrieved from http://www.cec.sped.org/AM/Template.cfm?Section=Evidence_based_Practice&Template=/TaggedPage/TaggedPageDisplay.cfm&TPLID=24&ContentID=4710

Detrich, R. (2008). Evidence-based, empirically supported, or best practice? A guide for the scientist-practitioner. In J.K. Luiselli, D.C. Russo, W.P. Christan, & S.M. Wilczynski (Eds.), *Effective practices for children with autism: Educational and behavior support interventions that work* (pp. 3–26). New York, NY: Oxford Press.

Digennaro-Reed, F.L., & Reed, D.D. (2008). Towards an understanding of evidence-based practice. *Journal of Early and Intensive Behavior Intervention, 5*(2), 20–29.

Drake, R.E., Latimer, E.A., Leff, H.S., McHugo, G.J., & Burns, B.J. (2004). What is evidence? *Child and Adolescent Psychiatric Clinics of North America, 13,* 717–728.

Dumas, J., Wolf, L., Fisman, S., & Culligan, A. (1991). Parenting stress, child behavior problems, and dysphoria in parents of children with autism, Down syndrome, behavior disorders, and normal development. *Exceptionality: A Research Journal, 2*(2), 97–110.

Families for Early Autism Treatment. (1996). *"Doctor, My Child Doesn't Talk:" The importance of early autism diagnosis* [Video]. Available from Families for Early Autism Treatment, P.O. Box 255722, Sacramento, CA 95865.

Ferreri, C.A. (2002). *Neural organization technique.* Retrieved from http://www.positivehealth.com/article/neurological/neural-organisation-technique

Fertel-Daly, D., Bedell, G., & Hinojosa, J. (2001). Effects of a weighted vest on attention to task and self-stimulatory behaviors in preschoolers with pervasive developmental disorders. *American Journal of Occupational Therapy, 55*(6), 629–640.

Fletcher, J., & Martinez, G. (1994). An eye-movement analysis of the effects of scotopic sensitivity correction on parsing and comprehension. *Journal of Learning Disabilities, 27*(1), 67–70.

Florida Senate. (2002). *A resolution recognizing April 2002 as Craniosacral Therapy Awareness Month.* Retrieved from http://archive.flsenate.gov/data/session/2002/Senate/bills/bittext/pdf/s2398.pdf

Fraenkel, J.R., & Wallen, N.E. (2003). *How to design and evaluate research in education.* New York, NY: McGraw-Hill.

Goodman, K.S. (1992). Why whole language is today's agenda in education. *Language Arts, 69,* 354–363.

Grandin, T. (1992). Calming effects of deep pressure in patients with autistic disorder, college students, and animals. *Journal of Child and Adolescent Pharmacology, 2,* 63–72.

Green, C., Martin, C.W., Bassett, K., & Kazanjian, A. (1999). *A systematic review and critical appraisal of the scientific evidence on craniosacral therapy.* Vancouver, Canada: British Columbia Office of Health Technology Assessment, University of British Columbia.

Green, V.A., Pituch, K.A., Itchon, J., Choi, A., O'Reilly, M., & Sigafoos, J. (2006). Internet survey of treatments used by parents of children with autism. *Research in Developmental Disabilities, 27,* 70–84.

Gutstein, S. (2000). *Solving the relationship puzzle: A new developmental program that opens the door to lifelong social and emotional growth.* Arlington, TX: Future Horizons.

Gutstein, S.E., Burgess, A.F., & Montfort, K. (2007). Evaluation of the relationship development intervention program. *Autism, 11*(3), 397–411.

Gutstein, S., & Sheely, R.K. (2002a). *Relationship development intervention with young children: Social and emotional development activities for Asperger syndrome, autism, PDD, and NLD.* New York, NY: Jessica Kingsley.

Gutstein, S., & Sheely, R. (2002b). *RDI beginning seminar for professionals.* Houston, TX: Connections Center.

Hanson, J., & Zane, T. (2009). *The association method for autism treatment: Much ado about nothing.* Unpublished manuscript.

Jacobson, J.W., Foxx, R.M., & Mulick, J.A. (Eds.). (2005). *Controversial therapies for developmental disabilities: Fad, fashion, and science in professional practice.* Mahwah, NJ: Lawrence Erlbaum Associates.

Jacobson, J.W., Mulick, J.A., & Schwartz, A.A. (1995). A history of facilitated communication: Science, pseudoscience, and antiscience. *American Psychologist, 50,* 750–765.

Katsiyannis, A., & Maag, J.W. (2001). Educational methodologies: Legal and practical considerations. *Preventing School Failure, 46*(1), 31–36.

Kranowitz, C.S. (1998). *The out-of-sync-child.* New York, NY: The Berkley Publishing Group.

Lerman, D.C. (2008). An introduction to the second issue of *Behavior Analysis in Practice. Behavior Analysis in Practice, 1*(2), 2–3.

Lerman, D.C., Sansbury, T., Hovanetz, A., Wolever, E., Garcia, A., O'Brien, E., et al. (2008). Using behavior analysis to examine the outcomes of unproven therapies: An evaluation of hyperbaric oxygen therapy for children with autism. *Behavior Analysis in Practice, 1*(2), 50–58.

Letso, S., & Zane, T. (2008, May). *Relationship development intervention: A review of the research.* Paper presented at the 26th Annual Issues in Autism Conference, Atlantic City, NJ.

Metz, B., Mulick, J., & Butter, E. (2005). Autism: A late-20th-century fad magnet. In J.W. Jacobson, R.M. Foxx, & J.A. Mulick (Eds.), *Controversial therapies for developmental disabilities: Fad, fashion, and science in professional practice* (pp. 237–264). Mahwah, NJ: Lawrence Erlbaum Associates.

Newsom, C., & Hovanitz, C.A. (2005). The nature and value of empirically validated interventions. In J.W. Jacobson, R.M. Foxx, & J.A. Mulick (Eds.), *Controversial therapies for developmental disabilities: Fad, fashion, and science in professional practice* (pp. 31–44). Mahwah, NJ: Lawrence Erlbaum Associates.

New York State Department of Health. (1999). *Clinical practice guideline: Report of the recommendations. Autism/pervasive developmental disorders, assessment and intervention for young children (age 0–3 years).* Albany, NY: Author. Retrieved from http://www.health.ny.gov/community/infants_children/early_intervention/disorders/autism

No Child Left Behind Act of 2001, PL 107-110, 115 Stat. 1425, 20 U.S.C. §§ 6301 *et seq.*

Parham, L.D., & Mailloux, Z. (1996). *Sensory integration.* In J. Case-Smith, A.S. Allen, and P.R. Pratt (Eds.), *Occupational therapy for children* (pp. 307–356). St. Louis, MO: Mosby-Year Book.

Ramey, S.L., & Ramey, C.T. (1999). Early experience and early intervention for children at risk for developmental delay and mental retardation. *Mental Retardation and Developmental Disabilities, Research Review, 5,* 1–10.

Rossignol, D., & Small, T. (2006). Interview with Dr. Dan Rossignol: Hyperbaric oxygen therapy may improve symptoms in autistic children. *Medical Veritas, 3,* 944–951.

Sagan, C. (1996). *The demon-haunted world: Science as a candle in the dark.* New York, NY: Random House.

Sasso, G.M. (2001). The retreat from inquiry and knowledge in special education. *The Journal of Special Education, 34*(4), 178–193.

Schopler, E. (1999). Behavioral issues in autism. In E. Schopler & G.B. Meesibov (Eds.), *Current issues in autism series* (pp. 65–94). New York, NY: Plenum Press.

Simon, D. (2006, June). *Truth, American culture, and fuzzy logic.* Paper presented at the Cleveland State University NAFIPS conference, Cleveland, Ohio.

Smith, T., Mruzek, D.W., & Mozingo, D. (2005). Sensory integration therapy. In J.W. Jacobson, R.M., Foxx, and J.A. Mulick (Eds.), *Controversial therapies for developmental disabilities: Fad, fashion, and science in professional practice* (pp. 341–350). Mahwah, NJ: Lawrence Erlbaum Associates.

Stagnitti, K., Raison, P., & Ryan, P. (1999). Sensory defensiveness syndrome: A paediatric perspective and case study. *Australian Occupational Therapy Journal, 46*(4), 175–187.

Umbarger, G.T. (2007). State of the evidence regarding complimentary and alternative medical treatments for autism spectrum disorders. *Education and Training in Developmental Disabilities, 42*(4), 437–447.

Upledger Institute (2008). Discover craniosacral therapy. Retrieved from http://upledger.com/content.asp?id=26

VandenBerg, N.L. (2001). The use of a weighted vest to increase on-task behavior in children with attention difficulties. *American Journal of Occupational Therapy, 55*(6), 621–628.

Watling, R.L., & Dietz, J. (2007). Immediate effect of Ayres's sensory integration-based occupational therapy intervention on children with autism spectrum disorders. *American Journal of Occupational Therapy, 61*(5), 574–583.

Zane, T. (2005). Fads in special education. In J.W. Jacobson, R.M. Foxx, & J.A. Mulick (Eds.), *Controversial therapies for developmental disabilities: Fad, fashion, and science in professional practice* (pp. 175–191). Mahwah, NJ: Lawrence Erlbaum Associates.

Zane, T., Davis, C., & Rosswurm, M. (2008). The cost of fad treatments in autism. *Journal of Early and Intensive Behavioral Intervention, 5*(2), 44–51.

13

Bringing Social Competence Interventions to Scale in Autism Spectrum Disorders

The Next Challenge

Daniel Crimmins, Ginny Van Rie, and John Lutzker

This volume eloquently speaks to the growing development and refinement of interventions that enhance social competence in children with autism spectrum disorders (ASDs). The research presented has evolved to place greater emphasis on interventions in natural settings—home, school, and community—and with typically developing peers. There is growing sophistication, relevance, and appreciation of naturalistic interventions in the everyday lives of individuals with ASDs.

By its very nature, research is conducted under controlled conditions, with motivated children (or at least their families), committed investigators and therapists, and physical settings that are often "better than average." Research allows us to identify active components of interventions, learn about the circumstances when intervention is warranted and where it may not be likely to succeed, and perhaps develop a clear protocol outlining the future delivery of the approach. As research studies accrue, using a range of methods and increasing degrees of scientific rigor, researchers might even say that an intervention has achieved the status of being an evidence-based practice (EBP).

In many ways, defining a pool of EBPs is an end unto itself. In the last several years, numerous independent efforts have undertaken reviews of interventions for children with ASDs, with the goal of identifying evidence-based, established, and emerging practices to assist in intervention selection and delivery. Five examples over the last decade include a National Academy of Sciences report on educating children with autism (National Research Council, 2001), the New York State Education Department's autism program quality indicators (Crimmins, Durand, Theurer-Kaufman, & Everett, 2001), the National Standards Project (National Autism Center,

2009), the National Professional Development Center on ASDs (Odom, Collet-Klingenberg, Rogers, & Hatton, 2010), and the Vanderbilt comparative effectiveness report (Warren et al., 2011). Although each example represents somewhat different approaches to the endeavor of identifying effective practices, there is a clear and emerging consensus that there are several specific strategies or interventions with proven effectiveness in enhancing social interaction skills (among others) in individuals with ASDs.

However, as important as it is to identify that interventions are available to support individuals with ASDs in improving social and adaptive behaviors, it is perhaps of even greater importance to ensure that these practices reach all individuals with ASDs who could benefit from them. There is an ever-growing awareness of the increase in the prevalence of ASDs among children in the United States, most recently estimated at 1 in 88 (Centers for Disease Control and Prevention, 2012). The call for early intervention and the entitlement to special education mean that increasing numbers of children will require educational and other therapeutic supports, including communication and social skills—and the call should be for the provision of effective practices. Thus, this field faces an impending need for the widespread delivery of EBPs to a growing number of children and adults—a phenomenon referred to as scaling up. It is, unfortunately, a need for which practitioners are largely unprepared.

BRINGING EVIDENCE-BASED PRACTICES TO SCALE

Let us first examine the phenomenon of scaling up. As interventions evolve and evidence accrues in the area of social competence for individuals with ASDs, researchers confront the imperative that the interventions be disseminated widely *and* effectively. Obviously, effective practices can benefit only those individuals who receive them, and reaching a meaningful number of individuals suggests the need for organized support and standards of practice that require specific approaches employed at scale. In educational settings, one operational rule is that an intervention is considered at scale when 60% of the students who could potentially benefit from an intervention have access to it *and* it is implemented with fidelity (Fixsen, Blasé, Horner, & Sugai, 2009). The best resource for a more thorough review of research and practice in the area of implementation is *Implementation Research: A Synthesis of the Literature* (Fixsen, Naoom, Blasé, Friedman, & Wallace, 2005).

Fixsen et al. (2005) described how interventions are scaled up. Even though the examples were from the field of social welfare, they were presented in a manner that has direct relevance to education and community support for individuals with ASDs. There are six stages of implementation: exploration, installation, initial implementation, full implementation, innovation, and sustainability. Although they are briefly presented here in sequential order, they more likely operate in interactive cycles (Fixsen, Naoom, Blasé, & Wallace, 2007).

Exploration

Deciding to implement an intervention at scale is a large undertaking. During the exploration stage, each process required for scale up is thoroughly considered by the organization, emphasizing the goals of both successful implementation and sustainability. There must be a clear need for an intervention, ideally documented by systemic data, and a commitment by all stakeholders to move forward.

In general, the exploration stage is led by a diverse and representative implementation team that has the initial task of assessing the organizational readiness for change and the resources to support implementation. In some situations, the implementation team commits to pilot demonstrations to ensure that the intervention can be implemented with fidelity and result in positive outcomes prior to the installation and the full implementation stages.

The implementation team must anticipate how the change will affect the daily workings of the organization. In schools, for example, there must be a plan for school administrators to assess the new intervention, determine what features of the new intervention are not in place at their sites, determine how to implement those features within their available structures, and decide whether the new approach will supplement or supplant existing strategies. The implementation team should develop a readiness checklist that would allow school administrators to determine whether they are prepared for the implementation of the intervention at the school and school district levels.

A well-articulated communication plan must be designed prior to implementing a large-scale intervention in an organization. Ongoing and open communication within and between stakeholder groups is vital to successful implementation. All involved must be familiar with the intended outcomes of the intervention, and those outcomes depend to a large degree on the intervention being implemented with fidelity.

After the communication plan is developed, the team must plan for the actual implementation and the sustainability of the intervention. Considerations here include plans for the initial and the ongoing training of teachers, coaches to support implementation, monitoring systems for effectiveness and fidelity, and feedback loops for successes and concerns. Data should be used to determine whether the intervention should be adapted, modified, or changed at the practice level to ensure the truly improved the lives of the students who received it.

The exploration stage is critical to the successful large-scale implementation of an intervention. One of the major reasons that interventions fail when scaled up is that the system was not ready for change (Fixsen et al., 2009). After the implementation team has planned for the successful large-scale implementation of an intervention and a decision is made to implement the intervention, the exploration stage ends, and the installation stage begins.

Installation

During the installation stage, the nitty-gritty elements required for implementation are put into place, including creating detailed budgets, creating job descriptions, hiring the necessary staff, purchasing materials, setting up offices, assigning staff to new roles, and arranging initial training (Fixsen, et al., 2007). Each element is imperative for the successful implementation of the intervention. These essential factors must be in place before moving to the initial implementation phase.

Initial Implementation

As an intervention is being introduced, all parties are learning new roles and responsibilities, and practice is required to achieve proficiency. This predictably requires time, coaching, and communication; many interventions fail during this stage because time and support for change are provided.

Full Implementation

An intervention has reached the full implementation stage when the majority of the intended providers are implementing the intervention with acceptable fidelity (Fixsen et al., 2007). There are several challenges to reaching full implementation. One challenge is the turnover of trained personnel; in schools, this would include teachers, coaches, supervisors, and administrators. Each time a staff member leaves and is replaced, there are losses of both training time and effort for the departing staff member, delays while a replacement is trained, and a general slowdown in system-wide fidelity to the intervention. Moving through the stages from exploration to full implementation usually takes an organizational commitment of 2–4 years.

Innovation

After full implementation has been achieved, organizations can begin to innovate, making changes and adjustments to the intervention to simplify implementation—as long as the same outcomes are achieved. A significant concern is that many organizations want to streamline procedures without first ensuring the ongoing effectiveness of the intervention for the individual. Systems issues, such as cost, staff time, or ongoing training and supervision, become drivers in the decision process. It is imperative that organizations truly understand every nuance of the intervention and can implement it correctly before trying to make improvements. Innovations should be based on data collected while implementing an intervention in naturalistic settings (Fixsen, et al., 2009).

Sustainability

Sustainability must be an integral part of every stage, from determining feasibility during exploration; hiring qualified staff during installation; maintaining communication and persistence during the initial implementation; training and coaching; to fidelity monitoring during full implementation, to ensuring that modifications made during innovation can be maintained across time. Clearly, these require an ongoing commitment of resources to training, coaching, and monitoring; without these, the successful large-scale implementation of any intervention is unlikely.

SCALING UP INTERVENTIONS FOR INDIVIDUALS WITH AUTISM SPECTRUM DISORDERS

A major challenge in scaling up an intervention for individuals with ASDs is heterogeneity within the population. Because ASD is a spectrum disorder, there are not only similarities among individuals with ASDs but also vast differences between any one individual and others. There are, for example, wide ranges in academic, social, communication, and adaptive skills across the spectrum. Thus, an intervention may prove effective for specific subgroups of students with ASDs but may not be beneficial for all, making it crucial to clearly identify the characteristics of the individuals who are likely to benefit from an EBP within the population of individuals with ASDs.

Several factors must be considered in scaling up autism-related interventions, including instructional methods, specific content, contextual variables such as setting, social variables such as the role of peers, intended outcomes, and instructor training. For example, if an instructional method such as Pivotal Response Treatment (PRT; see Chapter 7) is scaled up, the content being taught may vary considerably depending on the child, but the instructional method and context will remain consistent. If a system of communication is scaled up, such as the Picture Exchange Communication System (PECS; Bondy & Frost, 2002), the content and the instructional method will remain relatively consistent, but the context may vary

216 Crimmins, Van Rie, and Lutzker

significantly. It is important to determine not only the broad category of skills that the intervention addresses but also what specific components of an intervention will be scaled up because the resources and training needed vary, based on the complexity of the task.

In both PRT and PECS, the fidelity of implementation is enhanced by manuals that describe each practice, widespread workshop and other training opportunities, and numerous active demonstration sites that allow potential adopters to see the intervention in a true practice setting. Decisions regarding which interventions can and should be scaled up must also be guided by professional standards of practice. The National Council for Accreditation of Teacher Education, for example, is in the process of creating standards for educating students with ASDs. After professional standards of practice are in place, the standards should be maintained and updated regularly to stay up-to-date with the evolving literature and research.

The Mandate to Scale Up

This chapter briefly spoke of the importance of scaling up, considerations in how to do so, and specific issues related to individuals with ASDs. With that, how likely will practitioners organize services and supports to focus on using EBPs?

Consider the bumper sticker "wisdom": "If you think education is expensive, try ignorance!" Scaling up EBPs and other effective practices may well be expensive. The steps outlined by Fixsen et al. (2007) are many, require an initial investment of resources, and confront numerous organizational hurdles to ensure sustainability. The associated costs can be substantial.

But is there a choice? What is the cost of doing nothing—or the cost of delivering services or supports that are inadequate or ineffective? This does occur—for several potential reasons, perhaps due to organizational inertia (e.g., these are the services that have always been provided), false economies (e.g., there is a desire to do more, but it is much too intensive or specialized [and expensive]), or controlling ideologies (e.g., practitioners do not provide an intervention because it does not fit with their specific intervention philosophy). The costs associated with not implementing an intervention are harder to quantify, but given the increasing number of individuals with ASDs, they are likely to be considerable.

On a final note and on a population level, practitioners know that there are significant disparities in access, quality, and outcomes experienced by individuals from ethnic and linguistic minorities for a range of health concerns. Although practitioners do not definitively know whether this is true for EBPs for individuals with ASDs, it is a logical extension of the health disparities literature to expect that it might be true. The call for scaling up is—in many ways—a call for equal access for all.

REFERENCES

Bondy, A., & Frost, L. (2002). *A picture's worth: PECS and other visual communication strategies in autism.* Bethesda, MD: Woodbine House.

Centers for Disease Control and Prevention. (2012). Prevalence of autism spectrum disorders: Autism and Developmental Disabilities Monitoring Network, United States, 2008. *Morbidity and Mortality Weekly Report, 61* (SS03), 1–19.

Crimmins, D., Durand, V.M., Theurer-Kaufman, K., & Everett, J. (2001). *Autism program quality indicators.* Albany, NY: New York State Education Department.

Fixsen, D.L., Blasé, K.A., Horner, R., & Sugai, G. (2009, February). *Readiness for change.* Retrieved from http://sisep.fpg.unc.edu/sites/sisep.fpg.unc.edu/files /resources/SISEP-Brief3-ReadinessForChange-02-2009.pdf

Fixsen, D.L., Naoom, S.F., Blasé, K., Friedman, R.M., & Wallace, F. (2005). *Implementation research: A synthesis of the literature.* Tampa, FL: National Implementation Research Network at the Louis de la Parta Florida Mental Health Institute, University of South Florida. Retrieved from http:// ctndisseminationlibrary.org/PDF/nirnmonograph.pdf

Fixsen, D.L., Naoom, S.F., Blasé, K.A., & Wallace, F. (2007). Implementation: The missing link between research and practice. *APSAC Advisor, 9,* 4–11.

National Autism Center. (2009). *National standards report.* Retrieved from http:// www.nationalautismcenter.org/affiliates/reports.php

National Research Council. (2001). *Educating children with autism.* Washington, DC: National Academy Press.

Odom, S., Collet-Klingenberg, L., Rogers, S., & Hatton, D. (2010). Evidence-based practices in interventions for children and youth with autism spectrum disorders. *Preventing School Failure, 54*(4), 275–282.

Warren, Z., Veenstra-VanderWeele, J., Stone, W., Bruzek, J.L., Nahmias, A.S., Foss-Feig, J.H.,…McPheeters, M.L. (2011, April). *Therapies for children with autism spectrum disorders: Comparative effectiveness reviews, no. 26.* Rockville, MD: Agency for Healthcare Research and Quality. Retrieved from http://www.effectivehealthcare .ahrq.gov/ehc/products/106/651/Autism_Disorder_exec-summ.pdf

Perspectives from Individuals on the Autism Spectrum, Family Members, and Service Providers

This section features commentary and responses from invited contributors who have a personal stake in autism research. These individuals were among a panel of participants at the convocation that included individuals with autism, family members, and service providers. They actively participated in the discussions and reviewed the final results and recommendations that the presenters made during the event. Their candid responses and recommendations on the pages that follow offer, at times, significantly different perspectives from those of the presenters—a humbling reminder about what priorities matter most and a resounding request that researchers and practitioners not forget to listen to the people they serve.

Adults on the
Autism Spectrum
Mentoring Children on the Spectrum

Linda Styles

This letter is written in response to an invitation from the hosts of the 2008 Organization for Autism Research (OAR) Applied Research Convocation. Those of us on the autism and Asperger syndrome spectrum who were invited to participate as observers wish to thank OAR and the Marcus Autism Center for the invitation both to attend as well as to respond.

At the convocation, we were asked for reactions and suggestions. Judging from the postconvocation discussion, those present with an autism spectrum disorder (ASD) and at least two of the mothers of ASD children present seemed to concur: The majority of the presenters obviously believe they are doing good work. We recognize that many of them are, even though some of us have deep reservations about the underlying methodology and the effectiveness of the approaches we heard discussed.

I have chosen to focus on one issue: the strong belief that there is a real need for qualified, competent adults on the spectrum to actively participate in the appropriate and case-specific mentoring of children on the spectrum.

My two points of feedback relating directly to this issue are important. In general, the convocation speakers exhibited an overt attitude of resistance to the idea that any adult ASD person would be capable of functioning as one of his or her colleagues in any capacity. This open dismissal, apparent to both parent and child, fosters a pervasive environment of hopelessness. Consequently, in too many cases, the mothers of ASD children take on themselves and impart to their children a desperate and lifeless depression. Mothers with no hope that their child will ever function and communicate in a "normal" way unwittingly become catalysts for more serious problems later in the child's life.

We feel that the combination of highly capable and specially trained ASD adults with invaluable, real-life experiences who are willing to serve as hands-on mentors to ASD children, coordinated with a real effort on the part of the medical community to correct the inexcusable lack of accurate and appropriate information for the parents of ASD children, will help improve the lives and futures of both parents and children and, by extension, society as a whole.

What seemed to be missing from the presentations was a true empathy and an understanding of the basic life of any ASD or Asperger persons: Their neurological wiring works significantly differently than that of neurotypical persons. As a result, these children will think and behave differently. Neurotypical behaviors are as odd and bewildering to them as their behaviors are to neurotypical people.

We are aware that the focus of this meeting was behaviorism, and we recognize that, in some cases, intense behavior modification may be necessary. It is our contention, however, that intense (and, to our minds, sometimes brutal) behavior therapy is often not the most effective starting point for an ASD child; if approached improperly, we believe behavior therapy will cause long-term harm to a child. Behavior therapy cannot be the sole solution vehicle.

Adults on the spectrum who have learned to live comfortably with their different neurological conditions are aware that there can be and often are useful and sometimes astounding results achieved by recognizing one simple fact: Not every spectrum child is in a deep, hopeless hole—if the child receives early and specifically appropriate mentoring. No one is looking for a handout here; self-sufficiency is the goal.

We have seen evidence in our community that persons at all points on the spectrum often have inherent talents and capabilities far more sophisticated than the majority of the convocation presenters seem to recognize. Individual interests and talents vary, and sometimes it is difficult to isolate deeply hidden capabilities. But it is an observed fact in our ranks that the typical odd behavior or difficulty with normal communication often masks a deep, intuitive understanding of complex ideas or systems, music, or virtually any specialized skill.

Although many neurotypical people have worked effectively as mentors to younger ASD persons, those of us in the community can state without hesitation that mentoring by an adult who has been through many of the same frustrating and seemingly pointless struggles can be a life-changing experience for an ASD child—very possibly the difference between a life on welfare or in a mental institution and that of a productive and valued member of the work force and society.

It is a great disservice to autistic and Asperger children everywhere to assume that their condition is a blanket "disorder" with no positive aspects. Although the condition can certainly include a variety of negatives, adult persons on the spectrum whom I know are personally offended by the term *high functioning*. Further, they firmly believe that they have achieved their successes specifically because of their different thinking systems, not in spite of them. To a person, not one would change the basic fabric of who each is by opting to become more behaviorally normal or socially adept if it meant losing the positives that each person perceives the neurological differences allow.

In spite of the stated goals, the current scientific and research climates that we heard represented do not seem to include working to help ASD children prepare themselves in any real way for success as an adult. It is unrealistic to expect ASD children to magically think and behave as neurotypical people, no matter how much behavior therapy they endure or which combination of drugs they are given. It is our strong belief that mothers with ASD children need to be aware that there is real hope beyond the terribly harmful, faddish, jump-on-the-bandwagon "defeat autism now" mentality. If treated with respect for the potential inherent in their different but sometimes restricted perception systems, the result often is a child who can develop into an independent, effective, and respected adult.

The early development of an effective communication system between the mentor and the child will lead to the discovery and the appropriate encouragement of talents. We do not maintain that every ASD child is a savant, but it is not unusual for an autistic child to be a savant, and the spectrum reflects degrees of this characteristic. It is an accepted statistic that better than 10% of autistic children are savant, compared to less than 1% of the general population. It follows logically that at varying levels of autism, varying degrees and types of talents likely exist. Discovery and nourishment of these sometimes near-savant skills—or any marketable skills—will go a long way toward instilling self-respect and preparing a spectrum child for a successful future.

The presenters at the OAR convocation focused on behavior modification to improve social skills and institute adaptive social behaviors, with no thought to exploring what oddly different intrinsic communication and learning skills a child might possess. Later, in adult life, these same children will wonder why they were trained like dogs to behave in an acceptable way, with no thought to developing the mind inside. As a result, many spectrum children display increasingly disruptive or unusual (sometimes even harmful) behaviors. The research community has failed them by maintaining a stubborn inability to grasp the basic facts of living on the spectrum in a neurotypical world

In addition, local caregivers and mentors have noted that once a spectrum child or adolescent realizes that he or she actually can be understood and has the possibility of developing a marketable skill, the social interaction issues generally tend to quickly resolve themselves.

The bottom line is that many of these children certainly do not have what they are taught to perceive as an irreversible and tragic disorder, low capability, and—by no means—low intelligence. These spectrum children would be better served by reevaluating the priorities and the attitudes of the medical and scientific communities with an open mind to the truth that many ASD children are doomed to lead wasted lives when it is not only not necessary but also morally wrong.

One of the members of our group, Bob Morris, who is himself a spectrum adult with a spectrum child, has helped found and develop Techniqual Mentoring Services (TMS) in the Atlanta metropolitan area, which has shown marked success with implementing some of the methods discussed here. The backbone of Morris's program is detailed, individual evaluations and a needs hierarchy tailored specifically for ASD adults, caregivers, and ASD children and their parents. Here is a descriptive quote from Morris himself: "We are identifiers and developers of eccentric expertise, mentors of real experience in eccentric expertise, and finders of and installers into niches. Then, we are real-world, getting-an-independent-life-as-soon-as-possible facilitators." We feel that Morris has a true grasp of the needs of ASD children and adults and has a solid start with TMS, so many wasted community resources, if made available, could be put into immediate and effective use.

All of us should have the same goal: To nurture and develop spectrum children in such a way as to maintain who they are and allow them to move into adulthood as independent, productive, and capable citizens. It is our sincere wish that both the autistic/Asperger and the neurotypical scientific communities will come together to work in a real way for that common goal.

Again, thank you for the opportunity to speak. We look forward to further open discussion.

It's All a Sham

Walt Guthrie

On the second day of the convocation, Dr. Thomas Zane gave a PowerPoint presentation titled "Pseudoscience in Social Skills Research and Intervention." For a brief moment, inadvertently, he almost hit on the truth.

There is little reason, other than this moment, to note the presentation. It was, from appearances, a seemingly hastily assembled, cut-and-paste job in which such odds and ends as a Unabomber quote and a Photoshopped caricature of an already-discredited scam were thrown into a mix with the belief that a coherent argument would somehow pop out at the end of the process. But one item in this gumbo is worth noting—a cartoon.

In the first panel of the cartoon, one man stands above another with his foot on his neck.

"Ouch! You're standing on my neck!" the prone figure complains.

"Well, that's one point of view," says the dominant figure in the next panel. "But one could also say that you are trying to trip me with your neck. You see, in the post-modern condition, we create our own reality based on our internalized preconceptions. Since there is no longer one objective truth, we are free to create our own truth. So you see, there is no right and wrong—just an infinite number of equally valid 'stories.'"

"But you're still standing on my neck!" the aggrieved figure protests.

"You never went to college, did you?" the straw man counters.

Apparently, Zane believes that someone is standing on *his* neck. Or, at the very least, the boot of some antiscientific or pseudoscientific cabal is planted firmly on the collective throat of the scientific community, which is represented by Zane and his colleagues in the applied behavior analysis (ABA) movement.

The cartoon, crude and didactic as it was, is not a very good one. But in some ways, it is an accurate representation of the situation. Yet Zane is dead wrong in his interpretation. ABA is not the aggrieved victim on the ground. It is, rather, the booted thug, blinded by its own rhetorical games-manship and pseudoscientific claptrap.

We've been here before.

In the early part of the last century, the proponents of eugenics made a similar claim to scientific respectability. Although it is true that they did employ some scientific methodologies, the epistemological foundation of their "science"—that the white race was superior to all others—was based on nothing more than a common social construct, one that was, at the time, intuitively and unquestionably obvious to both its practitioners and much of the dominant society at large. Indeed, the prejudices of the "science" and society reinforced each other. Its "scientific" findings provided a rationalization for miscegenation laws, forced sterilizations, and the ordering of a Jim Crow society.

Eugenics was ultimately invalidated as a science, but not by some profound new biological or genetic discovery. Instead, it was an understanding, following World War II and the uncovering of the crimes of the Nazis, of exactly where such "sciences" ultimately lead.

The treatment of homosexuality stands as another example. Its removal from *DSM-III* (*Diagnostic and Statistical Manual of Mental Disorders, Third Edition*) in 1973 was a result, not of some new discovery by researchers, but rather of evolving social mores and politics. Once a significant portion of society realized it was just a pathologized social construct, it ceased to be an abnormality, and the need for a cure disappeared.

The autistic person finds himself or herself occupying a relatively analogous position to the aforementioned, although the current labelers and categorizers would doubtless beg to differ. This time, the response is that the science is unassailable.

But is it? If real science is indeed involved in the process, little evidence of it was present at the official convocation. In Dr. Suzanne Letso's opening presentation, she submitted a "Parents' Bill of Rights," a set of principles that seem to have been dictated by the whims of professional and personal self-absorption and then snatched out of thin air. One of those discovered rights is the right of the autistic child to get prompt intervention, presumably from behaviorists like Letso. How wonderfully convenient!

The last of the rights was "Going to my grave in peace."

Really. Honestly. Is this science?

In the brief question session following her presentation, Letso was unwilling or unable to defend her use of the word *disorder* in reference to autism. She is unable to defend the use of a basic term that is a foundation of her whole area of expertise, but she is able to discern a "right" to "go to [one's] grave in peace."

This was not the objective truth of Zane's cartoon. Rather, it sounds as if Letso was creating her own truth based on her internalized preconceptions.

And so it went.

Dr. Eric Mayville, after mentioning during his presentation the autistic person's tendency to avoid eye contact, was asked if he knew why this was so. He didn't. Why not, he was further questioned, ask the autistics themselves? After all, plenty on the spectrum are quite capable of communicating why they do what they do or what various behaviors mean to them. Other researchers chimed in that that would not be "science."

Of course not. Let us not make the mistake of asking autistics to convey their inner thought processes. Better to conduct one's research with proper respect for Skinnerian techniques than to commit the fallacy of anthropomorphizing human beings.

Because the behaviorist is incapable of acknowledging in any meaningful way the inner life of the autistic, all that is left is the external manifestations of that life: behavior. Treatment becomes nothing more than modifying the behavior in accordance with the whims of whoever is picking up the tab.

Dr. Roy Sanders provided a laundry list of powerful drugs whose only purpose, in many cases, was to modify expressed behaviors from those exhibited to those acceptable to a third person. All talk of side effects was limited to the strictly biological and behavioral effects. As long as the child (the convocation primarily concerned itself with children) was behaving in a more acceptable manner and not suffering any overt physical reactions, then the treatment is considered a success.

This "Clockwork Orange" thinking raises a point that even the convocation had to address: If the goal is moving a child from one set of behaviors to another, how is success ultimately measured?

One suggestion, by an invited panel member, was to count the number of birthday party invitations received pre- and post-intervention and see if the number had gone up. More birthday party invites equals ABA success!

Ah, "science." Meticulously collating and measuring birthday party invitations to affix a childhood happiness index down to the third decimal. Would autistic children *really* be happier shoved into the noisy chaos of more birthday parties?

One could ask those on the spectrum. But of course that wouldn't be "science." Apparently, based on this convocation, what *is* "science" is to ask leading questions of an autistic child—such as "Would you like a friend?"—and then inferring from a child's positive response that that child wants to have every moment of his or her precious time alone stolen by faux friends set up by adult "experts" as part of some program.

Both the scientific and the pseudoscientific communities threaten the autistic spectrum community finds itself now threatened by both a scientific and a pseudo-scientific community. The scientific community works toward a "cure," which can mean only one thing: the identification and the isolation of the genetic markers for autism. Once this is achieved, a test for such markers can be developed. Then a genetic search-and-destroy campaign can be launched, eliminating the next and all future generations of autistics.

Of course, there is a huge chasm separating "can" and "will." The identification of markers for either freckles or red hair does not particularly bode ill for future generations who might possess those traits. But those people also do not face a campaign of unceasing blood libel perpetrated by such organizations as Cure Autism Now and Autism Speaks, where parents of autistic children can rattle on endlessly on their web sites and their propaganda videos about what a terrible burden their children are, sometimes with those very same children sitting right next to them.

Because the classification of autism as a disorder is a social construct, just as the classification of homosexuality was similarly classified 40 years previously, no amount of research or experimentation can falsify it, just as no amount of research could contradict that political dissent was a mental disorder in the former Soviet Union. Those with the power to label create their own truth, tautological as it may be.

There is no reason to doubt that the equally fraudulent and oppressive paradigms on display at this convocation should ultimately fare any better.

But the rapidity of that demise is dependent upon the autistic community itself. Those on the spectrum must come together to change the political and the social climate. This is already beginning to happen, thanks to the Internet, although it is likely that many of those at this convocation, professionally trained not to hear the ideas and opinions of the autistic community as anything other than behavioral symptoms of this or that pathology, will not even notice the climate change. When this finally happens, behaviorism will be rendered as irrelevant as eugenics.

Until then, behaviorists need to know the voice of our community will become only louder and angrier.

You're standing on our neck.

Get off our neck.

To Fit or Not to Fit

Patricia Lanaspa

When you become a parent, the truth is, you're not really completely prepared to face the challenges of this "profession." You're full of hope, best intentions, and expectations, but some of us find ourselves in situations that we never predicted, such as raising a child with a disability. In the case of children with autism, the worst "handicap" they may have is the capability to communicate with others and "fit" in a society that doesn't understand their way of being.

As a mother, you're torn between these needs to connect with your child and the acceptance of what he can become and letting him be "himself." I used to fantasize that, after we both passed away and would be in heaven (how optimistic I am!), I would be able speak to my son and tell him all the things I wanted to, and we could actually have a dialogue, not just an echolalic conversation. And he could tell me things such as "Mommy, that day my head really ached, but I couldn't say those words, so I just banged it against the wall" or "Mommy, how much I enjoyed going to Disney with you!"

I don't fantasize anymore. Instead, I've been very persistent, and every day I tell him like a hundred times, "Mommy loves you so much; you're my little angel," and he's able to reply, "I love you." Still, he can't tell me why he's crying, and it's difficult for him to choose between two options and give the answer orally, but I know we're deeply connected.

When I came to this convocation about social skills and adaptive behavior in individuals with autism spectrum disorders, I met several people who are on the spectrum, which really opened my eyes on how we contemplate our children. The range of this spectrum is so wide that it's not possible to generalize; it's better to see each case separately. There are parents among us who were never able to hear their child utter a word. Worse, these children show behaviors that can lead to severe injuries. Shall we try to modify this or just let them be because it's their right to be accepted the way they are? Shall we consider them "misfits" to society and try to change them, increase their vocabulary, modify their conduct, and apply any kind of intervention possible to help them "overcome their condition"? I dare say that this question should be answered first by the parents. What do I want to see in my child? What am I realistically able to modify? What is necessary to modify? When am I invading my child's right to be who he or she is? Again, the key is to see where along the spectrum your child is located.

During the convocation, we were able to listen to the voices of many adults with either Asperger syndrome or high-functioning autism, and, in these cases, most of them were validating their need to be respected the way they are. Who are we—the typical people—to tell them that they're wrong? That it's important to them to make eye contact; to practice interpreting the nonverbal clues of a conversation; to agree that there are many roads that you can take to one place, but you don't need to always follow the same street; and that changes in our schedule occur and that we need to adapt to them?

I believe these people are key for investigators, therapists, and professionals to understand—those who don't have a voice or can't make themselves understood. They're the ones who can explain the "mysterious ways" a person with autism functions. Is our vision of what a quality of life is the correct one? Why is it better than someone else's? Do they want to see their minds, attitudes, and behaviors dissected again and again? Again, these people should speak for those who can't do it and acknowledge the differences. As parents, we want to know the why. Why is he acting like that? Why is he bothered by this noise? Why doesn't he want to eat this food? Why is he crying? Why does such a device fascinate him? They cannot speak, and they cannot express their feelings, so it's really up to "the rest of us" to interpret their needs.

I'm open to all kinds of interventions that can be scientifically proved. The problem is, to get to "scientifically proven interventions," you have to experiment and speculate a lot. Am I willing to make my child available to researchers? I've already done so, but many parents choose differently. I believe that in only contemplating the individualities and hearing all the voices can we be successful.

The Middle School Dance

A Mother's Answer

Stacey Ramirez

I sat in the driver's seat white knuckled as I waited in a long line of cars to pick up Ryan from the eighth-grade dance. He was graduating from middle school, and this monumental event was being celebrated with a dance in the school gym. I was afraid that other students would not accept Ryan at the dance. After all, there was no teacher or paraprofessional assigned to make sure Ryan was included and smooth out any problems that might occur. I feared that my heartfelt commitment to inclusive education would be shown to be misguided—that my hopes and dreams were really delusions.

Middle school had been a long three years. The highs had not been very high, but the lows had been very low. Ryan has autism and has an individualized education program (IEP) for school instruction. During elementary school, Ryan had always been included in general education classes. His teachers and I worked together to ensure that everyone's needs were met, and he received supports that worked.

The team concept fell apart in the sixth grade, the first year of middle school. The sixth-grade educators did not seem to understand or appreci-ate the importance of inclusion for students with special needs. The teach-ers truly believed that he was neither accepted by his peers nor belonged in general education classes. By the end of sixth grade, we were engaged in legal action to get Ryan's education back on an inclusion track. It was difficult, but we recovered from the devastation of the sixth-grade IEP to complete his middle school career on a positive note. The experience had, however, left me questioning whether inclusion was right for Ryan. "Are accommodations in the general education class the right choice for a student with autism? Am I doing the right thing for my son? Have I been fighting the good fight but at his expense?"

Ryan had been talking about the dance for weeks. In his usual fashion, he had the date recorded on the calendar. We talked about the dance every day as it approached, and he somewhat obsessively planned the evening.

231

We got the perfect outfit, a black silk shirt with tan linen pants. And we practiced dancing. I tried to help him overcome the "Ryan Swing." He would hold his hands to the side of his head and move his hips side to side. It was fun to watch at home, but, as we learned from his older brother, definitely not good for the eighth-grade dance.

The day of the dance finally arrived. He got dressed in his new outfit and demanded we take pictures in our rose garden. As we arrived, girls in long flowing gowns and boys in tee shirts and jeans were getting out of cars in groups of three or four. A large group of students had congregated in front of the school. Ryan and I finally made it to the front of the drop-off line. He got out of the van, all alone. He disappeared into the crowd, and a tear wet my check as I drove away. The familiar "what if" questions began to flood my mind. "What if the other kids laughed at him for dancing funny? What if the girls all say no when he asks them to dance? What if the music is too loud and hurts his ears? What if he spends the whole night alone in a corner?" Oh, how I wished I had bought him that cell phone he had asked for so many times. Then I could run to his rescue when he called sad and lonely.

The 2 hours scheduled for the dance seemed more like 6 hours. I left the house 30 minutes early, even though it took only 5 minutes to get to the school. I wanted to be first in the car line. I was certain that Ryan was miserable and would want—no, need—my love and support. To my surprise, I was not close to being the first parent at the school. I was way back in an already long line of cars. A thought crossed my mind, "Could it be that I was not alone in my anxieties of having a child at the middle school dance?" I realized that having a child with special needs did not make me so different in this scenario.

As I sat in the driver's seat and waited anxiously, I wanted desperately to get to Ryan, but there was no way around the crowd. I could see that some of the kids were leaving the building and getting into cars. Slowly the car line crept to the front of the school. My heart was pounding as I finally made it to the gym. "Where is Ryan? Where is he?!" I wondered if I should park and go look for him. What if he was in the boys' room crying?

I relaxed just a bit when I saw him smiling as he finally emerged from a crowd of students. My heart soared as he got in the van and said he had a great time and danced with several friends. My anxiety transformed into elation when Ryan received a friendly farewell from a chorus of his classmates. In synchrony, the crowd yelled, "Bye, Ryan! Bye!" As we drove away, I even heard several friends shout, "I love you, Ryan."

As we drove home, tears streamed down my face, and Ryan began to study my face. His furrowed brow told me that it bothered him to see me cry. With a worried tone, he asked, "Why are you crying, Mom?" I explained that they were happy tears. I'd been worried that he might be sad and lonely at the dance, but now I was glad to know he had a great time. His response spoke volumes. "Why would I be sad, Mom? I was with my friends."

Many parents second-guess themselves and the decisions they make for their children—especially if they have a child with special needs. I received the gift of having my second-guesses and questions answered the evening of the middle school dance. I was assured that fighting the good fight for inclusion was right for Ryan. I willingly fought these battles because being included was important to Ryan. When asked about possible placements, he would eagerly announce that he wanted to be with his friends. For Ryan, being in a small group in a separate class was not an option. I always had some questions about how well he would do, but he has far exceeded all my expectations for classroom inclusion. Never had I dreamed that he would so completely break through the barriers and become part of his school community. For now, I am grateful for the answers and the life lessons brought to me by a simple eighth-grade dance.

In reflecting on the events and the conversations at the convocation, I can say only that I want for every parent to experience what I did at the end of the evening of Ryan's dance. Is social skills training, on its own, sufficient to help a student with autism be part of the school community? I'm afraid the answer is not likely. Is it important for Ryan to have social skills? The answer is yes, of course, but I think that training alone is not enough. Ryan has friends because of who he is—lovable, friendly, funny, and sociable (to a point). But is this enough? The answer, once again, is probably not. Ryan and I worked together as a team for him to be included. Ryan has "typical" friends because he was given the opportunity in the general education class to get to know "typical" peers, and they got to know him. I think that this is an important and necessary part of any program. I love Ryan and see him as an incredible force. With the help of his parents and school staff, he created his own perfect storm and established himself as a member of his school community. I wish that all kids had the opportunity to be this welcomed.

"Refl-Ex-ions"
on OAR 2008

Rosa I. Arriaga

According to Gerhardt, the idea behind the 2008 OAR Autism Research Convocation was to "bring the best minds in the field together with other professionals...to illuminate topics and priorities for research" (2008, p. 2). In June 2008, I was in the "other professionals" category. I had just finished my second year on the faculty in the College of Computing at the Georgia Institute of Technology (Georgia Tech). To some, my title of senior research scientist concocts notions of a person with deep knowledge of networks, databases, and software development. But, alas, I am a developmental psychologist. On hearing this, some might imagine a person with an in-depth understanding of autism spectrum disorders (ASDs) and perhaps able to contribute to the topic at hand—social skills and adaptive behavior in individuals with ASDs. That was not the case either; I had spent my graduate career trying to understand whether babies are born knowing about number. However, having embarked on a new career at Georgia Tech, my goal at the convocation was to learn as much as possible from those in the "best minds" category and see whether any of what they had to offer could be enhanced by technology. We had already shown some success in supporting other areas of autism (Gillette et al., 2007; Hayes et al., 2006; Kientz, Hayes, Grinter, & Abowd, 2006).

Gerhardt concludes that the convocation was an "extraordinary success" (2008, p. 2) and that its primary goal of "providing a comprehensive review and summary of the current state of ASD-related research on one specific topic and, subsequently, offer recommendations in terms of best practices in that particular area and identify future research priorities," was accomplished. I couldn't agree more. As a novice in the area of social and adaptive skills research, I left with a sense of what the state of both the art and the science were in the area and a notion of what technology might offer. I took this knowledge back to my students and colleagues, and from it, a new research program emerged. This led to a number of publications (Boujarwah, Abowd, & Arriaga, 2012; Boujarwah, Hong, Isbell, Arriaga, & Abowd, 2010; Gillesen, Hong, & Arriaga, 2009; Riedl et al., 2009a, 2009b), and a doctoral dissertation (Boujarwah, 2012). In brief, the system we developed presents individuals diagnosed with high-functioning autism spectrum disorder (or Asperger syndrome) with social problem-solving exercises. These are presented as scenarios that have obstacles and a set of solutions that the individual can choose from. At the end of the exercise, the individual gets to reflect on the social scenario he or she just experienced. Our system, Refl-ex, gets its name from the constant loop of *ex*periences and *refl*ection activities that the individual gets to practice. (See the demo at http://research.hsi .gatech.edu/reflexstudy/index.php; login: oar; password: oar2008)

The "experience" component of the system is presented from a first-person perspective with engaging illustrations and scenarios that guide a player through the activity. First, a predictable scenario is given (a boy is dropped off at the movie theater by his caregiver). In this scenario, nothing goes wrong, and the player just reads through it to become familiar with the setting. Next is a sabotaged scenario, which starts off in the same manner as the predictable scenario but encounters a problem (e.g., the movie he was going to see is sold out). Then the player must decide from among three different courses of action, with one or more options that may be appropriate for the setting (e.g., choose to see the same movie at a different time or do another activity at the mall). The narrative of the scenario then branches depending on the outcome that the player picks (e.g., if he sees a movie at a different time, then he must inform his caregiver that he will not be ready to be picked up at the agreed time). The "reflection" component allows the player to reconstruct experiences with the scenario via virtual puzzle pieces, creating a narrative that can be assessed by a clinician. The data from the experience and the reflection components can be a form of measurement that reports the narrative and the social capabilities of the player. During the course of our research, we considered using artificial intelligence techniques so that the data from previous sessions with Refl-Ex enables the system to automatically determine the degree of complexity of the new scenario (Riedl et al., 2009a, 2009b).

Gerhardt (2008) summarized some of the consensus points taken from the convocation. Here I highlight how the Refl-Ex system addresses these points:

- *A more comprehensive approach to investigating issues related to social skills is needed if significant change is to be possible.* In particular, the field needs to move from targeting individual social skills to targeting contextual social competence. We decided to address issues of social competence from the angle of enhancing problem-solving skills. The scenarios are designed to highlight environmental contexts that an individual may experience, such as dealing with unexpected events that may occur during a preferred outing (such as going to the movies) or a scheduled event (lunchtime).

- The vast majority of research in social skills is focused on younger learners on the spectrum. *There is, therefore, a need for greater research attention toward both adolescent and adult learners.* Our target audience includes adolescents or young adults who may have a diagnosis of Asperger syndrome or high-functioning autism.

- *There is a very real need for research and intervention protocols that allow for greater input by individuals on the spectrum and their families.* Our long-term goal is to put our system online, where parents and teachers can suggest scenarios, and online community members can help design the outcomes (including both narrative and artwork). We have also created an authoring system to help parents, therapists, and the individual with autism to create richer scenarios to be used with Refl-ex (Boujarwah et al., 2012).

- *Many of the so-called evidence-based interventions for developing social skills fail to easily generalize to daily practice, whereas interventions with a limited evidence base continue to flourish.* Research into more effective means of translating research into practice is indicated. For our user study, we had planned to administer standardized problem-solving tests and looked at problem-solving profiles to see whether repeated experience with our system would change the individual's core aspects of social competence. Here we had had limited success and found that we fell short on this mark. However the "generalization" goal is one that we strive to achieve in new systems that we are building.

In closing, I believe that the model of the convocation of bringing together the "best researchers" and providing "professionals" with tutorials on research topics is a formula for success. Although our research is in its infancy, the response from the computing and autism community has been very positive. This is evidenced by the papers we have published and the interest our studies continue to generate. As technologists, we are mindful that our work can have impact only if the ASD research community embraces it, and we hope to receive further input from these colleagues as we present our work at relevant conferences. We also look forward to future convocations for new research opportunities.

REFERENCES

Bourjarwah, F.A. *Facilitating the authoring of multimedia social problem solving skills instructional modules.* (Unpublished doctoral dissertation). Georgia Institute of Technology, Atlanta, GA.

Boujarwah, F.A., Abowd, G.D, & Arriaga, R.I. (May 5-10 2012). *Socially computed scripts to support social problem solving skills.* To be presented at The International ACM SIGCHI Conference on Human Factors in Computing Systems 2012 (CHI '12), Austin, Texas.

Boujarwah, F.A., Hong, H., Isbell, J., Arriaga, R.I., & Abowd, G.D. (2010, March). *Training social problem solving skills in adolescents with high-functioning autism.* Proceedings of the 4th International Conference on Pervasive Computing Technologies for Healthcare, Munich, Germany.

Gerhardt, P. (2008, July). Best minds in autism field gathered for 2008 OAR Autism Research Convocation. *The Oaracle* [E-Newsletter]. Retrieved from http://researchautism.org/resources/newsletters/2008/July_2008.asp#two

Gillesen, J., Hong, H., & Arriaga, R.I. (2009, October). *Refl-Ex: Towards designing an interactive and intelligent tool for social skill development of individuals with HFASD/AS.* Paper presented at the International Conference on Designing Pleasurable Products and Interfaces, Compiegne, France.

Gillette, D.R., Hayes, G.R., Abowd, G.D., Cassell, J., el Kaliouby, R., Strickland, D., et al. (2007, April). *Interactive technologies for autism.* CHI '07 Extended Abstracts on Human Factors in Computing Systems, San Jose, CA.

Hayes, G.R., Heflin, J., Abowd, G.D., Gardere, L.M., Matthews, E., Kientz, J.A., et al. (2006, June). *Evaluating a selectively archived video recording system for functional behavior assessment in schools.* Poster presented at the International Meeting for Autism Research, Montreal, Quebec, Canada.

Kientz, J.A., Hayes, G.R., Grinter, R.E., & Abowd, G.D. (2006, November). *From the war room to the living room: Decision support for home-based therapy teams.* Paper presented at the ACM Conference on Computer Supported Cooperative Work, Banff, Alberta, Canada.

Riedl, M.O., Arriaga, R., Boujarwah, F., Hong, H., Isbell, J., & Heflin, L.J. (2009a). *Toward assisted authoring of social skill scenarios for young adults with high functioning autism.* Paper presented at the International Joint Conference on Artificial Intelligence, Pasadena, CA.

Riedl, M.O., Arriaga, R., Boujarwah, F., Hong, H., Isbell, J., & Heflin, L.J. (2009b). *Graphical social scenarios: Toward intervention and authoring for adolescents with high functioning autism.* Paper presented at the Association for the Advancement of Artificial Intelligence Fall Symposium, Arlington, VA.

An Open Response to Dan Crimmins and Peter Gerhardt, et al.

A Response to the Organization for Autism Research and the Applied Research Convocation

Bob Morris

A SERIOUS QUESTION

The Organization for Autism Research (OAR) was coming to town, noting a longtime, low quality of life among learners with autism spectrum disorders (ASDs) and their families. I ardently agree. OAR also heralded its intent to follow a process of using good science in researching interventions, whose purpose would be to improve the quality of life of learners with ASDs and their families. My eyes lit up. I read it again and again.

OAR uses the term *pseudoscience* to indicate disdain for a plethora of futile treatments that have sprung up during what I call the long and painful 65-year history of notably disappointing results in the understanding of autism. I deeply appreciate OAR's use of *pseudo* and the idea of improving interventions and lives. This has been too long in arriving.

The goal of the convocation was to assess the current state of research and practice in the area of social competence and adaptive behavior for learners on the autism spectrum and then offer recommendations for future research. In my mind's eye, those words foster the concept that OAR wishes to be perceived in the most positive of perspectives—a good guy, standing out in a ragtag crowd. My own experiences around autism solidly bring agreement that such a standout is *sorely* needed.

The exercise of writing this response brings to mind again my lifetime of struggling to answer questions faced by many desperate parents. I recognize the question's complexity, difficulty, and possibly blunt directness. However, the problem ACs (*autistic cousins*—a term by which many within the online autistic community have chosen to identify themselves) face, particularly as they age, is very *real*, unnecessarily *huge*, and *massively* affected by the question's answer.

So what is the question? In light of the following statements, just how does a maxed-out, challenged, driven to distraction, desperate parent or, more critically, an adult AC (or anyone else) easily tell just who is a good science guy and a bad science guy—particularly when history clearly and repeatedly shows that, more than occasionally, a good guy performs as a bad guy, and some other guy comes closer to appropriately helping? Here, then, is some of what those searchers face—even today.

- Ph.D.s and M.D.s, male and female, of all races, nations, and faiths, are on both sides; various other highly lettered professionals, nearly all with very glib jawbones, are on both sides.

- On both sides is a long history of myopic assumptions and failed approaches, all accompanied by great volumes of baffle-gas words: some called rogue science, some pseudoscience, and some science, but mostly it's "not-considering-the-whole-truth-science." (Want to bet? Read on.)

- Historically on both sides, academic experts of autism have said, "Trust us, we know what is best to fix your child." Yet to date, *no one* understands the real problem, and there is no official, stable, simple definition for autism. Guesswork abounds, and, to date, very few, if any, have ever listened to the horizon-expanded people with real-life experiences. Also, very few, if any, have understood that not paying attention to the concept of the *hierarchy of use and need* can and does do serious harm.

- On both sides, there have been and are legions of behavior analysts, who haven't or don't realize that they are working with only 20% of the necessary information—information that is available but has remained unknown for more than 60 years. I have lived through this time. And from personal experience, I can speak of results such as the following:

  a. Naively trying to fix symptoms of a problem without even knowing what the problem is has proven unreliable.

  b. Different analysts have observed different phenomena; with insufficient information, they have gone off on a "fix 'em" tear, focusing on only a small part of the issue and never fully integrating the entire situation with other observations or observers.

  c. There have been many people badly damaged (in the name of therapy) and left twisting in the wind.

- The medical psychological academic community (MPAC) euphemistically tells itself in professional conferences that contact with their aging patients is lost between 16 and 24 years of age. Adult ACs use the more direct terms *ignored* and *abandoned*. This paints an accurate picture of hurtful, naive therapy followed by abandonment.

- The natural course of these actions is as follows: There are no less than six notably divergent agendas, all claiming to be *the* way to accomplish whatever "fix" for an AC that the agendites cook up, all for a problem that they are naive about, while calling it "curative therapy." This brings to my mind that they are likely using the wrong tool(s) and don't or can't even realize it.

- On both sides, the representatives selling five of these agendas—and splinters thereof—are sales-force types, with obligatory dress-for-success slick suits, smiling, notably handsome, slick-talking people all rigged so that desperate parents will—well—"salivate." There are even husband and wife teams to better handle, cultivate, and rope in distraught parents. The general gist of sales is the illusion of helping parents fix their kids instead of finding out what is really wrong and addressing it.

- This "fix 'em" mania is, of course, rooted in old habits and assumptions within the naive learned literature and the diagnostic attitude. If an older AC asks the representatives about real problems…guess what? Sympathy groups are blindly collecting sales spiels as information and are becoming springboards for the smooth-talking representatives. (Many parents will have great difficulty distinguishing between information and knowledge.) When older ACs try to draw attention to an "intervention myopia," these information-collecting groups will say, "Where is your degree? What do you know about it? Show us your credentials or sit down, shut up, and keep your place."

- Cure groups, all operating from myopic assumptions related to the *Diagnostic and Statistical Manual of Mental Disorders (DSM)*, the naive learned literature, and the diagnostic attitude, have long noticed the stalled progress and are pushing to advance *relief*, and they are encouraging vast projects to be attempted without the benefit of full understanding. (The vast majority of parents will have no way of knowing that *DSM* is *not* a scientific document.)

- Dangerous and aggressive practitioners exist today, with new ones appearing from the woodwork, especially (but not always) where the "good guys" do not tread. Yet the good guys are not visibly and appropriately addressing the use and the sales of dangerous and aggressive versions of anything, much less the rogue and pseudo stuff.

These statements should demonstrate the problems that parents face. So, Peter and Dan, I place the question to you to try to tell me, other adult ACs, or any of the parents mentioned at the top: "Just how does one tell a good guy from a bad guy?" I'm glad to furnish a straightforward, practical, bone simple, answer to the question—an answer that is addressed from several perspectives within this response.

The OAR web site seems to indicate that OAR is trying to address these same issues—that many treatments don't work—but there is something sort of ambiguous (possibly amiss) at least within my understanding of the situation that OAR is looking at. The OAR web site does not specifically say so, but the vast majority of the time spent in this convocation turned out to be behaviorism oriented, and, to my knowledge, behaviorism-oriented professionals are in the vast majority within the MPAC that is concerned with autism (MPACCWA). In my observation, behaviorists have been in control of the research into autism for 70 years. There are approaches other than behaviorism, but, again in my observation, behaviorists themselves have a *powerful* tendency to disregard those approaches. I hope Peter or Dan can offer some explanation.

For the purposes of this response, I hold to the presumption that behaviorists consider themselves as *the* way to go, simply because they behave that way. Therefore, when I refer to either the MPAC or the MPACCWA, I am essentially speaking to behaviorism.

PREFACE

My "think" processing is in some kind of complex imaging, with at least 7 degrees of freedom. Words, being essentially linear, are clunky. In other words, I cannot think in words very well at all, and every time I try euphemistic or diplomatic palaver, things can get really balled up. With those facts in mind, I trust you can live with direct language. I also emphasize that the contents of this response must not be construed as pointed to any particular person, except where named.

Taking OAR's words to mean what they say, this response includes comparing OAR presenters to other folks with whom I have had long experiences within the industry: the MPACCWA. I am playing the part of the child depicted in "The Emperor's New Clothes." To wit, the industry has been rigidly fixated only on children and has been stuck on "correcting" their behavior without understanding what causes their behavior. This situation is summed up as chasing symptoms without addressing the real problem: "trying to fix what ain't broke." The cause is very real, folks; I live there.

People living as ACs have long lived with various poorly recognized vulnerabilities and have long been perceived as having behavior problems, often unpredictable, and a serious drag on family life. However, we at Technical Mentoring Services (TMS) in Atlanta, Georgia, have found that a consequence of constantly trying to fix what ain't broke—while ignoring the real problem—fosters what is in disarray becoming worse. Cooperating with OAR's words, this response supplies some knowledge of practical remedies, and I can supply more. At TMS, we are forming a handle that facilitates the understanding of autism, one that your industry has long been talking about searching for but in the wrong place(s). This handle will become apparent within these pages. The following list starts the process in a first-things-first order:

- Please note, I didn't say *cause*, *cure*, or *fix*. I said *handle*, a place to get a real-world grip on the issue, a grip that your industry has never achieved. Hence, for this and other reasons, your industry is unable to define autism in a simple, direct, and stable manner. Guesswork—partly on target yet also misleading and obfuscating—has reigned for 70 years.

- There will be emotion in these pages—a powerful basis for such results from the unnecessary naiveté of the industry.

- Frustration and the impossibility of escaping it, including an inclination to seethe or fester, has been incessantly drummed into nearly all ACs. Some have had this basis more vigorously inserted, let's say, "hammered" in. I would hope it is unnecessary to describe the effect of a level of even stronger perpetration, that of "aggressive treatment."

- Vulnerable children, living with poorly recognized, differently thinking, and differently communicating minds and neurological systems, are highly susceptible to this form of unnecessary festering infection, an infection that often cannot be retired by simple means. Please remember that vulnerability in ACs is a major point within the MPACCWA's 70-year naiveté. There are other points as well, all involving various unskilled defenses.

- I perceived a strong yet naive desire to "help" at this meeting; therefore, this emotion is presented *to but not directed at* the convocation and its participants.

In simplest terms, the emotion in this response is directed at the industry, which, for whatever reason, has long and perhaps inexcusably failed to connect the dots within a sizable quantity of common and tangible facts concerning ACs and the way they relate to their environment.

I also restate for another reason. I hope this response will help you recognize that the failure to realize and understand the *real* problem, while essentially concentrating on fixing and correcting the resulting behavior in children, has created an inescapable, highly emotional situation within the affected individuals—a situation that is an artifact of naiveté, a situation that has cognizant individuals typically painted with having an impossible disorder, treated with disrespect, and finally ignored into abandonment.

This response is both highly congratulatory of your effort to gather together, and, because of speaking frankly about the apparent evidence, I must warn you that it may appear to rake your industry over the coals, when the only intention is to *finally* crack the shell of unnecessary blindness.

I will also follow a rule of good practice, which is to never seriously point out the shortcomings of anything without politely suggesting a thought-out, workable solution. Are you ready?

Please read this response with the idea that I would be glad to discuss all points calmly when and if you ask. However, please keep in mind that I don't think in the same manner as approximately 98% of the population, and there is no way that I can. Neither do I want to because the way I think has allowed me to solve difficult situations that the usual neurotypical (NT) way of thinking didn't or can't solve.

Someone took a risk inviting adult ACs to this meeting that you called a convocation. I wish to genuinely thank you for that, and I hope it will lead to some sorely needed but heretofore lacking knowledge exchange between the MPAC and adult ACs who have been lucky enough to have the needed horizon expansions.

I hope you can understand that we—the attending adult ACs—took a risk as well. An appalling fact is that adult ACs have been trying to communicate with the MPAC since at least 1969 that the reality of AC life and the picture painted by the MPAC were not the same. For whatever reason, these efforts were fruitless. From known MPAC habits, it is likely that their efforts were willfully ignored.

That particular time in space could not possibly have been under either Dan's or Peter's control, but hopefully we might now have a chance to begin what should have started 40 years ago.

I think we all are aware of the political climate within the MPAC approximately 70 years ago, in the late 1930s and early 1940s when Leo Kanner and, independently, Hans Asperger, made some very astute observations, including Kanner's observation of apparent genetic connections. But because of in situ politics, Kanner had to "drop" some of his observations and go another route. The communication of "different" ideas into the existing MPAC was, to say the least, difficult.

Resulting from MPAC naiveté and in situ politics, even the parents of the kids in question were painted as offenders. During that situation, there was not much of a chance in hell that AC communication could have begun sooner than about 1971. There was perhaps a chance to begin communication in the last quarter of the 20th century, when a group of parents found out about some inappropriate "effective" treatments, using aversives and restraints, but the rigid, boxed-in habits of the MPAC prevailed.

I do not wish to nitpick these multiple past issues, beyond simply achieving a mutual understanding that *they were and still are* bad behavioral practices. One presenter spoke of knowing about but downplaying such bad practice(s). There may be more of the same out there than you are willing to admit. At TMS, we have members who have experienced some of these bad practices and now have what amounts to posttraumatic stress disorder and have so far failed to live as independent adults.

There is a major "point-set" buried, perhaps entrenched, within your industry's learned literature and diagnostic attitude, a complex fact bearing heavily on the issue at hand, that I did not hear discussed at all. Even up to the early 1990s, when the terms *AC* and *NT* were established, the buried issue was notably effective, yet still there was not much of a chance in hell for adult ACs to communicate with the MPAC. As you might imagine, we find the same rigid, boxed-in habit(s). I certainly hope that now, roughly 16 years later, the statements made by OAR about evidence-based practices and improving lives will allow a reality-based bridge so that we can truly begin communication.

The points I mentioned soon follow…but first…should you accept the challenge herein, which is a recommendation for a certain kind of mutual help, the need here will likely stretch the limits of your considerable communication skills. Your acceptance of what we offer will also go a long way toward making it possible for your individual organizations' current marketing spiels to come true, possibly within your lifetimes.

The price is simply that some NTs (neurotypicals) within MPAC will have to perceive horizon-expanded ACs as colleagues, albeit oddball, and allow us to show you how to communicate in a rather different way of relating with the environment and in a different way of thinking—features that ACs are born with and can do nothing about, yet we can and do use those inherent capabilities to solve notably complex problems. That described concept is something your researching predecessors had *extreme* difficulty with. By the way, the potential rewards are great, perhaps *huge*.

We attended the convocation because we represent the children you are trying to "fix":

- The adult ACs attending the convocation have lived with and are still living through comparable sensory, perception, and reaction issues, including the resulting frustrations, anxieties, inescapable disappointment and depressions, and concepts that seem intangible to 98% of the world's population, including most of the presenters.

- Adult ACs know about useful stuff resulting from the neurological condition that your target kids are living with, and we can offer a certain guidance and consequently better success in what to do with the "autism problem" that they share with us.

- I believe that we agree that by current life expectancy indicators, all humans will spend something like 79% of their lives beyond 16 years of age. With that, ACs have solid grounds to state that your MPAC predecessors have repeatedly tried to solve a poorly understood situation while steadfastly remaining something more than approximately 80% naive of the situation's real living requirements. They have looked at only the 20% of the information available and have been trying to "fix" kids. We hope to help correct that problem—not the kids but the MPAC naiveté.

- We came because it is *us* that the MPAC is doing complex, far-reaching, and terrible mental surgery on. To date, the MPAC has never bothered to pay appropriate attention to *us*.

At TMS, we have found that by looking at any personality in the order of SPRATS (sensory issues, perception issues, reactions to both sensory and perception issues, abilities, and consequent thinking systems), then sorting ACs from NTs becomes much more reliable, and sorting ACs according to how their minds work becomes rather fascinating because we seem to uncover useful patterns—both talent wise and vulnerability wise.

The acronymic sequence of SPRATS is according to the ascending mental processing required, but it also has another superimposed order. Beautifully simple for what we can learn, this order is a hierarchy of use and need, where A is primary to B, then the combination of AB is primary to C, likewise ABC is primary to D, and so forth. *However*, the addition of B also adds greatly to the quality of A, and C likewise adds greatly to AB, D is necessary for the quality of ABC, and so forth.

Because my own set of native SPRATS does not include much ability to think in words, almost everyone can word things better and more quickly than I can. However, my particular thinking system and insights are much more effective elsewhere—some have said notably powerful. Years ago, at an event of complex conceptual training, with high-end technological equipment, the experts at the time compared my conceptual grasp to that of a steel trap, when "all" I did was build an "image of understanding" in my mind. I can join such an image virtually and swim around within it. I have attempted to describe such an AC thinking system. If you folks are interested, just ask about matrices and spaghetti bowls.

We hope to help you realize that there remains a great deal of old, damaging habits within the MPAC that the presenting group didn't seem aware of. That is, there were some harmful, exceptionally same-old, same-old ideas. For example, during the convocation, there were some welcome perceptions that encouraged my expectations of the OAR goals. I heard and appreciated some serious, well-meaning work, but I also found seriously dangerous, unexplained omissions. Hence, this response is constructed as a reaction to the apparent general belief within nearly all the presenters that few, if any, ACs have the mental wherewithal to deserve respect as capable individuals, much less as colleagues.

Pardon me for saying it this way, but I know that I am so AC-gullible that I have a personal survival rule hammered into me. I wait for actions before I finally decide what any new acquaintance, organization, or person meant to say about almost anything. In the past, I have believed too much of what people said; I have been a real sucker for euphemistic baffle gas, something in huge overabundance in autism meetings. Therefore, I am forced to remember I was potentially pleased to meet this group, and all seemed notably pleasant people. However, among the majority of the presenters, I eventually distilled an essence of a varied but nearly always high percentage of nonsuccess at really understanding people with autism, much less their real-world applications. This is a firmly established dangerous situation for ACs. We attempted to help with that at the convocation with a brief indication of a better way to help, and we do so again in this response.

THREE LAST "PREAMBLISH" COMMENTS

Comment I

I have lived longer than the entire named autism experience. That is, I was an AC before AC was cool. I have lived through many "incidents" of misunderstanding by so-called responsible authority figures, starting perhaps in the third grade. I was lucky, talent wise, so I didn't experience the devastating emptiness that can result from not knowing what I was. I have, however, lived to some degree with the anxiety, the emotional frustration, the eventual depression, and almost whatever else that "AC-ness" may imply.

My wife and I have spent more than 20 years trying to get appropriate help for our second son, always running into something or other with the various consultants indicating incomplete understanding at best and more often a failure to understand the kid at all. Recollecting this series of events brings a refrain to mind, politely stated, "If you can't dazzle 'em with brilliance, then you must use large amounts of euphemistic baffle gas to justify your invoice." In the end, we had to wrestle the appropriate diagnosis from the MPAC. The very month before the appropriate diagnosis was agreed on, vocational rehabilitation system testing diagnosed him wrong *again*. There is a long, insanely expensive, and huge frustration within the rest of the story accompanying these events, which extends beyond 2005. My wife, family, and especially myself have more than paid the dues to be plain spoken and direct with the MPACCWA and various sympathy groups. The other adult ACs attending the convocation also have had more than adequate qualification to speak plainly.

Comment II

I have associated with and communicated well with a sizable and varied, strangely creative group of people from my early teens through all my adult life. (Okay, they were and are geeks, somewhat similar to me, as I'm a bit geeky, too.) They say airline captains are grizzled veterans at 40,000 duty hours. I am an AC, a spectrumite, with something over 622,000 duty hours of direct, hands-on experiences. I grew up with and have long used my own unexpected and different thinking and learning system and know it works. All told, I can add probably more than 175,000 hours encouraging older ACs to develop themselves as opposed to fruitlessly worrying about how to be what they aren't.

I already knew my second son was a geek of some sort when, in great distress, he quit school, never to return. Referencing the idea of this convocation to improve the life of AC learners and their families, I will simply say two things:

1. As many parents, my wife and I have tried the ideas presented at the convocation and found them not addressing our son's needs.

2. We are parents of a now 38-year-old adult AC who was unemployable in 1995 but is now recognized in his field as a sought after eccentric expert. Such a profession doesn't allow unpredictable, disturbing influences even close to the $20 million pieces of equipment that he works on and around every day, with vastly improved social skills and adaptive behavior and remuneration to match.

The *whole* object of rearing a child is to prepare that child for success as an adult. But therein lies a rub—what kind of adult? My wife found a way to keep the home and family operating during the complete uproar, challenge, and unnecessary exercise. After we found that the MPACCWA was going to be somewhere between zero and too little help with our by then adult son, the onus fell on us to figure out a course. I attended conferences and presentations galore, all around the country, finding *nothing* really fitting real-world, adult AC situations. There were occasional attractive titles and lots of glib smiles, but there was little practical substance beyond the same-old, same-old MPAC thinking. I found good people really wanting to help. I even met a guy named Gerhardt about 8 years ago in Tampa whom I thought was really trying but did not appear to know how to go deep enough in his understanding of what an AC's problems are.

In 1998, I spent 6 months as a delegate to an official statewide committee for the State Plan for Autism, where, with the benefit of 20 or so people making pointed phone calls around the United States, we found that through high school, there was precious little practical working knowledge of the needs of real-world ACs lives, with *none* beyond high school. Although several delegates from over the state kept asking for a beyond high-school program, along with my own inadequate bleats to request actually listening to the adult ACs already known in the state, nothing was ever addressed, save finding that numerous other states also had nothing beyond high school and precious little up to that point. This seemed to take pressure off state mental health personnel because when pressed to do something, all they have to do is point to this committee and say, "Do what?" This always brings up the cry for more research.

My wife and I, relying a lot on my lifetime of AC-ological experience, eventually worked out something close to a best practice, a general way to prepare AC young for success as adults in an NT world. (*Note:* This is *not* success as a broken NT adult but as a *fully functioning* adult AC. There is a *big* difference between the two.)

There are three major points of relevance that those of us at TMS have learned by using these hierarchies as guides:

1. ACs can and will have unexpected, and often notably differently operating, thinking, learning, and communication systems.
2. ACs must know and be comfortable with how to apply their differently operating thinking and communication systems.
3. If you do not operate in a manner to build positive self-esteem and capabilities when working with these built-in, differently operating systems, you will not improve the life of an AC learner. "Teaching" social skills to an AC with low self-esteem is out of order and gets the individual nowhere near success as an adult.

The bottom line of qualifications is that after a lifetime of involuntarily having to use a confusing but what eventually became an uncommonly powerful form of thought organization, one that I eventually called a "three-dimensional image of understanding," I have developed a solid esteem of its capability in understanding complex system interactions. This has allowed me to become, after about 11–12 years of deep, concentrated work, a notably rare and capable mentor of and for older ACs and a service provider working to help older ACs prepare themselves for success as functioning adult ACs. I repeat, there are various reasons for *AC individuals to know and be comfortable with whatever their different thinking system is and can do.*

I hope that knowing a lot of what I am doing with older ACs will allow you to view me as a specially qualified, experienced consultant and colleague. I describe myself as an "expert of actual experience." In my humble opinion, TMS is currently at least 15–25 years *ahead* of the MPACCWA in understanding ACs and helping them prepare themselves for success as adult ACs, including help in understanding all the issues of independent living. These "different" thinking systems—if and as we can identify them and if we can help the individual break out of the usual "entrapment-prison"—are usually notably useful, but, I must stress, useful in a restricted way.

Many ACs, in spite of impressive capabilities in certain—even at times many—places, cannot comfortably approach what is commonly known as a fully, well-rounded education. In spite of some well-meaning but naive educators pointing to No Child Left Behind, the AC's education must be "individualized" in a similar manner as the old saw about "individualized services" that sympathy groups always spout.

Here are some examples of powerfully different thinking systems (there are many, many more):

- Albert Einstein called this "my 'imagination,'" where I put my thoughts together. Logic will get you from A to B. But imagination will take you everywhere. The true sign of intelligence is not knowledge but imagination.

- Einstein also connected his intuition into his thinking system: I am enough of an artist to draw freely on my imagination. Imagination is more important than knowledge. For knowledge is limited to all we now know and understand, whereas imagination embraces the entire world and all there will ever be to know and understand. There comes a time when the mind takes a higher plane of knowledge but can never prove how it got there. There is no logical way to discover these elemental laws. There is only the way of intuition, which is helped by a feeling for the order lying behind the appearance. The only really valuable thing is intuition.

- Temple Grandin calls her system "thinking in pictures." I have never spoken with her about how she views intuition, but I am rather certain she has one.

- I call mine my "image of understanding," and this image is known to employ 7 degrees of freedom. I am certain my intuition employs something else. I have never had the benefit of grappling with such thinking with a similar mind. I need to do that because discussing and respecting the thinking system is a way of improving geekish communication.

I'm not saying that any amount of ACs will compare to Einstein's strength. I'm saying that many ACs, now trained (possibly inadvertently) to be waste, can be developed into happy and productive, well paid, eccentric experts within their niche. I'm saying that ACs, if helped to find their niches, soon enough may very well tend to think and act as the "self-actualized personality" that Abraham Maslow described.

Comment III

We have no desire to punish, upstage, or insult anyone with this direct language. We have a strong desire (and qualifications) to point out a better way to help ACs succeed in the NT world. I will not consciously insult a difficult-to-attain academic degree. I also have a few letters behind my name. I know these degrees require a great deal of study, dedication, and work. However, there is a strong precedent indicating that unless very special precautions are taken, a certain form of blindness and an attitude (including in situ politics) often develops among the MPACCWA. Mindsets of habit, rigid box-bound thinking, tunnel vision, and a huge resistance to consider added facts that don't fit the "official" local definition are all involved. There is clear and regular evidence over more than 65 years that politics have often outweighed science.

Indeed, as far as adult ACs are concerned, such a problem of professional attitude has been true for more than the last half of the 20th century. With many of the old attitudes and habits grandfathered in and even apparent in many convocation presenters, I do not know if the blindness and tunnel vision are trained in or are part of politics of an acquired attitude, but they do exist. The ACs attending the convocation picked up the essence of seriously box-bound thinking, almost no knowledge of many realities of a young AC's life, and much less any of the looming visceral facts of an adult AC's life. This situation, existing for more than 65 years, tends to indicate that there is no recognition within the MPACCWA of any appreciable value within the AC's mind.

At times, there is solid reason to train psychological professionals to remain distant from certain problems, but many lessons exist around ACs indicating that proximity is required, *particularly* to find real understanding. My take of all of the convocation presenters, save for a very few, was and is that professional "distance" and the naiveté of detail that comes with said distance is the modus operandi.

The overall blindness in question also involves the fact that the MPACCWA, for at least 40 years, has *chosen* to know essentially nothing of adult ACs—what makes them tick, how they think, how and where they live, and so forth. The irony here is that adult ACs are a major source of useful knowledge and are currently the *only* knowledgeable and operating full-life resource on how to prepare AC kids for success as functioning adult ACs, not as broken adult NTs. Adding fuel to that fire, the MPACCWA has painted such a distorted picture of ACs that some parents of ACs avoid considering themselves as ACs, and the MPACCWA certainly doesn't want them to. But you do remember the genetic connection—don't you?

Adult ACs, and parents of ACs, once kids themselves, have been nearly totally ignored and abandoned by your predecessors. I seriously wonder, "What will be the record of this presenter group?" To date, you have been following the lead of your predecessors, all carefully referenced in their reading reference lists. The majority of the presenters' discussions, interactive among themselves, in this convocation clearly demonstrated in my mind that unless someone with better insight does something, the overall blindness to the reality within AC life ain't gonna get better anytime soon.

The reason is simple: If you are not looking in the right place with the right information in mind, you aren't likely to find what you need.

MAINSTREAM MPAC PERSONNEL AND THEIR RESEARCH INTO THE "AUTISM PROBLEM"

I think in three-dimensional images, a powerful tool to figure out relationships in systems. I won't bore you with much talk about this, but the thoughts making up these images interconnect and also interact in fluid ways, which renders describing stuff in a linear manner difficult. I can easily imagine myself swimming around within an amorphous matrix.

This way of thinking is a major part of my earlier-mentioned difficulty with words. As I developed this response, I tried to stay linear but couldn't fully do it. Some of this response may appear to get ahead of itself or go around the same path twice. Sorry, if you need to explore a good-sized building and must visit every section, sometimes because of the way the building is constructed, you must travel some halls multiple times.

The MPAC has been researching autism for at least 70 years. This section is a perspective of that research from the adult AC side of things. It also has perspectives within perspectives. It is, at once, incomplete and also foreboding of the truth in Einstein's words. I have used the term *incomplete* because I have limited the subject matter in this section to the details gleaned from the convocation, from and of the presenters, details or the lack of, that made the strongest impression on me and are easiest to explain, with solid backup information.

In this perspective, I am also speaking as a graduate advisor might to a group of high-level, respected graduate students who have been stalled or misled by a serious lack of insight and inexperience beyond an unfortunately tautologically tight focus—a situation where "analysts" are repeating assumptions but have failed to analyze.

Here are three examples of missing analysis in this convocation:

1. The *whole* object of rearing a child is to prepare that child for success as an adult, yet the vast majority of the convocation presenters appear to know very little of what it means to be an adult AC.

2. There is reason to strongly suspect or believe that the AC spectrum definitely could be, and likely is, the world's major source of deeply insightful and intuitively powerful creativity. I perceived hints of this from my days of working at the Georgia Tech Engineering Experiment Station in the 1960s. At TMS, we are continuing to find that many deep geeks display various notable AC traits. In fact, we already feel that we can draw a *spectrum organization line*, a line of cumulative dis-

An Open Response 253

comfort or oddity: "A spectrum line of decreasing comfort within normally expected (NT style) thinking and communications, extending
from regular thinking and communication, through odd, to distinct
difficulty with, so-called NT thinking and communication."

This line, starting, say, at the caricature of a certain kind of highly
focused academician (the eccentric professor) through the gifted yet
moody, to bipolar, to Rett syndrome and obsessive-compulsive disorder,
to Asperger syndrome, to Tourette syndrome, to autism, to *deep* autism,
and finally to seizures. (There is more detail, but you get the point.)

This being even close to true, there is a huge need to point out that
the AC spectrum is not the mindless black hole assumed, perpetrated
by the teachings of the MPACCWA and its accumulated learned literature and diagnostic attitude over the past nearly 70 years. Such a
situation presents a larger need to counter the harm being done by the
results of that same paint job.

My pointed question is why has this information taken so long
to penetrate the official awareness of the MPACCWA—an industry
long claiming to research the "autism problem." I think the answer
is enclosed within poorly fitting, rigidly boxed-in thinking that the
MPACCWA has so carefully clung to for 70 years. Please note: *There
is nothing that improves a life more and at lower cost than finding out you are
worth something after all—particularly if such a perception is coming from
your coworkers.*

The current convocation of well-meaning people, operating under
the flags of "good science" and "improving lives," is seemingly somehow unaware of both the age-old naiveté and the resulting plethora
of destructive practices of their teachers and the fact that notable psychologists and other qualified individuals have been pointing to the
idea of something more to autism than the naive and dismal picture
described by their teachers and apparently subscribed to by the majority of the presenters. Incidentally, at TMS, we have found that if you
do pay attention to the SPRATS hierarchy, after a client realizes that
his or her value originated within the actions and the attitudes of peer
appreciation, a graph of the AC's social skills and adaptive behaviors
performance *will* go through the roof, automatically. We even have a
pretty good idea why.

3. Whenever you approach a complex and unfamiliar or oddball system,
you have a situation that long ago became known for difficulties in avoiding misinterpretation of observations, various kinds of other odd errors,
and the resulting highly embarrassing failure. Special tools of scientific
research were needed and developed with blood on the notebooks.

Here are tools for good scientific and engineering practice that are *vital* in analyzing complex dynamic systems. Because some systems *are* hard to understand, you *must use* these tools to get reliably useful results.

1. *Reality checks.* Particularly with qualified natives, reality checks are vital. For 70 years, these have not been done by the MPACCWA and apparently are not even considered, although, perhaps, OAR has actually started to consider this. In complex, unfamiliar, and not understood systems, it is difficult to fully comprehend multiple aspects of all that is going on, so hypotheses get written and tried, to find out how well you sized up the situation. "Missed" targets are as educational (or should be) as "made" targets. As you progress, reality checks save huge surprises, which often amount to huge misses. Why hasn't the MPACCWA used reality checks?

2. *Occam's razor.* Simplicity appears to have been totally ignored for more than 60 years. The learned literature and the diagnostic attitude are literally overstuffed with decades-long accumulation of complex, divergent hypotheses springing from incomplete observations, nearly all with shaky assumptions attached. We can show that for a minimum of 40 years, qualified natives can and have tried to offer practical simplification toward understanding their differences. I will ask the question shortly, attempting to find a good reason for the failure of the MPACCWA to use the offered help. Adding Einstein's opinion, he said, "If you can't explain it simply, you don't understand it well enough."

3. *Completing the scientific method.* Science is, after all, about pursuing the *whole truth*, but what is the record of the MPACCWA? After 7 decades of seriously less-than-stellar success and multiple debacles, your industry still only tries to correct the behavior of frustrated, frightened, and/or thoroughly worn-down children, without really understanding the real root problem and the appropriate behavior to handle the associated vulnerabilities. The industry still doesn't have a stable definition of autism, and adult ACs say what they do have is not acceptable, and there is a notable refusal to learn any lesson from the failures or look for clues in the other 79% of an AC's life into which those children all too quickly grow and find themselves abandoned. The industry still has no official idea that there are notable positive aspects of autism, much less their considerable value, and still pursues fixes outside of and ignoring the limits of first things first.

Please carefully consider "What is wrong with the picture concerning these three tools?" There *will* be a quiz. There is also a fourth tool coming.

Here is a quick review of a few relevant facts on the issue—there are more:

- As you were taught before graduation (or were supposed to have been taught), sometimes in solving difficult problems—because most humans are usually notably fuzzy when more than four or five dynamic things are rapidly happening at once—it is convenient to make an early iteration by not considering all of the information available. The first iterations must be reexamined as newly iteratively acquired information and the unconsidered *are* included. Sometimes this is done through parameters.

- Approximately 79% of a current AC's lifetime can be expected to be spent as an adult. People, your teachers have *never* seriously looked at adult ACs. They have *no* knowledge of what adult ACs encounter every day, or what they can do. They don't know what happens to the adults who become totally ignored; let's say that valid explanation seems in short supply.

- Your teachers also have *never* looked at what happened with adults resulting from the damaging therapy, treatments, and training that those individuals got as kids, and the teachers also forgot the assumptions made—to temporarily ignore what they ignored.

- Your teachers have ignored the basic SPRATS layout of the people that they have treated. SPRATS is a simple way to understand how a mind works with its body to relate to its environment. They also ignored powerful indications in Maslow's *hierarchy of needs*, which was first published in 1943.

- Your teachers have ignored for decades the critical information about a genetic connection that Kanner tried to point out in his 1943 thesis. A genetic connection is a powerful shortcut to looking at older ACs, and they still haven't seriously considered that access port as a route to learning what older ACs are capable of, if developed appropriately. To my knowledge, the genetic connection has been used to only merely augment diagnosis. Does anyone have knowledge as to why?

Here are two examples of the "forgetful" assumptions:

1. One says that AC kids should grow up to be NTs or, at the very least, behave that way. After decades of failing to understand autism, and a massive accumulation of less-than-stellar success, do they ever remember the original assumptions and rethink the issue? Or figure out what is wrong with the original tenets? No. Please take it from real-life experiences: If one's S, P, R, and A (of SPRATS) are different, there is no choice but to have different thinking because one's native communication with one's environment behaves differently and is different in performance. If anyone needs a list of practical rules for investigations into unfamiliar systems used by other branches of science, just ask us at TMS. You certainly won't find such in the MPACCWA's learned literature.

2. A common assumption, particularly around the MPACCWA, is "if you can't measure it or perceive it, ignore it." This assumption is commonly used in the physical sciences to make an early iteration of solutions to a complex problem. The practical way of handling this is to always remember that it is one possible solution, and any politically affected thinking will often forget the lesson involved with the use of assumptions. If you ignore your assumptions and forget about such, the way to spell "ass-u-me" will crop up. The events leading to the *Challenger* disaster had this kind of unknown involved. A major problem within the MPACCWA is that somewhere, somehow, this use of assumption in the study of autism was forgotten.

I am jaded because I have lived through the entire time of this series of events concerning autism. I have also possessed one of those "AC memory systems" most of my life. Am I the only investigator to be somewhat aware of what has happened?

Speaking about the notice of the MPACCWA falling into a notably rigid, boxed-in kind of thinking brings back a long memory of mine and that of other AC's: frustration with the well-known tunnel vision and a certain kind of blindness. I was misled as a kid and misled and ignored as a parent. I have been often shunted off to one side because as a searcher for what respectfully works, I have politely asked difficult questions to some "expert" members of both the MPACCWA and big sympathy groups. If an adult AC asks a difficult question, he or she is put off and shunted to the side 99.41% of the time. Here are two examples:

1. My son and I were invited to *not* come to a state-funded resource center for autism for services because they were too busy.

2. Even various management people of some big sympathy groups have prevented, headed off, and discouraged the presentation of the *positive* aspects of autism at local conferences because I didn't (or couldn't) sound like a professional and would "send the wrong message" to the attendees—that autism doesn't need "fixing."

You must form your own opinions, but to me, so far, the entire series of events concerning autism demonstrates that your teachers decided to make conclusions while looking at only about 20% of the needed and very available information concerning an AC's life—choosing to use information gleaned from frustrated, frightened, and thoroughly beaten-down children. Let me reinforce that. They used limited information drawn from *known* shaky sources and ignored 79% or likely more of very available and better information and are trying to pass themselves off as experts in autism.

In my experience and the experience of many older ACs and their mothers, I make the following observations:

- For generations, the MPACCWA has demonstrated a powerful indication of some kind of obsessive fixation, a zealous effort to ignore what is in favor of what has been long assumed.
- There is a powerful resistance to accepting and explaining reproducible factual information that doesn't "fit" the old, poorly informed assumption set.
- There is a refusal to think outside their poorly fitting, yet stoutly rigid box, which is apparent through their lectures, personal opinions, and published learned literature. All of this existed as your teachers passed this fixation problem down to you.

I certainly hope *you* do not forget that science is all about the *whole* truth because otherwise it is just plain embarrassing to the industry.

Here is the fourth tool I mentioned previously would be coming: *Become aware of the real-world effects of projects: Independent living needs must not be assumed or guessed at.* This is a reality check, but although this may at first seem similar to the first tool, the reality being checked here is the *real* final outcome—not the outcomes chosen in hypothesis—but what the results of the project are as it is worked into the really big picture.

My deepest heartfelt thanks to Peter Gerhardt for using the term *NT* and delving into sexuality issues. He was the only presenter to do such delving and only the third presenter to touch on sexuality *at all.* Peter's presentation indicated that he has been actually listening to real-world AC living problems, an accomplishment apparently uncommon within the rest of the group. That observation frames an upsetting revelation: His presentation was cutting edge to the group, yet he spoke only of the most elementary stuff. Gerhardt was speaking about a powerful, built-in need/drive that people supposedly preparing AC children for adult life have no knowledge of what the kids face. If a need/drive this important is unknown to this cutting edge group, what does that say about the rest of the needs?

During the discussion time, Peter got a refreshingly honest and to the point comment from Joanne Gerenser, indicating that certain "circumstances" interfered with her and her colleagues having the best knowledge of the issue as it affected their clients. As I recollect, at the time I indicated to Joanne a serious appreciation of her remark. I remain still in deep appreciation because that remark helped me translate my thoughts to this response. Thank you again, Joanne.

Later on, Gerhardt asked how I liked his presentation, but I was so frazzled by then that I could not describe what was in my mind. I told him, perhaps inadequately, that "it was in the right direction." I will take this opportunity to soundly thank him for his efforts and strongly encourage him to look deeper. I emphasize the idea that his effort was only exposing the tip of the MPACCWA's iceberg of naiveté about unsupplied or unsatisfied needs relevant to ACs as they grow up.

Apparently, circumstances have somehow prevented the MPACCWA from recognizing that human nature is based on physical, emotional, and intellectual considerations, and there will be a pattern of needs attached if you expect any kind of predictability at all. The MPACCWA has also failed to consider that there is a powerful hierarchy of these needs, expressed as "first things first." If a more primary need is not being met satisfactorily, the individual will tend to display an abnormal prioritization, an irrational (possibly unconscious) and repetitive action, perhaps a craving, any of which can or will suddenly change if the order of satisfaction of more primary needs is worsened or repaired.

The individual's motivations and values displayed while trying to satisfy a higher-priority need will intermask with lower-priority needs, obfuscating both and possibly appearing as arrested development or even disordered personality, until such time as the prior needs are satisfied, at which point their values and motivations will seem to suddenly mature.

Sexual function in humans is built into the master design with greater complexity than most other terrestrial species. In humans possessing a normal sex drive, exercising sexuality is a major quality-of-life factor, and sexual health impacts an individual's physical, emotional, psychological, and even intellectual well-being. Consequently, for a young human with different SPRATS and something even more complex than the usual vulnerabilities, there is a *huge* need to understand a great deal of what is going on. This statement does not even mention that, in some cultures, odd or bizarre behavior can bring on remarkably negative reactions.

I might presume that because of the presenting group's qualifications in their chosen fields and because the convocation was about social skills, adaptive behavior, and improving lives, with a massive concentration on children, the thoughts of AC sexuality issues may not have seriously occupied the presenters' minds. At TMS, we know that this need in young ACs has solid beginnings as early as 6–8 years of age. I myself have often been asked questions from desperate mothers about handling such issues, while their kids were still dependent on their parents for a bath.

I assure you that sexuality in ACs will involve the idea of the SPRATS excursion signature. Senses, perceptions, reactions, abilities, and thinking are all involved. In this case, I can also assure you that where oddities in an individual's SPRATS signature interact with sexuality, we have 70 years of indication that genuine success with such will require attention by someone who really understands ACs.

Sexuality issues become more acute as a preteen grows into a teenager and a young adult. At TMS, we know that ACs will need AC-grade

information, where in our experiences, on receipt of such, the problem can
and will alleviate. But the longer you wait, the longer it will take to achieve
optimum results—that is, a person comfortable with himself or herself and
with others.

CIRCUMSTANCES THAT THE
PRESENTERS HAVE NOT CONSIDERED

Perhaps Joanne's statement about circumstances preventing the MPACCWA
from knowing all you need to know while launching into vast projects is because the learned literature, always referenced in MPACCWA papers, makes
no serious mention of those "disordered" ACs being worthy of consideration
as having unsatisfied needs, much less rational and reliable minds. Peter and
Dan, you know where to send someone willing to work *with* adult ACs, as
opposed to *on* them.

   Here is an allied observation: Apparently your teachers have planted
the seed of naiveté for so long—more than a half century—that ACs are so
terribly disordered and have so little predictability and brain horsepower,
and so forth, that anything you decide to do will "help." But from my
lifetime of working with older AC geek types, I know that what really exists, mind wise, is the unexpected existence of a decidedly different way of
relating to surroundings, thinking, and communication—a notably poor
recognition of same as well that is attached to a rigid, boxed-in naive way
of thinking. Such an unfortunate naiveté is illustrated: If you do not follow
an appropriate priority of need as you "help" them, you likely will be doing
harm, good intentions or not.

THE SCORE OF MPACCWA
RESEARCH AND ACTIONS AFTER 70 YEARS

The following list from history is a brief and incomplete summary of some
facts for OAR to keep in mind in its efforts to use good science. This is
some of the situation you face now.

- There is no agreed-on specific definition, just lists of varying symptoms
  depending on who made the observations.
- The mainstream learned literature is full of dismal diagnostic attitudes and comments, with no positive aspects mentioned, in spite of
  many qualified natives repeatedly saying there *is* something you are
  missing.
- Seventy years of less-than-stellar success, all the while speaking of un-
  fathomable variations in AC children, in spite of 40 years of qualified
  natives, speaking of striking commonalities.

- No one has made an organized list of vulnerabilities; sensory issues, the easiest to spot, have been ignored for at least 50 years.

- No knowledge of adult ACs—how they live, what they can do, and what their living needs are—in spite of qualified natives (and others) telling the MPACCWA that they should be looking at more than what they are looking at.

- Seven decades of notably less-than-stellar success by people of the doctorate caliber indicates a serious blindness, particularly in the face of many qualified natives, who for 40 years have been saying the picture painted by the MPACCWA doesn't match reality.

- Seventy years of less-than-stellar success by working *on* ACs compared to working *with* them.

- Seventy years of less-than-stellar success of trying to correct the kid without understanding what is going on. This without doubt amounts to "never time to do it right but always time to do it over."

- What do you want to call it? Naiveté? Ignorance? Arrogance? Arroignorance? Confusion? Misguidance? Human failings? Politics? Head in the clouds? Silliness? You name the poison, but remember that in reality, as far as really researching ACs is concerned, the entire MPACCWA has been and still is somehow violating or ignoring *all* four proven complex system research tools.

In my opinion, anybody claiming to know how to do autism research should be embarrassed by an industry with that record, especially when these tools and concepts have been tested and found practical and solidly effective for centuries.

THE REAL FINAL
OUTCOME OF MPACCWA-STYLE
INTERVENTIONS AFTER THE SAME 70 YEARS

Numerous ACs are damaged in the name of therapy and abandoned, in spite of good intentions.

More than 90% of the AC population is unemployed or seriously underemployed. The national average income for luckily employed ACs is only $6,000 per year—*that's no typo*. All an AC can usually expect from the typical MPAC outcomes is menial work in something of low responsibility and expectations in the fields of "food, flowers, and floors," and, more than likely, even that will be limited to part-time employment. I am not aware of any MPACCWA outcome that teaches that people with autism are very capable of performing extremely responsible and highly remunerated tasks where their SPRATS fit well.

Industry hasn't been told or shown by the usually recognized experts that these people often have very high potential even though it comes with a different but individually consistent way of communicating. Industry gets the message only that is orchestrated within the ilk of *DSM*: People with autism have a terrible and permanent disorder and are an unpredictable and disturbing influence. How do I know? From my personal experiences working with ACs and getting them placed. Note that I said working *with*, not *on*.

The MPAC too often is highly ecstatic to see a client get the equivalent of a $24,000 annual income; this is so rare that it is poster material. At TMS, we take strong exception to the MPACCWA's continuing history of bad assumptions, naive guessing, disrespect, and damage in the name of therapy. We are about demonstrating a better way. We heartily support using good science and relevant and valid research to develop the whole person according to each person's individual needs.

OAR COMES ON THE SCENE

I got the drift from the invitational messages sent to me that OAR might also be impatient with the MPAC. After all, OAR came to town to talk about relevant and valid research aimed at improving the quality of life of learners with ASDs and their families. This objective and OAR's web site imply that it knows something of what it wants to talk about.

At TMS, we are up to our ears in addressing, organizing, and satisfying real-life requirements and needs for older ACs, particularly adults. Therefore, social skills and adaptive behavior are subjects that TMS is interested in as well, yet just in a slightly different order.

Simply because the announcement indicated that a set of presenters was actively seeking the lead in a knowledge of what works, there was no way I could come to the convocation better prepared than being ready to listen. How could I assume anything until I had a chance to see and hear what the presentations were? Therefore, I was prepared to listen. So, remembering many conferences and much learned literature, I arrived with the following questions in mind:

- How will the OAR presenters stack up next to the old-time score of the MPACCWA's learned literature and diagnostic attitude?
- Do the OAR presenters really know that the AC kids that MPACCWA keeps "fixing" grow up? Do they know that adult ACs even exist?
- Will the OAR presenters understand that naive choices of methods and target outcomes can and does render AC life, particularly adult life, into a deeper layer of hell?

- Do the OAR presenters know what ACs really need? Are they on the right track to know?

   Okay. I went to listen carefully to the presenters to hear what was new. I had no idea about the space and the scheduling constraints ahead of time, but for next time, I have several comments and suggestions from an adult AC point of view.

My Quick Opinion of the Meeting Layout Itself

First, the food, the refreshments, and the choices thereof were second to none. This was particularly helpful because ACs often frazzle quickly when exposed to a large energy expenditure, which is required to exist around and communicate with a crowd of NT people. I lasted the full meeting, partly due to the room's acoustics and partly the chow and the refreshments available. That part of the meeting was superior.

   Second, within a rapid-fire presentation schedule, there was very little time allotted for the thinking horsepower required to handle the messages buried within and perform composing of any needed verbal reply concerning the solid feedback that we have. I had a noticeable difficulty with the crammed-in schedule and the seating: no desk and no wiggle room. Granted, I am an old geezer, but even *one-arm seats* would have made writing notes a lot easier and considerably less stressful.

   Third, as is usually the case around autism conferences, the clergy/faculty seemed to have assumed that only "fix 'em" cheerleaders would be there and *perhaps* the usual token ACs, gullibly hoping for help. The word *help* frames a perception problem here. What ACs need has never been understood by the MPACCWA, hence appropriate help still hasn't happened after 7 decades. Are the presenters trying? I definitely believe so, but the problem is that the learned literature doesn't say. The majority of the presenters were operating with old assumptions as to what help might be—stuff showing poor results for 70 years.

   We caught this group claiming the best of expertise in improving the lives of ACs and families, not thinking about the common difficulties that ACs have. Here is an example of a specific difficulty (or vulnerability if you will): I must receive and translate the thoughts presented into my own thinking system, process, and bring them back out and retrotranslate them to speak with the presenter. I came prepared to do that, all the while listening. I even requested an earpiece that allowed me to be sure I heard the speaker without side interference and even listen when I was out of the room. But schedule wise, there was no provision for a relatively common (among ACs) basic thought system such as mine.

Old MPACCWA habits are insidious and pervasive. So what else is new? There is no awareness that ACs commonly have different thinking. No, I'm *not* complaining about such because an experienced adult can handle such, and the earpiece furnished at my request did its job. This fact is just one of many that convinced us that what I'm going to say in the following sections *must be said.*

Here is an example of *good* stuff: I very much appreciate the advertised follow-up efforts; perhaps the intended interaction was that with a relatively hectic meeting, communication would be better with a personality attached to the later written word, where some folks feel less schedule pressure. This is a good idea to try; I do hope this works.

Presenters' Content During the Convocation

There were twelve 55-minute presentations and two 30-minute presentations: All were pleasantly delivered, and most were well prepared. My impression of each presenter was that he or she was at times a bit too fast but well rehearsed and reasonably comfortable to listen to. Though some were better than others, each displayed efforts to present useful points. Unfortunately, nearly every presenter appeared entrapped in old industry habits around and within that aforementioned rigid box of thinking, which so poorly fits many ACs. Though one presenter came much closer than the rest, from my real-life experiences, not one presenter indicated a real understanding of AC life.

It is vitally interesting to note that usually the well-rehearsed concept kind of means this is the way a speaker tends to think or wants the audience to think that is the way he or she thinks, particularly because almost no presenter drew attention to the many situations that don't seem to fit. I know that there are many occurrences of ACs not fitting in the said box. That unfortunate box can be personified as a diagnostic attitude that is both highly and overly complex and terribly myopic.

The MPACCWA Record

There is a *long time* failure to understand and the consequent failure to stabilize a definition of autism. Many mistakes exist in this time span, and there is little or no evidence of learning from those mistakes.

The OAR Approach

Five presenters advertised that they were members of the OAR scientific council; three were also board-certified behavior analysts (BCBAs). In all, seven of the presenters advertised that they are BCBAs.

These are notably respectable credentials. Because of this high percentage of analysts, I arrived hoping that perhaps some of them were beginning to analyze and get a clue as to why AC behaviors exist. The OAR did post definitions on social skills and adaptive behavior. *That is new* and a positive innovation for change from the many other autism meetings I have attended. But within the definitions and the presentations, I came to believe there was an undercurrent of seriously misunderstanding—perhaps even a total *lack* of understanding—why ACs behave as they do.

Sadly, after listening to several presentations, the answer to my arrival "hopes" became apparent. There still has been no significant analysis of the *real* cause of AC behavior, and there was not much of any realization as to what adult ACs have been trying to communicate for 40 years. I concluded that the traditional habits of the MPACCWA ruled.

The MPACCWA Record

There is an overall tendency to believe the ilk of the *DSM* (which is *not* a scientific document) and the old assumptions within the learned literature and the diagnostic attitude; there was only halfway listening to parents of their subjects—such as when the parents said they missed something in their observations—or not listening at all as to what rational adult ACs have been saying about errors for 40 years. This was followed by a total failure to seriously consider the existence of horizon-expanded adults on the spectrum.

The OAR Approach

Hey! OAR is doing this thing called a convocation. But the vast majority of the presenters seemed to be deeply buried in old MPACCWA habits and ideas. I asked more than one presenter how to improve the delivery of the ignored information message into MPACCWA. I found an extreme likelihood that they were not expecting such a question, and there has been no time to yet obtain meaningful answers.

Yet there is some *good news:* OAR people at least listened to the question.

Unfortunately, the *bad news* is that the vast majority of the OAR presenters have essentially zero knowledge of real-world adult AC issues, so the need to prepare an AC kid for success as an adult AC still seems to be hamstrung, in spite of their desire to help. No one could answer this question: "Why is autism called a disorder?" No presenter had any idea of the end results of their "fixing" on kids, such as when the kid becomes an adult, and none presented any apparent plans to find out. Perhaps one or two had some idea, but the group didn't know enough of anything about what ACs face in everyday life. Is this their fault? Not exactly; they are just following what they learned from their teachers.

The MPACCWA Has Been Stalled on "Disorder" for 70 Years

After looking at only approximately 20% of an AC's life, the presenters have never done reality checks, and they ignore Occam's razor. Their overall tendency is to disrespect abnormality, disregard AC wiring, and ignore vulnerabilities. There is a constant desire to fix, convert, or correct ACs into NTs—to force ACs to emulate performance contrary to what they are.

The MPACCWA Is Also Stalled on "Worthlessness"

There is absolutely no teaching of the positive attributes of autism. This combination attitude has led and still leads many people to take the avenue of "*any* effective treatment" no matter what the cost to the AC kid. I think I can infer from the attitudes of the presenters that the more aggressive "correction" treatments amount to torture methods and the Prussian forceful harshness that are supposedly discouraged now, at least in cases that the presenters know about or are willing to admit.

Beyond this point, however, it was hard to find any real change in the low respect of value of an AC mind, even though I was seriously looking for it. There was no direct mention of the more notable, still existing, more aggressive and forceful treatment centers with the euphemistic names. The outcomes that the presenters were targeting were the usual normalizing of kids' behavior that the industry has been chasing for 70 years. They considered measuring success by the number of birthday parties a kid was invited to.

The problem here, known from direct experiences, is that *adult* ACs know that this is so shortsighted and *not* the major need for survival and success as adults, where ACs spend approximately 80% of their lives.

Goodish News

I missed it, which I regret, but another invitee told me that there was one presentation that did observe that flexibility and resources are on the NT side of the table, so perhaps NTs will do a better job of adapting to ACs.

I must say that is a *most* welcome observation, and it sounded like a good start in the right direction, but I do not believe that this presentation was accompanied with any observations of significant value for AC minds to be protected. Yes, that presenter's thinking was welcome in the idea that this would help ACs, but real-life experiences show that such will not happen beyond a really forward-thinking treatment center, unless the MPACCWA actually breaks away from old habits and announces with plausible conviction that the "behavior problem" that they have been try-ing to "fix" for so long actually indicates the value of a differently thinking AC mind and its creativity, which are worthy of development and applica-tion instead of being dismissed as disordered and permanently disabled.

There are now a few respected people, researchers, scientists, and engineers who are actually advocating paying attention to the value and the creativity of these differently developed minds, but none was men-tioned at the convocation, which was *all* correction of so-called behav-ior problems. MPACCWA has an overall tendency to refuse to admit any positive aspects of the neurological condition. OAR still exhibits the same-old, same-old habit of assuming autism is all bad and must be *trained* away. There is no knowledge of positive aspects—what horizon-widened adults can and have done. The vast majority of presenters were fixated on correcting kids' behaviors, with absolutely no idea of what the real major need might be or the real over-a-lifetime cost to kids who were and are the target of the "fixes."

OAR, Hey! Good News

OAR really did ask the natives for constructive criticism. Wow, I wonder if this is real. I do believe we fully cooperated and offered them the best we could with what we had with us. But with 40 years of zilch, I must say that any demonstrated actions with minimal delay will be of extreme interest to adult ACs worldwide.

The MPACCWA has ignored real sensory issues and other SPRATS issues for so long that there are rampant and uncountable splinter "treat-ments." Also, your MPAC forebears have done and disciples still do their own unjustified "treatments."

OAR, has, as it should, knocked the rampant "treatment/cure" sales hype spiels. OAR called the splinter treatments "pseudoscience." *However,* apparently all the presenters knew very little about any of the genuine va-lidity within the basis for the needs that many splinter treatments attempt to and do fill. Uh-oh! True to MPACCWA teachings, the presenters missed a major real-world point: They appear to have no idea why the treatments sprung up, OAR (sorry about the pun) what to do about repairing said why.

A full hour presentation was spent on the need to get data. Not mentioned, unfortunately, was the MPACCWA's own long history of refusal to get useful and *needed* data, which resulted in bad guesswork and multiple debacles of failed treatments. No mention was made of the MPACCWA's notable lack of learning from its mistakes—no reality checks with those ignored adult ACs, not even the thought of such over a time span of 7 decades.

Nothing was said about the long failure of applied behavior analysis (ABA) to connect AC behaviors with SPRATS issue *vulnerabilities*, even though sensory, perception, and reaction issues are the very basic blocks of personality, and many luckier adult ACs have been trying to warn your industry of the mistake for 40 years. Also, Maslow's works have been before behaviorists for more than 65 years.

Still, there was a small ray of hope. Dr. Ala'i-Rosales indicated that she thought our (the five adult AC panelists) behavior during the convocation fitted well with a form of undeserved rejection—a reality that she had personally lived.

Because of their own steadfast naiveté and resistance to really learning about ACs, your teachers have looked for outcomes to suit their own naive notions and those of ill-informed, desperate parents. The MPACCWA has never analyzed full AC personalities or noticed the eyebrow-raising, extreme agreement with standard impedance-matching practices. Consequently, their attitudes have always come up myopic and are notably disrespectful, dismal, without hope, and with treatments to match that haven't fixed much of anything.

These presenters seem to be much more approachable people than many conferences I have attended, but the expected outcomes still appear molded from an old myopic habit within the MPACCWA. They seem unaware of the thought of looking for what happens to their clients as adults—the real eventual outcome.

I do hope that real communication can commence because unilateral pontification from experts of academia who have never lived the problem has, at the very least, proven the truth in both Einstein's and Maslow's words. I suggest that OAR in general and these presenters in particular keep the following in mind: It is *upon us*, the ACs everywhere, that the worldwide MPACCWA is performing far-reaching, complex, and "terrible" psychological surgery without understanding and then losing contact with (abandoning) their product. I say "terrible" and "abandoning" because in more than 60 years, the MPACCWA has not come close to understanding the root problem *or* evaluating the *real* final outcomes and apparently has never even tried.

Until now, the MPACCWA has never bothered to pay appropriate attention to us (adults ACs), particularly those of us who have been lucky enough to expand horizons far enough to present rational evidence of their errors.

STRAIGHT TALK, FOLKS:
DIRECT THOUGHTS FROM THE TRENCHES

For your consideration and with a request for frank discussion, here are some *accumulated, nagging, analytical thoughts*—all from the perspective of unvarnished real-life experiences of multiple adult ACs who are survival experienced and relatively horizon expanded.

Because TMS has on its client list many adults suffering the results of naive "treatment" encounters, relevant resultant emotions are involved in this section, emotions that are an artifact of *longtime* naive "help." In military palaver, I could say these clients are suffering from "friendly fire attacks"—*highly* emotional events.

It seems strange that behavior analysts *cannot* connect the facts to understand that AC behavior is often a form of communication that requires further analysis, rather than an immediate justification for various forms of concentrated "assertive" correction. In my opinion, you researchers have inherited an onerous situation from your predecessors. This is both a request and a challenge to get such out in the open and start real understanding.

Because other AC people are offering similar messages, people who are much more word oriented than myself and have been misunderstood or ignored for more than 40 years, including myself for at least 14 years, this seems to indicate and require that I must try harder to be effective. I will try to be polite, but it seems that I must be more direct or even blunt to know the point is posted and *un*ambiguous, as I frame what has been wrong and offer practical guidance for a better approach to the "autism problem."

Because of the complexities involved, these thoughts are in no particular order. Each stands alone, but all interact.

SHORT SNORTS

Except for a very few names throughout recent history, the MPACCWA has operated in an extreme shortage of even beginning to understand autism. Instead, its in situ politics always seems to squelch understanding, with the idea of an overpowering defect, which practitioners use as both an excuse and the need for correcting behaviors before any worth or respect can be granted to an individual.

I came away from the convocation discouraged but not with the usual inescapable depression of failing to get across a message of the positive aspects within autism, an indication of real value, of a real hope needed by many desperate parents, and ACs in *deep* trouble. The meeting closed with people saying "It is a start." I certainly do wonder what *that* means.

I tried to introduce the SPRATS sequence and how that would greatly help sorting out vulnerabilities. With zero time allotted, I thought some folks listened. But I've already spoken of my known gullibility, and after many such meetings, believing that I had finally found some appropriate thinking, yet the resulting actions have so far come to nothing.

My discouragement was and is based on the realization that if these adult ACs had not been there, the convocation presenters still would not even think of checking with a horizon-expanded adult AC for who knows how many more years to come. That complacency seems to come from industry habit, policy, and a shell of inexcusably rigid, boxed-in thinking. I am trying again to get through the shell within this requested response.

I know that this situation is not OAR's or directly the presenters' fault, but I submit that it is your responsibility to realize that the presenters' habits so strongly resemble what they were doused with: a set of unchallenged basic tenets based on assumptions of naiveté and industry politics that are buried within the historic learned literature and the diagnostic attitude, which they all keep referring to in bibliographies, and they will have great difficulty in truly "improving lives" as they touted.

I also submit that "behavior corrections," long done with naive purpose and some done with terrible disrespect, even assault young ones without awareness and respect of that powerful but abnormal thinking system—the system that your industry has denied, ignored, and laughed at for its gullibility (remember the joke about the name on the cookie?). This naiveté and disrespect of a young and vulnerable abnormal thinking system is more likely to do permanent harm than you realize.

In fairness to the MPACCWA, Einstein, Max Planck, and others observed the same sort of politics problem within the systems they worked. However, it was not to the massive extent of the MPACCWA's 40-year "stonewall" attitude toward so many adult ACs. This stonewalling is appalling, all the way from Kanner's diversion through 12 other debacles, innumerable mothers, and even more ACs, and then the ACs that got mainstream published. What *is* this?

On thinking awhile, there are at least two similar and appalling circumstances, but these are from history: essentially a factually naive and politically charged "establishment" against single individuals. The current issue is modern, involving far-from-ignorant researchers knowing that they had a longtime unsolved problem. These researchers did not bother to heed repeated, independent, and carefully worded notice of the fact that their hypotheses didn't fit reality very well at all.

The people with the sharpest imaginations (Einstein-style) are notably rare. They are called "genius" a lot. People with somewhat less powerful imaginations (Einstein-style) are not as rare, yet they are called "geek" a lot. In polite circles, most geeky people are perceived as "eccentric experts."

I am reasonably certain that Peter and Dan would agree that most of the presenters did not present as geeky; therefore, we could perceive most of them as NT experts by academia who somehow became known as autism experts. But they clearly have never learned what *real* AC life is. Because they demonstrated that they do not know much about *real* AC life, from where did they get their expert knowledge? I also note that they did come across as if ACs were to be fixed, not appreciated or even developed, *just trained.*

This leads me to believe that the presenters' expertise is highly dependent on the input of teachers and the learned literature: Teachers who have *never* understood autism while espousing old assumptions that have never been rectified; teachers who have passed down diagnostic attitudes based on unrectified old assumptions from their own teachers who never understood autism.

Whether you agree or not, I will remind you that the world's major supply of geek creativity appears to be on the AC spectrum. Incidentally, no real geek objects to being called a geek because there is no other word as easy to pronounce and remember as a description.

Contrary to old and naïve, tightly clung-to assumptions, older, productive, and communicative ACs actually do exist, and we have ample indication that they have for centuries, some notably successful and some not. At TMS, we have found a pattern that has always existed within the older ACs that we have been exposed to. This pattern is most simply described as SPRATS that have enough excursions away from an NT base zone, some to varying degrees above and below typical levels. Often, some have gaps or missing spots. Partial color blindness is an example of a gap.

At TMS, we find notably good correlation with AC behavior when comparing SPRATS signatures. In short, ACs are highly likely to have oddball SPRATS, and their individual behaviors are highly likely to relate to SPRATS issues. Creativity also seems to relate to oddball SPRATS. In summary, we fully expect to identify a large number of data points relating both AC behavior and creativity with oddball SPRATS. We know that this SPRATS situation exists in younger ACs and will be of immense help in understanding their behavior.

By examining biographical information, within resource constraints, we have found that highly creative people in history as well as today have many times shared these oddball SPRATS issues, which are also behavior related.

For whatever reason, the MPACCWA has long chosen to ignore the genetic connection—looking at the kids' parents. However, we know that Kanner himself noticed strong family traits, including SPRATS, but was deliberately blocked from within the MPAC of pursuing such avenues. Asperger also noticed and strongly suggested working with the notable high SPRATS capabilities in the people he studied.

In my opinion, the MPACCWA's narrow focus on "fixing" or "normalizing" frustrated, frightened, and worn-down children and their total failure to pay attention to adult ACs—some of whom were right there with Kanner's kids—and their consequent *failure* to inform later desperate parents of what could have been learned *have done irreversible harm.*

The operative word *fixing* means somehow training ("forcing," no matter how euphemistic the words) the kid to behave as the local professional expert thinks the kid should. First and foremost harmed are the numerous kids who have suffered a bunch of "fixes" that have not worked beyond teaching them of their *lack* of value, and then they were simply forgotten or abandoned. That, of course, translates into the phrase *damaged in the name of naive therapy regardless of the intent.*

As we listened during the convocation, it became plain to me and the other ACs that the behaviorist bent of the presenters was consistently operating as if they were oblivious to the real needs of ACs. This could solidly reinforce the idea that the MPACCWA, in its fixation, has been "fixing what ain't broke and thereby making what is in disarray worse."

In fairness to the MPAC, I *do* agree with the old observations of many patients that resulted in the MPAC's old saw (diagnostic attitude) that we (ACs) all seem so different that they can't figure us out, and we behave so oddly that we must be broken. I *don't* agree with the naive assumptions and "conclusions" and the grandfathered, inbred attitudes that followed. This is, of course, because I have the full benefit of adult experience as an AC (i.e., I'm not guessing) and have the benefit (now, 40 years later, beyond where I should have had the information) of knowing many of the whys about where I am good and where I need help and how to handle it. Also, by being "lucky," I have acquired a healthy self-esteem and this odd capability, and I'm going to guide that acquisition with every older AC that I can.

I again remind you that since at least 1969, rational adult ACs have been openly published trying to tell the MPACCWA that there were and are notable details that the MPAC was not paying attention to, and the MPACCWA's working assumptions had problems. I again suggest you look at the ideas behind the two acronymic sequences I have presented as a much better way to sort out ACs.

A major commonality among ACs of any age that affects behavior and life in general is that by blindly following the NT way—the MPACCWA's way of doing things—we are forced to operate permanently in a state of disappointment, frustration, doubt, and depression. There is a combination of reasons for this. The good news is that this doesn't usually require serious medication after the individual AC has reached appropriate understanding of self and capability. We sincerely thank Dr. Sanders for realizing that less medication is better.

REALITY CHECK AND SPRATS

In all branches of science (except the science around autism), an accepted and regularly applied reality check is as follows: "In any project, if you have applied good people and haven't achieved good results in a reasonable time, something must be wrong with the basic tenets." Yet after 7 decades, heeding this reality check has not happened in the science (or the politics) around MPACCWA. In three inadequately emphasized sentences, these facts stem from my more than a decade of point work:

1. *We ACs are different in our sameness, but largely the same in how we are different from the NT archetype.* Vulnerabilities are nearly always involved, coupled with the individual having no idea of the best defense.

2. *We ACs are definitely neurologically abnormal, clearly illustrated in the SPRATS excursion chart concept.* We operate quite well within certain individual limits (most easily described on a SPRATS chart)—both with stability and reliability.

3. We ACs are generally known to respond extremely well to the expectation of performing as if we were unique instruments, *carefully imped-ance matched to an individualized particular class of insight or related task.*

Impedance matching is an important concept in any physical science and most living conditions. Electronic engineering people "wrote the book," but the application is universal. For any task, using appropriately matched tools, supplies, and knowledge is the only way to optimize the results produced at minimal loss.

A BRIEF EXPLANATION OF
SPRATS AND THOUGHTS ON THEIR SIGNIFICANCE

SPRATS is a way to describe a complete personality via hierarchies for the use of both *system* and *mental processing*. I list them from the bottom up to emphasize where the foundation is. The higher positions are built using the lower positions as foundations and are therefore also highly and dynamically dependent on the lower positions for function as well as architectural support.

- *Thinking systems (TS).* Of course, thinking is the king of processing. This is where one's mind perceives its environment and originates interacting functions of itself and its container (the body) with and within the environment. TS is very dependent on the functioning input–output (I/O) interactions with the body's S, P, R, and A systems, which are the mind's only known ways to communicate outside itself. That is, if your S, P, R, and A I/O systems are different, the TS has no choice but to operate with and as the differences require. Also, because differences at the S, P, R, and A levels will behave cumulatively, whether or not synergistically, we should expect surprising differences at the TS level.

- *Abilities (A).* Abilities involve senses, perceptions, and reactions plus significantly more processing. Complexities—similar and increasing the level of hierarchy above that already listed with S, P, and R—apply. S, P, R, and A (besides sounding like a railroad) really is a complex operating network with many variations available that may *not* be easily NT.

- *Reactions (R).* Reactions are an individual's response to S and P. Varied processing exists, but now actions (the response) and the two-way impulses and the processing required to control them are involved. Some reactions are automatic, and some are voluntary. Some are subliminal, and some are not. Some reaction signals are not sent from brain. Some reactions come from the brain only after a long delay.

- *Perceptions (P).* Perceptions can be viewed as sensory information with some amount of processing included. Some perceptions require more processing than others, and different perceptions require different processing, including but not limited to other mental and sensory inputs.

- *Senses (S).* Sensory signals are raw materials, so to speak. They are impulses in a circuit and require basic (minimized) processing to function. Some sensory signals require no thought processing to create action.

Please remember that there are more than five senses. Also remember that vulnerabilities start here but do not stop here. In other words, because an AC individual's TS has its input from S, P, R, and A, systems are not organized in the same manner as those of NT individuals. The resulting thinking development will be dynamically different or *differential* in nature when compared with NTs. From this SPRATS picture, stating it bluntly, the MPACCWA, while tightly focusing on correcting "defects," has naively failed to explore the entire upper two thirds of the SPRATS chart and its many ramifications.

Early on in this convocation, it became apparent to me that nearly every presenter operated as if unaware of (perhaps even oblivious to) the most basic of SPRATS issues—some notable sensory and perception differences—that we ACs constantly live with. I tried to describe the importance of the SPRATS chart concept of sorting out ACs because after approximately 11 years of working with SPRATS, I know it works. We should keep in mind that depending on what you find in an individual's low or missing SPRATS, you need to know which has priority for attention, what can be developed or worked around as first things first.

As said at the convocation, we ACs are working on a list specifically to help various mentors understand the importance of keeping first things first. The list can be used to help the MPACCWA understand ACs because it supplies a solid handle on why so many confusing facts exist. It can be used to help inexperienced mentors understand what to look for, to truly help an AC without damage. The list can also be given to maxed-out parents to more clearly delineate what's happening. It should become a notably convenient handle to calm much of the "splatter" accumulated from too many unrectified assumptions.

We already know of a few better thinking people who are beginning to plug in their observations of something more to autism than the "fix 'em behaviorists" allow in their rigid thinking. Walt Guthrie brought up a solid point: Beginning in the middle 1940s, many of your predecessors committed various forms of assault with high impunity. The industry, the MPACCWA, has essentially forever treated ACs without respect, just as if we are Skinner's rats. This bad behavior must be eliminated: first, last, and always. Our brains and bodies have been attacked in the name of "doctor always knows best," with "therapy" that included little real respect if any at all. Although on the surface treatments are not as rough as they have been, to this day, the habits of disrespect remain strong, and appalling treatment still exists with ineffective effort on your part to stop it. Your industry, the MPACCWA, has been fixated on fixing kids at almost any cost (who remain the same self but involve higher costs as adults)—all of this without really understanding the needs and the utility of an AC life, particularly as an adult.

I am almost certain that this agenda began in response to loud and long demand from desperate parents; however, something else happened during this time. Both rogue and pseudoscience came on strong, and multiple divergent agendas (pseudo based or not) sprang up. I noticed that the convocation did not mention rogue at all.

The MPACCWA has long indicated to the world that we ACs have a permanent and terrible disorder, low capability, and mostly low to average intelligence; therefore, we are fair game for any method possible to fix or repair daily. As far as autism is concerned, the *DSM* is a political (not a scientific) document, and its attitude, if nothing else, opens the door for other people, some who are "less qualified" but who really do notice valid and addressable facets of AC SPRATS, where the vulnerability can be alleviated and do so. For reasons known only to the MPACCWA, there are still many facets of autism that the *DSM* and the MPACCWA ignore; hence the so-called pseudo treatments spring up in all their incomplete glory with, of course, their own marketing agendas.

The common target outcome held up at this convocation was that kids should act more normally, as in *normal* for an NT. This rather strongly indicates that the presenters seem to be following the old MPAC habits and have not analyzed the behavior carefully enough to realize why ACs do what they do. As their teachers, they have not looked at adult ACs to get better handles on how ACs think, what they have to live with, what they can do, and what they have done. Mind you, they would need to find adult ACs with more expanded horizons, but no one looked.

A VALID CRITICISM OF SALES HYPE: PSEUDOSCIENCE GRADE WAS PRESENTED, BUT NOTABLE, HIGHLY RELEVANT, RELATED FACTS ABOUT THE UTILITY OF THE HYPED PRODUCTS WERE NOT MENTIONED

From my perspective, this wave of pseudoscience that OAR has been trying to bring out into the open was brought on by the MPACCWA's own failure to notice and react productively to multiple valid facets of an AC's needs. That MPACCWA's habit of "omission" effectively allowed and encouraged people who did notice and react to start their own marketing campaigns. Indeed, in our adult AC eyes (as people who are forced to the back of the bus), this rings similar to some common logos and posters used by various groups.

Yes, indeed, selling is important, vitally important, but a higher priority need is to get the target correctly identified before sending adult ACs down the garden path. There is little excuse for professionals to not know that first things first is a good idea.

I was frazzled enough that Friday afternoon and had no place to write notes, so two examples of a presenter's concentration on spiel as opposed to what the product was all about is all I could manage. There were more spiels discussed, but I made no notes as to check with users about the practical utility of the product as compared to the spiels. I fully agree with the presenter that the *hype* is trouble.

To get hype-filtered information about respectful and effective improvements of ACs' lives as guided by the published hierarchies of use and need that we are actually using to develop ACs for success as ACs, the plan at TMS is to include a consumer reporting service. This is similar to how service of the Consumers Union operates today: no advertising, no hype, and what product or service works how well in a defined application. The following are two example criticisms of pseudoscience without understanding what really worked.

Example #1

There was a notable pseudoscience criticism of the marketing spiel for Irlen lenses. In my opinion from years ago, I agree that the Irlen sales spiel was and still is kinda cockamamie. However, a fact of the matter, the lenses are an operating adaptation of optical color filters, which are known to do their job. The presenter failed to recognize that the lenses themselves do good work, and the implication that we who wear them are silly, when they reduce unnecessary vulnerability while making us much more comfortable in a significant sensory issue, is unjustified.

This optical vulnerability has other known SPRATS connections: These filters are needed by some ACs with optical energy input interference problems. I must add that visual SPRATS are often associated with notably useful skills. I mentioned my own sensitivity to a certain band of yellow. When my eyes are "attacked" by such exposure, the result can almost totally block rational thought (and I suddenly shift to really undesirable social skills). In that case, don't you think I need an optical color filter?

Here is a fact that is very interesting to professionals willing to admit the positive aspects of autism and actually pursue their application: ACs sensitive to certain colors can pick up the presence of plant or animal abnormalities well before the NT. Another fact of a notably useful color filtering SPRATS issue is as follows: *Color blindness was grounds for rejection from military service in World War II until they found this condition made it possible to "spot" camouflage as if it was a lit up roadhouse at 2 a.m. on a moonless night.*

Example #2

I definitely agree with the criticism of the sales hype for hyperbaric chambers, as I myself can and have accomplished the same effect with a much lower cost (to me) using a simple oxygen hose and a rebreather, similar to the faddish "oxygen bars." But, again, why are we silly for doing what makes us feel better?

I am reiterating that the MPACCWA has established a solid history of ignoring reality checks, and any adult ACs politely trying to say something was amiss. I am again sincerely thanking OAR for organizing this convocation, which does appear to be intended as a genuine reality check.

THE GOAL OF MPACCWA

Around the autism spectrum, make no mistake, there is a lot of pain, often the intense anguish of never understood great frustration. The perception of pain is a powerful motivator, and intense pain can cause humans to do what they would not, even could not, ordinarily do. In a gross understatement, the presence of intense pain causes rational beings to appear irrational and can foster a desperation of biblical proportions among the people it surrounds.

This combination of irrationality and desperation can be compared to a jug of aged nitroglycerin, which is very sensitive to handle and has powerful consequences stemming from naive handling. In the case of autism, there are many vulnerabilities and other exciters, but the exciter of least valid reason is, like it or not, the politics surrounding appalling consultant naiveté or blindness or whatever the MPACCWA wishes to euphemize or ignore instead of getting data and analyzing the results.

For 70 years, the MPACCWA has been concentrating on the wishes of maxed-out parents who have never been given sufficient information and the professionals' own notions as to what these kids should be like, as well as the internal politics of the MPACCWA. The parents seem to say in chorus, "Fix my kid, fix my kid—make him normal! Social skills are terrible—won't look you in the eye"—and more. Over 70 years, the MPACCWA has had its own brand of worries, including economic, internal politics of various kinds, and finally does not know what is really up with these kids.

The upshot of all this is as follows: After those 70 years, the MPACCWA, including this convocation's cutting edge group, is still thinking in the same-old, same-old box. The historic box has been restricted to correcting the kid's behavior (per parent entreaty), without really understanding the kid's problem first or at all.

The best information source for understanding a kid's problem has been almost totally ignored; thus the goal of solving the real problem remains elusive. Rabbit trails abound, and the goal of giving parents the information they really need to know about the potential that these kids may have is consistently swept under the rug. So what is currently happening?

- I am well aware of the marketing problems of obtaining grant money and staying employed.
- I am well aware of stories with "axes to grind" nature, and spin controls operated by "interests," commercial or otherwise. A really effective one, done by the Phoenicians, was about whole ships sailing off the edge of a flat world while being chased by huge sea monsters. That one gave later navigators (highly educated people of the day) fits, not to mention the worried and desperate sailors.
- I am well aware of herd thinking, thinking in a box. If you ain't the lead dog, the view is always the same.
- I am well aware of the problems of rainmaker politics. Even Kanner was sidetracked in deference to such a situation.
- I am well aware of some of psychology's internal politics, the necessity of keeping face, by going with the flow, and staying on the good side of the rainmaker. I know that swimming upstream can be difficult.
- I am well aware of the value of assumptions in early iterations of solving complex problems. Indeed, there is a common assumption, particularly around the MPACCWA: "If you can't measure it or perceive it, ignore it." The problem with that particular assumption is that it is one, and as such has been ignored in favor of the heavily politically affected,

same-old box thinking. Such thinking will and does often forget how the word *ass-u-me* is spelled.

- I am well aware of the comforts of working for or alongside people of political power and habit and the dangers of depending on them to think about the real universe instead of local fiefdoms.

- I am well aware of the difficulties with habit guided (misguided) senior officers and invested teachers. Here are some examples: Maginot Lines, dependency on battleships for sea power, Earth-centric astronomy, and so forth. In my opinion these difficulties offer no valid reason for highly educated behavior analysts to not use the many indications that something was and is wrong with the basic tenets held onto all this time.

Reiterating the major inexcusable points from the perspective of horizon-expanded adult ACs:

- Not seeking horizon-expanded adult ACs' help in understanding the abnormality and consequently from ignorance "trying to fix what ain't broke and thereby making what is worse."

- A teaching dismissal as disordered and disabled.

- Abandoning the results of naive actions on vulnerable kids, while encouraging more kids to be similarly "fixed."

The following is what to expect from always thinking within the comfort of a box, where well-meaning analysts are failing to think clearly, perhaps failing to think creatively at all, reality checks aren't done, and so forth:

- Battles are devastatingly lost before they begin.

- Huge amounts of unnecessary pain and waste occur.

- Smart people come up looking embarrassed.

(Refer again to the wisdom of Einstein, Maslow, and Planck.)

SEVERAL ACTUAL ULTIMATE OUTCOMES OF THE MPACCWA'S LONGTIME FIXATION ON THE GOAL OF "CORRECTING" THE KID'S BEHAVIOR

The industry attitude forces me to lay the following out with gritted teeth:

- A very real ultimate outcome, so far, is that more than 90% of the AC population is unemployed or seriously underemployed, and the national average remuneration for the luckily employed ACs is $6,000 per year. All an AC can usually expect from the typical MPAC outcomes is menial low-pay, low-responsibility work in the fields of "food, flowers, and floors," and, more than likely, even that will be limited to part-time employment.

- Another very real ultimate outcome (i.e., how an adult AC's life is impacted) from fixating only on normalizing behavior and social skills training for AC kids prepares the child to do the following:

  - Politely accept the public dole or politely accept becoming an inmate.
  - Politely accept getting fed Risperdal and low-pay, low-responsibility food, flowers, and floors jobs.
  - Politely accept poverty.
  - Politely write a *suicide note*.

How do I know how so many adult ACs have such an inescapably low self-esteem, that the vast majority can't escape by themselves, and that the current thinking of the MPACCWA as demonstrated in this convocation offers nearly zero or even negative help to adult ACs, which the kids all too soon grow into?

This, of course, means that the so-called sympathy and cure groups have been given a myopically wrong message. This in turn gives state and federal people a myopically wrong message. *Dare I mention parents?*

Does this picture of hard facts better illustrate that the inescapable misunderstanding of vulnerability problems and the aggressive fixation on trying to fix what ain't broke can absolutely make what is damaged worse? The following are other outcomes:

1. I was disturbed, after 2 full days of listening to the presenters, that only one presenter barely touched on one of OAR's major reasons to exist, which is printed in *OAR's Best of the OARacle:* There is a knowledge gulf between practitioners and scientists. That presenter actually said (and seemed to very carefully gloss over the total reality) that there are some bad ABA practices out there. This presenter actually came and spoke at length with the adult ACs attending in extended, purposeful conversation. Seeking out adult ACs was and is a rarity; only the presenters who didn't seek us out can explain why. Meanwhile, such is added into the 40 years of ignoring the worth of AC minds, a behavior so firmly adhered to by your predecessors, your teachers.

2. It took a few days, but I finally figured out another point of what seriously disturbed me in such a smooth-running meeting with notably pleasant people. (I have the work of Maslow, Herb Lovett, Barry Prizant, Howard Gardner, Elisabet Sahtouris, Gail Gillingham, and others, even Skinner to some degree, to back me up.) This convocation bore the unmistakable essence that nearly every presenter was acting as if totally unaware of the 7 decades of the MPACCWA's avoiding the whole truth, while continuing to make wrong judgments negatively affecting the lives of many trusting people. They even seemed totally unaware of the practice of abandoning older individuals once

entrusted to their failed care and then simply forget about it. At the very least, no one loses any sleep over the problems of such causes.

In direct language, there is a *gulf* between the scientists themselves with the same gulf having arm extenders going even deeper in separating scientists from the realities of their subjects' lives. It seems to me that the vast majority of these presenters have never come to grips with the mess their teachers have swept under the rug. If they have, they certainly didn't mention it.

HOW THESE OUTCOMES FIT
TOGETHER: A LOGICAL CONCLUSION

Nearly every presenter, in spite of an apparently genuine and strong desire to help, appeared to be continuing in the wrong direction and seemed blissfully unaware of a serious need to identify the *real* root problem and follow an appropriate (checked out with natives) hierarchy of use and need.

Coupled with their continuation of the age-old fixation on children, to the extent of forgetting that the children rapidly become ignored and trapped as adults, this forces me to the following conclusion (I regret not knowing how to say this more gently.): It appears that the *major* vector of the MPACCWA has been in some way always locked into a box of seriously rigid thinking, a box that poorly fits an AC's needs, which has always been to protect the politics of a behaviorist's brand of "*not considering the whole truth science.*" This conclusion, unless someone can show me or successfully explain otherwise, is solidly reinforced by the facts of 70 years of the MPACCWA's less-than-stellar success in the face of qualified people informing them of something wrong for a minimum of 40 years, which in turn is being stonewalled by the MPACCWA and finally capped by the accumulated ultimate outcomes mentioned in this response.

I didn't know much of Maslow's teachings at the time of the convocation, but the presenters convinced me that the essence of the MPACCWA closely matches the essence predicted by Maslow's words: "The [preoccupied (exclusive)] study of crippled, stunted, immature, and unhealthy specimens can yield only a cripple psychology and a cripple philosophy."

A Notable Hole in the Real
World of Today and Everyday Social Skills
and Adaptive Behavior Attitudes That I Have
Witnessed in This and Innumerable Other Conferences

Only three presenters even touched on the looming stumbling block of AC sexuality.

One seemed upset with becoming aware that she had no idea how to satisfactorily handle her son's "adult problems." Another was asked to chemically take sexuality issues away. The third, the only presenter using the term *NT*, seems to have the right direction in mind but danced too much around the issue. It is quite possible that he didn't have the time to set up the situation as he would have liked. There was too much information to cover in 2 days, much less the 55 minutes allotted for each presentation. This issue alone causes me to wonder: Was there only one presenter who has *ever bothered* to listen very much? Have the widespread stories of inappropriate public behavior not registered with behavior analysts and not indicated any form of a communications need?

Remember the many incidents of AC memory and gullibility. ACs are told various degrees of baloney, by "unassailable expert authorities," commercial media, and various misguiding how-to publications; believe it all hook, line, and sinker; and remember it for a long, long time. This causes great internal argument when they see reality and try to justify baloney. I see such *every day* as I work with individuals who have been trained to believe that they have no value because they live with differently operating thinking and communication systems.

These Upside-Down Situations
Should Not Be and Do Not Have to Be

In our experience at TMS, adult ACs are capable and willing and unemployed or underemployed.

- We adult ACs have in our ranks many high school graduates with okay social skills *who can't work because...*
- We adult ACs have in our ranks many college graduates with okay social skills *who can't work because...*
- We adult ACs have in our ranks brilliant and highly useful Techniqual experts who by themselves can't make it past the drummed-in personal esteem of zero value *who can't work because...*
- *Withdrawal happens.* By themselves and without a certain honest and unassuming respect and trust, they are paralyzed with the anticipation and the certainty of still another deeply wounding attack on their vulnerabilities, sagging self-respect, and any remaining tatter of some slim remaining belief of always promised "help" (that never happens appropriately) and have no effective defense.

I'm not asking anyone to stop thinking about social skills and adaptive behavior. I'm asking for the presenters to look at horizon-expanded adults to learn what needs have higher priority, such as a healthy and a positive self-esteem and self-capability and sufficient positive experience in the application of both. This is because we already know that pursuing such will also tend to resolve social skills and adaptive behavior issues automatically.

By following a system of hierarchies of use and need, one that is well tuned to ACs, by horizon-expanded (qualified) ACs, it is easier to understand that if a prior priority need is not met, there will be a kind of need back charge, perhaps a craving with roots in the prior need that obfuscates and intertwines with later priority needs.

AN OFFER TO HELP YOU OUT OF THE COMING PROBLEMS

In these days of the Internet, with vastly improved communication among ACs and their families worldwide, ACs will come to realize the realities of their situation. They will find out what they really are:

- I don't think they will be all that proud of being trained to act more "normal" as children, while real and higher priority needs and capabilities were and still are ignored.
- I don't think they will be all that proud of the failure to encourage their different development needs, self-esteem needs, and marketable skills.

Should they be proud of the MPACCWA's "normalizing" record? The one now 70 years old with real-world ultimate outcomes of more than 90% unemployed or seriously underemployed; the one with average potential income somewhere less than one third of poverty level; and the one where they are abandoned and left, at best, to a dole system itself in deep trouble?

I tried to get across that we know from direct experience that developing the trapped eccentric expert is a much more practical and ultimately more efficacious way to improve social skills; improve adaptive behavior; and promote happiness, success, and independent living as an adult AC. I will reiterate that developing the eccentric expert even in elementary school (age appropriate) will start the "social skill" aspect toward unheard of heights of accomplishment—all on its own. I know that there are great opportunities and rewards in doing a much better job solving the knotty technological problems springing up now in time (and will arrive at an even greater pace in the near future) that cannot be best solved while sitting around in a social group singing "Kum Ba Yah." (Thanks, Temple!)

A great deal of evidence exists indicating that numerous highly creative people (past and present) tend to display AC characteristics. A great many AC people also tend to display the characteristics of highly creative people, particularly if the positive aspects of autism are put to useful application. It is time for the MPACCWA to connect the dots. At TMS, we are learning how to take any AC and give him or her a hand up from serious anxiety, depression, and unemployability to become some kind of eccentric expert and hence into high potential for real employment and then on into a real independent life as far as possible that may individually imply.

You see, *we* know from real-world experience that ACs need a life, not a life sentence, as has been the case for at least 70 years. Currently, to prevent or commute this said life sentence, we must repair enough of the damaging occasions—in home, school, outside, and the doctor's office— that misunderstanding was despotic, the message to us was/is disrespect, and the idea that SPRATS and life needs that we were born with are not acceptable. If we know what's good for us, we had better conform.

At TMS, we are respectful identifiers and developers of eccentric expertise while we respectfully and most thoroughly learn of the individual's vulnerabilities. Then we are mentors of real experiences in eccentric expertise while showing how to handle vulnerabilities and then finders of and installers into niches. Finally, we are real-world, getting-an-independent-life-as-soon-as-possible facilitators.

In this we are about giving a respectful hand up. We also know that in this proximity we can learn to reliably separate bad behavior from a geek's frustration, as in anyone operating in handout mode quickly learns it doesn't work, but someone pulling his or her weight will get the information needed.

If and as the occasion arises during the entire process, we also mentor know-how in "survival politics" because only under very special circumstances should anyone tolerate destructive, damaging, behavior—whether done in ignorance *or* cognizance.

All of this is individualized and respectful of the AC because both ACs and ourselves can learn more that way. At the same time, we are continuing to firm up ideas within the SPRATS acronymic sequence. We have been performing the ideas Maslow put forth in our TMS process. We have been supplying the ignored needs of the AC and are having remarkable success, as we learn how best to do such.

NOTE

Referring to the humor above, our throughput so far, we have all had social skills go through the roof "just because we supplied and customized the application of some primary needs." Yet we are not social skillets; we are finders of empty need slots, with the capability of understanding the appropriate fill for said slots and the know-how to make it work. We all know that currently the MPACCWA has a terribly long way to go to achieve what TMS is attempting to do now. We expect to solidly demonstrate that we are well ahead of the mainstream MPACCWA.

The best I can say is *stop* trying to make the problem fit the same-old tool that hasn't worked for 70 years. Instead,

- Look at the entire situation and then develop or adapt a tool to help fulfill a system of appropriate hierarchies of use and needs for an individual.
- Develop the abnormal talents, their utility and their diversity, that nature has demonstrated time and time again as nature evolves. The old MPACCWA habits of not reviewing tenets or not ever thinking outside the same-old box do not even come close to evolving.

Do you genuinely want to help ACs (and their families) notably and permanently improve their lives as soon as possible? You can, by letting us (horizon-expanded adult ACs) help you. But to do that, we need to get around the fact that your industry has habitually demonstrated the thinking that ACs are devoid of genuine respect of capability, and your industry has trained that unfortunate habit into uncountable experts of academia, researcher and practitioner alike.

We must say that the convocation caused depressing disturbance in the life of each AC attending. From this response, I hope you have gathered that the experts of academia within the MPACCWA have long been guessing and guessing badly while somehow ignoring multiple qualified sources for better information. To make real progress, what you really need are some qualified experts of actual experience with the knowledge, the confidence, and the spirit to call the bluff on habitual assumptions and rigid boxed-in thinking.

DEDICATION

May a more complete picture of the real problem, and what works to help improve lives across the full life span, bring about a true awareness of the reality around autism.

May a real cooperation occur to look at the whole situation in rectifying an unnecessary and damaging state of affairs that has and will continue to be an embarrassing debacle if we don't cooperate.

There are great opportunities and rewards in doing a much better job than done over the last 70 years.

Afterword

Reflections
on the Convocation

Daniel Crimmins, Shahla Ala'i-Rosales, and Peter F. Gerhardt

In the summer of 2008, a group of scholars convened to review, analyze, and reflect on the state of applied research related to social and adaptive skills. Each scholar presented a review of the current state of a particular area, made recommendations for translating scientific research to applied settings, and suggested future research directions. There was time for debate, discussion, and commentary by peers, people with autism spectrum disorders (ASDs), family members, and community stakeholders. The primary goal of this event was to encourage the translation of research into everyday practice and, by doing so, change lives for the better.

This book presents the results of those presentations and discussions, which were marked at times by divergence in views, values, and priorities. Each presentation and the resulting chapters in this book reflect the effort of the authors to understand and provide a meaningful context for the research evidence on increasing social and adaptive skills in people with ASDs. At the end, everyone agreed that every convocation participant was committed to increasing the happiness of people with autism and their membership in caring communities. Everyone also agreed that there is clearly a long way to go to make lives meaningful for too many individuals with ASDs.

THE NEED TO DO EVEN MORE
TO IMPROVE SOCIAL AND ADAPTIVE SKILLS

By definition, people with autism have difficulties communicating and socializing and have restricted interests that are often not shared by others (Volkmar, Paul, Klin, & Cohen, 2005). The convocation offered insight into the everyday lives of children and adults with ASDs with regard to their social and adaptive skills. Socials skills reflect an ability to adapt to the environment through verbal and nonverbal communication. Adaptive skills allow a person to achieve independence and a level of responsibility referenced to the individual's age and social group. Social and adaptive skills are widely viewed as essential for achieving independence, economic productivity, personal safety, and well-being at home and in the community.

Yet, despite increased attention and efforts in the past several decades, there is a widespread lack of confidence that individuals with ASDs will be able to master these skills. According to a survey of more than 1,650 parents with children with an ASD, fewer than 20% feel that their children will be able to make major life decisions, have friends, be valued by the community, or have regular opportunities for recreation; in addition, only 29% believe that their children with autism will *always* have a place to live (Easter Seals, 2008). The survey also revealed that 900 parents of children who are typically developing felt very differently; that is, the majority of these parents felt certain that their children would have friends, be valued by the community, have recreational opportunities, and live independently as adults—a sad, disquieting, and discordant set of statistics.

The concerns of parents about the future for their children with ASDs are unfortunately supported by limited research on long-term outcomes. Howlin, Goode, Hutton, and Rutter (2004), for example, found that most adults with ASDs remained dependent on families and other support services and had few close friends, limited employment, poor communication skills, and continuing interfering behaviors. Overall, less than one fourth were described as having good or very good adult outcomes. Even when they have jobs, many adults with ASDs are underemployed or employed in positions that are inappropriate given their skill set (Barnhill, 2007). Research also suggests that the difficulties in forming and maintaining social relationships, poor communication, and restricted behavioral repertoires represent critical barriers to full and meaningful community inclusion (Cederlund, Hagberg, Billstedt, Gillberg, & Gillberg, 2008; Garcia-Villamisar & Hughes, 2007). Assuming that instruction and support to improve social and adaptive skills are directly related to improving these long-term outcomes, practitioners clearly have far to go.

IT IS BECOMING CLEARER
WHERE TO START AND WHAT TO TEACH

The positive news is that advances in the science are occurring every day. Researchers know much more today than even 5 years ago about providing critical supports to children with ASDs and their families.

Gerenser (see Chapter 5) focuses us on the increasing recognition of the importance of joint attention as a gateway behavior; that is, most very young children readily engage others by looking at an object in the environment and then looking at the other person. The typical response to this is a comment on the object or some action with the object by the other person.

Children with ASDs demonstrate significant difficulties with joint attention, which is often one of the first signs that differentiate them from peers who are typically developing or children with other developmental delays. Joint attention is considered an important skill because of its potential relationship to engagement and language development. The good news is that joint attention can be taught. What is unknown is whether teaching joint attention results in a child who is able to do so not only when others initiate but also when the child initiates on his or her own. It is also unclear whether this will necessarily lead to enhanced language and social outcomes for these children.

Anderson (see Chapter 8) cites a range of findings supporting the impact of early intervention on long-term adaptive functioning. Anderson suggests that there may be a core set of skills that serve as the building blocks for learning self-help skills, including sustaining attention to an activity for 5–10 minutes, responding to one's name, following simple instructions, and imitating the actions of others. Evidence shows that when taught to young children, these skills promote the development of long-term independence.

Openden (see Chapter 7) cites four areas for intervention with young children within the model of Pivotal Response Treatment (PRT): enhancing motivation, ensuring responsivity to multiple cues, supporting self-management, and increasing self-initiation. Similar to the skills named by Anderson, these are seen as critical to the metaskill of learning to learn. Complicating matters, implementing PRT requires, at a minimum, three additional considerations: early intervention, intervention in natural environments, and parent training. These relate directly to the context of instruction and support the premise that positive outcomes require intervention by the right people at the right time in the right places. Skills developed within this learning-to-learn framework are, however, more likely to be generalized across settings, maintained across time, and used spontaneously.

Kasari, Locke, Ishijima, and Kretmann (see Chapter 10) explore the dimensions of social skills intervention in children with ASDs, finding that the critical end point must focus on social reciprocity among children with ASDs and their peers. These researchers also examine how the right people and places for intervention are different for school-age children with ASDs, examining peers and school and home as environments, with friendships as the ultimate goal.

Weiss (see Chapter 3) reminds us that social skills are elusive targets for instruction, and the results of interventions to date have been modest. One aspect is that children are not intrinsically motivated to learn such skills because they often lack the social interest and the ability to comprehend social nuances. A second aspect is that social skills are multidimensional by nature, requiring an understanding of how complex social interaction really can be, judgment in determining how to use each instructed skill, and perspective on when to use it. These complexities underscore the difficulty in teaching such skills to the point that they will effectively and thoroughly serve the individual in the natural social environment.

Gerhardt, Zawacki, and Satriale (see Chapter 9) address concerns related to adolescence and early adulthood—ages that are all too often forgotten in research, although there are clearly a vast number of individuals with ASDs who require support throughout their adult lives. They frequently must develop skills for social interactions in the workplace, community settings, and the home. Many require support in dealing with the day-to-day aspects of living that fall under the heading of adaptive behavior.

AND IT IS ALSO CLEARER HOW TO GET THERE

In addition to an awareness of the importance of specific skills, the field has become more sophisticated in terms of measurement and context. Researchers have definitely not resolved every issue related to these factors, but they do have a better platform from which to begin the journey.

Mayville (see Chapter 2) outlines the myriad approaches—from rating scales, to direct observation, to curriculum-based assessment of social skills and social competence for individuals with ASDs. These are critically important for science to have reliable and valid measurement of the constructs that practitioners use to identify a condition and define the impact of interventions. Mayville cites an expanding literature supporting enhanced capacity for measurement but also points out two significant limitations in assessment methods: There is still far too little research that addresses social behavior in natural contexts, and adults with ASDs are woefully underrepresented in the measurement research.

Schwartz and Chen (see Chapter 6) outline a strategy for incorporating autism-focused interventions into a broader context of positive behavior support for building social relationships in school settings. They discuss common elements for supporting *all* children in school, such as providing a safe, nurturing, predictable, and reinforcing environment that explicitly provides instruction in social behavior. They also point out that many children are unlikely to develop social interaction skills without focused and structured teaching. Similarly, students with ASDs may require a higher intensity of support, perhaps with a greater emphasis on ensuring fidelity with the selected instructional method, while also emphasizing the importance of teaching skills in natural contexts. If social relationships with peers are an important goal for students with ASDs, then students must be taught these skills across different activities, in varied settings, and with multiple partners.

Koenig (see Chapter 4) discusses the need for considering group interventions as one way of scaling up. With that, she cautions that controlled research has yet to demonstrate strong improvements for the intervention group relative to controls. She notes the need for clearly adhering to the fidelity of an intervention to better understand what works and what does not work.

THE WORLD IS STILL MESSY:
FIDELITY, DOSAGE, AND FUNCTIONALITY

Several authors raised questions related to intervention to improve social and adaptive behavior for individuals with ASDs. Included among them are what practitioners wish to do for students with ASDs; why they wish to do it; why they think a selected approach is superior to another; and how exactly they want it carried out, by whom, and with what frequency.

Zane (see Chapter 12) raises concerns about the quality of evidence that is used to define whether an approach is an evidence-based practice (EBP); too often, claims of effectiveness are made with totally inadequate evidence. Zane cites standards used, for example, by the New York State Department of Health (1999), and Koenig (see Chapter 4) cites the work of Chambless and colleagues (e.g., Chambless & Ollendick, 2001), which includes elements such as multiple studies by multiple researchers, rigorous methods and systems of measurement, and the availability of detailed intervention manuals.

Koenig provides a brief history of the randomized controlled trial, from its origins in the history of clinical medicine to its application in today's social sciences. She cautions that many of the assumptions that underlie comparisons for diseases are far less likely to be applicable to ASDs.

Sanders (see Chapter 11), for example, strongly emphasizes that not all ASDs are the same; the signs and symptoms of ASDs likely result from many different etiologic factors. Although Sanders emphasizes that an understanding of the etiology of an individual with an ASD is critical to selecting medication (alone or in combination), this recommendation is likely to generalize across considerations of any and all intervention options.

With all these advances, there is still a tension associated with selecting intervention options and supports for individuals with ASDs. Although researchers know the many ways that individuals with ASDs are similar *and* dissimilar to those without ASDs, they still often have no basis in the literature to say which children will respond to which interventions delivered at which intensity. Families and increasingly older individuals with ASDs are sometimes confronted with multiple options—but more likely presented with a single choice—about a course of intervention to address core ASD signs and symptoms. When offered, the teachers and the therapists providing the intervention may be highly skilled but could quite possibly be relatively untrained novices; supports may be available at adequate levels of intensity (e.g., several hours per week) but more likely may be scheduled only a few minutes per day or once per week; and the approach may have a high level of support in the published literature, but little is known about whether it will work for a specific child from a specific family.

CONSIDERING FRIENDSHIP AND CONTEXTS

Among the overarching findings of the convocation was the need to continue to expand the framework for the goals of an intervention, which is made more difficult by the fact that social and adaptive are contextually dependent constructs that are moving targets. Letso (see Chapter 1), for example, urges us to shift the focus from education in the least restrictive environment to life in the least restrictive environment. Her argument is that families (and individuals) require support to lead successful lives at home and in their communities. She notes the potential importance of family support, parent training, advocacy skills, and how skills are routinely recommended. But she also cautions that these supports are in many ways subjected to the same considerations related to effectiveness, fidelity, and dosage that were identified earlier in this chapter, with the likelihood of inconsistent outcomes and increased burden on families.

Schwartz and Chen (see Chapter 6) discuss the importance of interventions that support the interaction of *all* children in socially valued rituals and routines in typical settings and contexts. They suggest that the preparation of an individual to be a member of a group or a learning community is a higher order goal than the development of discrete social skills.

Similarly, Kasari and colleagues (see Chapter 10) emphasize the importance of peer relationships as the route to friendship. These relationships must be fostered, however, because their mere presence in an inclusive environment does not ensure social belonging. Shared experiences and the coaching of peers have both proven useful in increasing reciprocal social relationships in the context of school and play dates. Important to understanding this intervention is the recognition that students with ASDs express interest in having friends and feeling as if they belong, but the cautionary note is that this appears to require intervention in the broader context of other students, friends, and family members. This begs the larger question of the degree to which future interventions (and research to demonstrate their effectiveness) should focus on social contexts rather than social competence.

These emerging data certainly support the notion that schools and social networks are appropriate targets for change efforts—toward the goals of increasing tolerance, cooperation, acceptance, and even kindness to be experienced by all students. As researchers consider the social demands of everyday life (e.g., living in a family, with roommates, or among loved ones; negotiating the grocery store, the gym, or public transportation; getting along with multiple personalities that compose varied workplaces), it may be important to consider large-scale interventions to promote civility, tolerance, and social justice for all—including and in no way limited to only those with ASDs.

WHAT EVERYONE LARGELY AGREED ON

The convocation presentations and discussions were lively—and as can be seen in the commentaries, at times even heated. Great effort was extended to ensure that all felt that they had been heard, although that sometimes required follow-up discussions during breaks and meals. When the convocation was over, consensus had been achieved on several points, including agreement on the state of the art and emerging trends in research on social skills, gaps in the ongoing research, and several points on which everyone could only agree to disagree. The research cited in this volume demonstrates that we have made significant gains along several dimensions and are moving in a number of positive directions:

- A shift is starting to occur from a focus on social skills to a broader emphasis on social competence. Furthermore, this shift is beginning to look at the natural ecology of social relationships and take into account context, meaningful outcomes, and clinical significance.
- The concept and the process of joint attention and its role in social skills and competencies development needs continued investigation.
- There is increased interest in examining interventions on social settings and networks beyond work focusing on behavior change in individuals with ASDs.
- Methodological rigor is increasing among published studies, but effect sizes are often small in group studies. There is continued need to focus on clinical as well as statistical changes in behavior.
- Many social skills interventions have strong supporting evidence but are not adopted because, in part, they are difficult to implement or fail to generalize to everyday use in typical settings.
- Many interventions with limited supporting evidence continue to flourish, despite the lack of evidence, difficulty in implementation, and similar failures to generalize to everyday use.

The presenters and the panelists also identified several gaps in ongoing research efforts:

- One of the largest concerns practitioners face is getting EBPs into wide-scale practice. This requires far more attention to the training of the implementation workforce, organizational commitments, and ongoing monitoring of fidelity and quality.

- There is increasing need for reliable and valid systems of measurement to demonstrate the long-term use and usefulness of social skills in real-life contexts.
- There is also a need to expand the focus of measurement to capture a range of outcomes valued by individuals with ASDs and their families, such as friendship, participation in social networks, happiness, quality of life, and independence.
- Because it is not considered a core impairment in people with ASDs, adaptive behavior has received scant research attention in the last 20 or so years, yet many individuals with ASDs remain dependent on others for lifelong support in this area.
- The majority of research in social skills has focused on preschool and school-age children with ASDs; there is, therefore, a desperate need for greater attention to understanding needs and strategies to support adolescents and adults.
- There is far too little known and understood about the natural evolution of social relationships across time. To what degree, for example, should friendships and social networks be extended and enhanced versus being terminated because they are not meaningful to the individual?
- There is an increasing recognition of the need for research and intervention protocols that allow for greater input by individuals with ASDs and their families.

AND WHERE DID EVERYONE AGREE TO DISAGREE?

The discussions did not allow enough time to "officially" agree to disagree, but there were several points that divided those representing the viewpoint of the "science" and those representing the "lived experience" of ASDs. From the standpoint of the lived experience of ASD, the plea from adults with ASDs had several elements that generated extensive discussion. These elements are posed as questions to the research community with regard to the social competence of individuals with ASDs. With the exploding prevalence in the identification of ASDs, the following are critical questions for the next 50 years:

- How and when can individuals with ASDs be accepted as whole human beings—with strengths, gifts, talents, and, granted, some idiosyncrasies—but without the requirement to adhere to a social norm? When does the research focus shift to decreasing societal intolerance of differences?
- When will researchers focus on the unique abilities of individuals with autism and design environments to support the expression of these abilities?

- Who is the client when parents make decisions to place extraordinary effort at having their children with ASDs become more normal? Can the spectrum be viewed on a continuum with the struggles that occur between "typical" adolescents and their parents? And when is enough, enough—in reference to efforts to change nondangerous behaviors for children with ASDs?

- What do researchers really know about the lives of adults with ASDs? How do their life trajectories compare with those of their brothers and sisters, their classmates, or fellow citizens? What jobs do they find and hold? Where are they highly successful and where repeated failures? What do their friendships and marriages look like?

These questions emerged from the discussion; each question speaks to social and adaptive behavior in individuals with ASDs, and each is potentially researchable. Are there more issues to be resolved? We certainly expect so, but time will tell.

Disagreement from the research side focused more on how the requirements of science are often not understood by those it intends to benefit:

- A continuing emphasis on measurement is necessary, even though the people being measured express discomfort at being reduced to the operational definitions needed for a phenomenon.

- Science is not static, but it is often slow with studies building on earlier work. An appreciation for incremental gains in understanding what researchers are studying is ingrained in research training; it does not come naturally to those without that training. Everyone has probably encountered the phrase *they had to do research to study that!* in framing some research activities as trivial or unnecessary. And because this may be true at times, it also reflects a very different way of approaching the world.

- In many ways, this convocation demonstrated that research in social competence has made huge advancements in the 2000s, but these advances have at times been overshadowed by societal events occurring at a far faster pace than the research. The increase in the prevalence of ASDs, the mandate for including students with ASDs in the least restrictive environment, and the push for meaningful lives as an outcome of intervention are three social phenomena that have underscored the need to know more about how to support individuals with ASDs in everyday settings.

SO WHAT IS NEXT?

In the end, everyone collectively committed to interventions that produce meaningful, sustained changes in natural environments, across time, and across important contexts. Accomplishing this will require an acceptance by the research community to continue to broaden the analysis of interventions for social and adaptive behavior—their long-term benefits and possible unintended consequences, provided alone and in combination with other intervention efforts (e.g., pharmacological, educational, vocational). This will also require the continued development of ecologically valid systems of measurement, a commitment to the role of the evidence of efficacy and effectiveness, and an enhanced understanding of what it means to bring effective practices to wide-scale implementation.

Practitioners are collectively committed to individuals and families receiving the supports and services that contribute to leading meaningful lives—where meaning is defined in terms of overall well-being and purpose. But practitioners acknowledge that families (and increasingly individuals) confront tremendous immediate pressure to make decisions about interventions, often in the face of conflicting claims and inadequate evidence. It is the responsibility of the scientific community to disseminate what researchers know but also to admit the limits of that knowledge.

REFERENCES

Barnhill, G.P. (2007). Outcomes in adults with Asperger syndrome. *Focus on Autism and Other Developmental Disabilities, 22*, 116–126.

Cederlund, M., Hagberg, B., Billstedt, E., Gillberg, I.C., & Gillberg, C. (2008). Asperger syndrome and autism: A comparative longitudinal follow-up study more than five years after original diagnosis. *Journal of Autism and Developmental Disorders, 38*, 72–85.

Chambless, D.L., & Ollendick, T.H. (2001). Empirically supported psychological interventions: Controversies and evidence. *Annual Review of Psychology, 52*, 685–716.

Easter Seals. (2008). *Living with Autism Study*. Retrieved from http://www.easterseals.com/site/DocServer/Study_FINAL_Harris12.4.08_Compressed.pdf?docID=83143

Garcia-Villamisar, D., & Hughes, C. (2007). Supported employment improves cognitive performance in adults with autism. *Journal of Intellectual Disability Research, 51*, 142–150.

Howlin, P., Goode, S., Hutton, J., & Rutter, M. (2004). Adult outcomes for children with autism. *Journal of Child Psychology, Psychiatry, and Allied Disciplines, 45*, 212–229.

Volkmar, F., Paul, R., Klin, A., & Cohen, D. (2005). *Handbook of autism and pervasive developmental disorders*. New York, NY: Wiley.

Index

Tables and figures are indicated by *t* and *f*, respectively.

Sensory integration therapy (SIT), 198, 200–202
Sertraline, 189
Sexuality, *see* Adults with autism spectrum disorders (ASDs)
Shaping, 143–144
  see also Prompting
SIB-R, *see* Scales of Independent Behavior, Revised
Sign language, 37
Signal-detection devices, 152
SIT, *see* Sensory integration therapy
Skillstreaming (curriculum), 84
Social autopsy, 44
Social cognition
  see also Social skills
Social Communication, Emotional Regulation, and Transactional Support (SCERTS), 25
Social competence
  assessing, 18, 22–23
  defined, 17–18, 69, 109
  developing, 111–120
  employment outlook and, 76, 123, 160–161
  impairments in, 19
  interest in, 33, 109
  joint attention and, 69, 71
  measuring, 53, 78
  quality of life and, 76, 109, 113
  role of, 76
  scaling up interventions, 211–216
  see also Social skills
Social Competence Inventory (SCI), 57–58
Social comprehension, 36–46
Social language, *see* Language
Social motivation, *see* Motivation
Social networks, centrality of, 180, 180*f*
Social reciprocity skills, *see* Social skills
Social relationships
  facilitating, 84–85
  friendships, 171, 172–174, 175, 179, 181, 232–233, 292
  importance of, 83–84
  initiating, 34
  play dates, 117, 173, 177–178, 292
  quality of life and, 84
  schoolwide positive behavior interventions and supports and, 95–98

  see also Social skills
Social Responsiveness Scale (SRS), 21, 25–26, 27
Social skills
  adaptive behavior and, 164–165, 165*f*
  assessing, 20–25, 290
  challenges in, 33, 53–54
  children versus adults, 28
  components of, 34–35
  curricula for teaching, 53, 57, 178
  data acquisition in, 10
  defined, 6, 17, 57
  domains of, 6, 17, 64
  functionality of, 99, 101–102
  generalizing, 6–7, 39, 43, 85, 179, 181
  impairments in, 18, 34, 58–59, 137–138, 160, 189–190
  importance of, 233, 289–290, 292–293
  interventions for, 85–89, 179–181, 289
  language development and, 19
  learning, 11
  observing, 23–24
  outcome measurement after interventions, 59–62
  qualitative aspects of, 35–36
  quality of life and, 85, 160
  recommendations for, 26–28
  remediating, 46
  research and practice in, 11, 25–26, 175–179, 236–237
  stimulating, 19–20
  teaching, 33, 56–58, 64, 89, 101–102, 109, 165
  see also specific skills and interventions
Social skills groups, 93, 96, 97, 178–179
Social Skills Rating System (SSRS), 22, 27
Social Stories
  effectiveness of, 101
  role of, 37–40, 41, 57
  sentence types for, 38
  video feedback in, 38–39
Social validity, 100–101
Spectrum organization line, 252–253
  see also Autism/autism spectrum disorders (ASDs)
Speech
  communication and, 138